RHETORICAL POWERS

COLUMBIA STUDIES IN INTERNATIONAL
ORDER AND POLITICS

COLUMBIA STUDIES IN INTERNATIONAL
ORDER AND POLITICS

Stacie E. Goddard, Daniel H. Nexon,
and Joseph M. Parent, series editors

The Columbia Studies in International Order and Politics series builds on the press's long tradition in classic international relations publishing while highlighting important new work. The series is founded on three commitments: to serve as an outlet for innovative theoretical work, especially that work which stretches beyond "mainstream" international relations and cuts across disciplinary boundaries; to highlight original qualitative and historical work in international relations theory, international security, and international political economy; and to focus on creating a selective, prominent list dedicated to international relations.

Before Colonization: Non-Western States and Systems in the Nineteenth Century,
Charles R. Butcher and Ryan D. Griffiths

Beyond Power Transitions: The Lessons of East Asian History and
the Future of U.S.-China Relations, Xinru Ma and David C. Kang

Governing the Feminist Peace: The Vitality and Failure of the Women,
Peace, and Security Agenda, Paul Kirby and Laura J. Shepherd

States and the Masters of Capital: Sovereign Lending, Old and New, Quentin Bruneau

Making War on the World: How Transnational Violence Reshapes Global Order, Mark Shirk

RHETORICAL POWERS

HOW RISING STATES SHAPE INTERNATIONAL ORDER

SASIKUMAR SUNDARAM

Columbia University Press
New York

Columbia University Press
Publishers Since 1893
New York   Chichester, West Sussex
cup.columbia.edu

Library of Congress Cataloging-in-Publication Data
Names: Sundaram, Sasikumar author
Title: Rhetorical powers : how rising states shape international order /
Sasikumar Sundaram.
Description: New York : Columbia University Press, 2026. |
Series: Columbia studies in international order and politics | Includes index.
Identifiers: LCCN 2025020657 | ISBN 9780231207829 hardback |
ISBN 9780231207836 trade paperback | ISBN 9780231557139 ebook
Subjects: LCSH: Language and international relations—Case studies |
Language and international relations—India |
Language and international relations—China |
Language and international relations—Brazil |
Bangladesh—History—Revolution, 1971 |
Haiti—History—Coup d'état, 2004 |
Syria—History—Civil War, 2011–
Classification: LCC JZ1253.5 .S86 2026
LC record available at https://lccn.loc.gov/2025020657

Cover design: Milenda Nan Ok Lee
Cover image: Christine Waterstone / Shutterstock

GPSR Authorized Representative: Easy Access System Europe,
Mustamäe tee 50, 10621 Tallinn, Estonia, gpsr.requests@easproject.com

TO RACHEL

CONTENTS

Acknowledgments   ix

INTRODUCTION   1

1. RHETORICAL POWER POLITICS:
A FRAMEWORK   25

2. REPERTOIRE OF POWER POLITICS IN INDIA,
BRAZIL, AND CHINA   63

3. INDIA'S RHETORICAL POWER POLITICS
IN THE EAST PAKISTAN CRISIS, 1971   96

4. BRAZIL'S RHETORICAL POWER POLITICS
IN THE HAITIAN CRISIS, 2004   129

5. CHINA'S RHETORICAL POWER POLITICS
IN THE SYRIAN CRISIS, 2011-2020   160

6. RHETORICAL POWERS, FLIPPED SCRIPTS,
AND GLOBAL DISORDER   188

Notes   205
Index   271

ACKNOWLEDGMENTS

This book examines a distinct form of rhetorical power politics in the international hierarchy. It emerged from discussions with several mentors, friends, family members, colleagues, and lucky acquaintances on the journey. First, I thank the reviewers and specifically editors of the Columbia Studies in International Order and Politics series: Dan Nexon, Stacie Goddard, and Joseph Parent. Dan spent several hours discussing the ideas underlying the book, clarifying them to me rigorously, and he graciously tolerated my mistakes along the way. Dan gave the intellectual life support for this project. I have yet to address all his questions because it would take another decade to finish the book. This book would never have started without Patrick Jackson. At various points, I had several opportunities to meet and talk to PTJ, and he has been a great source of encouragement. Dan, Stacie, and Jo were generous in providing much needed insightful comments on the first full draft. I also want to thank my editor at Columbia, Caelyn Cobb, who remained steadfastly supportive throughout my extended writing and revision process. I was incredibly fortunate to meet and work with these mentors. All errors of fact and interpretation are mine alone.

In researching this book, I owe a huge debt to several institutions. In India, my research was possible with the support from the Manohar Parrikar Institute for Defence Studies and Analyses. Staff at the Nehru Memorial (now Prime Minsters') Museum and Library, United Service

Institution of India, Observers Research Foundation, the libraries of Jawaharlal Nehru University, University of Madras, and Anna Centenary Library in Chennai were very helpful. I must thank the staff at the Tamil Nadu Archives and Historical Research, even if I did not use the wealth of those materials in this book. In Brazil, I am particularly grateful to the São Paulo Research Foundation for generous funding under the São Paulo Research Foundation FAPESP Grant #2017/10021-6. The immense support from the Department of Political Science (DCP) at the University of São Paulo (USP) and access to research material at the Center for Research and Documentation on Contemporary Brazilian History (CPDOC) of the Getulio Vargas Foundation have been important. I also particularly thank the staff at the Library of Congress in Washington, DC. The idea underlying this book began during my time at the Central European University (CEU), Budapest/Vienna. I am grateful to CEU, the finest academic institution that funded my research early in my career and offered a challenging intellectual environment to experiment, fail, and restart several times.

I owe my greatest debts to mentors and friends in all these institutions. At CEU, I encountered Friedrich Kratochwil, Xymena Kurowska, Paul Roe, Alexander Astrov, and Erin Jenne, all of whom took pains to help me think carefully about international politics. My greatest intellectual debt at CEU is to Xymena. In India, I owe thanks to Raja Mohan, Rajesh Basrur, Rajesh Rajagopalan, Ananya Sharma, Abhijit Singh at the Observer Research Foundation (ORF), Priyanka Pandit, and Kapil Patil. In Brazil, I am particularly grateful to Rafael Villa, who shaped my thinking about Brazil and Latin America. I can never repay Rafael's kindness in supporting this project. On successive trips to Brazil, I had opportunities to meet and talk with Maíra Siman Gomes, Kai Kenkel, Janina Onuki, Matias Spektor, Feliciano de Sá Guimarães, and Leonardo Ramos. I owe a huge debt to all. In writing this book at City St George's, I was fortunate to get comments and suggestions on different chapters at various points from Inderjeet Parmar, Amnon Aran, Geoff Swenson, Sandy Hager, Tom Davis, Neil Loughlin, Viktor Friedmann, Andri Innes, and Laust Schouenborg. I am profoundly grateful to Amnon for enabling me to clarify my thinking and to Inderjeet for helping me make bold arguments. I am fortunate to have such fantastic colleagues.

A number of mentors and friends supported me while I connected the dots. I am profoundly grateful to Dan Nexon, who once again came to the rescue, spending literally all night with me in DC. I am most grateful to Stefano Guzzini for helping me think about power politics over several years. Jeff Legro read an early draft and helped me to avoid unnecessary jargon. Naeem Inayatullah and John Hobson have been a profound source of inspiration. Both took a big portion of their time to talk and offered constructive feedback, and I learned so much about what and how to write and why from these discussions. I am fortunate to know Adam Lerner and Vineet Thakur, who graciously read some chapters on short notice. Both have been crucial in helping me sharpen the argument. Evan Ramzipoor provided brilliant editing on the final version of the book and showed unfailing commitment to ensuring clarity in prose and attention to detail with unfailing kindness. Even with all this outstanding support, all remaining problems and errors are mine alone.

My largest gratitude goes to my family, especially my parents, for their unwavering support. To my wife, Rachel, I owe more than words can convey. She read drafts, stood by me during the most challenging moments of writing, and patiently put up with my vagaries and rhetoric. I am fortunate to be surrounded by her wisdom. Rachel was confident in my ability to complete this project, trusting me to navigate the darkness. What she may not realize is that she was the one holding the light all along. I dedicate this book to her.

RHETORICAL POWERS

INTRODUCTION

"**I**ndia is struck in a new world disorder," wrote a global affairs journalist. "New Delhi wants to be friends with Moscow and Washington, but the war in Ukraine has underscored the contradictions in its global visions."[1] With the ongoing global power transition from the West to the rest, it is not surprising that such commentaries have become mainstream.[2] On February 25, 2022, the day after the Russian invasion of Ukraine, the United States and its allies raised a resolution at the UN Security Council. It rebuked "Russia's aggression against Ukraine in violation of Article 2(4) of the UN Charter," which prohibits the threat or use of force and calls on all members to respect the sovereignty, territorial integrity, and political independence of other states.[3] Russia unsurprisingly vetoed the resolution. At that time, India was serving as an elected member of the UN Security Council. It abstained from the resolution, surprising many interlocutors attentive to India's commitment to the so-called rules-based international order. Such abstentions continued throughout the year.[4] This pattern irked many Western policymakers across Europe, who compelled India to stand on the right side of history.[5] Indian policymakers wasted no time in defending their interests in the context of the Russia-Ukraine War, and they resorted to a well-rehearsed playbook: anticolonial and anti-imperial rhetoric.

India's external affairs minister, S. Jaishankar, launched a rhetorical salvo: "Europe has to grow out of the mindset that Europe's problems are the world's problems, but the world's problems are not Europe's problems."[6] Later, he added, "The Global South, especially, is feeling this pain very acutely. India, therefore, strongly advocates a return to dialogue and diplomacy."[7] India's prime minister Narendra Modi has also frequently challenged the so-called colonial mindset.[8] This time, he appropriated Mohandas Gandhi to articulate India's position on the Russia-Ukraine War and emphasized that "today's era is not an era of war."[9] India's defense minister Rajnath Singh "cited Mahatma Gandhi's famous quote on peace: 'there is no way to peace, peace is the only way.'"[10] In keeping with its rhetoric, India dramatically increased its import of Russian oil, benefitting from the discounted price of Russian crude, and continued its legacy partnerships with Moscow on weapons procurement, effectively defying Western sanctions. Indian policymakers also condemned the exclusion of Russia from international forums and future UN negotiations. And in the opening session of the Voices of the Global South summit in January 2023, Modi volleyed another round of anti-imperial rhetoric: "Most of the global challenges have not been created by the Global South. But they affect us more." Furthermore, he said, rich nations "do not factor in our role or our voice." He added, "In the last century, we supported each other in our fight against foreign rule. We can do it again in this century, to create a new world order that will ensure the welfare of our citizens."[11]

Many policymakers, pundits, and academics see contemporary India's anti-imperial and anticolonial rhetoric as self-defeating, contradictory, irrational for a rising power, and archaic under the so-called liberal internationalism of our times. Janis Lazda, a former policy adviser in the White House and U.S. Senate, questioned, "How can one prop up this war's undisputed aggressor, while claiming to be on 'the side of peace?'" And he rhetorically asked "so, is this still the country of Gandhi?"[12] Sumit Ganguly, an academic and a commentator in the United States on India's foreign policy, was perplexed on the rhetoric coming from New Delhi: "Although India's foreign-policy decision-makers seem to think they can take a contrary stance on an issue of global concern and get away with it, there may be limits to the tolerance of the United States and other partners." And he added, "India's failure to stand with the United States and other democracies on the Ukraine question could lead to some diplomatic isolation."[13] Others astutely observe that the Indian prime minister, a member of a Hindu nationalist ideology group, is "utterly at odds with the capacious and open-minded worldview of Gandhi" but was cleverly deploying rhetoric using anti-imperial and anticolonial tropes.[14] For many commentators, India's seemingly irrational, confused, and contradictory rhetoric also appears self-defeating. Instead of talking like a rising power or a great power, such rhetoric undercuts the country's rise and weakens its engagement in international politics. For Modi, however, resorting to such a rhetorical strategy offers a lever for lifting India's position in the context of an international political crisis. What appears to commentators as irrational and contrarian is actually a rational strategy undertaken by shrewd political actors.

India is not the only state deploying seemingly self-defeating anti-imperial rhetoric in an international crisis. Brazilian president Luis Inácio Lula da Silva (Lula) was sworn in January 2023, replacing the far-right conservative Jair Bolsonaro (2019–2022). Lula condemned the "violation of Ukraine's territorial integrity."[15] But in an interview with *Time* magazine, he said: "Putin shouldn't have invaded Ukraine. But it is not just Putin who is guilty. The U.S. and the E.U. are also guilty."[16] Brazilian policymakers called for a ceasefire, rejected unilateral economic sanctions on Russia, and frowned on countries supplying arms and ammunition to either side.[17] Lula flipped the commonplace claim that if you oppose Ukraine defending itself, then you are pro-imperialism, not antiwar. Lula instead argued that if you support the war, then that support is a continuation of imperial warmongering: "Russia does not want to stop, and Ukraine does not want to stop. And if you don't talk about peace, you are contributing to war."[18] Under Lula, Brazil sought to position itself as a peacemaker. Lula met Chinese president Xi Jinping to plan a "peace club" over Ukraine and to bring warring parties to the negotiating table.[19] Brazil also abstained from resolutions that suspended Russia from the UN Human Rights Council and the Organization of American States (OAS).

Brazil's anti-imperial rhetoric again appears irrational and inconsistent to many policymakers, pundits, and academics. U.S. National Security Council spokesperson John Kirby accused Lula of "parroting Russian and Chinese propaganda."[20] Media pundits called Brazil's rhetoric and its actions "hyperactive, ambitious, and naïve."[21] Many academics saw a "blatant self-serving contradiction in the Brazilian position" because its leaders focused on "commercial and political prerogatives rather than simply staying quiet on the issue" and sending mixed signals about its leadership that were "inconsistent" with a risk-averse position.[22] Even Sean Burges, who has studied the ambitions of the "South American giant," found it "confusing" that "a reflexive anti-American ideological position amongst Lula's foreign policy coterie appeared to trump Brazil's very vocal claims to pan-Southern solidarity at the expense of Ukraine."[23] Guilherme Casarões, a prominent Brazilian foreign policy analyst, wrote: "Overcoming the Brazilian left's outdated views on authoritarian socialism and anti-imperialism may be as daunting a challenge for the Lula administration as leaving a sound diplomatic legacy."[24]

China, too, has levied anticolonial and anti-imperial rhetoric on the Russia-Ukraine War. On February 4, 2022, China and Russia reinforced their bilateral partnership as a friendship with "no limits" to defend a world order based on international law, the UN Charter, and the democratization of international relations.[25] Twenty days later, as the Russia-Ukraine War unfolded, Chinese policymakers squarely blamed the so-called imperial and colonial attitude of the West for the war.[26] In March 2022, Xi Jinping reiterated that "the legitimate security concerns of *all* countries must be taken seriously" to arrive at a peaceful settlement of the crisis.[27] Foreign Minister Wang Yi called on the West to discard its "Cold War mentality." Yi added, "We will continue to firmly oppose all hegemonies and power politics and resolutely uphold the legitimate rights and interests of developing countries, especially small and medium-sized countries."[28] At the same time, China's rhetoric targeted Western double standards and hypocrisy. Beijing pressed specifically on NATO's "constant eastern expansion since the Cold War,"[29] problems of unilateral sanctions, the role of arms exporters who add "fuel to the fire,"[30] and the spillover of crisis in the "Indo-Pacific strategy" affecting the peace and stability in the "Asia-Pacific region."[31] Its official policy of neutrality and democratic values belie the fact that Beijing uses anti-imperial rhetoric that enables Russia's breach of Ukraine's territorial integrity and sovereignty.

Xi Jinping's rhetoric confirmed Washington's view of China's threat to international order. In a special report on how the People's Republic of China (PRC) seeks to reshape the global information environment, the U.S. State Department argued that "PRC government officials and state media have since routinely amplified the Kremlin's propaganda, conspiracy theories, and disinformation about the war while officially purporting to be neutral, giving Moscow significant rhetorical cover even as Russia's forces engaged in alleged war crimes in Ukraine."[32] In the early months after the Russian invasion, U.S. secretary of state Antony Blinken stated that Chinese rhetoric was not only "echoing Russian propaganda around the world," it was also "shielding Russia in international organizations" and "shirking its responsibility as a P5 member."[33] Daniel J. Kritenbrink, U.S. assistant secretary of state for East Asian and Pacific affairs, believed that China's rhetoric confirmed its "might-makes-right mentality." Washington's goal was "not just to preserve the international order, but to "modernize it."[34] China's anti-imperial rhetoric seemed self-defeating, apparently aimed at hastening a showdown with the United States rather than dissipating it.

The force of the anti-imperial and anticolonial rhetoric of India, Brazil, and China in the Russia-Ukraine War is only one of the many signs of the changing dynamics of a global landscape. The growing assertiveness of these states marks the global transition of power from the West to the rest. Thus, many scholars focus on refashioning a new international order that includes the rest.[35] The prevailing wisdom holds that, for the first time in history, an interdependent world will be populated by numerous power centers with multiple versions of modernity.[36] According to Charles Kupchan, "The challenge for the West and the rest alike is to forge a new and pluralistic order—one that preserves stability and a rules-based international system amid the multiple versions of modernity that will populate the next world."[37] John Ikenberry aims to retain the mantle of reform with the liberal West: "There is widespread dissatisfaction today with the existing international order, a view held inside the West as well as in the global East and global South. But the liberal states in the West are in the best position to offer leadership in the reform of this order. Neither the global East nor the global South really have new ideas about how to replace the existing order with something fundamentally different. What it needs is reform."[38] But the anti-imperial and anticolonial rhetoric that comes from non-Western states is baffling to such views on international order. This rhetoric seems neither to embrace the multiple modernities view nor to endorse the discourses of liberal order.

This debate on the durability of Western hegemony against assertive non-Western states and the nature of reform required to uphold the liberal international order entirely misses and misconstrues the politics of non-European states because they don't focus on what I see as one of the fundamental fabrics of our modern world: the histories, consequences, and legacies of Western imperialism and colonialism. The prevailing wisdom about the challenges of arriving at the next world by design, represented by John Ikenberry for upholding the global West and Charles Kupchan for preserving multiple versions of modernities, fails to see the subtle and not-so-subtle imperial and colonial continuities in international ordering. These scholars fail to see the anti-imperial and anticolonial scripts—and the strategic ways in which clever policymakers use and flip these scripts—to change the world.

Failure to study new forms of power politics because anti-imperial and anticolonial rhetorical claims are old-fashioned and have no place in the liberal international order would be a big mistake. These tropes have landed squarely in the heart of contemporary global politics. In the wake of the Russian invasion of Ukraine in 2022, Vladimir Putin rhetorically asserted Russia's place as a leader of a global anticolonial movement and inspired policymakers in Asia, Africa, and Latin America when he argued that the United States seeks to impose a "global neo-colonial dictatorship" on the world.[39] In the run-up to the U.S. presidential election 2024, both Donald Trump and J. D. Vance engaged in carefully orchestrated anti-imperial rhetoric as antiwar rhetoric to challenge the rules-based international order. In speaking about the problems of liberals on democracy and the rule of law, J. D. Vance, the newly appointed running mate and now vice president, said: "You know, the EU has kept billions of dollars of promised aid away from Hungary, because of its views on Ukraine. It captured billions of dollars of promised aid from a previous government in Poland, because of the conservative Polish government's views." He added, "That's not a rules-based order. That's Europe, from Brussels and Berlin, imposing liberal imperialistic views on the rest of the continent."[40]

In response to anti-imperial rhetoric among Republicans, journalist Jeet Heer asked: "Amid the sordid crimes of the American Empire, running from the Mexican-American War under Polk to the Forever Wars that have marked the 21st century, there have been a few brave souls who have stood as the nation's conscience. These dissidents have repeatedly mounted principled opposition to plunder, torture, and conquest. The roll call of anti-imperialist heroes includes Henry David Thoreau, Mark Twain, W. E. B. Du Bois, Helen Keller, Martin Luther King Jr., Noam Chomsky, Bernie Sanders, and Barbara Lee. Does former president Donald Trump deserve a place in this pantheon?"[41] His answer was a resounding no. However, Heer also pointed out that there are two rival forms of imperialism in the United States. The one that Trump favors "is an imperialism of naked territorial conquest, resource plunder, and alliance with local comprador autocrats." The other that liberals favor is "imperialism in the name of international law, human rights, and free trade." He added that Trump must be rejected because his view "legitimizes militarism just as much—if not more—than mainstream liberal internationalism."[42] These debates on the imperialism of liberal internationalism are not new.[43]

The point is that anti-imperial and anticolonial rhetoric is part of our political reality across the left and the right and in the so-called West and the so-called non-Western states. The world is heading toward increasing tensions because of the West's unwillingness to fashion a new order and the demands of the so-called "Global South" states.[44] Some large and ambitious states, such as India, Brazil, and China, explicitly position themselves as leaders of the Global South. Not only will there be strategic challenges between the West and the rest but also intense competition between these self-proclaimed leaders of the global majority. Perhaps *the* important task at hand is to study the workings of non-Western power politics. It is important not only to examine the dynamics of Western imperialism and colonialism but also to examine how it bears on the present as power struggles. As Western political actors increasingly use the anti-imperial rhetorical playbooks that were the mainstay of non-Western actors, studying the causes, uses, workings, and effects of this rhetoric will allow a proper diagnosis of global order and disorder. The alternative is wishful thinking about forging a negotiated consensus in a divided world, where pundits appear to know the concerns of the rest but remain oblivious to imperial and colonial legacies and their strategic appropriations in our world.

THE ARGUMENT

The fundamental argument of this book is that anti-imperial and anticolonial rhetoric is the power politics of actors to advance political objectives in statecraft and change the international order. This book is not the first to study power politics, defined as "a condition in which politics 'turns into a fight *for* power, a prelude to political action *by means of* power; the *means* of politics' thus 'becomes the *goal* of the politician.' "[45] It is, however, a key contribution to the study of rhetorical power politics and its nature and transformation in statecraft under the hierarchical international system. In this book, "rhetoric" is defined as an instrumental and strategic use of language and arguments by policymakers in public speech to persuasively move multiple audiences or coerce them into submission to a political project. Rhetoric, in other words, is emotionally laden strategically deployed public communication—a language game—deployed on audiences for "persuasive or symbolic purposes."[46] Rhetoric is narrower than discourse and narrative (which includes the private, as in autobiographical narrative), but it is also connected to it. Narratives are stories people tell about themselves and the world; a narrative without rhetoric is toothless, while rhetoric without the backing of a compelling, broader narrative is meaningless.[47] As Aristotle long ago pointed out, all political actors engage in rhetoric "to conduct investigations and to furnish explanations, both to defend and to prosecute." But "some perform these tasks haphazardly, other by custom and out of habit" and "it would also be possible to do them by a method."[48] In this book, I argue that rhetoric for non-Europen states, particularly this habit and custom in rhetorical power politics, is a fundamental product of the hierarchical international system.

The hierarchy-centric scholarship in international relations (IR) places the patterns of super- and subordination at the center of the study of world politics.[49] Alongside the material and military hierarchy, scholars point out that the international system is deeply hierarchical and that it is based on civilizational, racial, class, and gender inequalities and social stratifications that corral some states into stratified relations in the pecking order.[50] The social hierarchies came into full force in the nineteenth century. The West established the norms, rules, and principles of the international system that have had an enduring influence on the present.[51] In other words, the now seemingly standard norms and rules of the international system were "improvised out of the colonial encounter" and then violently fixed and sustained to retain the unequal order.[52] There are enduring imperialisms and spectacles of colonial culture that cling, as Ann Laura Stoler put it, "to the present conditions of people's lives."[53] Such legacies continue in "high politics"[54]—the arena of diplomacy, security, war, and peace. But underdogs were not always silent victims in the hierarchy.

This book argues that rhetoric is a strategic instrument to challenge the silencing, disempowerment, and exclusionary practices in the hierarchy. Without rhetoric, underdogs will simply not be heard in such a system. Rhetoric, in James Scott's famous phrase, is "a weapon of the weak."[55] Against the history of the Western empire, imperialism, and colonialism, anti-imperial and anticolonial rhetoric for non-European states was a weapon of the weak. While previous studies tend to focus on rhetorical politics in this way, this study focuses principally on the unseen side of how some determined states develop a rhetorical repertoire in statecraft. Repertoire is understood as a set of routines learned, shared, and acted out as products of struggle.[56] Thus, this book hones in on how lessons of anti-imperial and anticolonial rhetorical performances in the struggles against Western empire and imperialism became part of their repertoire of statecraft. Policymakers have learned that the content of an argument does not always translate into effectiveness under the deeper social dynamics of international hierarchy and stratified power relations. In the hierarchy, policymakers have thus sharpened these lessons to expose and exploit the contradictions in the legitimating principles, norms, and rules of the international system. The flipping of anti-imperial and anticolonial rhetoric to challenge the international order is thus part of deep-rooted power political performances.

This book is the first to argue that distinctive rhetorical power politics in the international hierarchy will define our world, and actors who innovate on their repertoire and flip colonial and imperial scripts to exercise power by showing the contradictions of the international system will be the dominant players. Some foresee that many states will embrace Western values, others see the emergence of the Asian century, and many others argue that our world will have no center of gravity. This book contends that anti-imperial and anticolonial power politics will upend the liberal order. How it unfolds will define the next world.

Understanding such workings of rhetorical power politics requires unpacking specific histories of Western imperialism and colonialism.[57] Thus, this book begins with an account of the legitimating principles of Europe's and North America's overseas expansion and conquests, which took a decisive turn in the nineteenth century. Multiple European empires and nation-states, including the United States, expanded at a rapid pace. In that period, it is estimated that the British Empire gained

"4.5 million square miles and 66 million inhabitants;" "France gained 3.5 million square miles and 26 million people; Germany 1 million square miles and 26 million people, and Belgium through Leopold's Congo Free State, 900,00 square miles and a population of 8.5 million."[58] The United States engaged in continental expansion, expanded its territorial holdings by more than 2 million square miles, and ruled 2.5 million colonialized subjects by the end of the century.[59] John Hobson called such aggressive expansion the "earth hunger" of New Imperialism.[60] "By the 1930s, almost 85 percent of the world's territory either was part of an imperial system or, as in the case of much of Latin America, had formerly been European colonial holdings."[61] The rapid global expansion of the West rested on the principles and norms of the standards of civilization, racial superiority, capital accumulation, and exclusionary nationalism. In the "might is right" worldview, these legitimating principles were also aimed at managing intra-imperial competition, keeping the balance of power, and protecting international order.

These dominant principles, norms, and rules of the international system humiliated non-European states and the millions of colonized people because of their purported incapacity to govern themselves in an orderly manner. The narrative was that the uncivilized, barbarian, racially backward, and feminine natives and savages representing various sovereign and semisovereign territories and colonies required disciplined and civilizing leadership.[62] Such a view backed by Western military and economic power created enduring political and economic inequalities between the West and the rest. The "non-European states and colonies were encumbered with onerous obligations" to meet the strict conditions of imperial norms and rules "and had only limited or conditional rights," as Adom Getachew writes.[63] Empires also embraced different institutional modes of governing the colonized natives. "Imperial formations" extended from outright annexation, federation, and protectorates to the commonwealth, among others.[64] At the beginning of the twentieth century, this form of governance became entrenched as a distinctive stratified approach to managing the international order. Thus, the West used the authority of the League of Nations to continue the formal and informal exclusion of non-European states and their voices for managing order. Article 22 of the covenant of the League of Nations placed "people not yet able to stand by themselves under the strenuous conditions of the modern world" under the "sacred trust of civilization." In effect, it meant "tutelage of such peoples entrusted to advanced [European] nations."[65] The dominant legitimating principle to maintain international order thus reflected the hegemonic imperatives of great powers.[66] The West became "entitled to command," the rest "obligated to obey," and the relationship "regarded as right and legitimate by both."[67]

But many anti-imperial and anticolonial elites from Asia, Africa, and Latin America have scrutinized the legitimating principles of the international system more closely. The norms and rules of the international order might reflect the visions of the powerful, but they have also acquired a life of their own that has fueled the challenges of anti-imperialist actors. Many ideas circulating in the transnational sphere have provided inter-colonial connections, solidarities, and foundations for their contesta-tions. For example, throughout the nineteenth century, many elites from Asia, Africa, and Latin America used and inflected ideas of liberalism, antiracism, federalism, social Darwinism, nationalism, anarchism, and spiritual revivalism, among others. In this way, non-European elites compelled the West to conform to principles they had enunciated and pointed out the contradictions in practice. This pattern of anti-imperial contestation circulated throughout the transnational network and spread to different parts of the colonized world via people, goods, and the mass circulation of newsprints.[68] As Christopher Bayly puts it, by 1900, non-European leaders engaged in "anti-government protests in places as far distant as Santiago, Cape Town and Canton" and "invoked the notion of their 'rights' as individuals and representatives of nations."[69] For the West, whose reach of the global was violent but also patchy and precari-ous, patterns of anticolonial contestations threatened the order as well as the material, racial, gendered, and class inequalities that sustained their empires. So what did the West do?

By the mid- to the late nineteenth century, European and North American political actors *silenced* contentious and quarrelsome activists, sovereigns, semisovereigns, and colonies from Asia, Africa, and Latin America.[70] This book shows that foreign policy elites in the metropole followed a unique path of silencing contestations on high politics by attributing *incompetence* to non-Europeans on matters relating to inter-national ordering.[71] Such silencing through attributing incompetence was evident across a diverse set of institutional challenges to imperial rule, from individuals to collective actors. For example, the West viewed anti-imperial individual activists with disdain. Referring to Gandhi, the arch-imperialist Winston Churchill said: "It is alarming and also nauseating to see Mr. Gandhi, an Inner Temple lawyer, now become a seditious fakir of a type well known in the East, striding half-naked up the steps of the Viceregal Palace, while he is still organizing and conducting a defiant campaign of civil disobedience, to parley on equal terms with the representative of the King-Emperor."[72] Europeans also silenced the diplomatic claims of semisovereigns because speakers of this group were not worth hearing.[73] For example, Thomas Lawrence, a famous international lawyer, noted that it would be absurd to "expect the king of Dahomey to establish a Prize Court, or to require the dwarfs of the central African forest to receive a permanent diplomatic mission."[74] And the West formulated unequal treaties against grand old civilizations such as China, Japan, and the Ottoman Empire because of their incompetence in high politics. The 1919 report of the American Section of the International Commission on Mandates noted that Turkey is held by "people whose incompetence to convert nature's gifts into use or profit is historically patent." There is "hideous mis-government [*sic*] and massacres of the Turkish rule," and Asia Minor must be divided because of "Turkey's utter inadequacy to the strategic world position in which she is placed."[75]

The foundations for this pattern of silencing emerged in the conduct of the European Great Powers—France, Britain, Austria, Russia, and Prussia—that had assumed a position of authority in high politics since 1815. But silencing non-Europeans is intricately connected to the late nineteenth- and early twentieth-century Atlanticist (that is, European and North American) ways of managing international order and remaking the world in its own image based on the export of democracy, secular nationalism, and capitalism as the truly universal value of the modern world. With material superiority, such silencing patterns were reproduced durably in the superpower competition and remain steadfast in the character of today's American empire. For example, in the Cold War period, the West viewed Vietnam as an incompetent state, "vilified as a threat to order in Southeast Asia." Thus, its claim to a right to self-defense against the "cross-border killings by the Khmer Rouge" was silenced in the face of the geopolitical interests of superpowers. Compare that to the expansive doctrine of self-defense assumed by the United States in Iraq in 2003. For Gerry Simpson, this discrepancy is not the result of the "historical development of the norm or the changing technologies of terror" but the entrenched view that the "doctrine of self-defence does not apply to middle powers."[76] In 2025, Israel as a middle power demonstrated a commitment to self-defence with the entrenched view that the doctrine does not apply to people in Gaza under its occupation. The reproduction of silencing is part of the deep hierarchy of the international system.

This book maps three ways in which the silencing practices of the West work in international politics. First, the West determines that states from Asia, Africa, and Latin America lack the *capabilities* to influence regional and global geopolitics, and therefore the views of their policymakers don't matter. Second, Western policymakers engage the world as though non-European states and their political actors cannot exercise *objective judgments* on managing international order. Third, the West views these states as agents *without authority* to command and enforce the rules of international society. That the subordinate actors do not get to weigh in on matters relating to international order is not a natural condition of world politics. It arises from the Eurocentric nature of world politics, power relations in the colonial encounter, and what Edward Said called the "dreadful secondariness" of colonized people and their cultures.[77]

Although hierarchy and postcolonial studies in IR have often underlined these long stories of exclusion, silencing, and stigmatizing practices as unique moments in our world, stopping the story at that point is one-sided. It misses the ways in which actors on the lower rungs of the hierarchy challenge these silencing and disempowerment practices of international ordering. In the interconnected global space of the nineteenth century, "anticolonial activists had created a terrain of anti-imperial global critique,"[78] which provided the material and cultural foundation for renewed challenges against the empires at the end of the century. In other words, people in the lower rungs of the hierarchy have formed connections and fought back and challenged and, in doing so, have also pursued power. The view that non-European states were always silent victims is thus misplaced.

For example, the Afrikaner fight against British imperial power in the Boer War (1899–1902) was followed closely in China and informed their challenges against the West.[79] Many Arab, Turkish, Persian, Vietnamese, Indian, and Indonesian nationalists celebrated Japan's defeat of Russia (1905) and viewed the event as the beginning of the end of Western imperialism and forged anticolonial connections to that effect.[80] W. E. B. Du Bois shrewdly praised Japanese imperialism against global white supremacy. He understood rhetoric as the means to cross the abyss of "the color line."[81] The black internationalism of Marcus Garvey reached into Aboriginal activist communities. The First International Council of Women in 1888 marked a tradition of feminist internationalism even as anti-imperial Iranian women "boycotted European textiles at virtually the same moment that Indian women participated in *swadeshi* [Indigenous manufactures] protests."[82] These interconnected, inter-imperial activists with different ideological affiliations went on to challenge the West and set the stage for the reordering of the world.

This book argues that these non-European activists found *rhetoric* to be an important weapon for standing against the growing material dominance of the West and defying its silencing practices. Their emotionally loaded anti-imperial and anticolonial rhetoric also became a necessity because most non-European activists believed that they could not simply voice their views politely without being crushed under Western silencing pressures and the jingoism in the imperial system. Thus, rhetoric was a necessity that was creatively put to use under hierarchy. Because the normal and polite ways of articulating the challenges were defanged, anti-imperial and anti-colonial *rhetoric* instead of emotion less language became central for non-Europeans to play their game in international politics.

Mohandas Gandhi, for example, put rhetoric into action when a journalist asked him what he thought of Western civilization. "I think it would be a good idea," he replied. In the midst of the struggle, he also added, "The tendency of Indian civilization is to elevate the moral being, that of the Western civilization to propagate immorality."[83] In the wake of European intervention in China and the onset of the Opium Wars, Commissioner Lin Zexu rhetorically chided Queen Victoria in 1839: "Let us ask, where is your conscience? I have heard that the smoking of opium is very strictly forbidden by your country; that is because the harm caused by opium is clearly understood. . . . How can you bear to go further, selling products injurious to others in order to fulfill your insatiable desire?"[84] Later Sun Yat-Sen and Mao Zedong scorned the "robbers" of Versailles and unequal treaties with fierce rhetoric.

This pattern of anti-imperial and anticolonial rhetoric emerged, as Christoper Bayly puts it, as a central "counter preaching"[85] instrument designed to "subvert the contemporary self-confidence of colonial elites," their "moral failures," and the "degeneracy of British and European domestic society."[86] Some political actors have also used rhetoric to point out the contradictions, hypocrisies, and disorder in the legitimating principles of international ordering. Ashis Nandy once argued that "under oppression, when survival is at stake, there is regression to infantilism" and "generations of subjection can diminish the habit of dignity and teach grown men the strategy of the little child."[87] In the colonial world, rhetoric represents this infantile strategy. It has put imperialists and paternalists abroad on their back foot while also working to critique fellow nationalists and colonized elites at home who have failed to engage in popular mobilization against domination.[88] Some rhetoric-wielding, ambitious non-European actors were also pursuing power at the same time. Their rhetoric espoused exclusionary nationalism and territorial expansion and looked to emulate the ascent of the Atlanticist world. Some of these non-European states had "their eye as much on other global imperial powers as they did on the indigenous people they aimed to colonize," as Tony Ballantyne and Antoinette Burton write.[89]

This book shows that some ambitious non-European political actors—specifically India, Brazil, and China—developed a *repertoire* of anti-imperial, anti-Yankee, and anticolonial rhetoric in statecraft to exploit the contradictions in the principles, norms, and rules of the international order to their advantage.[90] Any repertoire is a "body of items that are regularly performed" and, unlike habits, they emerge reflexively when actors perceive reliable and effective ways to produce the intended performance and become part of their stock of skills as know-how, but it also remains eminently amenable to innovation, creativity, and change. "Repertoires are thus not simply inventories of elements that need to be combined in order to be able to conduct a given type of project, and/or achieve a given epistemic goal; crucially, they include knowledge of how to align such inventories of elements so that they can be effectively used to acquire the resources, capacities, and expertise needed to pursue an inquiry."[91] In this light, deploying anti-imperial and anticolonial rhetoric is a useful, appealing, and tractable political instrument for non-Europeans in the international hierarchy.

Political actors in the international hierarchy have frequently used and improvised on this rhetorical repertoire in their struggles against the exclusionary practices of international ordering. They learned from the magical force of anti-imperial rhetoric to garner a voice under silencing practice and highlight the contradictions in the legitimating principles of the imperial ordering practices. In a double move, policymakers often rely on the rhetorical repertoire in statecraft and often flip the scripts to exploit the contradictions in the legitimating principles of the international system. This book argues that such moves should be seen as creative innovations in their power politics to maneuver strategically within hardened hierarchical network structures. The enduring and manifold lessons of struggle against Western empire and colonialism, coupled with the demands of forging independent statecraft, mean we will see more of these innovations in the future. The West's approach to liberal ordering based on universalizing its values and institutions triggers non-Western policymakers to continue to use anti-imperial and anticolonial rhetoric, fine-tuning their know-how each time, to engage in effective claim-making performances and improvise and innovate on them in an international crisis.[92]

This book shows that policymakers from India, Brazil, and China relied on rhetoric to stand against the deep and enduring silencing practices when managing international order. Their anti-imperial and anticolonial rhetoric and affective performances became regular tools in their tool kits and, in many ways, necessary instruments in the international hierarchy. Many Indian, Brazilian, and Chinese policymakers used these scripts creatively to expose and exploit the contradictions in the legitimating principles, norms, and rules of the system. In chapter 2, I will show how such rhetorical repertoires of power politics became part of the statecraft in the long struggle against empire. The underlying logic of such rhetorical power politics seems to arise from the idea that they must exploit the established rules to survive.[93] If creative use of anti-imperial and anticolonial rhetoric in relation to multiple audiences came to represent a strategic way to pursue power under hierarchy, we must notice that different political actors use different colonial scripts depending on the time, socially specific conditions, and global power dynamics. This book theorizes three ideal-typical ways in which policymakers rely on their rhetorical repertoire to exploit the contradictions in the international system in pursuing power politics. The expectations derived from simplified ideal types provide benchmarks for the analytical study of the real phenomena.[94]

First, in an international crisis, these postcolonial policymakers focus on the colonial nature of the reigning norms and rules of the international order with a public claim to help the other people and states. By highlighting the contradictions in the dominant principles, they enact rhetorical claims similar to their claims during the colonial and imperial periods. Policymakers use subtle and not-so-subtle anti-imperial rhetoric to stratify norms that advantage their strategic interests. They use this rhetoric to probe different audiences and engage in dialogue only with audiences who are sympathetic to their claims. The underlying logic is that one must break the rules to survive. As their rhetorical repertoire centers around the unequal international order, we can expect that political actors seek to innovate on their claims to break the rules and create a wedge among audiences using the rough anti-imperial and anticolonial scripts and might also flip these scripts to achieve their objectives.

This book shows that Indian policymakers engaged in this kind of rhetorical power political strategy in the East Pakistan crisis of 1971. The Indira Gandhi administration worked against patterns of silencing replete in the crisis and innovated on its rhetorical strategy by looking back to the anti-imperial and anticolonial past and shaping the crisis by representing India as fighting for the oppressed Bengali people. In this rhetorical strategy, Indira Gandhi's rhetoric exploited the contradictions in the legitimating principles of the Cold War international order and cut archenemy Pakistan to size. As this book will show, the anticolonial rhetorical strategy of the Indira Gandhi administration was not very different from that of Mohandas Gandhi, who, as we saw, engaged in a "counter-preaching" rhetorical strategy. Today, Modi's appropriation of Mahatma Gandhi or his calls for self-reliance and resistance in similar anti-imperial and anti-colonial language is not accidental, even if the rhetorical modality is ruthless anger, violence, and resentment.

The second ideal-typical way in which anti-imperial rhetorical repertoire unfolds as power politics rests on how political actors want to work within rather than explicitly defying the rules and norms of international ordering. This book will theorize that some policymakers focus on anti-imperial rhetoric to signal inclusivity and solidarity with other institutional members, playing on past scripts. Again, by enacting the contradictions in the dominant principles, these policymakers use their rhetoric to show the continuing imperial nature of international ordering. Instead of standing alone or stratifying norms as in the previous type, however, we can expect that they rhetorically present themselves as strong supporters of institutionalized local, regional, and cultural prescriptions and proscriptions and seek solidarity. The conceptual framework expects that political actors deploy anti-imperial rhetoric in statecraft to bind themselves to other anti-imperial interlocutors, present themselves as strong supporters of working with these members, and articulate their claims as though they fit within established anti-imperial conventions.

This book will show that Brazilian policymakers engaged in this kind of anti-imperial rhetorical power politics in the Haitian crisis of 2004. The Lula administration challenged the patterns of Western silencing using rhetoric against American interventionism and Yankee imperialism in the Latin American region. The rhetoric of the Lula administration is not very different from the historical quest of anti-imperial Latin American policymakers who sought autonomy from the domination of the United States. This continuity in rhetorical power politics means anti-Americanism is not an idiosyncratic approach of the Lula administration but a tool that worked strategically with the anti-imperial views that resonated with other Latin American states.

Third, some policymakers use anti-imperial and anticolonial rhetoric to defend pluralism aggressively in the international order. By showing the contradictions in the legitimating principles, norms, and rules of international ordering, these policymakers deploy anti-imperial rhetoric to challenge the Western ideological dominance in the system. Within the ideal-typical conceptual framework we can expect that political actors use such anti-imperial rhetoric to accuse, denounce, and reproach other interlocutors. In this rhetorical process, they shame Western interlocutors holding the reins of power. Again, this is a repertoire learned in the struggle against imperial powers. By speaking up for pluralism in statecraft, their rhetoric emphasizes alternative ways of resolving an international crisis. The objective is to avoid outright confrontation with leading powers while preparing for threats and opportunities that are likely to emerge in the future. This book shows that Chinese policymakers engaged in such an anti-imperial rhetoric in the Syrian crisis of 2011–2020. The Xi Jinping administration was dissatisfied with Western perceptions of China's incompetence in managing international order outside its region. Alongside anti-imperial rhetoric around the Syrian crisis, the administration emphasized its authority as a guarantor of principles of sovereignty and self-determination. It denounced and reproached the West and shamed other interlocutors for creating disorder in the Middle East. As with India and Brazil, the rhetoric of the Xi Jinping administration drew from a repertoire of engagement with colonial and imperial powers of the past.

Such theoretical mapping is not exhaustive. Multiple rhetorical strategies often overlap, and political actors frequently use many strategies in a single episode. However, rhetorical power politics emerges as an innovative strategy that draws and adjusts from a corpus of effective anti-imperial rhetorical repertoire from the past. It is useful for cutting across the structural inequalities of the hierarchical system. Rhetorical powers can pry open the system and, in the process, reorder the world.

RETHINKING POWER POLITICS AND IR THEORY

Rhetorical power politics under the hierarchical international system—particularly the use and exploitation of the anti-imperial and anticolonial tropes—is a ruthless enterprise that challenges silencing practices in which actors cleverly establish their competent engagement in international ordering. One of the central aims of this book is to bring into the same conversation the different strands of IR theory on power politics—such as realism, rhetorical entrapment, and postcolonial studies—that are currently separate and siloed. This book contends that the realist focus on power struggles and realpolitik is important. But by focusing on material hierarchy and ignoring the social hierarchy and the silencing practices of the hierarchical international system, realists miss the complex ways in which states pursue power politics. This book also agrees with the extensive constructivist literature on rhetorical power politics as a weapon of the weak. But by equating skillful argumentative content with effectiveness, these scholars miss the enduring colonial and imperial legacies in the international system and how, as a matter of course, claims advanced by those on the lower rungs are different from those put forth by top dogs. Finally, the suffering of actors as a consequence of imperialism and colonialism is a real problem, as the extensive postcolonial scholarship shows.[95] The reality of the grief and miseries of the Indigenous and the stateless are tragic. However, some ambitious postcolonial states are not just victims but also power mongers. Painting all non-European states with a single brush based on their past colonial predicaments would be an error.

Political realists might look at rising India, Brazil, and China facing the military hierarchy of the West and treat their behavior as a pursuit of self-interest in anarchical international politics. The common view is the power transition from the West to the East.[96] It is true that these states are pursuing realpolitik, but not in the manner that realists describe. Focusing on military and economic hierarchies ignores symbolic and discursive instruments central to these states' political strategies. Realists reject the problem of silencing and epistemic violence in the international system. They underestimate the enduring injustices, racist humiliation, and violence against non-Europeans and in turn neglect the fundamental form of power politics of non-European states.[97] Policymakers sometimes challenge the legitimacy of the Eurocentric order that supports colonial practices and pursue political projects even when they are materially incapable of overturning the status quo, and some realists call this behavior irrational domestic politics and attribute these choices to domestic pressure rather than international strategy.[98] If the focus is to study the struggle for influence in world politics, political realism must also pay attention, as constructivists point out, to nonmilitary instruments and the social dynamics of the international system, which policymakers use to achieve realpolitik goals.[99]

Most recent constructivist IR works that examine discursive and symbolic struggles between actors have focused on norm contestation and rhetorical entrapment.[100] Conscious of the importance of legitimation strategies in the international order, constructivists argue that political actors contest norms to secure their political objectives. Scholars of rhetorical entrapment apply this argument to power politics.[101] Actors' ability to wield rhetoric by "speaking the same words as their potential adversary, but using them to justify its expansionist policies" marks an important aspect of international power struggles.[102] The literature has enriched our understanding of how different political actors use rhetoric as weapons of the weak to pursue political projects. Many actors deploy strategic rhetoric in international politics. But colonial legacies and thus the different positions of actors in the stratified social hierarchy affect their rhetorical choices.

Think, for example, of Libya between 1992 and 2003. The country faced sanctions for its involvement in the bombing of Pan Am Flight 103, the infamous Lockerbie bombing. As Ian Hurd shows, the Libyan rhetorical strategy publicly championed the norms of liberal internationalism to show that both U.S. and UK investigators placed punishment ahead of judicial hearing, thus disrespecting the procedural justice of international law.[103] Libyan rhetoric is certainly a weapon of the weak. But Hurd offers no account of the histories of Italian colonialism and perceptions of Western imperialism or how these factors might have affected the rhetoric of Muammar Gaddafi, the ruler of Libya at the time, and his realpolitik concessions in accepting responsibility for the bombing.

For many postcolonial states under epistemic silencing, rhetoric is the only way to be heard in international politics, similar to "how violent outbursts are the only recourse of slave rebellions" because of the "lack of access to other more legitimate forms of protest."[104] Existing works on political rhetoric and norm contestation have neglected the histories of Western empires and have paid less attention to how colonial hierarchies shape rhetoric in world politics.[105] As this book will show, some ambitious non-European states that have developed a repertoire of anti-imperial and anticolonial rhetoric aim to upend the international system. By relegating norm contestation and rhetorical framing to the implicit liberal domain, existing works on rhetorical entrapment ignore the complicity of liberal internationalism with imperialism and the central idea from postcolonial studies that the hierarchies and exclusions of colonial rule continue to inform the dominant norms, rules, and principles of international politics.[106] Establishing hierarchy as a constitutive element of the way we study discursive struggles in international politics will enable us to understand how non-Europeans in the international hierarchy have understood these problems and flip the colonial scripts in their power politics.

Postcolonial criticism and skepticism are not without their limitations. Postcolonial scholars paint most non-Europeans as victims of colonial trauma and thus complement Marxist perspectives written from the perspective of the colonizers.[107] Both these accounts resort to an exceptional account of the West in global transformation, however, and ignore the anticolonial critiques and the fierce struggle for power and freedom among the colonized in the imperial network.[108] For example, Black communities in Brazil reimagined a novel sociospatial geography called marron settlement, or *quilombos*, to defend against the brutality of chattel slavery. Black members in these communities escaped slave owners, articulated a new idea of freedom, and later challenged the myth of racial democracy in the country. As new historical studies show, the strategies and politics of Indigenous communities such as the Maoris changed the conception of rights in global politics despite defeat.[109]

Taking a comprehensive view of the dynamics in the Western empire means that we cannot essentialize the binaries of the oppressive West and stigmatized or traumatized rest. Ayze Zarakol rightly focuses on social stratification but views agency and status concerns in the face of socialization pressures as an internalization of stigma and victimhood of the larger society. Focusing on the collective trauma of colonialism, Manjari Miller also argues that a "mentality of victimhood" is part of India's and China's "national identity and international outlook."[110] However, the colonial past is not only a tragic trauma; the erasures and silences in the colonial practices can engender shrewd power politics. Many other states opt for the extreme in capitalizing on collective trauma. Benjamin Netanyahu's Israel is engaging in a ruthless military action in Gaza that shows how the weaponization of collective trauma in the past enables state policymakers to justify the systematic genocide of stateless Palestinians.[111] And North Korea has developed nuclear weapons in response to the national trauma of U.S.-led UN forces waging war against the country in the Korean War of 1950. Understanding power politics requires us to see the reality of ambitious states appropriating the past for strategic use.

Today many Western policymakers are using the anti-imperial rhetoric and playbook of non-European actors in international politics.[112] In this introduction, I wrote about the anti-imperial and anticolonial rhetoric of Vladimir Putin as well as that of Donald Trump. But radical demagogues in the West also seek to re-create the imperial past or cherry-pick anti-imperial ideas to conjure notions of "alternative facts" and "posttruth politics."[113] Some ultranationalists in the non-Western world appropriate postcolonial debates to prop up hatred, rewrite national histories, and glorify violence. In this light, even if there are surface similarities between the rhetorical strategies of, say, Donald Trump and Narendra Modi, the latter plays on colonial scripts of defiance while the former draws on rhetorical strategies that center on an imperialist past of American expansionism. Focusing on how political actors use colonial scripts in rhetorical politics can enable us to rethink how these complex power politics work in the hierarchical system.

ROAD MAP

Chapter 1 will unpack the theoretical framework that guides this book. The argument moves in three steps. First, it looks at the existing IR scholarship on power politics, focusing on realism and rhetorical entrapment schools of thought. From a postcolonial sensibility, I critique but also build on these research programs to show how deep social hierarchies influence power political choices, rhetorical content, and the effectiveness of rhetorical deployments in politics. Second, it elaborates on how—in the brief but significant period of Western imperialism and colonialism—empires engaged in international ordering through the systematic silencing of non-European actors. It will pay attention to synchronic and diachronic aspects of top-down domination for theorizing the practices of attributing incompetence to non-Europeans on matters relating to international order. Third, this chapter theorizes on the resistance and challenges to silencing practices and the impact of these practices in the development of a repertoire of statecraft. Political actors from Asia, Africa, and Latin America learned the art of using rhetoric as a product of the struggle against silencing, but they also innovated on it to exploit the contradictions of the system. The chapter will also theorize this aspect of rhetorical repertoire and elaborate on the ideal-typical ways in which political actors perform their rhetorical power politics against the legitimating principles of the system. This chapter will then establish the interpretive research method appropriate for this theory and what one should expect in the empirical world if the theory is plausible against competing alternative explanations on the workings of rhetorical power politics.

Chapter 2 will examine the rhetorical repertoire of India, Brazil, and China in international politics. It will focus on the origins of rhetorical strategies in these states in the struggle against Western imperialism and colonialism. The chapter will track the ways in which political actors from these states engaged in anti-imperial and anticolonial rhetoric and exposed contradictions of international ordering. In learning from successful rhetorical moves that challenged the empires in high politics, the community of practitioners built their statecraft by innovating on these original passage points. As chapter 2 will demonstrate, the use of anti-imperial and anticolonial rhetoric continued both implicitly and explicitly, the interwar period solidified their repertoire, and political actors innovated on these strategies throughout the Cold War and the post–Cold War period. Rhetoric is not central to every aspect of a state's foreign policy. We must be careful not to examine every foreign policy practice in the light of an inevitable rhetorical onslaught. In statecraft, not being rhetorical is itself a carefully planned rhetorical strategy to achieve political outcomes. Thus, the rhetorical repertoire is one among multiple power political repertoires that these policymakers developed.

Chapters 3, 4, and 5 will focus on rhetorical power politics in India, Brazil, and China, respectively, as deployed during humanitarian crises abroad. This rhetoric is not limited to humanitarian issues alone. However, reconstructing the rhetorical power politics of India in the East Pakistan crisis (1971), Brazil in the Haitian crisis (2004), and China in the Syrian crisis (2011–2020) enable us to see that these states' behaviors are not simply reactive—they are examples of shrewd statecraft centering on flipping the colonial script. Chapter 6 concludes by returning to the practice of rhetorical power politics of Global South states and the current controversies with which this book begins.

Power politics is a disruptive enterprise; rhetorical power politics is no less so. Taking the argument of this book seriously will enable us to understand how power works from below and the implications on international disorder. It is not surprising that many of these ambitious Global South states silence local, tribal, and Indigenous voices in international politics, thereby re-creating violent imperial projects of their own. Even if the rhetorical instrument of power politics does more damage to the project of meaningful living, it will remain the centerpiece of their international politics.

1

RHETORICAL POWER POLITICS

A Framework

Why does anti-imperial and anticolonial rhetoric remain central for many states in contemporary international politics, including for the so-called ambitious rising powers such as India, Brazil, and China? Coming from a rising power, such rhetoric would be self-defeating. It certainly differs from the strategies of past rising powers, such as the United States or Prussia, in the nineteenth century. In many ways, ambitious states in the Global South do not speak like rising powers in the Global North or like aspiring great powers on the global stage. As the introduction to this book showed, the rhetoric of anti-imperialism and anticolonialism was evident in the Russia-Ukraine War in 2022. Many policymakers, pundits, and academics saw such rhetoric as futile, contradictory, and irrational given the dynamics of the so-called liberal international order. International relations (IR) scholars agree that there is a global transition of power from the West to the rest, see increasingly assertive postures of the non-European states, and accept the necessity to refashion a new international order. Nevertheless, IR scholars seem divided on how to make sense of the fierce rhetorical battles and performances on the international stage.

Assertive rhetoric from India, Brazil, and China clearly involves realpolitik moves in navigating the world. But our IR scholarly idiom for studying these power-political games in the hierarchical international system is limited. Realists focus solely on the shifts in the relative power of states, emphasize military and economic capabilities, and view rhetoric as "cheap talk" in the anarchical international system.[1] They rightly focus on realpolitik but miss the symbolic and discursive side of power-political competition. Rhetorical entrapment scholars, in general, offer greater attention to symbolic aspects of power politics and view actors' resort to rhetoric as a weapon of the weak in the battle for legitimacy. Both realism and social-constructivist accounts are important for my conceptual framework, but they do not fully explain how the choice of rhetoric might itself be the consequence of social hierarchies arising from Western imperialism and colonialism. Here, postcolonial sensibilities allow us to see the continuities of imperial projects, the persistence of racist discourses, and the enduring "civilizing" missions in the hierarchical world. Yet non-Western political actors are not merely repressed, stigmatized, and marginalized victims. Rhetoric-wielding actors exercise power by working within and cutting across the legacies of Western empire and imperialism. In this chapter, I bring elements of this diverse literature into conversation with each other to build a novel framework of rhetorical power politics.

My conceptual framework unfolds in three ways. Building on existing IR scholarship on the hierarchy of the modern international system, this chapter argues that Western international practices frequently treat non-European states as *incompetent* in managing order. This is epistemic violence, which refers to practices that silence the voices and ideas of marginal subjects.[2] As I point out in the introduction, states continue to exist in a world shaped by the legacies of Western empires and imperialism. In world-ordering practices, demarcating who is competent and who is not is a form of power exercised by top dogs. I theorize how this pattern of silencing non-European states works by focusing on three interconnected imperial practices: refuting the ability of non-European states to employ material capabilities to protect order, rejecting their ability to exercise objective judgment, and challenging their authority to manage international order. These three practices have structural consequences in the sense that they consistently position Asian, African, and Latin American political actors as secondary, if not irrelevant, when thinking about world ordering, which constrains these states' normal ability to voice their views or justify and legitimize their policies in an interconnected world.

In response to silencing practices, non-Western political actors in the mid- to late nineteenth and twentieth centuries used rhetoric to challenge their incompetent status. In unequal relations, rhetoric is a weapon of the weak, as social-constructivist IR scholarship shows. However, there are deeper social stratification and racial, gendered, and even civilizational inequalities that drive this weapon. And with different rhetorical content, these actors in the lower rungs of hierarchy respond to and challenge the enduring silencing practices of the international system. Silencing and disempowerment practices give rise to the necessity of rhetoric. It manifests, among others, as anti-imperialism and anticolonialism in international politics. Such rhetoric crucially enables policymakers in the lower rungs of hierarchy to dissect the legitimating principles, norms, and rules of international ordering; counteract claims and offer counterclaims; and exercise agency. Thus, using rhetoric for exploiting the contradictions in the legitimating principles, norms, and rules of the system is a strategy that less powerful states developed under hierarchy. Over time, this anti-imperial and anticolonial rhetorical strategy evolved into a repertoire in statecraft for speaking out and speaking up about the international order.

Innovating and improvising this form of rhetorical instrument in statecraft and building a repertoire of exploiting contradictions in the principle, norms, and rules of the system, are creative ways to flip the colonial scripts to upend the international order. Social hierarchies that are shaped by imperialism and colonialism thus affect the choice to deploy rhetoric, the actual content of the rhetoric, and its political effectiveness. This chapter maps this rhetorical power politics under social hierarchy in ideal-typical terms. Then, the chapter outlines an interpretive research method for investigating its manifold workings in international politics. In this way, the conceptual framework offers a novel avenue to study power politics. The framework established here sets the stage for empirical investigation of the evolution of this rhetorical repertoire as well as the unfolding of the creative power politics of India, Brazil, and China in distinct issue areas and political episodes.

IR AND POWER POLITICS

Most observers of the assertive rhetoric of India, Brazil, and China in international politics tend to say that these states are exercising power. The question of power lies at the heart of much IR theorizing about international politics. Power is an "essentially contested concept," which means that an authoritative definition (intensions) and its set of referents (extensions) are characterized by endless disputes led by both scholars and practitioners.[3] As Stefano Guzzini, a leading theorist of power, argues, power involves multiple meanings and stands in for resources or capabilities, influence, rule, authority, and legitimacy; for individual disposition, autonomy, impersonal biases; and as an emergent property, among others.[4] And a relational understanding of power—A has power over B to the extent that A can get B to do something that B would not otherwise do—requires a contextual analysis of shrewd statecraft practiced by political actors in specific interactions.[5] For this reason, the common view that India, Brazil, and China are exercising power requires a careful investigation of what power, why it is exercised, and how political actors exercise it in world politics.

A thoroughly relational account of power must also consider the production of intended and unintended effects. Power is a performance that political actors enact in practice, affecting the practices of others.[6] In practice, there is an endless process of power politics. Max Weber saw power condition as "a condition in which politics 'turns into a fight *for* power, a prelude to political action *by means of* power; the means of politics' thus 'becomes the *goal* of the politician.'" Building on these lines, Stacie Goddard and Daniel Nexon define global power politics as "involving politics based on the use of power to influence the actions and decisions of actors that claim, or exercise, authority over a political community."[7] With power, many political actors aim to structure the relations and conduct of other actors. Power politics brings change but also leads to hubris, miscalculations, and misjudgments, which is a tragedy of political life.[8]

In this section, I focus on two prominent IR accounts that theorize the power politics strategies states use in international politics. I focus specifically on recent advancements in realism and rhetorical entrapment schools. Examining these frameworks through a postcolonial lens shows the limits of these approaches to studying power politics under the racial and imperial social hierarchy of international politics.[9] A postcolonial perspective in IR also requires improvement to match the changed conditions of diversity among postcolonial states. In moving beyond these existing frameworks in IR, the discussions serve as building blocks for a practice-based perspective on power and a foil for my conceptual framework in subsequent sections of this chapter. We will see why the rhetoric of India, Brazil, and China, specifically the anti-imperial and anticolonial claims, which seems so self-defeating, is a distinct form of power politics.

REALISM AND REALPOLITIK

Realist scholarship in IR is diverse and wide ranging, but much of it shares a fundamental feature marked by an emphasis on the struggle for power in international politics. As Hans Morgenthau, one of the fathers of classical realism in IR, puts it, "[International] politics is a struggle for power over men, and whatever its ultimate aim may be, power is its immediate goal and the modes of acquiring, maintaining, and demonstrating it determine . . . political action."[10] For many so-called classical IR realists, the tragedy of history is cyclical, where efforts to build order ultimately succumb to disorder and war. Here, military preparedness and economic capabilities, including alliances, are necessary to survive. Morgenthau also showed, however, that the pursuit of concrete policies in a power struggle "requires the wisdom and strength of the statesman," and it needs prudence in making sense of social conventions rather than the "rationality of the engineer."[11]

Kenneth Waltz's neorealism starts with the understanding that, in the anarchical system, states lack a common authority to enforce rules, and thus states rely on their military and economic capabilities, watching others, to ensure their survival. As Waltz puts it, "When the distribution of national capabilities is severely skewed, concern for absolute gains may replace worries about relative ones."[12] Prudence requires "estimating one another's capabilities" and maximizing security by preserving the balance of power.[13] Other realists like John Mearsheimer call for maximizing power. "Even when a great power achieves a distinct military advantage over its rivals, it continues looking for chances to gain more power. The pursuit of power stops only when hegemony is achieved."[14] But hegemony may culminate in a formal empire or overextension.[15] Thus, the so-called neoclassical realists argue that this "myth of empire" or any distortions to the systematic workings of the balance of power is often a problem arising from diversionary domestic politics. It involves deranged elites and institutions in a domestic setting such as the military-industrial complex that capture the levers of state power toward particular and not national interests.[16] Thus, most versions of realism study power politics as a product of the distribution of material capabilities and the perceptions and misperceptions that arise in an anarchic international system.

Some sophisticated realist accounts focus on the relational and interactional aspects of power relations. David Baldwin argues that power is not a property but a relation.[17] In the Vietnam War (1955–1975), Americans had superior capabilities but almost no influence over the Vietnamese people and soldiers to shape the outcome toward victory. Under inter-dependencies and asymmetrical relations, we must recognize strategic bargaining in a contextual situation. Thomas Schelling argued that "adversaries watch and interpret each other's behavior, each aware that his own actions are being interpreted and anticipated, each acting with a view to the expectations that he creates." Schelling added that the power to constrain an adversary may depend on the power to bind oneself; that in bargaining, weakness is often strength, freedom may be freedom to capitulate, and to burn bridges behind one may suffice to undo an opponent."[18] This was an important point for studying power politics under anarchy.

Realists and game theory rationalists thus joined forces to study how even materially weaker players could win in a bargaining process.[19] They study political actors' promises and lies, information asymmetry between bargaining players, diversionary tactics, costly signaling, audience cost, status and reputation of actors, and cunning appeals to legitimacy, among others. This has led to important insights into conventional and nuclear deterrence, alliances, arms control, crises, and wars.[20] For our purpose, what is important is that the debate between power-as-capabilities and power-as-relations works within an understanding that states and its policymakers use fixed material capabilities to articulate their strategic interests. Policymakers' language of power is either a reflection of rump materialism or it is confirmation, disguises, or pretexts in conveying this information to gain the upper hand against adversaries in a contextual bargaining game. Rhetoric is relevant, as some realists note, to convey information to adversaries. Jack Goldsmith and Eric Posner sum it up well: rhetoric serves a strategic purpose, and even if it is "largely a ceremonial usage," it can reveal "private information when nations have sufficiently similar interests or are disciplined by the presence of multiple audiences."[21] Therefore, realists view language as a strategic pursuit because armed coercion is expensive, and "their discursive practices reflects [sic] shifts in payoffs from coordinating with different nations" for security or power maximization.[22]

However, realist ways of studying power politics in the rhetoric of India, Brazil, and China are limited. Such an assessment stems from three fundamental limitations of realist theory in IR. First, realism fails to see the variegated meaning of realpolitik language in strategic interactions because of its commitment to a universal understanding of state behavior under anarchy. It does not matter if rhetoric-wielding political actors are located in an imperial core or the colonized periphery as long as they are engaged in maximizing security or power. But this is a bizarre assumption when social and racial hierarchies in the international system offer different meanings for policymakers who reflect on and challenge their "station" in the system. For underdogs, social hierarchies create a novel space for distinctive realpolitik content. For example, Frantz Fanon put it in a radical polemic interpreting economic capabilities and advocated for revolutionary violence: "The wealth of the imperialist nations is also our wealth. . . . Europe is literally a creation of the Third World." And he added, "Violence is a cleansing force" to free the native from inferiority complex.[23] Mohandas Gandhi developed an anti-industrial radicalism that was no less realpolitik in its consequentialist analysis of world politics.[24] Very few IR realists would consider the realpolitik of Frantz Fanon or Mohandas Gandhi, partly because their claims are not made in the idiom of bargaining and payoffs in an anarchic matrix.

Recent IR scholarship shows that even before the start of a "situationally specific" strategic game, actors are part of an international social hierarchy with rules, norms, and legitimating principles that establish different entitlements to capabilities and resources.[25] Social hierarchies based on race, culture, or identity and inequalities based on class, capitalism, and development stage skew bargaining and interactions among actors in power struggles. We will see more of this social hierarchy issue in the next section. The point is that political actors are part of this uneven social world, and even while performing power politics, they pursue (collective) action as part of a group enmeshed in norms and rules of social hierarchies. Political actors do not resemble laboratory-tested rational autonomous individuals calculating payoffs based on capabilities. However, all realist accounts, including relational ones, focus on material hierarchies alone. As Rebecca Adler-Nissen and Vincent Pouliot point out, "Capabilities pre-exist power relations as exogenous, latent resources: they are already there, so to speak, waiting to be activated in a particular context."[26] From such a perspective, a realist analysis of the rhetoric of anti-imperialism and anticolonialism from India, Brazil, and China would only continue to problematize their guns and tanks in different idioms, thereby ignoring the more complex realpolitik game these policymakers play within social hierarchies of international politics.

Second, the greatest strength of realism as a forward-looking theory in terms of future threats and uncertainties remains impoverished by its rigid scholarly vocabulary and methodologies. Realist-rationalist scholars distinguish between deceptive language and actual power politics, where material capabilities cause the former to affect the latter. In other words, language is a reflection or a representation of power politics but not constitutive of it. This is a problem because "a master does not 'cause' a slave; instead, both, and their respective powers, are constituted through this master-slave relation."[27] In recent years, IR research has advanced sophisticated ways to study language games, practical reasoning, misrecognition, and the meaning and interpretation of actors involved in power struggles.[28] Constructivists contend that language is power.[29] As Ronald Krebs puts it, "In politics, language is a crucial medium, means, locus, and object of contest. It neither competes with nor complements power politics: it *is* power politics. Through language, actors exercise influence over others' behavior. Through language, political subjects are produced and social relations defined."[30]

Thus, rhetoric, as I defined in the introduction, is as an instrumental and strategic use of language and arguments by policymakers in public speech to persuasively move multiple audiences or coerce them into submission to a political project. Using rhetoric actors exercise power and move audiences in the social world. Rhetoric is narrower than discourse and narrative (which includes the private as in autobiographical narrative) but also connected to it.[31] In making the distinction between rhetoric and discourse, Chaim Perelman reminds us that rhetoric "is central to discourse because its role is to intensify adherence to values, adherence without which discourses that aim at provoking action cannot find the lever to move or to inspire their listeners."[32] All political actors engage in rhetorical performances. The performance of not being rhetorical is itself an act of rhetoric to be heard. In such a view, we are in the realm of the Aristotelian idea "that rhetoric is as it were a kind of *offshoot of dialectic and the study of ethics* and is quite property categorized as political [emphasis in the original]."[33] We are looking at different power dynamics, opportunity structure, and strategic games than that assumed in realist theory.

Epistemologically, realists also draw an artificial line between social science and politics. However, the explicitly contradictory positions of most academics on self-defense, territorial integrity, and expansionist policies on the Russia-Ukraine War (2022) and the Israel-Gaza War (2023) show that such lines are ideological, political, and increasingly rude. The readiness to criticize Putin's Russia is not evident against Nethanyahu's Israel even when both are power hungry dictators. Pretending such objectivity through a realist analysis of India, Brazil, and China repeats the same problem of realism that neglects social hierarchies and the weaponization of institutional rules that drive power politics. We must not dispense with realpolitik but make it political. As Partha Chatterjee remarks, all "interpretation acquires the undertones of a polemic. In such circumstances, to pretend to speak in the 'objective' voice of history is to dissimulate. By marking our own text with the signs of battle, we hope to go a little further towards a more open and self-aware discourse."[34] Postcolonial sensibilities to realism require us to focus on the vagaries of the political, not evade it.

Third, using a realist lens to study the strategic rhetoric of India, Brazil, and China would fundamentally ignore the role of Western imperialism in the very foundation of realism. As Matthew Specter shows, realism and its tenets in the study of realpolitik are not neutrally focused on the balance of power and equilibrium in the anarchical system. Instead, realism descended from the concept of Weltpolitik, which is "based on a British model of noncontiguous or spatially deterritorialized imperialism, a combination of colonies and preferential access to trade" to maintain "American and German imperialism."[35] Imperial undertones in realism continue to thrive as an Atlantic realist tradition. As the chapter will show, many non-Western political actors are aware of this connection and cleverly flip colonial and imperial scripts to challenge the order.

In line with its ignorance of imperialism, however, realism maintains that international orders emerge spontaneously. For Waltz, order is the result of "struggles to achieve and maintain power," which means "order is spontaneously formed from the self-interested acts and interactions of individual units."[36] For Mearsheimer, in contrast, the new international order in the interdependent multipolar world involves both "full-throated economic and military competition," as was the case during the Cold War, and a deep involvement "in managing the cooperative aspects of the global economy, which was not the case during the Cold War."[37] Repeating these mantras ignores the imperial connection of realism to the creation and maintenance of international order and its impact on the culture and values of interlocutors. For example, Baldwin and followers of Schelling do not study the imperial basis of power but argue that the effect of military capabilities or resources depends on the values and preferences of the parties. However, the origin and sources of these values are rooted in the colonial and imperial legacies, which remain hidden and uninterrogated. Ignoring these developments and treating rhetoric as strategic only in a realist sense would be to repeat an impoverished agenda. It would miss much more interesting power politics in the anti-imperial and anticolonial rhetoric and remain unable to offer a robust basis for studying the various challenges to international structure and order.

RHETORICAL ENTRAPMENT AND REALPOLITIK

In contrast to realist accounts, a growing body of liberal-constructivist scholars take political actors' strategic language seriously and study the legitimation battles of political actors in international politics. Legitimation means justifying policies within the norms and rules of the international system. When actors speak the language of legitimacy, they turn "brute coercion into authority" and exercise power that "becomes palatable" and "seemingly benign."[38] Working within and against the linguistic turn, which was a major development in the philosophy of language in the West in the early twentieth century, some IR scholars have argued that the meaning and effect of material power and interests depend on the rules, norms, and social structure of the system. Alexander Wendt observes that there are different cultures of anarchy based on "different kinds of roles in terms of which states represent Self and Other."[39] As he put it, "Self mirrors Other, becomes *its* enemy, in order to survive. This of course will confirm whatever hostile intentions the *Other* had attributed to the Self, forcing it to engage in realpolitik of its own, which will in turn reinforce the Self's perception of the Other, and so on [emphasis in the original]."[40] It follows that anarchy is not a natural condition but a product of distinctive acrimonious state interactions based on which norms they think are legitimate.

Such an intervention led to bourgeoning empirical and normative research in IR on socialization, understood as states learning to behave according to the logic of legitimacy and appropriateness in the system.[41]

The power politics twist in socialization is manipulating "social facts"; that is, actors manipulate values, cultural norms, and collective beliefs.[42] As Frank Schimmelfennig argues, "Actors manipulate norms to avoid or reduce the cost of socialization" and rhetorically "frame their preferences and actions as norm consistent."[43] Not unlike game theory rationalists, early constructivists interested in power politics saw strategic discursive practices using norms as cost conscious actors manipulating the adversary.

However, a significant advancement in this constructivist tradition came from IR scholars who focused on the tensions between the rule-governed practice of language and the norm-governed practice of the international social system. The pursuit of strategic objectives requires that actors carefully maneuver, on the one hand, between the language of collective identity, for example, as a member of a nation or religious group. On the other hand, actors must also navigate the stringent "collective understandings for the proper behavior of actors within a given identity."[44] For example, political actors work within the normative legitimacy of the international system that privileges human rights, not slavery, and prohibits using military force for debt collection, even if these might have been legitimate in the past.[45] Using norms and rules in legitimation battles, actors who engage in power politics are not merely using strategic discourse to hide or manipulate reality but also construct a reality.[46]

An example is the recent power politics of Russia. The invasion of Ukraine and the power political strategies were based the desire to construct a collective identity of a Russian nation and as a great power that has the legitimate right to reject the dominant norms about maintaining the sovereignty and territorial integrity of its neighbors. Vladimir Putin put it this way in July 2021: "The determination of nationality, particularly in mixed families, is the right of every individual, free to make his or her own choice. But the fact is that the situation in Ukraine today is completely different because it involves a forced change of identity. And the most despicable thing is that the Russians in Ukraine are being forced not only to deny their roots, generations of their ancestors [sic] but also to believe that Russia is their enemy. It would not be an exaggeration to say that the path of forced assimilation, the formation of an ethnically pure Ukrainian state, aggressive towards Russia, is comparable in its consequences to the use of weapons of mass destruction against us."[47] On

February 24, 2022, Russia invaded Ukraine despite the high costs, universal sanctions, and low payoffs.

This is power politics of a different kind, where actors use language to interpret the norms and rules of the international system and construct a new reality to make these principles reflect the priorities and identities of their state. Military power and relative capabilities are central in such constructions through intersubjective relations, understood as shared meaning that actors bring to bear on these material things in the bargaining process. But there is no brute material power outside the realm of interpretation. For thick constructivists—those who take actors' linguistic dynamics and their role in the contingency and historicity of norms and rules—however, power politics through strategic language is practical reasoning that requires careful attention to the intersubjective understanding of actors and the rules of the game. Power politics is not clockwork or "costs largely in our heads," as realists assume.[48] Despite the claims that Putin is mentally ill, there is an army of soldiers and millions of Russian people who partake in the realpolitik rhetoric against the West. Power politics done with the language of legitimation is ruthless.

The study of the power of language and the language of power in this thick constructivism is wide ranging. Consider three related versions of this scholarship. First, some constructivists focus on how actors engage in international politics with language games, like playing a game of chess, using norms and rules to advance their interests. Karin Fierke, for example, examines how actors negotiate social rules through complex language games and systems of meaning that impose boundaries on what can and cannot be said within its rules in security politics.[49] Antje Wiener focuses on norms as meaning-in-use and contestations of these meanings among interlocutors in discursive practices.[50] In this view, how political actors debate using shared meaning systems and enact their political objectives is more important than calculating their shifts in payoff.[51]

Second, some constructivists claim identity informs political choices. A recent advancement in this framework is the so-called ontological security research program. Jennifer Mitzen, in her seminal study and critique of realism, argues that "physical security is not the only kind of security that states seek," states also seek ontological security, which is the "need to experience oneself as a whole, continuous person in time." When both these securities are in tension, "even a harmful or self-defeating relationship can provide ontological security," and in a perverse sort of way, "states can become attached to conflict." Mitzen concludes that "no realist argument fully captures the identity effects of persistent conflict, because none acknowledges the social construction of state identity."[52] In other words, ontological security research shows that power struggle is a self-fulfilling prophecy. It is a product of autobiographical narratives of the self, the commitment to keep a particular narrative going in relation to the other, the psychological and social needs that arise from foreign policy routines, and the acute anxiety that arises from the disruption of routines, which gives rise to pathological power struggles. IR scholars extend these claims about power struggles in novel ways, where the focus is on the sociopsychological side of realpolitik behavior.[53]

The third major branch within this thick constructivist theorizing of power politics focuses on rhetoric—as a weapon of the weak—in legitimation battles, and scholars bring to bear a thoroughly relational study of power struggles without psychological reductionism.[54] Rhetorical coercion or entrapment is a process where materially weak political actors use norms and rules to legitimize their behavior and, in the process, trap and corner their superior opponents into publicly accepting claims they would otherwise reject. Opponents accept the rhetorical moves because the cost of not accepting those claims might affect their social standing. Recall the discussion in the introduction of Libya's role in bombing Pan Am Flight 103. Libyan actors used the norms of liberal internationalism to trap more powerful political actors such as the United States and the United Kingdom to relax sanctions in line with the procedural justice of international law.[55] Theorizing on these dynamics, Ronald Krebs and Patrick Jackson argue that rhetorical coercion works in legitimation because both the claimant and opponents "must craft their appeals with an eye to some audience which sits in judgment of their rhetorical moves." In public argumentation, "when the opponent, regardless of private beliefs, can no longer sustain its opposition" in the eyes of the audience, they are rhetorically trapped in the game.[56] Rhetorical legitimation that can deprive opponents' maneuvering space in this way is an integral part of power politics.

Many scholars look at rhetoric this way to study the working of the weapon of the weak in legitimation battles to mobilize support, build coalitions, and demobilize opposition in international politics.[57] A focus on rhetorical practices challenges realists on their own turf to show that material hierarchies are not the only indicators of success and even weak actors can successfully engage in legitimacy battles in their rhetoric to exercise power. These approaches provide a wealth of insights on public rhetoric and its connection to intersubjective meaning, how political actors weaponize norms and rules in the system, and how they bring creative linguistic moves in public battles that are not mere "window dressing for power and interests" but "an integral part of power politics."[58] These advancements have brought forth a renaissance in the study of rhetoric and power politics. My focus on rhetoric builds on these socioconstructivist advancements.

Nevertheless, existing IR conceptualizations of rhetoric are also limited and cannot be applied directly to study rhetoric and the distinctive power politics of India, Brazil, and China. Hierarchy and postcolonial studies in IR show us the continuities in Western imperial practices and different social stratifications that make up the international structure. We briefly saw the background of the effects of Western imperialism and colonialism in the introduction. Ayse Zarakol and many other hierarchy-centric scholars correctly argue that the international system is underwritten by deep structures of civilizational, racial, economic, and gendered hierarchies of the past and that these stratifications reproduce in manifold ways to affect present-day insecurities.[59] The central problem with constructivist accounts, particularly those found in the rhetorical entrapment model led by Jackson, Krebs, and Stacie Goddard, is that they ignore deep colonial and imperial structures and how variation in the structural location of actors affects their rhetorical choice in power politics.

Krebs and Jackson, for instance, link the content of rhetoric with effectiveness to demonstrate rhetorical coercion, but they generally ignore the international hierarchy within which rhetorical games of actors unfold. Because these studies challenge the realist obsession with material capabilities to account for power politics, however, the focus is on the ability of weak actors to prevail against the strong. The larger focus on international stratification and the unequal position of actors in the power hierarchy is obscured. Goddard focuses on multivocal rhetoric in legitimation battles with little consideration of how some states on the lower rungs of the hierarchy may engage in different rhetorical content and performances within the normative order, resembling a layered form of multivocality. In other words, there is no attention to how rhetoric might be interacting with the deep social hierarchy, legacies of colonialism, and civilizational and racial stratifications that hierarchy scholars in IR point out. The super- and subordinate power relations in which the actors are embedded affect both the choices of their rhetorical content and its effectiveness in pursuing power politics.

Many existing ontological insecurity and postcolonial studies suffer from another difficulty. These research programs rightly call attention to the "impressive ideological formations of imperialism" that create stigmatization, trauma, anxiety, and the precarious nature of colonized subjects in the unequal international system.[60] It is right that the experience of deep hierarchy—its socializing effects—"teach actors to play certain roles, including having certain interests and expectations."[61] But ontological insecurity and postcolonial research programs view these conditions solely through the lens of victimhood of the periphery. They do not see the diversity of experience of disempowerment in the colonial period and how "subalterns" found creative ways to exercise power in the unequal but interconnected global system. Zarakol focuses on a self-fulling prophesy as "socialization driven by a desire to escape stigmatization [that] can actually perpetuate the established-outsider figuration" and the agency available in stigma-coping strategies that are status and self-esteem concerns deliberately picked from a menu offered by the West.

In the existing ontological insecurity and postcolonial accounts, there is an exceptionalist view of Western imperialism as one that paralyzes, stigmatizes, and traumatizes the non-Western world. The peripheral actors are frequently subjected to blame, shame, stigma and have status concerns within the Eurocentric world.[62] However, as John Hobson and Alina Sajed rightly show, "Either the non-West is portrayed as a silent victim, unable to escape the overwhelming hyper-agential power of the West, or it is portrayed in terms of enacting grandiose and sometimes heroic or romantic forms of open defiance-resistance that are frequently viewed as having little or no impact upon global politics."[63] Because of this portrayal, there is no attention to how the repertoire of power politics developed under domination and the experiences of disempowerment might produce realpolitik and rhetorical moves that constructivist scholars point out. In other words, hierarchy scholars are right that the consequences of international socialization are stratification and stigmatization. Stigmatized victims deliberately play through their status concerns in international politics. However, the consequence of stratification is also shrewd realpolitik maneuvering in which the scripts that underdogs use involve a deeper repertoire of past power political practices. The recent emphasis on the study of international practice responds to these problems by focusing on performances and enactments of power politics on the world stage.[64] But the right sort of attention to practice must be attentive to the unequal playing field and the legacies of imperialism and colonialism, and must not assume away the impact of the brief but world-transforming era of Euro-American global dominance.

RECONCEPTUALIZING RHETORICAL POWER POLITICS

Bringing a critical stance of postcolonial perspective to enduring social hierarchies and imperial legacies resolves the many tensions in studying power politics in the realist and constructivist approaches. I have already argued that realist emphasis on realpolitik, and constructivist emphasis on rhetoric and discursive practices are basically right, but they do not go far enough. A postcolonial perspective suggests that the international racial, gender, military, and economic (capitalist) hierarchies are structured over a long time and have homeostatic tendencies, meaning they are sticky and multifaceted, and these hierarchies do not change automatically when a state's gross domestic product (GDP) changes. This is because relational practices between top dogs and underdogs congeal into a hierarchical structure based on continuously unfolding assessments of competence and incompetence of interlocutors who are working to manage order, which relies on silencing practices.

Despite the pernicious features of Western imperialism, non-Western agents were not just spectators to the unfolding of the drama of international politics. They challenged, stood up, resisted, and fought back. Rhetoric was a central instrument—a necessary instrument—against the silencing practices of the hierarchy. With rhetorical power politics, however, non-Western political actors reconfigured the world and won independence and decolonization. It became part of their repertoire of statecraft. Uncovering this pattern of politics is to rethink the workings of power under hierarchy in international politics. The next two sections expand these two ideas—silencing practices and a rhetorical repertoire that, in fits and starts, become part of statecraft and unfold in creative performances of power. Conceptualizing power politics in this way provides novel insight into why underdog political actors use and then flip the anti-imperial and anticolonial scripts in rhetoric to maneuver in the system. It is an innovation in their power-political games in the unequal liberal order.

SILENCING: HOW HIERARCHY BUILDS INTERNATIONAL SYSTEMS OF POWER

As we saw in the introduction, the modern international system is fundamentally hierarchical, divided between the West and the rest, and it has remained that way since the late 1700s.[65] The first age of global imperialism between 1760–1770 and 1830 began with the Seven Years' War. Britain and France fought in both hemispheres, with Britain gaining control of much of India and North America. Thereafter, imperialism unfolded in the context of war between European empires across four continents between 1793 and 1815, in which Europeans systematically exterminated the Indigenous populations in the Americas.

As Jürgen Osterhammel shows, the "new imperialism" or "high imperialism" between 1880 and 1918 came about through the intertwining of economic integration, new technologies of intervention, the collapse of peace in the European system of states, and the rise of Social-Darwinist interpretation of international politics.[66] The Great Powers—France, Britain, Austria, Russia, and Prussia—and weaker European powers such as Belgium took the mantle to "civilize the natives." They partitioned the African continent through the Berlin Conference in 1884, paving the way for additional imperialist endeavors across continents and culminating in the carnage of World War I.

Against the racially discriminatory backdrop of mandates instituted through the League of Nations, the third age of global imperialism began with the Japanese invasion of Manchuria in 1931, continued with the expansions of Nazi Germany, and extended into the end of World War II. The inter-imperial competition between the United States and the Union

of Soviet Socialist Republics (USSR) during the Cold War and the renewal
of the American empire after the Cold War with the Gulf Wars, the Iraq
War, the War on Terror, and now the Russian invasion of Ukraine mark the
fourth and fifth waves of globally interconnected imperialism, respectively.

Each period of Western imperialism was sustained by various "legitimating principles," articulated and defended by the reigning superordinate
power(s) and agreed upon by subordinates. These legitimating principles
are "core norms that establish what counts as acceptable behavior and
allow states and other political actors to adjudicate the legitimacy of competing claims."[67] For example, "keeping the balance" was the dominant
legitimating principle of the nineteenth-century Concert of Europe. This
principle involved grading and measuring the different material capabilities of states and establishing a social role, as Edward Keene shows, for
"a new kind of *élite* in international society [emphasis in the original],"
who, as one of the Great Powers, "asserted the right to intervene" against
the sovereignty of lesser powers to maintain order after the Napoleonic
Wars.[68] And self-determination was the dominant legitimating principle,
famously led by U.S. President Woodrow Wilson, in the early twentieth
century. In our times, human rights and democracy take a central role. In
any international system, legitimating principles are important because
they allow political actors to use the rules, norms, and values associated
with these principles to interpret what counts as acceptable behavior, hold
each other accountable, and adjudicate competing claims in the system.[69]

The legitimating principles, norms, and rules of the hierarchical international system provided meaning to interlocutors participating in international politics. It also bolstered Western military and economic power.
These principles offered the nearly exclusive justification for imperialism
and colonialism, which sought to civilize outsiders and manage order.
And world ordering using these principles is a continuous process.[70]

It is now common knowledge that the Western empires have historically
imposed an unequal order, stacking and refining it over time with discriminatory social logic. From categorizing people in different non-European
worlds as savages, barbarians, racially inferior creatures, and feminine,
and as members of backward, decrepit civilizations, such discriminatory
practices have tilted the balance in favor of the West.[71] Although this hierarchical relationship is recognized as right and legitimate by super- and
subordinate states, the latter are integrated unequally into the practices of

the international system. As Adom Getachew shows, "Non-European states nations were excluded from the full rights of membership but remained subject to the obligations of inclusion."[72] International hierarchies imbued with discrimination and inequality undercut the opportunities for any form of equal dialogue between the West and the rest on the legitimating principles of the system. Although the decolonial narrative has revived the demand for equality and nondomination, this is an unfinished project.

The hierarchy scholarship in IR is bringing these inequalities to the foreground in world politics.[73] Scholars discuss military and economic capabilities hierarchy,[74] class divide,[75] status hierarchy,[76] racial hierarchy,[77] gender, and patriarchy,[78] among others and show the fundamental continuities of these hierarchies in the present international system from the colonial and imperial period of the past. Different political actors experience and respond to such social logic of hierarchies differently.[79]

A common thread underlying the workings of all social hierarchies in international politics is the practice of silencing—the way powerful actors eliminate the voice of subordinates.[80] Non-European actors experience silencing far more than their European peers.[81] Silencing constitutes epistemic violence when audiences do not respond the way speakers want them to respond because the speakers belong to a group that is perceived as unworthy of hearing.

Kristie Dotson shows that several kinds of harm result from such silencing practices.[82] Patricia Hill Collins's work in *Black Feminist Thought* shows that "black women are less likely to be considered competent due to an audience's inability to discern their credibility beyond 'controlling images' that stigmatize black women as a group."[83] By systematically disempowering Black women this way, audiences reject their agency, undermine their history, and doubt their testimony. This conditions Black women to remain silent. For example, some Black women hesitate to report domestic abuse lest the stereotypes of violence in Black families are painfully reinforced in public.[84] In hierarchical international politics, the situation of the subordinate states is similar. Hierarchy studies in international politics have examined silencing practices and demonstrated rich analysis of blame, shame, stigmatization, infantilization, and opprobrium of states by examining hidden histories. When the West rules over the historiography of events that transform the world, it removes the historical salience of non-European politics and identity.[85]

Can *you* exercise judgment?

Do *you* have
capabilities?

Do *you* have
authority?

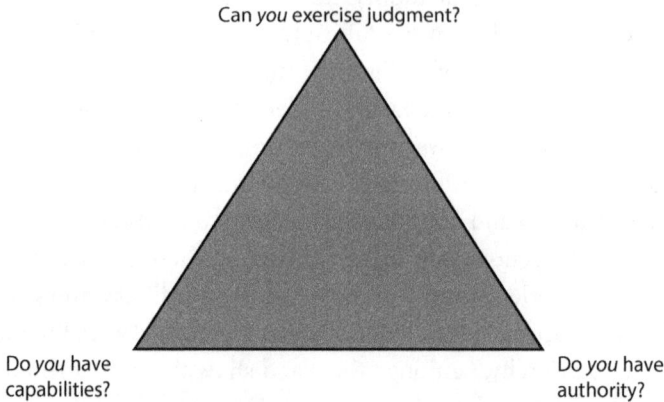

FIGURE 1.1 Practices of attributing incompetence in international ordering

The most common ways of silencing non-European actors have focused, however, on international ordering and became systematic from the mid- to the late nineteenth century. The "rhetoric of empire" involved demarcating *competence versus incompetence* on matters of high politics, understood as the arena of diplomacy, security, war, and peace.[86] In this way, Western states preserved their privilege while excluding non-Westerns in the current ordering process but keeping doors open for the future. As Uday Singh Mehta shows, such exclusion is defiantly self-confident, "defended by reference to the 'manifest' political incompetence of those to be excluded and justified by a plethora of anthropological descriptions that serve to buttress the claim of incompetence."[87] Thus, attributing incompetence to non-Europeans is at the heart of this silencing. There are three mechanisms through which this practice of silencing functions in managing order: refuting the ability of non-European states to employ material capabilities to protect order, rejecting their ability to exercise objective judgments, and challenging their authority to manage international order (see figure 1.1). These patterns of silencing are structured across time and space, and I elaborate on them below.

1. Incompetent in Employing Material Capabilities

Silencing practices involve a process of Western policymakers refuting the ability of non-European states and their political actors to employ their material capabilities to protect order. It is a form of boundary draw-ing in the claims-making process that Asian, African, and Latin Ameri-can actors don't have the military or economic resources to bring changes to the social and political conditions of international politics. In general, silencing practices based on material capabilities put super- and subor-dinate relations in a tight hierarchical network. Superordinate powers advance two key claims. First, only Western actors have phenomenal economic and military capabilities and thus enjoy the right and duty to change regional and extraregional politics and the political geography of the world. Second, even when non-Western members of the interna-tional system acquire material capabilities, their competence is deemed legitimate only within acceptable bounds of the meaning of material real-ity established by the West. Superordinate powers assign the dominant meaning of material reality in international politics.

The Western treatment of non-European actors as incompetent in using material capabilities has a systematic continuity across time and space, at least from the mid-nineteenth century. The Western focus on "grading of powers" is a long practice.[88] The early rhetoric of the West against China proves this point. As David Spurr shows, political actors in the Western empire firmly believed that "the Chinese have 'stumbled upon things': they stumbled on gunpowder, on the mariner's compass, and on the printing press five hundred years before Gutenberg," and the goal of American Protestantism "was to awaken the Chinese capacity not only for reason and invention, but also for the more worldly benefits of entrepreneur-ship."[89] The British slogan, "Whatever happens, we have got, the Maxim [machine gun], and they have not," coined by Hilaire Belloc in 1898, belies the fact that non-Europeans had also used advanced military technolo-gies in warfare. For example, Emperor Menelik II of Ethiopia inflicted the worst defeat on Italy in 1896 at Adwa in Ethiopia, using millions of rounds of ammunition with an advanced French Libel rifle.[90] Nevertheless, social stratification based on racial and civilizational lines have persisted.

In 1930, British High Commissioner Henry Dobbs submitted a report to the Permanent Mandate Commission of the League of Nations that "Iraq had all the working machinery of a civilized government and could stand alone administratively, even if it cannot do so militarily or econom-ically, and that was sufficient" for the British mandate over Iraq.[91]

In the aftermath of World War II, the development of the economic capabilities of third world states became the concern of superpowers. Many developing countries focused on racial equality and called for the "right to development."[92] But many Western countries opposed this as an incompetent interpretation of human rights yoked to developmental capabilities.[93] In 1986, the United States Representative to the United Nations General Assembly Third Committee said, "The totalitarian nations often had recourse to the creation of [endless] new rights in order to hide the fact that their peoples had no political, civil, economic, or social rights."[94] Developing countries sought a New International Economic Order (NIEO) in 1974, a proposal to end economic dependency through plans such as technology transfer and regulation of transnational corporations, among others.[95] The West treated the NIEO projects for improving material capabilities as incompetent performances. As Anthony Anghie shows, Henry Kissinger "began a concerted campaign to organize the rich against the poor" and the "legal aspects of the NIEO campaign were inevitably contested by the developed states and the lawyers supporting their position."[96] The right to development and the NEIO collapsed alongside the strengthening of neoliberalism, which attributed the problems in the material capabilities of the non-West to their incompetence in engaging in free trade reforms.

Today, there are marked continuities in attributing incompetence to non-Europeans on material capabilities to protect international order. That is why the top dogs manage the International Monetary Fund (IMF) with higher special drawing rights (SDRs);[97] in international law, superordinate powers define and demarcate definitions of aggression and who is prosecuted in international criminal courts;[98] and in the UN, powerful states serve as penholders.[99] The problem is not that the non-European states, acting in their role as speakers, have not offered sufficient evidence of their military or economic capabilities to justify their role or alternative principles of world ordering to Western audiences. Rather, Western audiences neglect to meet these speakers halfway. This undervaluing through the perception of incompetence also means rejecting Global South states as knowers of the appropriate way to manage international order or resolve economic problems in international politics.

2. Incompetent in Exercising "Objective" Judgment

Silencing also involves Western policymakers rejecting the ability of non-European actors to exercise "objective," meaning impartial, judgments for managing international order. In other words, superordinate actors in the hierarchical structure see cultural prejudices and psychological biases in the judgments of subordinate actors. In general, such assessments involve stereotypes, including implicit and explicit racism and character assessments, that render these actors unable to partake in managing international order. The practice of silencing here is twofold: Western audiences refuse to see non-Western states as impartial, and non-European speakers respond by truncating their voices on the international stage. This twofold problem manifests strikingly whenever subordinate actors hold viewpoints on international ordering that differ from the political projects pursued by the West.

These two features of silencing practices are also evident across time and space in international politics. For example, in the Haitian Revolution (1791–1804), slaves emerged victorious and established an egalitarian society. In response, President Thomas Jefferson of the United States called Haitians "cannibals of the terrible republic" and doubted their ability to maintain order in the Western Hemisphere.[100] As the eminent historian Robin Blackburn shows, "Whatever his high-minded protestations about republican liberty and some future emancipation of slaves, Jefferson's determinate allegiance was to the slave order."[101] Many European states that had previously recognized the United States did not recognize an independent Haiti. In 1829, David Walker, a great abolitionist, published "An Appeal to the Colored Citizens of the World." But at the same time, the United States "passed new laws banning the teaching of slaves to read and write, and prohibiting, too, teaching slaves about the Bible."[102]

In the second half of the nineteenth century, such prejudiced assessments of the judgments of non-Europeans continued. For example, the 1865 Morant Bay Rebellion in Jamaica against injustice and poverty was viewed by the British Empire as a "confirmation of the incapacity of colonial subjects for liberal reform."[103] As Karuna Mantena puts it, the difficulty of "civilizing" the colonial subjects led to new culturalist essentialism in the imperial repertoire for a moral disavowal of others: "the error was understood to lie less with the structure of imperial power (and the contradictions that ensue from its attempt to elicit social transformation through force) than in the nature of colonized societies."[104] Decades later, in the British Empire, the Ilbert Bill (1883) gave Indian magistrates in the Indian countryside the right to try charges against British subjects of European descent. Europeans and the British, including Anglo-Indians, vehemently rejected the idea that educated Indian natives could have any commitments toward the rule of law or have entitlements to try and punish "Whites legally."[105] Many Anglo-Indians dismissed the bill on racist lines, and James Fitzjames Stephen, a famous English lawyer, argued from a commonplace racist view that Indian magistrates did not have the competency to judge the minds of Europeans.[106]

Such assessments were further reproduced in the twentieth century with new vocabularies. For example, in the famous Bandung Conference in 1955, many Asian and African states aimed to safeguard their newly achieved independence and exercised their judgment in statecraft to maintain a nonaligned position, distancing themselves from superpower rivalries. Indonesia's Ahmed Sukarno, India's Jawaharlal Nehru, Algeria's Ahmed Ben Bella, and Egypt's Gamal Abdel Nasser offered nuanced claims and counterclaims on anti-imperialism and nonalignment. However, in 1956, U.S. Secretary of State John Foster Dulles charged the Non-Aligned Movement (NAM) as an "immoral and short-sighted conception."[107] The infamous U.S. diplomat George Kennan argued that people in Africa, Asia, the Middle East, and Latin America were too "impulsive, fanatical, ignorant, lazy, unhappy, and prone to mental disorders and other biological deficiencies" to help the West in the superpower rivalry.[108] Such views were not unique to the United States. The Soviet Union also advanced similar practices against the revolutionary judgments of the third world. For example, when Fidel Castro rose to power in Cuba in 1959 *without* Moscow's support, "[Nikita] Khrushchev and his colleagues quickly came to perceive the Cuban revolution as both a reflection of the Soviet past and a vision of the future," and Khrushchev removed Soviet missiles from Cuban soil without consulting Castro.[109] The struggle to protect the Soviet reputation became a fight against the judgments of its client states.

There is a remarkable continuity in such assessments of the limits of the judgments of non-European states through today. The Western-led North Atlantic Treaty Organization (NATO) overthrew Muammar Gaddafi in the 2011 Libyan crisis. India, Brazil, and China, as rising powers, challenged this practice of violent regime change. Nevertheless, many Western states viewed their non-Western counterparts as biased, ideological, and wrong and deemed their judgments unworthy of consideration.[110] One finds remarkable continuity in such assessments of the so-called Global South states in the Russian invasion of Ukraine in 2022. Then UK foreign secretary James Cleverly said, "The West will be in trouble unless it learns to listen better to the Global South" and "it is very easy to slip into the habit of just telling people what we want them to do—we have to listen better."[111] In this way, Cleverly confirms the habit of the West. The silencing practices and, paradoxically, the recognition of the non-European world reinforce hierarchy.

3. Incompetent in Wielding Authority

In this analytical framework, silencing also involves Western policymakers rejecting the authority of non-Europeans in the international order. Authority is relational in the sense that one's rightful command becomes binding through the voluntary submission of others without violence or persuasion. As Hannah Arendt puts it, "When force is used authority has failed," and authority is also incompatible with persuasion, "which presupposes equality and works through a process of argumentation."[112] Thus, authority requires regular enacting, authorizing, contesting, and redeploying one's authority claims.[113] The practice of silencing comes from the view that only the West has the authority to manage the challenges of the international order.

Once again, we find continuities in this pattern of authority-centered portrayal of incompetence on non-Europeans across time and space in international politics. In 1882, for example, the British Empire occupied Egypt. British practitioners challenged the authority of the Ottoman Sultan in Egypt and rejected the nationalist movement led by Colonel Ahmed Urabi as anything but authoritative. In cooperation with Lord Harrington, Secretary of State for India, Lord Northbrook, the First Lord of the Admiralty, "enumerated his doubts about diplomatic solutions—the Sultan was impudent, Freycinet [the French Premier] was 'more than weak,' and Bismarck was meddling. 'Unless there be a real risk of war in Europe,' he concluded, 'we must then do it [intervene] ourselves.'"[114] Such imperial disdain for local authority changed in the early twentieth century with the increasing recognition of intermediaries for imperial projects.[115] Frederick Lugard, the British governor-general of Nigeria from 1907 to 1919, said that there is a "strategic value of the internal authority exercised by native rulers," which can be "part of the machinery of administration." This is similar to the use of native collaborators and intermediaries in the French colonization of Morocco.[116] At the end of World War I, the League of Nations mandates and colonies treated many political actors as "not yet" ready for an authoritative exercise of the right of self-determination.[117] And the United Nations, established after the end of World War II, was based on sovereign inequality that nevertheless continued the legacies of the League of Nations. As Tara Zahra shows, many "British leaders hoped that the United Nations would help sustain the authority of a 'civilizing' British Empire."[118]

The attribution of incompetence to non-Europeans on the authoritative management of the international order requires interpretive power over legitimating principles with a high degree of differentiation on the laws of war. A strict reading of the UN Charter prohibits the use of force except under self-defense, invitation by a host government, and UN Security Council (UNSC) authorization. On these lines, non-European humanitarian interventions have historically been perceived as lacking competent authority. For example, India's intervention against East Pakistan in 1971, Vietnam's intervention against Pol Pot in Cambodia in 1978, and Tanzania's intervention against Idi Amin in Uganda in 1979 did not qualify as "humanitarian intervention" or as an exercise of moral authority to prevent human tragedy.[119] But discarding such strict reading in the post–Cold War period, as scholars from the third world approaches to international law (TWAIL) show, Western leaders invoke the universality of humanitarian ideals and its moral authority to support unilateral interventions such as in Kosovo, Iraq, Libya, and Syria, among others.[120]

Political actors in Europe and the United States are now changing the fundamental laws of war. They are doing it alone because of the continuing notion of a lack of competent authority in the non-Western world in this domain. The Bush doctrine in the 2003 war in Iraq focused on preemption. Continuing this idea, most Western states agree on an expanded idea of self-defense norm in the so-called Bethlehem principles, which means preemptive use of force even when there is uncertainty on the place of the attack or nature of the attack. As Antony Anghie shows, couched in the language of imminence, "the Bethlehem version of the use of force was not so much a departure from the Bush doctrine but, rather, a refinement of it," so much so that "few powerful states have taken upon themselves the task of changing fundamental principles of the laws of war."[121] Israel's expansive interpretation of self-defense norms and the callous use of force in committing genocide in Gaza after October 7, 2023, is a continuation of this trend.[122] Despite China's authoritative position as a permanent member of the UNSC, Western states view China's or any non-Western state's challenge to such transformation of the principles of laws of war as incompetent performances against the bourgeoning threat of terrorism.[123] It is easy to dismiss China because of its lack of authority to follow human rights norms.[124] As TWAIL scholarship shows, however, the danger of authority hoarding is a continuation of imperial policies in novel vocabularies.[125] The sociogenesis of silencing non-Europeans extends across space and time.

STRATEGIC LOGIC OF RHETORICAL POWER POLITICS UNDER HIERARCHY

The above account shows that Western great powers are committed to an exclusionary world-ordering practice that renders them unwilling to listen to those outside their context. It largely aligns with what the bourgeoning IR scholarship on hierarchy tells us about the fundamental ways in which Western states ignore and sideline the rest. Silencing practices are continuous, sedimented, and inherently part of the international ordering process. Thus, underdogs must play by different rules compared to actors higher up on the international hierarchy. They rely on rhetoric.

Recall the constructivist IR discussion on rhetorical politics in the above section. Rhetoric is a strategic language game and a performance of practitioners to corner opponents and achieve political objectives. It is an instrument "to persuade, coerce, cajole, and incentivize others to engage in, or eschew, such joint action."[126] Rhetoric of speakers may also involve gestures and affective performances to influence audiences at the level of emotion through mastery of arguments.[127] This is all true. For subordinate political actors, however, rhetoric and its contents are also products of the international hierarchy, not just asymmetric power dynamics among bargaining actors but also of the deep power structures defined by racial, gendered, and imperial forms of silencing practices in the system.

To exercise rhetoric from the lower position in the social hierarchy is to exercise agency and, for policymakers, rhetoric and affective performances activate against the enduring silencing practices in international politics. Rhetoric is useful not because it is objectively good but because of its necessity, ease, tractability, and proud appeal in enacting such affective performances in relation to multiple audiences. As Elizabeth Anderson shows, "the powerful won't really listen to reason—that is, to claims from below—until they no longer have the power to routinely enforce their desires . . . the subordinated and oppressed must actively participate in that contention."[128] Like all rhetoric-wielding actors, these political actors weaponize international norms and rules of international order to achieve strategic objectives. Because the superordinate actors treat them as incompetent in managing order, however, they use rhetoric that explicitly challenges their silencing and disempowerment to show *contradictions* in the rules and norms of the international system. To speak about problems of the international ordering despite the overwhelming pressures of silencing is a form of rhetorical power. To put it in simple terms, rather than speak in normal polite terms, subordinate actors use rhetoric and affective performances to shrewdly exploit the contradictions in the legitimating principles, norms, and rules of the international system.

IR scholars recognize that the legitimating principles in the hierarchical international system are contradictory, not homogenous.[129] There are contradictions between the universal principles of equality and liberty and the norm of maintaining order and stability by justifying inequalities.[130] There are also tensions between the principles of nonintervention and militant humanitarianism, which the UN has adopted since 1945. Contradictions are not a modern feature. For example, Britain led the mid- to late nineteenth-century international order, bringing to life legitimating principles of "cosmopolitan liberalism," emphasizing the free movement of people, goods, and capital.[131] Its leading proponents also pursued free trade imperialism based on exclusionary norms and rules of racism and civilizational superiority. "World crises have always been, as [Karl] Marx once put it, 'the real concentration and forcible adjustment of all the contradictions of bourgeois economy.'"[132] All contradictions are a frequent source of contestation among political actors in international politics.[133] This view is also consistent with the constructivist emphasis that structures are not deterministic. Instead, the gaps and cracks in the international structure offer novel conditions of possibility for exercising agency. The contradictions in the legitimating principles, norms, and rules of the international system frequently manifest as political and economic crises, wars, disruptions, and global disorders, among others. These are opportunities for those ambitious policymakers in the lower rungs of hierarchy.

Some non-European political actors exploit these contradictions in their rhetoric, not to tame or resolve them but to put them on display and thus challenge their disempowerment and assert their competence.[134] At one level, this is not surprising. Powerful states are interested in ordering and not its contradictions, which more often manifest in disorder. And subordinate states are frequently at the receiving end of all the problems of international ordering and the failures that arise from the idealized standards of order. Thus, non-European political actors have historically recognized the contradictory principles of the modern political system and selectively used one against the other for survival. Chapter 2 will show how political elites in India, Brazil, and China enacted such contentious performances even under the hierarchical order of Western imperialism and colonialism.

Historians frequently point out the central role of the "periphery" in remaking the core. Christopher Bayly notes that, in the long nineteenth century, many "Indigenous thinkers generally selected the more conservative elements of liberal ideology which emphasized the history and organic unity of human communities, rather than those which asserted unmediated rights. These fitted well into local understandings of hierarchy and order."[135] In this way, they engaged in "counter preaching" rhetorical strategy to fight against the pressures of social hierarchy.[136] In the introduction, we saw the examples of Mohandas Gandhi, who engaged in a polemic attack on Western civilization, and W. E. B. Du Bois, who praised Japanese imperialism. These rhetorical tactics were strategic performances that put imperialists on their back foot. We tend to ignore these kinds of selections and strategies as realpolitik relations and consider them only when they conform to realism or rhetorical entrapment models. But subordinate states have always used rhetoric as a product of the struggle against silencing in the hierarchical structure, and ambitious leaders like Gandhi and Du Bois exposed the contradictions of the racial, gendered, and predatory capitalist international system that were hiding in plain sight.

In general terms, we can then say that rhetorical power politics is at work when political actors systematically push against the dominant power and deploy anti-imperial and anticolonial rhetoric to exploit the contradictions in the legitimating principles, norms, and rules of the system and disrupt international relations. In this sense, the notion of rhetorical power politics moves away from being a "weapon of the weak," as in holding top dogs accountable in a stand-alone situation, to habitually playing the role of top dogs from the position of underdogs. Many forms of constructivist analysis of rhetoric in IR nevertheless miss the colonial and imperial entailments in systematically resorting to rhetorical strategies. Rhetoric is a skill learned from the struggle against empires and, over time, some non-European policymakers develop the know-how to manipulate established scripts in statecraft.

To make sense of this distinctive rhetorical power politics where non-European political actors systematically exploit the contradictions of the international system, using anti-imperial rhetoric, we must understand these performances as part of their repertoires of statecraft. As we briefly saw in the introduction, repertoires are catalogs, stocks of skills, or inventories that an actor habitually uses in the world to navigate the world without reinventing the wheel every time in the process. As Doug McAdam, Sidney Tarrow, and Charles Tilly formulated the concept, repertoires are conventions in contentious performances of actors to mobilize for collective action. Like marches, demonstrations, and petitions and the associated scripts of contention, repertoires are "limited ensembles of mutual claim-making routines available to particular pairs of identities."[137] Stacie Goddard, Paul MacDonald, and Daniel Nexon refine these ideas on repertoire to understand international power politics. They view statecraft as a set of repertoires of power politics. As they put it, using a repertoires approach "draws attention to how the practice of statecraft not only reflects but creates power, either by mobilizing one's own power resources or by demobilizing the resources of others." They further add, "And all of this requires scripts that guide how actors engage in these activities."[138] Policymakers cannot pull scripts out of thin air. More often, they learn and innovate from established scripts, thus fine-tuning their repertoire each time. Repertoire are "historically evolving, strongly constraining, cultural products."[139] Yet policymakers frequently, even if incrementally, reflect and innovate these tool kits for action; thus, in this sense, repertoires are not unchanging habits of policymakers.[140]

Rhetoric is a repertoire of power politics in the statecraft of non-European states in the hierarchical international system. Anti-imperial and anticolonial rhetoric for many policymakers in Asia, Africa, and Latin

America includes established scripts of struggle against the domination and silencing of the West. Many policymakers used these scripts historically to exploit the contradictions of the system. A rhetorical repertoire emerges when these policymakers, as a community, perceive the use of this instrument as an effective way to assert competence in international ordering. Learning from interactions under silencing, they systematically use rhetoric and also creatively innovate these anti-imperial and anticolonial scripts by redeploying them in novel situations and flipping the scripts in other situations to achieve political objectives. In the rhetorical repertoire, policymakers rely on "obligatory passage points," which refer to sedimented challenges to silencing practices in the system that subordinate actors refer to to inspire and move the community of practitioners for pursing power. As chapter 2 will show, policymakers in India, Brazil, and China have long relied on such obligatory passage points to innovate the claims. Contemporary Indian policymakers like Narendra Modi exploiting the claims of Mohandas Gandhi, Lula da Silva using Baron Rio Branco, or Xi Jinping innovating the claims of Mao Zedong is thus not accidental. Rhetorical repertoires of power politics are like jazz music performance of a song—it is "important to not only know it (the items in the repertoire, e.g. the songs), but to know what to do with it, i.e. to enact it."[141]

How policymakers deploy rhetorical repertoire in statecraft also depends on the different lessons that political actors learned in the struggle against Western imperialism. Many subordinate actors have struggled against Western empires as agents from formal colonies, informal colonies, protectorates, annexed regions, or federations. Some, like Indian policymakers, deliberately choose anticolonial rhetoric against disempowerment and unfairness; others, like Brazilian policymakers, resort to claims of anti-Americanism and anti-Yankee rhetoric; and others, like Chinese policymakers, use anti-imperial rhetoric and ideological conflict. All policymakers mixed and matched anti-imperial and anticolonial rhetoric as they stood up against silencing and used a variety of affective performances against the excruciating pressures of silencing under hierarchy. Thus, there are variations in the way different policymakers under international hierarchy use and innovate their rhetorical repertoire against defanging and disempowerment and strategically use the contradictions in the system in the struggle. In chapter 2, we will see the evolution of the rhetorical repertoire in India, Brazil, and China in greater detail.

Traditional realist or rhetorical entrapment analysis does not pay attention to rhetorical repertoires of statecraft in international hierarchy. Rhetoric might appear as cheap talk or as a strategic practice to corner opponents. But there is more going on when we see that non-European policymakers improvise their rhetorical challenges to disempowerment and resort to colonial scripts again and again. For example, against the legitimating principle of human rights, their rhetoric enacting colonial scripts would leverage historical violations of sovereignty and humanitarian problems resulting from imperial interventions to promote liberal reforms. Pointing out hypocrisy is another way policymakers use colonial scripts in the rhetoric. Using lessons about the colonial and imperial periods, political actors show imperial continuities and conscious violation of proclaimed principles or selective adherence to these principles.

History is also replete with examples of subordinate leaders in the social hierarchy following anti-imperial and anticolonial colonial scripts in rhetoric, even in the period after the formal end of imperialism and colonialism, to negotiate and achieve political outcomes. For example, in refusing to accept the standard meaning of terrorism in 1984, the governments of Asia and Africa articulated that the "idea of terrorism includes South African apartheid, government-supported death squads in Central America, and International Monetary Fund policies." Such a move built on the anticolonial claims learned in the past.[142] In recent years, many policymakers from Asia, Africa, and Latin America also resort to rhetoric by deploying anti-imperial and anticolonial scripts supporting and opposing the meaning of democracy promotion in Iraq and Afghanistan, criticizing the imperialism of NATO but praising collective security and highlighting the problems inherent to the responsibility to protect against human rights violations. The way of flipping anti-imperial and anticolonial scripts in dealing with the Russian invasion of Ukraine in 2022 and for criticizing Israel's imperialism and colonialism in Gaza is part of the established rhetorical performances of power politics. If we focus on rhetorical repertoire, as I pointed out above, then this need not be seen as an aberration or an accident.

We can generalize about this rhetorical repertoire by focusing on how political actors use colonial scripts in a crisis and play with contradictions in the norms and rules of the system. I submit that it is not a general theory or a middle-range theory but ideal types in the conceptual framework to guide empirical analysis. Ideal types of the workings and innovations of rhetorical repertoire under the social hierarchy serve as standards to compare against empirics. As Patrick Jackson argues, "Researchers construct ideal types in order to create an idealization of a phenomenon's characteristics that can then be compared against other, related empirical instances. [Therefore,] ideal types will never accurately or exhaustively describe the concrete manifestations of a specific phenomenon, but they do provide benchmarks for the analytical comparison of real phenomena."[143] Thus, in an international crisis, we can expect that subordinate political actors will return to rhetorical performances focusing on the colonial nature of the norms and rules, exploiting the contradictions of the international system, and pursuing power. This can unfold in at least three ideal-typical ways.

First, in their rhetoric, some political actors contest, reinterpret, and stratify the norms of the international system, highlighting its imperial entailments. This is a radical interpretive process where political actors challenge the validity of norms as they did during the colonial period, outlining incompatibilities between the ways in which actors apply these norms and arguing for replacing one norm with another—one that is in line with the actor's preferred policy option. They also probe multiple audiences and their attitudes to gauge whether they might be receptive to their policy preferences. The audience's reaction to the rhetoric offers avenues for testing the meaning and significance of their colonial scripts and heuristically labeling them as friends, enemies, or neutrals in line with how the community of practitioners aims to achieve the political objectives. By enacting rhetorical claims similar to their predicaments during the colonial period, policymakers use their rhetoric to engage in a selective dialogue with friendly audiences, circumventing others to break the rules. Chapter 3 will show that the Indira Gandhi administration engaged in rhetorical performances and stacked different norms from human rights protection, self-defense, prevention of genocide, and maintenance of regional order, among others, in the 1971 East Pakistan crisis. Indian policymakers used anti-imperial and anticolonial scripts and also improvised their rhetorical repertoire to achieve their strategic objectives.

The second ideal-typical way of understanding how subordinate political actors use their rhetorical repertoire to achieve political objectives is to focus on how they use anti-imperial and anticolonial arguments to signal inclusivity with international norms and institutionalized conduct rather than stratifying norms and rules, as in the previous type. Institutions are "explicit arrangements, negotiated among international actors, that prescribe, proscribe, and/or authorize behavior."[144] Rhetorically working within these arrangements and appealing to the solidarity of other external members with their anti-imperial and anticolonial claims gives political actors novel avenues to demonstrate that their political projects fit within local, regional, and cultural norms and conventions. Using inclusive rhetoric as they did during the colonial period to build solidarity offers avenues for them to exploit the contradictions of the international system by managing radical opposition. We can expect that policymakers use their anti-imperial rhetorical repertoire to articulate myths, metaphors, analogies, and commonplaces to reaffirm collective identifications. Note the difference when political actors in the previous hypothesis aim to use colonial scripts to engage in selective dialogue versus here, where they seek joint commitment.[145] Chapter 4 will show how the Lula administration in Brazil strategically deployed its anti-Yankee rhetoric for intervention. Policymakers used established anti-imperial scripts to seek the adherence of other members in the region and then bound Brazil to collective Latin American institutional standards and conventions to achieve its strategic objectives in Haiti.

Third, the innovation and improvision of rhetorical repertoire can also unfold when political actors use anti-imperial and anticolonial scripts to circumvent the uncertainties of international politics. We can expect that rhetorical actors here outflank others by exploiting global ethics rather than just stratifying norms or expressing institutional solidarity. In their rhetoric, some political actors use anti-imperial rhetoric to articulate moral norms about the intrinsic duties of states in international politics. By strategically using this rhetoric in a political crisis, however, political actors engage in accusing, denouncing, and reproaching other interlocutors. Similar to the colonialized modality, this rhetoric uses obligatory passage points that resonate with their community of practitioners to shame Western interlocutors. But innovating on the rhetorical repertoire in this way garners opposition from audiences against their political project. For rhetorical power politics, this limelight is strategically useful to challenge the principles of international ordering. Using colonial scripts, we can expect that policymakers translate their conduct and strategically plead for pluralism and exercising leverage against opponents.[146] Chapter 5 will show how the Xi Jinping administration returned to its anti-imperial and anticolonial scripts, improvised its rhetoric, and strategically exploited the situation to assert the principles of sovereignty and territorial integrity in the Syrian crisis.

These broad generalizations on the different workings of rhetorical repertoire in statecraft are important for understanding the creative ways that policymakers exercise power under the hierarchy. They represent only a limited number of creative moves of rhetorical instruments and not a comprehensive range of strategies available for non-European states engaging in world-ordering practices. In an unequal playing field, non-Western policymakers play a rhetorical game by drawing on lessons learned from the legacies of Western imperialism and colonialism.

RESEARCH METHOD

For this study, I will use an interpretive research methodology that examines actors' meaning-making moves in international politics. The top-down rhetorical forms of ordering rely on Western policymakers interpreting the norms and rules of the legitimating principles, hiding the contradictions, and attributing incompetence to non-Europeans. In bottom-up rhetoric, non-Western policymakers reinterpret these norms in a series of contradictory and conflicting anti-imperial and anti-colonial claims to assert their competence and to pursue novel political projects. Thus, power politics is a densely interpretive process.

An interpretive analysis of power politics attends to the conscious and intentional use of language and examines the classifications and arrangements that actors impose on the world and their unintended effects in the social space.[147] In these discursive engagements, political actors work within their social practices, habits, shared understandings, or identities and cultures, among others, that constitute political conduct. The interpretive research in IR is replete with novel improvements on this research design in knowledge production and its political possibilities.[148]

Building on this scholarship, I use interpretive analysis to explore the politics of India, Brazil, and China. They are all self-proclaimed leaders of the Global South.[149] Studying these three ambitious states in international politics is important. As the Human Development Report of 2013 put it, "For the first time in 150 years, the combined output of the developing world's three leading economies—Brazil, China and India—is about equal to the combined GDP of the longstanding industrial powers of the North—Canada, France, Germany, Italy, United Kingdom and the United States. This represents a dramatic rebalancing of global economic power."[150] As we saw in the introduction and in this chapter, however, leaders from these states continue to deploy anticolonial and anti-imperial rhetoric in their political projects. They do not speak like rising powers. Putting the theoretical framework of this chapter into motion and elaborating the power political moves in these strategic discursive practices requires interpretation.

In this book, I will broadly interpret the historical evolution of the rhetorical power politics repertoire in India, Brazil, and China and examine how these lessons manifest in the context of managing humanitarian crises abroad. Rhetorical power politics is not confined to this domain. Yet the focus on humanitarian crisis and intervention—primarily a preserve of the West and a central pillar of its international ordering practices—can show the radical potential of their power politics. Humanitarian intervention is generally defined as "the threat or use of force across state borders by a state (or group of states) aimed at preventing or ending widespread and grave violations of the fundamental human rights of individuals other than its own citizens, without the permission of the state within whose territory force is applied."[151] Intervention has a long and contested history from the late eighteenth century onward, with the recognition of a superior class of great powers. As Edward Keene argues, humanitarian intervention emerged when a distinct class of great powers within international society "had the ability, and successfully asserted the right, to intervene in the affairs of those who, as sovereigns, at the same time belonged to an inferior group of lesser powers."[152] The normative duty to save humanity expanded from this intra-European concern to the wider world.

But many non-Western states have engaged in humanitarian interventions: India in Bangladesh in 1971; Vietnam in Cambodia in 1978; Tanzania in Uganda in 1979; the Economic Community of West African States (ECOWAS) in Liberia in 1990 and in Sierra Leone in 1997; multiple UN missions predominantly led by Global South states in UN Charter Chapter VII peace enforcement operations, in which Brazil played a role in Haiti in 2004, among others. The universe might be small, but it is connected to the broad semantic field of world politics, such as norms about warmaking, sovereign equality, great power status, the debates on the principles of human rights and the doctrine of nonintervention, social hierarchy, and international order. In the humanitarian domain, we can expect that the rhetorical lessons learned, and repertoires forged in the struggle against imperialism is unnecessary. There is no need to be rhetorical when the world is witnessing mass atrocity crimes. Thus, the humanitarian domain offers the opportunity for an expansive interpretive reconstruction of political processes from a small universe but with an intricately connected large number of observations.[153]

In this book, India, Brazil, and China are cases for the interpretive reconstruction of their politics in East Pakistan in 1971, Haiti in 2004, and Syria from 2011 to 2020, respectively. My interpretive analysis will map how dominant political actors interpreted India, Brazil, and China's incompetence in relation to the legitimating principles of international ordering during each of the crises. Then, I will reconstruct the contentious affective performances of elite political actors—particularly the Indira Gandhi administration in India, the Lula da Silva administration in Brazil, and the Xi Jinping administration in China. I will highlight the power political battles among policymakers and their interlocutors, activating their rhetorical repertories and using colonial and imperial scripts to pursue their political projects.

I will examine political elites and their speeches and writings, debates and discussions in the UN, debates in domestic legislatures and other public institutions, and press conferences. I will also rely on critical assessments and evaluations in media reports, editorials, and op-eds in English-language newspapers. I substantiate the analysis of the public performances through an engagement with some declassified documents. For the Indian case, I will examine the Foreign Relations of the United States 1969–1976, Volume XI, South Asia Crisis, 1971; Henry Kissinger Papers at the Manuscript Division, Library of Congress; declassified documents of the Ministry of External Affairs, Government of India, India-Pakistan Relations 1947–2007, Vol-I-X. For the Brazil case, I will examine debates in the national legislature and some declassified primary materials from the Getulio Vargas Foundation. For China, I will rely only on elite public argumentation in the UN and use officially translated English materials. I will also rely extensively on secondary historical works. With all this evidence, I will show the evolution of rhetorical repertoire and its concrete manifestations of the rhetorical power political processes in distinct humanitarian intervention episodes.

My analysis is interpretive in two senses. First, political elites and their audiences engage in rhetorical claims and counterclaims by contesting different norms in the legitimating principles for managing these humanitarian crises. But norms are not freestanding "things"; they are instituted by the practical attitudes of interlocutors who "take or treat these normative proprieties as committing and entitling other agents and themselves to further beliefs and actions."[154] Through contextual interpretive analysis, we can offer insights into how interlocutors use these norms to pursue their politics, adding meaning and sense. Second, norm use by rhetoric-wielding actors themselves or their audiences might be "wrong" or "confused" when compared against the unfolding humanitarian crises. In other words, political actors in India, Brazil, and China might not always be careful in using and abusing the validity and applicability of norms agreed upon by other interlocutors. Interpreting these processes from the third-person perspective as an academic analyst—who observes the observations of these policymakers—allows for a critical and explicit political analysis.[155]

2

REPERTOIRE OF POWER POLITICS
IN INDIA, BRAZIL, AND CHINA

For the first time in hundreds of years, non-European states are part of the nerve center of international politics. Between 1500 and 1800, European empires overtook the Ottoman Empire, China, and India in the East. Both European and North American imperial formations came to dominate the world over the course of the long nineteenth century and have continued to retain hegemony through today. But tectonic power shifts seem to be gathering force.

In 2015, Immanuel Wallerstein, "a sociologist who shook up the field with his ideas about Western domination of the modern world,"[1] argued that the "world system is in serious trouble" and asked what role the so-called BRICS—Brazil, Russia, India, China, and South Africa—play in the emerging world order. He said, "If one's definition of anti-imperialism is reducing the power of the United States, then the BRICS certainly represents an anti-imperialist force." But "if we look at the relations of BRICS countries to other countries in the South," particularly its immediate and distant neighbors, "it resembles how the United States and the old North related to them. They are sometimes accused of not being 'sub-imperial' but being simply 'imperial.'"[2] Wallerstein put his finger on the continuous predicament of power politics. BRICS has become a shorthand for hopes about a renewed force of anticolonialism and anti-imperialism among states who forged their connections in the inter-imperial networks of the nineteenth century and "third world" solidarities in the twentieth. BRICS is also a shorthand for despair about the BRICS countries' power politics playing out through colonial and imperial scripts.

Although debates about the different international roles of the BRICS are a recent development, their repertoires of power politics were forged much earlier and continue to direct their statecraft. As we saw in chapter 1, rhetoric is a language game in the public realm with persuasive or symbolic purposes and a necessity for those suffering silencing on the lower rungs of hierarchy. We also saw that this repertoire included established linguistic tool kits and inventories of contention that policymakers use and innovate in strategic ways to achieve their political objectives. Scholars who wish to understand non-Western states must look at the development of rhetorical repertoire in the histories of Western empires and imperialism. As recent historical studies show, colonized people were political actors who "worked hard to wrest power and authority from imperial governments" and had "long histories of intercolonial connection, collaboration, and of course also friction."[3] These political actors also worked hard to retain the hard-won power and turned ruthless in their ambitions, learning different ways of pursuing power politics. The goal of this chapter is to understand how anti-imperial and anticolonial rhetoric became part of the repertoire of statecraft and how political leaders put this lesson to use in power politics.

Using recent developments in BRICS history and politics to trace the evolution of a realpolitik repertoire serves three methodological purposes. First, it shows the ways in which political elites—in occupied colonies such as India, indirect colonies such as Brazil, and semicolonies such as China—were constantly innovating to challenge Western imperialism in the late nineteenth century and how these lessons structured the development of statecraft in the twentieth century. Their inter-imperial solidarities and connections helped them articulate and innovate selective claims, challenging the silencing practices in the hierarchical system. I focus on the interconnections between the colonizers and the colonized, which allows us to see innovations in statecraft in relation to entanglements in imperialism. Innovative rhetoric for statecraft has had implications for the structure of the hierarchical international system from decolonization to their justification of the right to advanced technologies such as nuclear weapons.

Second, this approach enables us to see how non-European elites articulated views of state power in contentious anti-imperial performances to pursue their selective "national interests." As this chapter will show, contentious and performative challenges—such as India's nationwide non-cooperation protest movement for swaraj ("self-rule"), Brazil's withdrawal from the League of Nations after its failed bid for a permanent seat, and the May Fourth movement in China that erupted with resentment over the Versailles Treaty—fed into their statecraft.[4] In these performances, elites wrestled against each other and learned to exploit skillfully the contradictions in the legitimating principles, norms, and rules of the modern international system. Looking back to the learned lessons of statecraft, we can see how their rhetorical power political repertoire came about, its features, and how and why it reproduces itself in the international system.

Third, looking at the specific histories of diplomacy and statecraft shows reflexive learning among non-European political actors and how they maneuvered within and against the intricate domination of Western empires. Reflective learning enables reforms "in response to perceived failures" or the search for "more effective solutions."[5] Indian, Brazilian, and Chinese political actors learned to use their rhetorical strategies in such a way that sometimes they bring an ostentatious display of anti-imperial and anticolonial rhetoric to the negotiating table. Other times, they rely on diplomatic negotiation without seeking the limelight but still flipping colonial scripts. Historicizing their engagement shows how learning to use rhetoric skillfully was central in statecraft in the social hierarchies, more than static public commemorations, to create a national narrative. This chapter will show that the interwar years—between 1918 and 1939—were a watershed moment for political actors in developing such a dynamic strategy. In this way, the chapter contributes to the ongoing idea among historians and postcolonial scholars that there was no sharp break between the Cold War and what came before.[6] The post–Cold War continuities in the power political repertoire of BRICS states, for example, have turned many explicit interwar rhetorical claims implicit.

The chapter will show the development of political repertoire as an instrument of resistance, its maturation as a weapon of the weak in the interwar years, and its use in the contemporary period. First, I will examine the rhetoric of non-European activists and politicians in the imperial network and show how they evoked their ancient culture and tradition to position themselves against the rise of European imperialism. Second, I will examine the continuities of such rhetoric at the height of New Imperialism, roughly between the last decade of the nineteenth century and the end of World War I. Between 1900 and 1919, many political actors from India, Brazil, and China decried their inferior position on questions of international order and stood up against the hierarchical system.

Third, I will show how these political actors in the interwar years frequently built on their predecessors to challenge imperial practices, honed their anticolonial and anti-imperial rhetoric, and systematically wielded it as a weapon of the weak. I will look specifically at intra-elite competition among these states and how they exploited the contradictions in the geopolitical principles, norms, and rules of postwar ordering. The inter-imperial period was important because elite debates in this period became mandatory passage points for the communities of policymakers on statecraft. Empires rebuffed such claims, of course, silencing by attributing incompetence to non-European actors. But non-European rhetoric using old scripts continued despite ignominious failures against the British Empire in India, American expansionism in Latin America, and European encroachments in China. The fourth section of the chapter will show the continuities and innovations of this power politics in the Cold War period, and the concluding section will examine the rhetorical power politics of these states against the American empire and the rules-based international order.

RHETORIC AT THE RISE OF
EUROPEAN IMPERIALISM

The start of the nineteenth century marked a critical moment for non-European, enslaved, and Indigenous people. The French and the American Revolutions in the last two decades of the eighteenth century inspired different people around the world to attempt their own independence movements. For example, by the early nineteenth century, Haiti had wrestled independence from France (1804); Mexico saw independence wars against Spanish control (1810–1821); Nepal (1814–1816) and Burma (1824–26) rose against the machinations of the English East India Company; India saw the great rebellion of 1857; and the Maori king declared the boundaries of its kingdom in 1858, standing against the British using the same narrative of the age of revolution.[7] This chain reaction of revolts and responses to revolts was so unprecedented that "empires came under scrutiny" from multiple interlocutors in the inter-imperial network.[8]

The British Empire used legitimating principles and norms of liberalism to "civilize" Indigenous people and engaged in colonial domination in the name of progress. Others, notably the French, also used the principle of *la mission civilisatrice*, or "civilizing mission," to transmit so-called European culture worldwide. All European empires were "garrison states," meaning military security were their top priority, seeking to rule over non-European societies to finance their wars and consolidate the "military and aristocratic character" of conquests.[9] Dynastic and aristocratic links among Europeans allowed for cooperation even if policymakers condemned the imperialism of the other.[10] Thus, in the wake of the Napoleonic invasion of Portugal in 1807, British warships helped the Braganza monarchy escape Portugal to Brazil in 1808. In a couple of weeks, Brazil changed from a colony (1500–1808) to a metropole (1808–1821) and later turned into an empire (1822–1888). Such developments also established British hegemony in Brazil and effectively relegated the country to a semicolony for resource extraction in exchange for preserving its imperial dynasty. The Opium War of 1839–1842 and the Second Opium War of 1856–1860 involved multiple Western powers collaborating and cooperating to exploit China. For most non-Europeans, all Western empires were cut from the same cloth of racial arrogance in service of aggressive profiteering.

In the early and mid-nineteenth century, some non-European elites challenged Western empires and their aggressive ideologies. In 1832, Indian reformer Rammohan Roy questioned the notion of *terra nullius* ("nobody's land") in India, which officials of the British East India Company used to justify their rule. Rammohan Roy's early rhetoric, what I call proto-strategic rhetoric, focused on the "longstanding popular sensibility that there existed a subcontinental cultural entity" called Hindustan.[11] He looked to its ancient constitutional customs as a repository of reason and focused on civic republicanism to assert that Hindustan was not "barbaric." His focus was also on reforming the British Parliament so that it could act as a proper "guardian" of India and replace the corruption of the British East India Company.[12] His contemporary Rama Raja (Ram Raz) looked back to Kautilya's *Arthasastra*, an ancient Indian treatise on statecraft, to suggest a long lineage of India's statecraft based on democracy and constitutionalism, and he confidently asserted India's rights in the international system.[13]

Rhetorical claims of anticolonial activists who leveraged tradition and culture were a global phenomenon and not confined to direct colonies such as India. The emergence of Brazil as an indirect colony of the British Empire was similarly accompanied by several revolts and republican challenges that engaged its cultural practices and traditions. For example, Brazil's radical priests Frei Caneca and Manuel Carvalho Paes de Andrade engaged in an anti-Portuguese revolt in Pernambuco in 1824. They challenged the emperor of Brazil, Dom Pedro I, who, after independence in 1822, aspired to a colonial reunion of Brazil with Portugal. These rebels fought against the emperor's dynastic conception of the incipient Brazilian nation and sought autonomy of its provinces. They were killed by Brazilian firing squads. However, sentiments of nondomination in statecraft remained central to Brazil's opposition to its "enslavement" through unequal treaties with Britain.[14]

In one corner of the British Empire, a Burmese prince talked about his nation, asserting that the "English have no rights to the eastern lands" and we will not "tamely submit to the foreigner."[15] Roughly around the same time, on the other side of the world, Brazil's José Bonifácio Andrada e Silva, as close adviser of Dom Pedro I, advocated building "a homogenous nation in the course of few generations, for, failing this, we will never be truly free, respectable, or happy."[16] He sought the abolition of slavery in 1823 (which would not come until the birth of the first republic in 1888). Thus, in the interconnected world, empires came under greater scrutiny from multiple agents from the metropole and the colony in the inter-imperial network, even as they stormed ahead with conquests and annexation.

The Qing dynasty stepped up its survival plans against the rise of European imperialism.[17] Political and intellectual elites selectively used the tropes of Confucian humanism to revive "interest in the school of statecraft" to maintain dynastic stability and build a sense of a nation.[18] Reformist Wei Yuan's ideas of learning from the "superior techniques of the barbarians," meaning the West, and using "barbarians against barbarians" were important rhetorical flourishes during the unfolding crisis in China.[19] It also involved a master plan to threaten the British in India using Russians, French, and Americans to preserve the Qing dynasty.[20] The Chinese also stepped up their attempt to build naval ships in line with the rhetoric of "learning from the barbarians," and later in the century, the Jiangnan Arsenal and a naval yard at Fuzhou were in operation.[21] Nevertheless, "China did not develop a nation-wide sense of urgency until more intense shocks stunned the Middle Kingdom."[22]

By the mid-late nineteenth century, the incipient rhetoric of non-European states became louder. At the end of the nineteenth century, India's literary star Bankim Chandra Chatterjee argued for an organic sociological unity that evoked ancient India and designed the slogan *Bande Mataram* ("Hail to the Motherland") in 1875 to assert nationhood.[23] Eminent thinkers such as Dadabhai Naoroji, Ganesh Joshi, Gopal Krishna Gokhale, and Mahadev Govind Ranade, among others, advanced the idea of protecting Indian culture and its political economy.[24] As Manu Goswami puts it, "Nationalists recast both the rhetoric and practice of laissez-faire economics as the coalition partner of Britain's global economic hegemony. Against the abstractions of classical economic theory, they sought to develop a conceptual framework that was at once explicitly historicist and nationalist."[25] In Brazil, the imperial state defended slavery as part of its tradition and culture despite facing incessant calls for reforms from elites within and outside the state.[26] As the U.S. Civil War (1861–1865) became a reference point for enslaved Brazilians, Brazil's imperial statecraft worked to stop its subjugated peoples from taking any inspiration from that war. As the governor of the maritime province of Maranhão reported, the slaves in the province of Anajatuba in 1861 did not have any "organized plan and only hope for their freedom." But "I will do whatever I can to neutralize any plans that the matter concerning the United States of America might create here among the slaves."[27] This is an important reminder that resorting to tradition was a conservative enterprise for self-preservations and a thoroughly rhetorical enterprise.

In some instances, semicolonies such as China sharpened their proto-strategic cultural rhetoric against the empires. The Qing Restoration, through a coup d'état in Beijing in 1861, brought Empress Dowager Cixi as regent headed by two Manchus, Prince Gong and Grand Councillor Wenxiang. Their rhetoric relied on traditional Confucian order because such tropes were readily available instruments for challenging European imperialism and suppressing internal rebellions. In this sense, reviving Confucian traditions such as *Chung* ("faithfulness"), *Hsin* ("trust"), *Tu* ("sincerity"), and *Ching* ("seriousness") offered a strategic space to protect

China's interests and build an exclusive nation based on ancient traditions and, at the same time, to "firmly reject several extra-legal requests" from foreigners.[28] Thus, elites in the Qing dynasty worked within the terms set by "civilized" powers.[29] But their incipient rhetoric simultaneously sought self-strengthening. They relied on polemical slogans such as "Chinese learning as the fundamental structure, Western learning for practical use," or "Western sciences borrowed their roots from ancient Chinese mathematics. . . . China invented the method, Westerners adopted it."[30] Li Hongzhang, a Chinese politician and diplomat of the late Qing empire, used these claims for military modernization. Also Sun Yat-Sen (1866–1925), the paramount leader of the 1911 Revolution, endorsed this rhetoric even if he challenged the pace of such modernization and also called for constitutional and institutional economic reforms.[31]

In sum, early political activists wielded rhetoric as a proto-strategic weapon against the globalizing empires. They leveraged cultural practices and traditions to strengthen their claims in the inter-imperial network. As Christopher Bayly puts it, "the need for self-strengthening" spread across all "extra-European civilisations, subject or partially independent," at the same time when "European dominance of the world reached its high point after 1850."[32] Rhetoric offered avenues to push back against the claims of superiority of Western civilization. However, these elites could not face the onslaught of the military and economic power of the Western empires without a concerted plan of resistance. Their ability to draw from their past to push back against Western silencing and maneuver in the hierarchical system became sharper in the subsequent period of imperial aggrandizement.

RHETORIC AGAINST THE HEIGHT OF GLOBAL IMPERIALISM

The onset of New Imperialism marked another shift in the strategies of the non-Europeans. At the height of global imperialism, geopolitics emerged as a core legitimating principle of the international order. The principle rested on social Darwinist ideas of the "survival of the fittest" and societies as organisms that would die if they did not expand. This sentiment gained prominence around 1880, peaked in 1918, remained strong through Nazi expansionism and the Japanese invasion of Manchuria in 1931, and culminated with the end of World War II.[33] This story is also well known.[34] But these geopolitical principles rested on several paradoxes, antinomies, and contradictions, as we will see below.

By the mid-1860s, Britain had moved away from protectionism and aggressively supported free trade, offered public goods, and celebrated geopolitical projects based on Greater Britain.[35] But most other empires opposed British free trade liberalism by nationalizing and erecting barriers to free trade and by relying on the very same geopolitical principles of territorial expansion and the exploitation of colonies.[36] Germany's Otto Van Bismarck demanded protection for iron and rye, Central European states established tariff walls, and the United States retained its commitment to national market protection. These exclusionary geopolitical principles contributed to a European international community that rested on militant nationalism. There was a "competitive alliance equilibrium" based on mistrust of other states.[37] These imperial powers pursued aggressive expansionist practices in the periphery to secure a "place in the sun," meaning in the tropical locations of Africa and Oceania, to rival the British. As we saw in chapter 1, this gave rise to aggressive silencing of non-European states.

But by the 1880s, heterogenous Pan-Asian, Pan-African, and Pan-Islamic movements emerged to push back against the geopolitical principles of these empires. When William Gladstone called the Ottoman Empire "one great anti-human specimen of humanity" in the context of the Ottoman suppression of the Bulgarian insurrection of 1876, many Ottoman intellectuals responded with counterarguments that "Islamic and European values of progress were not incompatible."[38] When Ernest Renan referred to Islam as an impediment to science and rationality, Nemik Kemal, famous for his statement that "Europe Knows Nothing about the Orient," accused Renan of "being full of delusions."[39] Thus, by the end of the century, the colonized space was already filled with rhetorical challenges that slowly became explicit instruments of resistance. In India, Dadabhai Naoroji and Romesh Chunder famously argued that the British "drain of wealth" from India was the principal cause of India's poverty.[40] Their drain theory inverted the idea of the progressive narrative of colonialism based on the view that it improves the ability of natives to acquire the benefits of scientific and industrial modernity. Instead, he wrote: "This India is 'bled' and exploited in every way of their wealth, of their services, of their land, labour, and all resources by their foreigners, helpless and voiceless, governed by the arbitrary law and arguments of force, and with injustice and unrighteousness—this India of the Indians becomes the poorest country in the world, after one hundred and fifty years of British rule."[41] Such arguments would soon swell to be part of the rhetorical repertoire of the state agents, as we will see in the subsequent sections.

Such claims came from long and sustained research by a dedicated community of young Indian reformers in the inter-imperial network who detested "the racial exclusiveness of British rule and the inappropriateness of its forms of law and sociality for Indian society."[42] In the Indian colonial ecumene, claims about the nation, protection of its political economy, and the limits of Western civilization became common tropes for those who specialized in statecraft. The Indian National Congress (INC), established in 1885, was made up of so-called moderate elites who were well versed in anticolonial rhetoric in the early twentieth century. Elites from the INC proclaimed, "Our industries need protection," and they set the stage for protests against foreign goods from the British Empire, calling instead for goods produced in one's country (*swadeshi*).[43] In this way, INC elites used the rhetoric of culture and tradition to chastise the empire. As Pherozeshah Mehta, a founding member of INC put it, "So far as the historical argument is concerned, we [the INC] have been successful in turning the tables upon our adversaries. We have shown that it is they who defy the lessons of history and modernity when they talk of waiting to make a beginning till the masses of the people are fully equipped with all the virtues." Mehta emphasized that it is because our traditions show that we can represent ourselves as a universal nation.[44] Other political actors who were part of the swadeshi style of contention against the British Empire would frequently borrow rhetorical claims from each other to assert India's quest for autonomy using principles based on social Darwinism to talk of an "organic" conception of the Hindu nation.[45]

Brazil became a republic in 1888 and, in 1902, the famous arbitration genius José Maria da Silva Paranhos Junior, the Barão Rio Branco, became Brazilian minister of external affairs under President Rodrigues Alves. The principal international problem in Brazil at that time was the demarcation of its boundaries, touching every country except Chile (Ecuador was still fronted on Brazil). The Barão of Rio Branco engaged in negotiations through the legal-geopolitical principle of *uti possidetis*, that is, to preserve the boundaries of the imperial-colonial state (formalized by Portuguese diplomat Alexandre de Gusmão).[46] Rio Branco settled the boundary problems, adding territory to Brazil that is equivalent to France and Germany and setting the stage for aggressive nation building.[47] Rio Branco worked with a team of men: Joaquim Nabuco, Ruy Barbosa, Francisco Viega, and Euclides da Cunha, among others. These elites sensed the pulse of global ideas of the twentieth century and actively participated in Brazilian statecraft in relation to Europe and the United States. They converged on rhetoric emphasizing Brazil's greatness. As Rio Branco put it, "Brazil resolutely entered the sphere of great international friendships, to which it is entitled through the aspiration of its culture, through the prestige of its territorial greatness and the strength of its population."[48]

Rhetoric in China turned fierce against the Western empires. In 1902, Liang Qichao, one of the influential reformist voices in the Qing dynasty, wrote a manifesto titled *On the New People*. It was based on social Darwinist principles and written even as the dynasty was limping and in tatters. He emphasized that all people have responsibilities and to fulfill them, we must preserve our lives committed to "rights consciousness" (*quanli sixiang*). Acquiring strength involves acknowledging righteous duties toward oneself and toward a general group. Yet rights are continuously disturbed. Like organisms engaged in the fight for survival of the fittest, the demonstration of strength must be continuous in a transitional period—not through "reasons" but through "trial by fire" so that the rights subsequently attained can never be relinquished.[49] Liang Qichao asserted that a great state is also a strong state, but it is also one with a concern for the world.[50] In this way, he asserted that a new China must be such a state. In 1905, Sun Yat-Sen became the head of the Revolutionary League, endorsed social Darwinist ideas, and focused on greater centralization for a strong Chinese state.[51] The anti-imperial and self-strengthening rhetoric of Liang Qichao and Sun Yat-Sen would continue to resonate among Chinese elites throughout the century, more than anything, to protect against predations of the West in its unequal treaty relations and of Japan in its imperial expansion.

Such rhetoric was not stagnant, partly because of the dynamic nature of violent rule practiced by imperial powers. Relentless protests and unrest in the colonized space played out every day in the twentieth century, and this affected the statecraft of the subordinate members in the social hierarchy. India's massive protests seeking swaraj, Brazil's diplomatic protests against its unequal treatment in The Hague Conference and the League of Nations, and China's storming protests in the New Culture/May Fourth Movement (1915–1923) stirred elites to think carefully about ways to maneuver in the hierarchical international system. These changes led to small innovations that focused on bold performances of diplomatic resistance in front of global interlocutors.

Such innovations were apparent in India after George Curzon, the viceroy of India, partitioned Bengal in 1905 in keeping with the principles of social Darwinism and a demonstration of racial superiority and arrogance. Many Indian reformers and nationalists challenged the partition immediately as a desecration of the Indian nation. Drawing on the previous claims about ancient traditions, religion, culture, and native political space (swadeshi), they marshalled old claims and advanced a new view of despoilation of the Indian nation *Bharat Mata* ("mother goddess"), calling for swaraj.[52] Aurobindo Ghosh, India's famous anticolonial fighter, looked to Bankim's song of *Bande Mataram*—meaning "I bow to thee, Mother" that personified India as mother goddess, inspiring deep patriotism—and weaponized the rhetoric of India's greatness in a Hindu vision by articulating an organic view of the Indian as a Hindu nation.[53] He said: "It was thirty-two years ago that Bankim wrote his great song and few listened; but in a sudden moment of awakening from long delusions the people of Bengal looked round [sic] for the truth and in a fated moment somebody sang *Bande Mataram*. The mantra has been given [emphasis in the original]."[54] A switch in the rhetorical repertoire from swadeshi to swaraj was possible because other elite interlocutors found this rhetoric an efficient way to resist empire and innovate ideas that drew on elites who articulated these claims previously. The so-called nationalist extremists Lala Lajpat Rai, Bal Gangadhar Tilak, and Bipin Chandra Pal—who formed a troika of Lal, Bal, and Pal—would frequently look back to Rammohun Roy and Kautilya's treatise on statecraft, establishing an obligatory passage point of the culture of Indigenous realpolitik in India to challenge moderate members of the INC. Mohandas Gandhi wrote a polemic draft about Hind swaraj: "The English have taught us that we were not one nation before, and that it will require centuries before we make one nation. This is without foundation. We were one nation before they came to India."[55] Such rhetoric was so disruptive that the colonial British state declared the proclamation of *Bande Mataram* illegal in public space. The British Empire annulled the partition of Bengal in 1911, not the least due to the rhetoric and public protests in India.

It is important to note that Indian elites who used such rhetoric had to contend with other elites, such as Muslim intellectuals and transnational political actors, to wrestle a distinct view of the nation. The struggle between Hindu and Muslim elites on the appropriate use of rhetoric for resistance defined the trajectory of the Indian and Pakistan nation-states. Nevertheless, a group of caste-based intellectuals innovated the rhetoric on tradition, culture, and practices to articulate another view of the state from the predominant Hindu variant offered by the majority of INC elites. For example, Iyothee Thass, a prominent anticaste activist from the south, asserted that the Tamil-speaking "Paraiyar community were the original Tamils and casteless Buddhists."[56] He steadfastly stood against the geopolitics of the colonial state's caste-based census (started in 1872). And his arguments on rights and duties set the stage for pan-Indian non-Brahmin consciousness, anticipating B. R. Ambedkar by several decades.[57] All this shows a fertile public sphere of performances, claims, and counterclaims in India.

In Brazil, a subtle shift in rhetoric on diplomacy and statecraft came from elites who were part of the ministry of external affairs of Baron of Rio Branco but who also saw new challenges for the state in the early twentieth century. Three elites played a central role.[58] In 1905, Joaquim Nabuco, an antislavery stalwart and an aristocrat, was appointed as the ambassador of the first Brazilian embassy in Washington, DC. He brought up the "traditional" debates on the importance of the Monroe Doctrine in Brazil and shifted from his erstwhile anti-Americanism to becoming an "emphatic Americanist."[59] Rui Barbosa, twice an official candidate for the presidency of the Brazilian republic and head of the Brazilian delegation to the Second International Peace Conference (1907) at The Hague, firmly believed that Brazil's foreign policy was "severely outdated."[60] Barbosa also witnessed the workings of the unequal international system when the United States, Germany, and the United Kingdom agreed to create a High Court of Arbitration at The Hague Conference, where "eight powers would have a permanent seat and the other nations of the world would have rotating seats."[61] He advocated for the equality of nations in the court and famously withdrew from The Hague. Manuel de Oliveira Lima, a journalist, historian, and diplomat, also took a stance for Latin Americanism.[62] He steadfastly condemned Theodore Roosevelt's big stick policy and opposed "American interventionism and imperialism in the continent."[63]

As sociologist Angela Alonso puts it: "The rhetoric of Barbosa was that of the equality of all nations, but his group of supporters were the delegates from Latin America [not the United States]. In that sense, the Brazilian stance ultimately appeared to be closer to Latin Americanism." Nabuco focused on "realpolitik" because equality might be "good as [a] principle" and argued that "'we cannot impose it on the world' since the economic and military inequality between the countries was a fact,"[64] but later in his life, he became concerned with "the growth of imperialism, suspecting that it would end, as it actually did, in a World War."[65] Thus, by the early twentieth century, diplomatic elites switched the traditional repertoire of Brazilian statecraft and focused on demanding, sometimes ostentatiously, Brazil's right to inclusion in the international system. In about two decades, Brazil stormed out of the League of Nations because it failed to secure a permanent position. Growing discontentment with Brazil's recognition in the international hierarchy underlies such performance, and rhetoric became more important to articulate discontentment.

Many Chinese elites in the republican period embraced similar rhetorical postures and improvised the claims from the past to challenge the presumptive normative principles of the international system. In a way, the rhetoric of China's political actors also shifted by the early twentieth century. Many of China's revolutionary elites saw significant problems with the Qing empire's statecraft on military modernization and challenges to the West. By the end of the nineteenth century, Japan's victory over China in 1895 led to the humiliating Treaty of Shimonoseki. When World War I started, Japan joined the Allies against the Central Powers, ousted Germany, took control of its colonies, including Shandong, and reinforced its dominance in Manchuria and inner Mongolia. It pressed to transform China into a Japanese protectorate through the infamous Twenty-One Demands of January 18, 1915.[66] In response to these developments, protests erupted across China to save the nation.[67] The radical rhetoric that emerged in response to this protest was a significant innovation.

Elites in the late Qing dynasty, such as Yan Fu, Kang Youwei, and Liang Qichao, had previously focused on radicalism, while Li Hongzhang and Wang Tao used Western learnings in the Self-Strengthening Movement. In contrast, the radicalism of the May Fourth Movement called for repudiating the weakness of the Chinese past and sought a "national awakening" that embodied China's cultural values.[68] As Edward Fung shows, the New Culture/May Fourth Movement led to at least four radical positions: Confucian radicalism, which called for reforms based on reading Confucian classics; anarchic radicalism that held an anti-Machu motif and called for a dissolution of imperial Confucianism; Radical Marxism, which inspired the communist movement; and Westernized radicalism, which believed in the superiority of Western culture and practices.[69]

The Republican Revolution thus witnessed forceful claims of many elites on statecraft based on national strength to fight inequality and an unjust international system. Hu Shi, pragmatic reformist; Chen Duxiu, founder of the Chinese Communist Party; and Liang Shuming, a philosopher and cultural conservative; and others brought forth new rhetorical challenges to reorganize the sociopolitical order. Hu Shi pointed out that a reorganization of national heritage meant a total revamping of old customs so that the "once a great civilization" could create a transformation by following the "universal path to progress."[70] He claimed that it was time to create a new Chinese "essence" (*ti*), which could be used to improve the collective "Great Self of Chinese society." Hu Shi advocated rights and freedom domestically.[71] In international politics, he advocated for a great state through military reforms, even working with warlords.[72] And even as the Beiyang government contributed Chinese laborers to the Western Front, Sun Yat-Sen, in 1912, hoped to rejoin China with the international community.[73] But Sun Yat-Sen switched the rhetorical game reflecting on World War I, which would resonate among multiple elites across the century. Sun Yat-Sen delivered his *Three People's Principles* as a series of sixteen lectures in 1924 and argued:

> Many year [*sic*] of fierce warfare had not been able to destroy imperialism because this war was a conflict of imperialisms between states, not a struggle between savagery and civilization or between Might and Right. So the effect of the war was merely the overthrow of one imperialism by

another imperialism; what survived was still imperialism. Now we want to revive China's lost nationalism and use the strength of our four hundred millions to fight for mankind against injustice: this is our divine mission. . . . We, the wronged races, must first recover our position of national freedom and equality before we are fit to discuss cosmopolitanism. We must understand that cosmopolitanism grows out of nationalism; if we want to extend cosmopolitanism we must first establish strongly our own nationalism. If nationalism cannot become strong, cosmopolitanism certainly cannot prosper.[74]

Other elites improvised the challenges to social Darwinism, which Kang Yuwei and Liang Qichao deployed, to return to the trope of China's humiliation at the hands of the Western powers in the last quarter of the nineteenth century.[75] Liang Qichao called for the "renovation of the people," which resonated with Hu Shi and Sun Yat-Sen and also anticipated Mao Zedong's focus on "people's rule."[76] At the 1919 Paris Peace Conference, Wellington Koo, C. T. Wang, and W. W. Yen worked on arguments for reforming the world and using international law for the liberation of China from Western dominance. Yet they doubted that Western leaders would concede to China's claims. This conviction led elites to develop rhetoric centered around unequal treaties. As Dong Wang shows, China was the "first nation to challenge the legal validity of its treaties with foreign countries" that subsequently helped reform "the received assumptions in international law to include an acceptance that a treaty imposed upon a defeated/weak state under duress is not viable."[77] Young Mao Zedong chastened Wilsonian ideas through bolshevism by charging that the connection between self-determination and imperialism was a "shameless" form of oppression.[78]

Anti-imperial rhetoric offered the space to wrestle with complicated views on statecraft despite the economic and military powers of the West and its silencing practices. Antihegemonic rhetoric also enabled ambitious political elites from India, Brazil, and China to innovate on old ideas based on tradition and culture and manage the state in the hierarchical international system. Their rhetoric espoused many of the same justifications for territory and space as their European counterparts. This became explicit in the interwar years.

INTRA-ELITE COMPETITION AND RHETORICAL REPERTOIRE IN THE INTERWAR PERIOD

The interwar period between 1919 and 1939 saw a distinctive consolidation of rhetorical strategies in India, Brazil, and China. The end of World War I saw many old empires crumble, such as the Hohenzollern, Habsburg, and Ottoman empires. It also witnessed the onset of nationalism inspired by Woodrow Wilson's ideal of national self-determination and the promises of Russian bolshevism. With the arrival of the League of Nations and formal institutionalized solutions to global governance, many Western interlocutors agreed to conduct diplomacy based on public legitimacy instead of a secret set of treaties agreed between monarchs.

Yet imperialism remained stable. In the League of Nations, non-Europeans were only an afterthought. As we saw in chapter 1, they were regularly found "not yet able to stand by themselves under the strenuous conditions of the modern world" and were placed under the tutelage of the British or the French Empire.[79] But many of these states would not take this disdain lightly.

One way of assessing this novel rhetorical innovation is to see how multiple elites in their intra-elite competition wrestled a conception of their "state-nation" in claiming their right to participate in the international order. Recall India's Bal Tilak, who participated in swadeshi and swaraj modes of contention against the British Empire. The colonial state barred Tilak from attending the Paris Peace Conference at Versailles and selected two loyalist delegates to represent India. Tilak instead sent a memorandum to the Paris Peace Conference arguing for sovereign Indian statehood. He used the arguments about self-determination and independence. He also strategically added the rhetorical view that "independent India would be an active agent of peace and security in the region, continuing to defend British imperial interests."[80] And Lala Lajpat Rai, who lived in exile in the United States between 1913 and 1919, met with W. E. B. Du Bois and saw the plight of "American blacks with the untouchables in India" and engaged in campaigns to present an anti-imperial case to Woodrow Wilson.[81] Yet he also viewed the fears of Muslims in Hindu India as "prejudice and an insufficiently developed feeling of Indian brotherhood."[82] Rai would join the Hindu nationalist club to redeploy his rhetoric against Muslim demands in India. They drew on past rhetorical debates to articulate a strategic ethno-nationalist cultural view of the Indian state.

Another group of Indian elites was attentive to geopolitical principles, attacked the moral superiority of empires, and worked to consolidate a distinct view of state power in geopolitical terms. For example, the Greater Indian Society in 1920, which included historians R. C. Majumdar and Kalidas Nag and philologists Suniti Kumar Chatterji and P. C. Bagchi, used the cultural rhetoric of previous debates to articulate a bold view of Indian culture as a superior civilizing force across all Asian land.[83] As Susan Bayly shows, members of the society focused on "imagined initiatives of an Indic colonising past with the life of moral and spiritual action prescribed for anti-imperialists and nation-builders."[84] The Greater India Society members were keen to say: "India also has its Napoleons and Charlemagnes, its Bismarcks and Machiavellis. But the real charm of Indian history does not consist in these aspirants after universal power, but its peaceful and benevolent Imperialism—a unique thing in the history of mankind."[85]

Recall Ram Raz, who used Kautilya's *Arthasastra* to assert India's realpolitik tradition and autonomy against the rise of Western imperialism. Now reference to *Arthasastra* became an obligatory passage point for many other elites. In the interwar years, the treatise triggered a huge debate in the public sphere.[86] Benoy Kumar Sarkar spearheaded the debates and claims about India's realpolitik by arguing for a Hindu theory of international relations.[87] He went back to the fourth century BC to show that Kautilya's *realpolitik* resonates with the speculations of Grotius in *Laws of War and Peace* (1625) and is in good company with Aristotelian justification of warfare. As Sarkar puts it, Indian views on statecraft reflect the "innate militarism that the human world inherits from 'beasts and birds.'"[88] India's thinking on the balance of power (*mandala*) prioritizes the adjudication of friends and enemies based on the geographical position of these states. And he argued that the world federation of the Hindus for universal sovereignty (*chakravartin*) "is identical with the [concept of] the *dominus omnium*" in the Western political thought and "*hwangti* [*sic*] of the Chinese [emphasis in the original]." More than anything, the underlying style of this argumentation understood global legitimizing principles and flipped the colonial script, which viewed India as primitive or medieval in dealing with issues of international order, to pursue statecraft.[89]

Such rhetoric also faced the challenges of the interwar world and brought out another group in the intra-elite competition. The end of World War I saw the renewal of imperial violence in the colonies. India witnessed the infamous Jallianwalla Bagh massacre in Amritsar in April 1919, in which, under the direction of General Reginald Dyer, the British army killed an unarmed crowd of Indians. Mohandas Gandhi led an unprecedented mass protest against the British in India from 1920 to 1922. After a pause to train the masses on nonviolence, he started the revolutionary noncooperation or *satyagraha* movement in 1930, aimed at securing Indian independence. Gandhi's anti-imperial rhetoric moved from the polemical Hind swaraj period, which saw English civilization as a "Kingdom of Satan," to a matured view that "it was the duty of every Indian to destroy the British Empire," and toward an ascetic view that to fight against imperialism one must begin with a self-authorized nonviolent action, which could "melt the stoniest heart."[90] Such claims substantiated his rhetoric about the decadence of Western civilization, capitalism, and modernity.

The Great Depression of the late 1920s and early 1930s affected millions of non-Europeans in disproportionate ways and exacerbated the plight of the poor. After the Bolshevik Revolution, some elites from the metropole and the colonies tried to engage in inter-imperial solidarity using novel revolutionary rhetoric, in which they spoke with and for the struggling nations in the world.[91] The Congress of Oppressed Nationalities in Brussels in 1927, which became the League Against Imperialism (LAI), played an important role in this development. The congress itself was a grouping of 174 delegates representing 31 states, colonies, or regions and 134 organizations.[92] In it, transnational anticolonial elites, from anarchists to radical Marxists, reflected on the exploitation and the unequal international system.

Jawaharlal Nehru, the future prime minister of independent India, participated in the Brussels congress. His participation fundamentally shaped his global statecraft, which centered on forging Asian solidarities and confronting American imperialism. At the congress, he emphasized that it was a matter of shame and sorrow that the British government sent Indian troops to coerce the Chinese. "Imperialism is trying to utilize one subject country to coerce another but in spite of her weakness India is not so weak today as to permit herself to be employed as a pawn in the imperialist regime."[93] In suggesting closer cooperation between LAI and the INC, Nehru used the rhetoric of ancient Indian culture for closer cooperation with China and other Asian countries. This was very much part of the rhetorical ecumene of the Greater India Society and the Hindu right. Such commitments made in LAI served as a precursor for Nehru's role in the Bandung Conference in 1955. Nehru deployed a rhetoric of anti-imperialism for global statecraft and flipped the colonial script by showing the contradictions of the continuing imperial geopolitics of the international system.

But Nehru also challenged the narrowness of worldviews that came from the Hindu right, including that of Mohandas Gandhi.[94] From his experience with the Brussels congress, he also asserted: "Most of us specially [sic] from Asia, were wholly ignorant of the problems of South America, and of how the rising imperialism of the United States, with its tremendous resources and its immunity from outside attack, is gradually taking a strangle hold [sic] to Central and South America." He added, "The great problem of the near future will be American imperialism, even more than British imperialism."[95] Nehru's views on the statecraft of an independent India focused on working with other "struggling nations of the world,"[96] took a universal view of anti-imperialism, and in 1929 declared that he was a socialist.[97] Many other elites viewed Nehru's challenges to the Hindu right inadequate. For example, during the interwar years, India's greatest anticaste activist, B. R. Ambedkar, publicly burned *Manusmriti*, the ancient caste-based Hindu book of law.[98]

To strengthen their state, elites across Brazil also engaged in intra-elite competition via rhetoric throughout the interwar period. This period marked the end of the First Republic (1880–1930), which ended with a revolution and the onset of the dictatorship of Getúlio Vargas (1930–1945). At the height of World War I, Afrânio de Melo Franco served as a key diplomat under President Arthur Bernardes. His immediate task was to negotiate Latin American support for the United States against the opposition of Argentina and Mexico. Recall Rui Barbosa's emphasis on equality and Oliveria Lima's rhetoric on Latin American solidarity. Melo Franco's rhetoric returned to Pan-American solidarity, which he adapted so that Brazil could be considered the "spokesman of the Pan-American conscience" at the international level.[99] At the League of Nations, Melo Franco argued about Brazil's role, claiming that "our greatness, our devotion to the ideals of the Society and our large population entitle us [that] we must have a seat on the Council."[100] Melo Franco also noted the "ignorance of European leaders regarding Latin America" and, like Rui Barbosa in The Hague, stood dissatisfied with Brazil's diplomatic isolation. He formally announced Brazil's veto on Germany's reentry into the League of Nations, withdrawing from the League of Nations in June 1926.[101]

Another group of elites focused on discontentment with Brazil not being placed on an equal footing as a white Western nation in managing the international order. Alberto Torres, the father of Brazilian national-ism, called for an awakening and the transformation of national character so that "Brazil would take its rightful place among the great nations."[102] Everardo Backheuser, an important Brazilian intellectual elite in the interwar years, worked in close cooperation with the state. He relied on social Darwinist ideas of this time and argued that the miscegenation of the Brazilian population with immigrants would develop a superior cul-ture that was consonant with the country's great size.[103] He also argued for solidifying Brazilian national unity, equalizing all provinces (*equipotên-cia*), and subordinating them to the center. The interwar years witnessed Brazil's consolidation of its national identity with important intellectuals like Manuel Bomfim, Gilberto Freyre, and Sergio Buarque de Holanda contributing to this racial identity project. Thus, the rhetoric of distinc-tiveness also allowed elites to use the geopolitical norms of the interna-tional system to consolidate a national identity.[104]

U.S. imperialism in Central America and the Caribbean was an important concern for elites across Brazil. The United States intervened in the Dominican Republic (1905) and Mexico (1914–1915) and occupied Nicaragua (1912–1933), Haiti (1915–1934), and the Dominican Republic (1916–1924). Many Spanish American elites, however, excluded Brazil from the debates about how to address collectively U.S. imperialism in Latin America.

Some elites, such as Oswaldo Aranha and Raul Fernandes, rhetori-cally used the tensions between the United States and Spanish American republics to advance Brazil's interest through mediation. Their rhetorical innovation played both sides. For example, Oswaldo Aranha, a princi-pal organizer of the revolution that brought Getulio Vargas to power in Brazil in 1930 and served as Brazilian ambassador to the United States, used the established rhetoric of the Monroe Doctrine and skepticism of

Spanish republics along with multilateralism. In 1935, Aranha wrote to Vargas, "The Indo-Spanish countries are our natural enemies; they cannot inspire confidence and even today they retain suspicions towards us inherited from Iberian struggles and heightened by continental rivalries."[105] And yet he also supported Franklin Roosevelt's Good Neighbor policy toward Latin America in 1930. In the interwar years, Vargas would use similar rhetoric to maneuver between the United States and other great powers such as France, Germany, and Italy to secure better trade deals and military modernization plans.[106]

Elite competition, tensions, and disagreements increased their reliance on anti-imperial rhetoric to defend their version of statecraft as superior to that of others in the public sphere. In China, after the end of the Qing dynasty in 1911, fierce competition among elites shaped the country's engagement in international politics. The late Qing dynasty had initiated a series of reforms that changed the rhetorical engagement of its officials. For example, in 1908, Wu Ting-fang, a Qing official to the United States, stated in Washington, DC, that "China has been dubbed 'The Sick Man of the Far East,' 'The Sleeping Lion,' 'The Tottering Empire'; but while this gloomy picture of the state of affairs might have been partly true of China of a few decades ago, it is no longer true now. The 'Sick Man' is rapidly convalescing, the 'Sleeping Lion' is awake, and the hoary and tottering Empire has had new blood injected into her system."[107] Even if the dynasty was soon to fall, the view of awakening resonated across the commitments of elites as diverse as Yuan Shikai, Sun Yat-Sen, Chiang Kai-shek, Li Dazhao, and Mao Zedong, among others. The competition to define the contours of China's statecraft led to several innovations in the interwar years, in which a common frame of reference included anti-imperial rhetoric. The first group of elites was composed of Sun Yat-Sen and his transnational revolutionaries, who established themselves across Asia, Europe, and the United States and were determined to overthrow the Qing dynasty. But after the end of the dynasty, Yuan Shikai became president and the regime faced numerous problems, including accepting the Twenty-One Demands in the Treaty of Shimonoseki, which led to a nationwide eruption of anti-imperial and antigovernment protests. After Yuan Shikai's death in 1916, China descended into a civil war between different warlords. Nationalist elites (Guomindang) were led by Sun Yat-Sen and included Chiang Kai-shek, Deng Yanda, and Wang Jingwei, among others. They converged on the rhetorical idea of the failure of the revolution. Sun Yat-Sen deployed his fierce rhetoric on the emptiness of the Republican revolution in Whampao military academy, which was formed in 1924. He said, "After thirteen years of revolution, the Republic is just an empty name and, even today, the revolution is a complete failure. . . . Our sole hope is to create a revolutionary army to save China from extinction. To achieve that, we must enact the Three People's Principles and the Five Power Constitution."[108] Recall Sun Yat-Sen's lectures, in which he emphasized that the nations that employed imperialism were advocating for cosmopolitanism, which was antithetical to Chinese nationalism. He added that once they elevated the standing of the Chinese nation, China could stand by the ancient principle "rescue the weak, lift up the fallen" and not replicate the imperialism of the West.[109]

Nationalist elites were able to articulate and improvise the ambitious anti-imperial rhetoric. Elites articulated China's rights in the League of Nations and drew on the rhetoric of antihegemony. In 1924, C. C. Wang argued for a council seat, saying, "China was an intellectual country at a time when Europe was in a rudimentary state of civilization," and, through skillful rhetoric, not only chastised the West but also pursued power.[110] In 1924, Sun Yet-Sen asserted that the Kuomindang government (KMT) would help small nations. But his focus was on establishing a confederation of weak nations in the form of the "Great State of the East" that included "Japan, Mongolia, India, Afghanistan, Persia, Burma, and Annam," effectively establishing the rhetorical foundation for dominating smaller nations.[111] After the sudden death of Sun Yat-Sen in 1925, Chiang Kai-shek and the nationalist elites continued to demonstrate China's role in the world. In his (ghostwritten) work *China's Destiny*, Chiang Kai-shek articulated similarly anti-imperial rhetorical views about China's role for a domestic and international audience.[112] In a synoptic view of five thousand years of China's history, he presented a spatialized perspective on China as a multiethnic amalgamation of Chinese, Manchu, Mongol, Tibetan, and Muslim peoples. He argued that all minorities were part of the Chinese nation (*zhonghua minzu*), and treated Mongolia and Tibet as part of its geopolitical orbit because that constituted the "local reality." He cut ties with the Soviet Union and slit the throats of many communists as well. Liang Shuming advanced the idea that China's "final awakening" did not require any emulation of the Europeans: "[We] must neither look to the outside [for help] nor retreat and degrade [ourselves]. It is only by fully developing and utilizing our strength and standing on our feet that we can strive [for success]."[113] In this way, the nationalist elites, intellectual elites, and the cultural-conservative elites in republican China found common ground.

The interactions between these elites in the republican era converged on the call for equality through a rhetoric of anti-imperialism, which exploited the geopolitical principles of the international system. Recall Hu Shi's emphasis on the total revamping of old customs. Hu Shi used the legitimating principles of the international system to "unreservedly accept the modern civilization of the West."[114] The old rhetoric of using "barbarians against barbarians" remained strong. Chen Xujing, a leading sociologist, wrote in 1935, "the Western culture is a culture of imperialism" and the "best means of overthrowing imperialism is to use its very culture and not our own culture of the kingly way—that is, not our culture of pacificism."[115] Hu Shi became China's ambassador to the United States in 1938 and used similar anti-imperial rhetoric to defend China's position in the international system. Members of the Chiang Kai-shek government called him "a model of old virtue within the New Culture. An example of the new thought within the framework of old moral principles."[116] This is not to say that the nationalist and conservative elites converged without tensions;[117] these elites acknowledged anti-imperialism; used it judiciously; and tried to steer the statecraft to secure growth, development, and a rightful place in the international system.[118] Such rhetoric was strategic to both retain power in the domestic system and face the ruthless geopolitical principles that guided imperial expansion in the interwar period.

Another group of elites was the communists, the founders and movers of the Chinese Communist Party (CCP), which included Chen Duxiu; Li Dazhao; and, of course, Mao Zedong. In China, CCP took several interesting turns, first competing and then cooperating with the KMT to fight warlordism and imperialism. The CCP then broke with the KMT and stood as its fierce rival in 1927. Finally, CCP cooperated with KMT to present a unified front against imperial Japan and, in a long civil war with KMT, took over China through a revolution. As products of the New Culture/ May Fourth Movement and inspired by the Bolshevik Revolution, a group of activists led by Chen Duxiu saw the problem of Western imperialism more starkly than others. Li Dazhao set the tone for future rhetoric in 1918, saying, "Red flags are flying everywhere," and a Russian-style revolution across the world cannot be halted, and "the dawn of freedom is breaking."[119] Recall Sun Yat-Sen's rhetoric about the emptiness of the republican revolution and the need for a revolutionary army delivered at Whampao Academy in 1924. Communist elites believed that the nationalist revolution of the 1920s was a bourgeois revolution. Thus, Chiang Kai-shek purged many communists in 1927 to "save the revolution."[120] The competition among communists, the prospect of persecution and defection on the right approach for a revolution, and partnership with the Third Communist International (Comintern) enabled these elites to reach anticolonial movements around the world, from Berlin to San Francisco and to many Southeast Asian countries.

Among many communist elites, Mao Zedong was instrumental in the Sinification of Marxist philosophy to focus on peasantry for the proletariat.[121] He accepted Vladimir Lenin's idea of capitalism-imperialism but also focused on understanding various classes in the countryside. In this context, the Japanese imperial influence in China starting in 1931 became unmistakably clear, and its invasion of Manchuria sent shock waves across China. The League of Nations found Japan at fault but refused to pursue military or economic sanctions. Mao launched a rhetorical salvo in 1932, calling the league a "League of Robbers by which the various imperialisms are dismembering China."[122] On December 9, 1935, thousands of students in China marched against Japanese imperialism. The GMD and CCP in the Sino-Japanese War were similarly united in defeating the Axis powers. The communist elites, led by Mao, subsequently embarked on a mission of liberating the world from imperialism, thereby restoring China's rightful place as leader of Asia. At the success of the communist revolution in October 1949, Mao rhetorically asserted that "the Chinese people have stood up" against imperialism and will not take insult and humiliation anymore.[123]

The intra-elite competition in India, Brazil, and China in the interwar period shaped the anti-imperial and anticolonial rhetorical repertoire of statecraft that elite policymakers continue to innovate today. Historicizing their anti-imperial rhetorical shows how elites challenged the silencing practices of the hierarchical system and used their arguments to turn rhetoric into an instrument of statecraft. They maneuvered under the pressures of the hierarchical system and learned to practice power politics

as a product of struggle by exploiting the exclusionary geopolitical principles of the international system. The interwar years thus set the stage for
bolder rhetorical moves during the Cold War.

RHETORIC IN THE COLD WAR

The end of World War II marked a continuity in the geopolitical principles of the West. The battle between American liberalism and Soviet communism had a long pedigree, starting in the early twentieth century; after
the war, these ideologies took center stage for superpowers in international politics. Many Western interlocutors continued their exclusionary
and racist policies, as well as their silencing practices, toward Asia, Africa,
and Latin America. The defeat of Nazism did not eliminate the racial prejudices that underpinned the international system. Instead, as John Lewis
Gaddis puts it, the American "empire by invitation" and the Union of
Soviet Socialist Republics' (USSR) "empire by imposition" reemphasized
geopolitics.[124] This meant continued exclusion and domination.[125]

For example, even as India's independence movement was at full speed,
Winston Churchill rebuffed its efforts and, in 1942, famously quipped
that he had not become the king's first minister to liquidate the British
Empire.[126] Brazil's interest in a permanent seat on the UN Security Council due to its "sacrifices in favor of the Allied forces" was rejected.[127] And
when Chiang Kai-shek, a trusted ally of the United States, challenged
the U.S. perspectives on world order, the "United States attempted to have
the Chinese leader replaced by other anticommunists who would be more
willing to listen to American advice."[128] In different ways, many African
states were subjected to racism and unequal integration despite persistent
debates in the West about a just and equal United Nations. When both the
United States and the USSR accepted a bifurcated world between capitalism and communism, they viewed non-Europeans as pawns in a global
chessboard. Under these conditions, politicians in Asia, Africa, and Latin
America returned to their anti-imperial and anticolonial rhetoric with
remarkable force. For many, rhetoric also gave them the attention they
sought in the exclusionary Cold War world.

Let us take a list of examples. In April 1955, representatives of
twenty-nine independent Asian and African countries convened at the

now famous Bandung Conference, which was the inaugural meeting of the so-called Non-Aligned Movement (NAM). Recall the Brussels league and the anticolonial solidarities forged by many policymakers from Asia, Africa, and Latin America through the LAI in the interwar years. At the opening speech of the Bandung Conference on April 18, 1955, President Sukarno of Indonesia said: "We are often told 'Colonialism is dead'" but "How can we say it is dead, so long as vast areas of Asia and Africa are unfree? . . . Colonialism has also its modern dress, in the form of economic control, actual physical control by a small but alien community within a nation."[129] In 1958, Prime Minister Kwame Nkrumah of Ghana articulated claims about anti-imperialism to pursue a nonaligned policy against superpower rivalries to ensure modernization: It was true that colonial masters did not deliver on their promise of modernization, but after independence, "we cannot tell our people that material benefit and growth and modern progress are not for them. If we do, they will throw us out and seek other leaders who promise more. And they will abandon us, too, if we do not in reasonable measure respond to their hopes. We have to modernize."[130] Such claims became common ways to seek autonomous terms of engagement with the United States and the USSR.

But policymakers from India, Brazil, and China shifted their rhetoric to focus on realpolitik that was not wholly concerned with fixing the system but upending it to fit their ambitions. Building on their anti-imperial rhetorical repertoire, they worked to exploit the contradictions in the legitimating principles of the international system but moving away from its proto-strategic rhetoric to now use it as an instrument in statecraft, like how great powers would use the instrument of economic sanctions, to reorient the system.

Much has been written about nonalignment and the India-Pakistan wars. But the rhetoric about nonalignment was India's realpolitik repertoire shaped to the new conditions. For instance, on April 22, 1955, Jawaharlal Nehru asserted: "Do honourable members of this Conference realise that the NATO [North Atlantic Treaty Organization] today is one of the most powerful protectors of colonialism? I say that explicitly. Here is the little territory of Goa, in India, which Portugal holds. We get letters from the NATO powers—mind you, Portugal is a member of NATO—and Portugal has approached its fellow members in the NATO on this point—telling us, 'You should not do anything in regard to Goa, you should not do this and that.'" He added, "The Republic of India told them that it is gross impertinence on their part. Let there be no doubt, we shall deal with this little matter in the way we like."[131] On December 18, 1961, some thirty thousand troops of Nehru's India annexed Goa, decimating the Portuguese troops.

Indian policymakers' rhetorical justification for intervention used anticolonial tropes, similar to how Rammohan Roy harkened back to civilizational continuities and how Bal Tilak challenged the partition of Bengal in 1905 and argued that Portugal's "vivisection of India" was unlawful.[132] Indian policymakers flipped the colonial script: "the fact that [Portugal] has occupied [Goa] for 450 years is of no consequence, because, during nearly 425 or 430 years of that period we really had no chance to do anything because we were under colonial domination ourselves. But during the last fourteen years, from the very day when we became independent, we have not ceased to demand the return of the peoples under illegal domination." Indian policymakers argued that the idea that colonial powers had sovereign rights over territories they won by conquest in Asia and Africa was unacceptable. An Indian representative stated in the UN, "It is the European concept and it must die. It is time, in the twentieth century, that it died."[133] A majority of UN Security Council members, including Portugal, vehemently condemned India and called for a withdrawal of Indian forces, which was blocked by a Soviet veto. Many Indian policymakers had previously viewed the partition of India as a "desecration of sacred geography,"[134] and Nehru retained Curzon's geopolitical view of India's territorial defense.[135] And with Goa, the claims in India's antiimperial and anticolonial rhetoric were realpolitik in the sense that India conquered the state despite opposition and marked a new high point of postcolonial power politics with anticolonial rhetoric.

This weaponization of anti-imperial rhetoric highlights India's ability to maneuver under the pressures of the Cold War and the ways in which political actors pursued a (masculinized) statecraft by exploiting the principles and norms of the imperial system. Although the majority of Indian policymakers have nuanced their anti-imperial and anticolonial rhetoric to achieve strategic ends, the realpolitik is frequently at the very heart of important political projects. Among the most well-known of these cases is India's engagement in the Bangladesh War in 1971, which will be a case study in the next chapter to demonstrate the mechanisms through which rhetorical power politics worked in practice. In the Cold War period,

India's participation in debates over decolonization in 1960, its nuclear weapons test in 1974, and its interest in the New International Economic Order (NIEO) in 1974 played with a similar rhetorical repertoire to pursue its interest and thus pursued its power struggles against imperial domination. Indian political elites frequently rely on the rhetoric of unity in diversity and emphasize that "the world is One Family" (*Vasudhaiva Kutumbakam*). Such rhetoric also harks back to the past and builds on the ideas of other elites who formulated such claims based on traditions of the Hindu civilization to protect the state against empires. When looking at the consolidation of this rhetorical repertoire in the interwar years and its function as a compass for many policymakers, the continuity of such rhetoric in the Cold War period and afterward is not exceptional.

Brazilian policymakers also played skillfully with anti-Yankee rhetorical strategies in the region throughout the Cold War, building on their repertoire of autonomy but also innovating on it to advance Brazil's ambitions on the world stage.[136] Juscelino Kubitschek (1956–1961) exemplifies rhetorical innovations for realpolitik in Brazil's foreign policy.[137] He relied on the same rhetorical tropes as Rio Branco to Getulio Vargas to show the importance of building a modern and industrial Brazil that was commensurate with its size and cultural superiority in Latin America. In 1956, Richard Nixon visited Brazil and pressed Kubitchek to help embark on an anticommunist crusade. Kubitschek "reminded Nixon that 'liberty is merely a word for those who live in extreme poverty'" and sought "consistent governmental effort—American official aid—in infrastructural areas that lacked attractiveness for private investors."[138] Exploiting the problems in the American anticommunist rhetoric enabled Brazilian policymakers to maneuver within the confines of the system. He reoriented Brazil's domestic geopolitical space by mobilizing 2 to 3 percent of Brazil's gross domestic product (GDP) to build a new capital city of Brasilia and shaped Brazil's regional geopolitical space by launching a multilateral Pan-American operation (Operação Pan-Americana) for economic development. Kubitchek also engaged with the Soviet Union and China to advance economic development. His rhetoric emphasized Brazilian agency between the West and the rest and retained its powerful political focus: "We wish to form [*sic*] part of the West, but we do not want to constitute its proletariat."[139]

When the rhetoric of Brazilian policymakers veered too much toward anti-imperialism and anticapitalism, the democratic regime was booted out with American support, setting the stage for the military regime from 1964 to 1985. But even the ardent pro-American position of the military regime, which contributed troops for U.S. intervention in the Dominican Republic in 1965, soon shifted its rhetorical repertoire to seek greater autonomy. As foreign minister in 1961, San Tiago Dantas called for *politica external independente* ("autonomous foreign policy"), showing that the state was willing to stand up to the pressures of U.S. dominance.[140] By the early 1970s, the foreign minister, Antonio Azeredo Silveira, looked back to the rhetoric of independent foreign policy and highlighted its economic growth to assert, "Brazil is ever more able to participate in the affairs of the world as a 'power' with its own political weight, thanks to the success of its national development. Today, Brazil is increasingly able to assert its presence in the world, and within the West."[141]

In response to India's nuclear tests in 1974, Azeredo informed President Ernesto Giesel of Brazil that Brazil cannot "reproach India" because the tests were in "accordance with the general policy of Brazil [on the right to peaceful nuclear explosions] in international forums." Nevertheless, he also argued that Brazil's adversary Argentina might consider "manufacturing a nuclear device" and "proceed to [seek] a solution similar to that followed by India."[142] But anti-Yankee rhetoric served more than ever as an instrument for the realpolitik strategy of using and working within institutions, and by the end of the Cold War, Brazil's realpolitik would lead to a nuclear agreement with Argentina to apply safeguards on all nuclear activities carried out within their territories.[143]

The fact that most Brazilian policymakers were practicing realpolitik within agreed regional conventions, such as in the Latin American or South American region, or in formal institutions, such as in the concerns for a permanent seat in The Hague, the League of Nations, or the United Nations, remind us that imperial experience created different spaces for elites to secure their interests. In chapter 5, I will show how Brazil, under the administration of Luis Inácio Lula da Silva, returned to anti-American rhetorical repertoires, engaged in realpolitik within institutions and conventions, and plunged into a humanitarian intervention in Haiti in 2004. The broader point is that the continuities in the rhetorical repertoire of statecraft, perfected over time and skillfully articulated in the interwar years, played an important role in Brazil's engagement in the Cold War.

Like Brazil, China used anti-imperial rhetoric as power politics throughout the Cold War and, in the process, changed the world. Mao emphasized from the start that the communist revolution was about building a strong multiethnic nation and that the People's Republic of China (PRC) stood up to the insult and humiliation of imperialism.[144] On February 14, 1950, both the PRC and USSR signed a thirty-year treaty of friendship, alliance, and mutual assistance. But soon multiple events knocked Chinese policymakers in rapid succession, which pushed them to familiar rhetorical repertoires of anti-imperialism. In three months, in June 1950, North Korea attacked South Korea. And in another three months, in October 1950, Chinese forces were fighting U.S. and UN forces across Yalu, forcing this powerful coalition to face an unprecedented retreat south of the 38th parallel. As John Garver shows, "Well before the US landing at Incheon, let alone the crossing of the 38th parallel, Mao said, 'if the US imperialists won the war, they would become more arrogant and would threaten us. We should not fail to assist the Koreans.' "[145] Then came the Indochina crisis. On January 18, 1950, the PRC recognized the Democratic Republic of Vietnam and emphasized a prolonged war against imperialists, training and advising Viet Minh forces. On May 1, 1954, Viet Minh forces decimated the French in the Battle of Dien Bien Phu. As the United States took up "arms against Communist imperialism," the PRC emphasized the danger of U.S. military intervention to compel Ho Chi Minh to accept the partition of Vietnam. Mao Zedong, Zhou Enlai, and other CCP elites, through careful realpolitik, ensured a territorial buffer between U.S. power and PRC borders.[146] Under rapid succession of multiple and overlapping crises, CCP leaders turned to rhetoric systematically and perfected its interwar repertoire for the Cold War world.

For example, on November 6, 1957, Mao gave a speech at the ten-year anniversary celebration of the Russian Revolution. He declared that American imperialism "will not stop six hundred million Chinese people from taking the socialist path. . . . The imperialist jackals must remember that the days are gone when they order about humanity at their will; the days are gone when they dominate the Asian and African nations."[147] Furthermore, "the imperialists are in decline as they are like the sun at six o'clock in the evening. . . . The Western countries have fallen behind. . . . The East wind was prevailing over the West."[148] Mao envisioned himself as the genuine successor to Joseph Stalin in the Marxist-Leninist pantheon.[149]

He started the Hundred Flowers Campaign in mid-1957 in a massive anti-right campaign supported by Deng Xiaoping, general secretary of the CCP, and Liu Shaoqi, chair of the National People's Congress. Mao's rhetoric of anti-imperialism turned against the Soviet Union in the 1960s. By the early 1970s, the PRC was moving for a rapprochement with the United States. When Nixon made his historic visit to China in February 1972, the PRC flipped the anti-imperial and anticolonial rhetoric and stated that "China will never be a superpower and it opposes hegemony and power politics of any kind." It added that China stands with "oppressed people and nations" and secured the U.S. intent to "reduce its forces and military installations on Taiwan as the tension in the area diminishes."[150]

After Mao's death, the rhetoric of anti-imperialism continued in the PRC in novel ways. Deng Xiaoping returned to the anti-imperial and anticolonial rhetoric and, in 1974, attacked both the superpowers with the claim that they "are vainly seeking world hegemony" to "bully the developing countries."[151] He also used anti-imperial rhetoric to crush the protests in Tiananmen Square in April 1989 and returned to Mao's rhetorical repertoire, seeing the protests as a "planned conspiracy." The rhetorical repertoire of anti-imperialism that was part of the period before the Cold War remained steady through the end of the Cold War.[152] But we see the constant innovation of such rhetoric from Xi Jinping, who sees himself as the legitimate successor to Mao. As Xing Lu shows, "Xi not only has upheld Mao's rhetorical legacies but also speaks like Mao" and "by employing similar metaphors used by Mao, making references to Mao's quotes, and following Mao's storytelling techniques."[153] Chapter 6 will show the ways in which the Xi Jinping administration further improved China's rhetorical power politics repertoire to achieve its political objectives of standing up against Western imperialism in the context of the Syrian crisis.

CONCLUSION: BUILDING RHETORICAL REPERTOIRE AMID CONTINUING STRUGGLES

Against the overwhelming military and economic supremacy of the West, anti-imperial rhetoric was perhaps the only meaningful way of engaging on questions of international order. But the extent to which elites could deploy rhetoric depended in turn on their reflections on preexisting polit-ical conditions, selective understandings of social change, and practical ways to channel the overwhelming power of the Western empires. In this sense, rhetoric was a learned reflective art that enabled Indian, Brazilian, and Chinese elites, for example, to offer vigorous claims on world order-ing practices and carve a space of their own in the process.

This study of rhetorical strategies shows how non-Europeans trans-formed the international order. Indian elites such as Rammohan Roy, Dadabhai Naoroji, Bal Tilak, M. K. Gandhi, and Jawaharlal Nehru; Bra-zilian elites such as Joaquim Nabuco, Rio Branco, Rui Barbosa, and San Tiago Dantas; and Chinese elites such as Liang Qichao, Hu Shi, Sun Yet-sen, and Mao Zedong, among others, played a central role in innovating their rhetoric and strengthening its repertoire. Their rhetorical force in statecraft evolved from proto-strategic recourse to referencing ancient tradition and customs, to an instrument of resistance and a costless weapon of the weak. And in its matured interwar and Cold War years, it was a realpolitik strategy that enabled political actors to exploit the con-tradictions of the system to achieve political objectives.

In India, Brazil, and China, this continuous and creative development of anti-imperial and anticolonial rhetorical repertoire as power politics remains a distinctive force. The lessons from the bottom rungs of the hierarchy have been consistent despite differences in domestic political environments because these countries have uniformly faced epistemic violence on questions of international order. Nevertheless, "simple bina-ries" between self and other, between those who set and meet social stan-dards in international politics and those who do not, are insufficient.[154] As Ann Towns and Bahar Rumelili remind us, there are "complex grada-tions of hierarchies" and the variegated strategies of the "underdogs."[155] As this chapter has shown, non-Europeans contested dominant norms to cut across the hierarchical system. In this light, the role of three big BRICS states is only a continuation of the rhetorical repertoire forged earlier as a product of struggle.

3

INDIA'S RHETORICAL POWER POLITICS IN THE EAST PAKISTAN CRISIS, 1971

On March 25, 1971, East Pakistan (present-day Bangladesh) faced a brutal military crackdown by the Pakistani army. By June 1971, this crackdown turned into a systematic genocide against Bengalis, the exodus of hundreds of millions of refugees to India, and a civil war for the independence of Bangladesh. The Pakistani army that started a regional and a global humanitarian crisis to maintain its regime in the name of maintaining territorial integrity shook the world. On December 27, 1971, Prime Minister Indira Gandhi of India gave an interview to the National Broadcasting Corporation (NBC) of the United States on India's successful war against Pakistan that led to the creation of Bangla Desh. She noted, "We feel that in this [war], India has spoken up not just for the people of Bangla Desh, not just for the cause of India, but the cause of oppressed people all over the world. We have always stood for this cause and I sincerely hope that we shall always stand for it." Indira Gandhi was then questioned on India's autonomy and credibility as a non-aligned nation in light of the Soviet Union's support to India in the war. She replied, "We are firmly committed to non-alignment," which means that we reserve our "right to judge things absolutely independently. We have fought for our independence not so long ago. The memories are very vivid in my mind. I was very closely involved. I simply cannot think that I would let the merest shadow be cast on our independence of decision or action for anything in the world."[1]

India's successful engagement in the war involved power politics. Henry Kissinger recognized it as such. In July 1971, Kissinger met Indira Gandhi and other members of the Indian government who were upset about the U.S. shipment of arms to Pakistan, which, in India's view, facilitated the genocide of Bengalis. Kissinger instead believed that "Indians were making a lot of noise in order to set up an invasion of East Pakistan." He believed that the Indira Gandhi administration was "playing power politics with cold calculations" and "even if the US shipped all $29 million worth of military equipment, it would not make any difference in the situation. So let's stop yelling about something that does not make a difference and talk might."[2] But this sense of inevitability also clouded Kissinger's understanding of the distinctive power politics that the Indian political actors wrestled with in the hierarchical international system.

For the Indira Gandhi administration, arguing and yelling against the unfolding East Pakistan crisis was might, which was often necessary in the hierarchy. From March 1971, multiple Western as well as postcolonial interlocutors had ignored, silenced, and sidelined the Indian version of the crisis. For example, President Richard Nixon believed that India was poor and heavily dependent on food and economic aid and thus materially incompetent to wage a war. He argued, "The Indians need—what they need really is a—mass famine. But they aren't going to get that. We're going to feed them—a new kind of wheat. But if they are not going to have a famine the last thing they need is another war."[3] And Kissinger asserted, "The Indians should be under no illusion that if they go to war there will be unshirted hell to pay."[4]

In the summer of 1971, Soviet premier Alexei Kosygin challenged India's judgment of the crisis. The Indira Gandhi administration's concern with the millions of refugees on its soil was understandable, according to Kosygin, but he viewed this concern as separate from the civil war in East Pakistan. The latter "was a legitimate question," but Kosygin suggested that "technically speaking . . . it can be resisted on the grounds of being a matter which relates to a domestic jurisdiction." West Germans concluded "with more than a touch of Orientalism that 'in Asia sober deliberations are often clouded by emotions.'" British officials referred to Indian diplomats worried about the East Pakistan crisis as "a bunch of psychotics."[5] For many interlocutors, India's incompetence under the Indira Gandhi administration to manage this regional crisis came from the view that India was materially poor, did not have authority under the superpower competition of the Cold War, and could not exercise rational judgment about its rivalry with Pakistan. As historian Srinath Raghavan writes, "The summer of 1971 in South Asia seemed to have shades of the summer of 1914 in Europe."[6] Yet with all odds stacked against India, the Indira Gandhi administration used the East Pakistan crisis to forge its unique path in power politics. In December 1971, Indian political actors achieved the strategic objective of refugee resettlement to Bangladesh and cut its archenemy Pakistan down to size.

Most international relations (IR) scholars have failed to examine the distinctive form of rhetorical power politics with attention to enduring silencing practices and India's position in the hierarchical international system. Some emphasize India's political project in terms of the ethical and juridical righteousness of a justified humanitarian intervention.[7] Others who focus on India's cold and calculating realpolitik are deterministic about the anarchical international system. They view India's performance in the crisis as archetypical of all regional hegemonic powers working toward tilting the balance of power in its favor.[8] Others claim this political episode was consequential mainly because international institutions such as the UN failed to work in an impartial or decisive manner.[9] Yet others have also argued that India used international law based on self-defense against "refugee aggression"[10] and have cited the dangers of setting such precedents for humanitarian intervention.[11] However, such explanations are not attentive to how India's realpolitik was predicated on its position on the lower rungs of the international hierarchy and how policymakers relied on established rhetorical repertoires and innovated them in statecraft. In other words, characterizing the power politics of the Indira Gandhi administration in conventional ways diminishes the regime's anti-imperial and anticolonial repertoire and the ingenious ways in which the administration updated a familiar repertoire to achieve its objectives.

The central argument of this chapter is that, during the East Pakistan crisis of 1971, the Indira Gandhi administration restaged its rhetorical repertoire, defined as the "limited ensembles of mutual claim-making routines," which actors had learned through the struggle against the Western empires described in chapter 1.[12] For Indian political actors, the familiar passage points of anti-imperial and anticolonial rhetoric, as in fighting for oppressed people, offered the space to shape the ongoing dynamics of interactions among interlocutors. The long history of the evolution of India's rhetorical repertoire in statecraft was discussed in chapter 2. The Indira Gandhi administration updated this rhetorical repertoire in statecraft, however, with ingenuity and labor. As Indira Gandhi put it in the midst of the crisis, "Mahatma Gandhi said that the way to peace was to live amidst strife and to struggle with all one's might to overcome it. This applies to nations no less than it does to individuals. Dreams must be accompanied by endeavour."[13] By using Gandhi and other ideas in the corpus of anti-imperial rhetoric, Indian political actors drove a wedge between multiple interlocutors, exploiting the contradictions in the legitimating principles, norms, and rules of the international system.

By drawing on historical works on the crisis, this chapter will show how Indian policymakers engaged in carefully staged rhetoric throughout the crisis to pursue power.[14] They flipped anti-imperial rhetoric to hierarchize different norms, such as human rights, regional stability, and self-defense, among others, at different intervals in line with their strategic interests; probed and delineated audiences through framing around fighting for the oppressed; and engaged in a selective dialogue with sympathetic audiences for strategically legitimizing a military intervention. By varying its anticolonial rhetoric in the fight for the oppressed in the East Pakistan crisis, the Indian policymakers derailed opposition and pursued their objectives of refugee resettlement and cutting Pakistan down to size. Indian political actors used an existing anticolonial repertoire and updated it with their own innovations in statecraft, which offers an important avenue to understand how hierarchy shapes rhetorical power politics and how shrewd political actors use innovation on these "historically evolving, strongly constraining, cultural products" in novel ways.[15]

The structure of the chapter is as follows. The first section will offer a brief background on the East Pakistan crisis of 1971. The second section will show India's position in the hierarchical international system and the silencing practices leveraged against the Indira Gandhi administration. The Cold War superpower competition between the United States and the Soviet Union, coupled with the history of India-Pakistan rivalry, reinforced the distrust of top dogs against third world states like India to manage the regional order. The third section will show how the Indira Gandhi administration used its established rhetorical scripts, updated its repertoire, challenged silencing practices in the hierarchy, and pursued power politics in the process. The final section will evaluate this explanation against alternative explanations in IR.

EAST PAKISTAN AND THE
CONTEXT OF CRISIS, 1971

The end of the British Empire in India came with a partition of the Indian subcontinent in 1947 into two independent states: Pakistan and India. Pakistan itself was bifurcated into two wings: West Pakistan (present-day Pakistan inhabited by Urdu-speaking Punjabi elites of about 55 million people during the crisis) and East Pakistan (present-day Bangladesh, a population who primarily spoke Bengali and was composed of about 75 million people). Over 1,500 kilometers separated East from West Pakistan. On May 21, 1947, Mohammed Ali Jinnah, the father of Pakistan, also called the great leader (*Quaid-i-Azam*) asked for a "corridor" through India connecting the two halves of Pakistan.[16] The corridor was never built. However, calls for a stronger link between West and East Pakistan grew into a campaign for a greater role for East Pakistan in national affairs. For a while, elites from both wings struck a compromise, and East Pakistani elites were content with procedural representation in the corrupt national offices.[17] However, a political mobilization of student protestors coalesced against the arbitrary policies of the Pakistani military regime led by General Ayub Khan, and these students forever changed the future of South Asia.

The global student protests took an anti-imperial and anticapitalist turn in South Asia. East Pakistani student protesters called for "full autonomy" within a federal constitution, leaving only defense, foreign affairs, and currency under the central government. West Pakistani protesters challenged the reigning corruption and called for a radical turn from a pro-American to a nonaligned foreign policy. As Srinath Raghavan writes, "The Pakistani students aimed at deposing the regime and effecting a fundamental transformation of the state," but they also "operated in an environment bereft of organized political forces or democratic structures. As a consequence, their movement had a more direct impact on the political trajectory of the country."[18] The Pakistani military regime believed that extinguishing the student protests required scaling up state power while paying lip service to democracy. In a bloodless coup, General Agha Mohammad Yahya Khan took over as Pakistan's chief martial law administrator and promised to hold a free and fair national election in both parts of the country. It looked as if a democratic election could usher in a new transformation. It did, but not in the direction envisaged by any of these interlocutors.

Pakistan's election result on December 8, 1970, came in as a bolt from the blue. It brought an unprecedented national victory to a moderate Bengali nationalist party—the Awami League—under the charismatic leadership of Sheikh Mujibur Rahman from East Pakistan. Rahman had championed East Pakistan's autonomy for a long time, a cause that merged with that of the radical student protestors. Under his leadership, the Awami League won 160 of the 162 seats in East Pakistan but no seats in West Pakistan. Nevertheless, the Awami League had a comfortable overall majority to form the national government. On the Western side, the Pakistan People's Party (PPP), under Zulfikar Ali Bhutto, won 81 of the 138 seats but no seat in East Pakistan. Bhutto was often suspicious of claims that East Pakistan's autonomy would spell the destruction of Pakistan. He worked closely with the military regime and viewed Mujibur Rahman's victory as a call for outright separatism even when East Pakistani elites explicitly sought autonomy within the bounds of a new unitary constitution. With the West and East Pakistani elites at loggerheads, the military assumed the self-proclaimed role of guardian of the state.

The Pakistani military feared a loss of its institutional position in the state, however, if power was transferred to the East Pakistani Awami League without "appropriate" constitutional arrangements. Bhuto's political party, the PPP, feared a loss of influence and prestige of the Punjabi community in the West if the power was transferred to "darker" Bengalis in the East. Thus, they both concocted tales about keeping Pakistan safe from enemies and emphasized parity rights in drafting the new constitution and a power-sharing agreement between political parties in the East and the West.[19] Although they won the majority in a free and fair national election, many in East Pakistan felt that these entrenched elites had engaged in political skullduggery. The National Assembly that was supposed to convene on February 15, 1971, to draft a constitution was postponed to March 3, 1971, and then abruptly canceled without any promise of a future date. At this time, East Pakistan erupted in a volcanic protest. On March 7, 1971, Mujibur Rahman referred to talks with Bhutto and West Pakistan leaders on constitution making and said: "There is still time for us to live as brothers if things are settled peacefully."[20] At the same time, however, West Pakistan troop reinforcement moved into the East with heavy weapons and artillery to "save Pakistan" from breaking up.

On March 25, 1971, the Pakistani army struck East Pakistan to "re-educate the Bengalis along proper Islamic lines" and to "eliminate secessionist tendencies and provide a strong religious bond with West Pakistan."[21] Mujibur Rahman was arrested as a traitor, and many members and supporters of the Awami League were systematically killed; others were hounded with impunity by the Pakistani army. As Gary Bass notes, "Any Bengali alleged to be a rebel or Awami Leaguer was 'sent to Bangladesh'—the euphemistic code for death without trial."[22] This resulted in the calculated genocide of Bengalis, and 10 million refugees entered neighboring India.[23] By December 1971, hundreds of millions of Bengalis were killed. "Estimates of the number of women raped range from 200,000 to 400,000" and victims were "imprisoned in camps where they were subjected to sexual assaults [every] day."[24] General A. A. K. Niazi, the West Pakistan military commander, referred to East Pakistan as "a low lying land, of low lying people."[25]

Under Indira Gandhi, India found itself in an environment of unprecedented uncertainty. In the recent 1971 election, Indira Gandhi had secured a substantial legislative majority and thus commanded large but incomplete support from the domestic public. Informed domestic groups, including major opposition political parties, keenly followed the crisis and kept the Gandhi administration on high alert.[26] Indian policymakers such as Principal Secretary P. N. Haksar, Intelligence Chief R. N. Kao, Foreign Minister Swaran Singh, ambassador to the Soviet Union D. P. Dhar, and Indira Gandhi, among others, were eagle-eyed readers of international politics. They all agreed that Pakistan's "internal" military actions would have consequences externally through the burdens posed by a flood of refugees into India. On March 27, 1971, the Indian government decided to provide relief to refugees on humanitarian grounds. On May 24, 1971, Indira Gandhi stated in the Indian Parliament that the cost of relief to the central exchequer might "exceed Rs.180 crores for a period of six months. All this, as Hon. Members will appreciate, has imposed an unexpected burden on us."[27] It became clear by September 1971, however, that "maintaining 8 million refugees in camps for six months at the rate of just 3 rupees per person per day would amount to 4,320 million rupees—about US 576 million."[28] This was an inordinate burden upon an impoverished state.

In this context, the Indira Gandhi administration started the ambitious project of centering India in the crisis and managing the regional order. As Gandhi put it, "Calculated genocide is resulting not only in the murder of tens of thousands of men, women and children but also forcing many more to seek refuge and shelter in India. It is a problem that threatens the peace and security of India and indeed, of South-East Asia. The world must intervene to see that peace and security is re-established and maintained."[29] But at its core, this project sought to exploit the East Pakistan crisis head-on by maneuvering under the unequal power hierarchy in relation to superpowers in international politics. This required work. Both the superpowers had their ideologically colored understandings of the competencies of actors in the management of regional order. Indian political actors were aware that much of the disruptions to order came from these powers arrogating special responsibilities in the management of regional orders. The powder keg of relations between India and Pakistan and between India and China, who fought a war in 1962 with a humiliating defeat of India and a newfound friendship between China and Pakistan, could drag many actors into an uncertain escalation that nobody wanted. The Indira Gandhi administration had to tread carefully in the face of these dynamics.

INDIA'S DILEMMAS IN THE HIERARCHICAL INTERNATIONAL SYSTEM

India's position in international politics in the early 1970s was materially precarious and socially frantic. On the material front, India was categorized as a third world country. It also faced problems because of the balance of payment crisis of 1966 and the devaluation of the Indian rupee in the expectation of aid from the World Bank and the International Monetary Fund (IMF).[30] On the social front, India's nonaligned policy had become frantic because the Indira Gandhi regime reached out to both superpowers for help and faced disappointments from enduring territorial problems with Pakistan and China. India received some material support from the United States in the Sino-Indian War of 1962.[31] After India's devastating defeat at the hands of China in this war, India's geopolitical quest to shape the South Asian regional order came into sharp relief. However, India did not have the much-needed money or material resources. This reinforced the frantic focus of policymakers on nonalignment.[32]

In 1963, Jawaharlal Nehru wrote that "a threat to India" would be a "threat to other countries of South and Southeast Asia." He added, "India's determination to resist aggression and retain her territorial integrity is, therefore, a vital factor in the safeguarding of peace and stability throughout this whole area." He acknowledged that the Chinese attack in 1962 had emboldened Pakistan to "press India to make all sorts of concessions" and that India needed weapons and military equipment "in the short run" and "in the long run manufacture [it] herself." Nehru also asserted, however, "We believe that any change should come about through our own volition, as a result of our own experience, and it should not be foisted on us through any kind of force or pressure. . . . This is not only in conformity with our larger interests, but also with the larger interests of the world."[33] When Indira Gandhi came to power with a huge domestic mandate in 1971, such Nehruvian commitment to nonalignment was at the heart of India's foreign policy. But the world changed in significant ways. Many prejudiced policymakers both within and outside India did not see a continuity between the moralpolitik of an elderly statesman such as Nehru and the young and unseasoned Indira Gandhi.

In international politics, this was also because, at the onset of the East Pakistan crisis, many interlocutors viewed India as inhibiting rather than enabling a resolution of the problem. In keeping with their prejudices, the superpowers also rejected Indira Gandhi's challenge to Pakistan's treatment of its own Bengali people in the crisis. In the introductory section to this chapter, we saw some examples of references to Indian political actors in the East Pakistan crisis as "emotional" or as "psychotics" who deserved "mass famine." The American administration also frequently referred to Indira Gandhi as "bitch" and a "witch." However, assessments of India's incompetent position in the crisis are not confined to harsh expletives alone. These assessments are a structural feature of international inequality and epistemic violence arising from instrumental evaluations of multiple audiences.

For example, at the beginning of the East Pakistan crisis, many interlocutors viewed the event as an internal affair of Pakistan covered by

Article 2(7) of the UN Charter, which says that the UN has no authority to intervene in matters within the domestic jurisdiction of any state.
Many saw India's complaints as an effort to manipulate humanitarian
issues to intervene in Pakistan's domestic affairs and thus benefit from the
crisis. Pakistani political actors in the UN claimed that India was engaged
in a "virulent propaganda campaign" and was flouting "the principle of
non-interference in the internal affairs of Member States."[34] The objective
of the Pakistani state was to prevent territorial disintegration.[35] Its political actors rejected arguments about liberation struggles in East Pakistan
as campaigns propped up by India. The Pakistani military regime thus
treated East Pakistan's Awami League and its members as "enemies" and
"subversives" of Pakistan.[36] Both the United States, in its "tilt" toward Pakistan[37] and China, in its "all-weather friendship" with Pakistan,[38] emphasized the norms of noninterference in internal affairs to save the Yahya
Khan's military regime from criticisms. Unlike Indian policymakers, who
were expressing "profound sympathy for and solidarity with the people
of East Bengal in their struggle for a democratic way of life,"[39] Pakistan's
formulation was within the conservative focus on sovereignty, territorial
integrity, and noninterference in the internal affairs of other states. As a
result, India's terms of engagement in the crisis faced an uphill battle.

Under UN Secretary-General U Thant, the UN prioritized peaceful
resolution disputes between states. Thant offered to mediate between
India and Pakistan to solve the crisis because the UN did not endorse
secession. But Thant also noticed the silence and "extraordinary apathy"
of the UN Security Council.[40] Most Western, nonaligned, and recently
independent postcolonial interlocutors converged on a conservative policy on the East Pakistan crisis as Pakistan's domestic affair. Indian policymakers aimed to shift the terms of engagement. As Gary Bass shows,

> But the results were disappointingly meager. Britain was lukewarm, with
> West Germany the most forthcoming of the European powers. India
> was particularly hurt by its near-total abandonment by the Non-Aligned
> Movement, particularly Indonesia and Egypt. Saudi Arabia, Libya, and
> Kuwait pressured Egypt to be even more pro-Pakistan. While India did
> get some donations for the refugees, the total sum was, senior Indian
> officials noted, miserably inadequate. In Parliament, the Prime Minis-
> ter was accused of "taking a begging bowl to other countries." As India's

ambassador in Paris reported, "The problem really is of India, and the world, in general, is not directly affected."[41]

In the face of this prejudice and indifference, Indian policymakers saw a dog-eat-dog world. As Indira Gandhi put it, Indians were disappointed with the "unconscionably long time which the world is taking to reach to this stark tragedy"[42] and "we cannot depend on the international community, or even the countries which I have visited, to solve our problems for us."[43] In the East Pakistan crisis, it was not inevitable that interlocutors converged on such conservative viewpoints. If multiple audiences and the UN had agreed that the East Pakistan crisis posed a "threat to international peace and security" and debated a Chapter VII military intervention operation, then the politics would have easily turned into an UN-led institutional one to prevent the genocide of Bengalis. As Bass shows, the Indian government "would have been delighted to have a Chapter VII resolution," but that was not forthcoming. The United States and China were "resolutely opposed to even a multilateral humanitarian intervention for the Bengalis." Such Cold War instrumentalism was captured by Secretary of State William Rogers to Nixon and Kissinger: "In the Security Council we would be China, Pakistan, and the United States all on one side, so we've got some pretty good leverage."[44]

Two developments exacerbated India's dilemma on how to respond to the East Pakistan crisis. First, in the larger Cold War environment, interlocutors had ideologically converged on matters of "national interest" since January 1971.[45] All states including India, did not go beyond the immediate pursuit of temporary advantage in the sense that none saw a long and brewing crisis. Thus, the United States and the Soviet Union were enmeshed in superpower rivalries, and the suffering of hundreds of millions of Bengali people did not provoke their moral conscience. At this stage, none of the Great Powers took the 1948 Genocide Conventions seriously and, for them, Pakistan's military actions had no morally identifiable content other than understanding them as an internal affair. The grand geopolitical interest of the United States was focused on creating a new alignment with China. Nixon and Kissinger viewed India's claims on the "responsibility of great powers" during the East Pakistan crisis as an impediment to the American geopolitical visions. As Nixon put it, "I want to piss on them [the Indians] for their responsibility. . . . We can't let these goddamn, sanctimonious Indians get away with this [moral claims against Pakistan]."[46] In Dhaka, U.S. consul-general Archer Blood was perturbed by the misplaced U.S. strategic priorities in the face of genocide in East Pakistan. Yet his views were silenced by those espousing the judgments of U.S. national interests in the White House.[47] The Soviet Union, "(despite its dreadful human rights record) demanded that Pakistan end its repression," threw down the gauntlet against the United States and China, and upheld the Universal Declaration of Human Rights.[48] None of them, including India, resolutely believed in human rights. The ugly instrumentality in the crisis based on American geopolitical interest to shape the world by realigning with China (as we shall see below), Soviet ideological rivalry against the West, and postcolonial conservative focus on territory and sovereignty meant national interests rested on whoever wills the end also wills the means.

For the Indian administration, Pakistan's military policies that resulted in a massive influx of refugees into the Indian territory were not an unintended consequence but the military regime's attempt to eliminate a substantial Hindu population from East Pakistan.[49] Indian political actors covertly supported the Bangladesh independence movement. On April 17, 1971, Syed Nazrul Islam stood in a mangrove forest across the Indian border, and with the tacit support of India, proclaimed the government of Bangladesh, and requested immediate recognition of its independence by other states. In May 1971, India supported the East Pakistan regiment that mutinied in the wake of Pakistan's assault and provided arms and training for irregular and guerrilla forces to bleed Pakistan. In June 1971, Foreign Minister Swaran Singh believed that "when the war comes even if it is our action, we should be able to make a case that it has been forced on us."[50] The question was how to pursue power politics to bring about this solution.

Second, the dilemmas of the Indian political actors were exacerbated by their covert military support for the independence of Bangladesh. India's support was slowly becoming public knowledge, resulting in more demands for India to allow the UN access to refugee camps. These demands threatened to expose the Indira Gandhi administration's exploitation of the East Pakistan crisis. At the same time, the legitimacy battles among exiled members of the Awami League were becoming explicit.[51] For some members of the Awami League, securing independence became a central and uncompromising aim. Yet some of its members, like Foreign Minister

Khandakar Moshtaque Ahmad and Awami League general secretary Mizanur Rahman Choudhury, were "critical of the [exiled] Bangladesh government's relationship with India and called for diversification of its source of dependence."[52] For some time, Khandakar Mostaque viewed the United States and not India as "the only country that could successfully arrange a settlement."[53] Others, like the self-proclaimed prime minister of Bangladesh in exile in India, Tajuddin Ahmad, faced challenges to his authority from Sheikh Fazlul Haq Moni, a nephew of Mujibur Rahman. As historian Srinath Raghavan puts it, "In consequence, New Delhi thought it 'politic to adopt a policy of watch and wait' " until "the situation in Bangladesh crystallizes further" and was "eager to avoid direct military intervention in East Pakistan."[54] The Soviet Union viewed its treaty talk and support for India only "as a deterrent" against aggression from Pakistan and China so that it could ensure peace across the subcontinent.[55]

The United States, China, and Pakistan were grouped against the members of the Awami League, the Union of Soviet Socialist Republics (USSR), and the Indira Gandhi administration. Such a concatenation of multiple audiences in opposite positions undermined the ties needed among different members to solve the East Pakistan crisis jointly in the interest of preserving regional or international order. As Nicholas Wheeler put it, the situation "prevented effective pressure being brought to bear on the growing conflict."[56] Without a common minimum denominator among interacting actors in the East Pakistan crisis, there was "anarchy" within the hierarchical international system, creating what scholars call a "heterarchical arrangement" among interlocutors. Heterarchies "typically have divergent or tangled hierarchies" or sometimes have anarchy within hierarchy when there is no one unit to dominate the rest.[57] In the East Pakistan crisis, this arrangement was based on a beggar-thy-neighbor perspective, in which the trust and sincerity of interlocutors were limited. Instead, silencing practices were accompanied by suspicions, misgivings, and outright hypocrisy among members. India's principal secretary to Indira Gandhi, P. N. Haksar, recognized it as such: "We cannot, at the present stage, contemplate armed intervention at all. It will not be the right thing to do. It will evoke hostile reactions all over the world and all the sympathy and support which the Bangla Desh has been able to evoke in the world will be drowned in Indo-Pak conflict. The main thing, therefore, is not a formal recognition, but to do whatever lies without our power to sustain the struggle."[58] In this dynamic environment, Indian policymakers used rhetoric to pursue their strategic objectives.

INDIA POWER POLITICAL REPERTOIRE
IN THE EAST PAKISTAN CRISIS

In chapter 1, I argued that rhetoric is a product of international inequality and silencing. It is a consequence of the stratified position of actors in the social hierarchy. In the context of Western imperialism and colonialism, political actors on the lower rungs of the hierarchy learned to use this instrument in the struggle against disempowerment and to improvise and innovate on it over time. For many non-European states, anti-imperial and anticolonial rhetoric has been an important script for challenging the silencing and disempowerment strategies in the hierarchical international system. Without rhetoric, these states simply would not be heard in this unequal system. Using rhetorical scripts to mobilize support and demobilize opposition to preferred policies, political actors develop a repertoire: a limited ensemble of claim-making routines that are learned, shared, and acted out as products of struggle.[59] The rhetorical repertoire in statecraft is exposing and exploiting the contradictions of the principles, rules, and norms of the international system.

As we saw in chapter 2, Indian political actors frequently experimented with and innovated on anti-imperial and anticolonial rhetoric and forged a repertoire to exploit contradictions and pry open the international system. In the East Pakistan crisis, Indian political actors returned to their familiar rhetorical repertoire to challenge contradictions in the international system and exercise their power. As Paul MacDonald points out, repertoires in international politics are strategic and not precision military drills in the sense that their "efficacy depends on the performer, the audience, and the stage on which a particular performance is taking place," and repertoires "constantly evolve in unexpected and unintended ways."[60] In the East Pakistan crisis, the Indira Gandhi administration relied on anticolonial rhetoric but quickly found that the crisis required further improvising on familiar rhetorical scripts to "fight for the oppressed" and in the process expose and exploit the contradictions of the international system.

For Indian political actors, these innovations were necessary because East Pakistan members themselves justified their choices using anti-imperial and anticolonial rhetoric. The Awami League, led by Shiekh Mujibur Rahman, viewed East Pakistan as being in a colonial relationship with West Pakistan. As Rahman frequently put it, West Pakistan intended to "keep Bengal as the colonial market and we are fighting for justice and fairplay [*sic*] and we shall continue fighting until we achieve our goal."[61] Exiled Bangla Desh prime minister Tajuddin Ahmed argued, "I want the Arabs to recall how they only fought to free themselves from the colonial rule of the Turks who were Muslims. Our struggle against West Pakistan–based colonialism is exactly analogous to their struggles against the Turks not very long ago." He "urged the nations of Asia, Africa, and Latin America to support their struggle in the same way as we supported their *struggle against colonialism and imperialism* [emphasis added]."[62] The Soviet Union and the Indian communist parties were also relying on anti-imperial and specifically anti-American tropes.

In this light, the Indira Gandhi administration deployed emotional anti-imperial rhetorical performances but focused on the pain of oppression and speaking for the oppressed. This was a lesson that Indian policymakers learned from past performances: not to rely on principled content alone in claims that can disappear under the practices of silencing. Instead, affective performances that expose the contradictions of the international system offered avenues to pursue political projects. How did the Indira Gandhi administration use this rhetoric to exploit the contradictions in international norms? In the Cold War international system, the boundaries of discourses on the norms of human rights, refugee resettlement, genocide prevention, and human rights enforcement were fluid. The two superpowers that put the world in a state of permanent crisis were unconcerned about fixing the meaning of such fundamental norms.[63] Indian political actors deployed rhetoric and hierarchized norms at different stages of their interactions with superpowers on the crisis, probed the attitude of different audiences, and engaged in a selective dialogue with sympathetic audiences in the strategic legitimation of refugee resettlement. For many Indian foreign policy leaders, the performance of the Indira Gandhi administration stands as an enviable yardstick of India's power politics through today.

HIERARCHIZING HUMAN RIGHTS NORMS
FOR REFUGEE RESETTLEMENT

As early as March 31, 1971, the Indira Gandhi administration had made a strategic commitment to refugee resettlement to East Pakistan. In the period between March 31, 1971, and October 24, 1971, at the height of Pakistan's crackdown on hundreds of thousands of Bengalis—which forced nearly 8 million refugees into India—the Gandhi administration directed its anticolonial rhetoric toward refugee resettlement that centered on safety, dignity, and honor. On March 27, 1971, the Indian government decided to provide relief to refugees on humanitarian grounds.[64] Nevertheless, flipping Mahatma Gandhi's way to help the oppressed, the Indira Gandhi administration emphasized that India could not be expected to demonstrate tolerance and embrace refugees from East Pakistan or permanently house them in India. Indira Gandhi argued, "The Government and people of India have always desired and worked for peaceful, normal, and fraternal relations with Pakistan. However, situated as India is and bound as the peoples of the sub-continent are by centuries-old ties of history, culture and tradition, this House cannot remain indifferent to the macabre tragedy being enacted so close to our border."[65] In other words, Indira Gandhi used the rhetorical repertoire based on traditions of ancient Indian culture and ties in the region to show that it cannot remain indifferent to the crisis in Pakistan. Nevertheless, India was not ready to accommodate the refugees but wanted instead to send them back. As Bass also shows, "Indians—themselves the victims of colonialism—found themselves explaining away the sovereignty of Pakistan."[66]

Throughout this period, however, India faced three uncertainties surrounding the East Pakistan crisis. The first was the proclamation of independence of Bangladesh by exiled Awami League members, which had Indira Gandhi's tacit support and encouragement. The Indira Gandhi administration, however, did not offer an immediate recognition of an independent Bangla Desh. Instead, the Indian Army's Eastern Command offered training and logistical support to guerrilla activities to carve out a liberated area in East Pakistan for a long and continuous resistance against the Pakistani military regime. At the same time, the Indira Gandhi administration faced domestic and international pressures for the recognition of Bangla Desh. As Indira Gandhi put it, "Every country has some movement of secession. Therefore, every country is afraid of what would happen to themselves if they gave support to Bangla Desh. But the situation is quite different—because it is not just a small part of the country that is asking for its rights. It happens to be the majority of the country, not a small part wanting to go away."[67] Keeping the problems of secession in Kashmir in mind, Indira Gandhi's rhetoric argued that it was the majority Bengali people who wanted to cede from other minorities held together by the Pakistan army. Such rhetoric was necessary to offset any claims about the independence or secession of Kashmir.

Second, leaders from both the United States and USSR were reluctant to take responsibility for the bourgeoning refugee crisis that threatened the regional order in South Asia. Relying on its familiar repertoire, the Indira Gandhi administration engaged in a counter rhetorical strategy. As Indira Gandhi put it early in the crisis, "The Great Powers have a special responsibility. If they exercise their power rightly and expeditiously then only can we look forward to durable peace on our sub-continent. But if they fail—and I sincerely hope that they will not—then this suppression of human rights, the uprooting of people, and the continued homelessness of vast numbers of human beings will threaten peace."[68] By activating the counter rhetorical strategy against both superpowers, the Indira Gandhi administration worked within the established tool kit of nonalignment and autonomy. However, the Soviet Union had proposed a treaty of friendship and cooperation in early 1969, and the Indian ambassador to the Soviet Union, D. P. Dhar, pragmatically suggested restarting talks in late April 1971.[69] Only by innovating its established practices of statecraft could the Indira Gandhi administration engage in a quasi-alliance with the Soviet Union and at the same time maintain its reputation in the nonaligned world. This created radical uncertainties among Indian policymakers.

Third, the Indira Gandhi administration had to weigh the role of China in the East Pakistan crisis. The traumatic war of 1962 and the close friendship between China and Pakistan, alongside Maoist China's support for separatist movements and small nationalities within India, worried Indian policymakers. The formal announcement of the opening between the United States and China in July 1971 exacerbated India's concerns.

In the context of these uncertainties, the Indira Gandhi administration was weighing how to solve the East Pakistan crisis without jeopardizing

India's interests and how not to waste the crisis for putting Pakistan in its place and asserting India's role in the regional order but without provoking the superpowers and the big regional neighbor, China. India's political actors updated their repertoire of anticolonial rhetoric to focus on oppressed people, their sufferings, and the Indian tradition of helping voiceless masses in despair.[70]

On May 24, 1971, the Indian prime minister stated in the Indian parliament, "We are proud of our tradition of tolerance. We have always felt contrite and ashamed of our moments of intolerance. Our nation, our people are dedicated to peace and not given to talking in terms of war or threat of war."[71] In August 1971, she asked, "How could we stop people from coming to us, knowing fully well that they would be certainly massacred in their homeland? This has not been our tradition."[72] The suppression of human rights by the Pakistani military regime in East Pakistan threatened peace. The Indira Gandhi administration performatively ranked human rights norms higher than the constitutive norms of Pakistan's sovereignty and norms of nonintervention in the internal affairs of other states. She said, "Conditions must be created to stop any further influx of refugees and to ensure their early return under credible guarantees for their safety and well-being. . . . If the world does not take heed, we shall be constrained to take all measures as may be necessary to ensure our own security and the preservation and development of the structure of our social and economic life."[73] As Indira Gandhi put it, "The refugees are prepared to undergo all this discomfort and deprivation here [in India] because in their own land, they face a brutal threat to their lives and honour."[74] In such a grave human rights violation and genocidal situation, Pakistan could hide behind the norms of nonintervention or sovereignty, which were precisely aimed at safeguarding human rights. As Bass argues, "Human rights became a mainstay of Indian government rhetoric."[75]

India's rhetoric on human rights norms was shrewdly designed within its anticolonial repertoire to fight for the oppressed Bengali people. Indira's rhetoric was accompanied by emotional performances, and the administration aimed to compel the international community to act in alignment with India's interests, but not because the administration believed human rights to be the most important norm in the international system.[76] Under conditions of uncertainty, the emphasis on human rights offered India the rhetorical ammunition to speak for the oppressed, to pry open the international system focused on sovereignty norms, and to shift audiences' interactions to focus on the moral problems in the crisis.

The Indira Gandhi administration's improvisation on its anticolonial rhetorical repertoire enabled it to accomplish five key objectives. First, by hierarchizing human rights, the Indian administration was able to claim that the crisis and flood of refugees were not an internal problem of Pakistan. Indira Gandhi categorically asserted: "What is happening in Bangla Desh has many-sided repercussions on our internal affairs. That is why I have said that this cannot be considered merely as an internal problem of Pakistan. It is an Indian problem. More, it is a world problem. The international community must appreciate the very critical character of the situation that has now developed."[77] With this rhetoric, the administration sought an entitlement to criticize Pakistan publicly: "We are, therefore, entitled to ask Pakistan to desist immediately from all action which it is taking in the name of domestic jurisdiction, and which vitally affects the peace and well-being of millions of our citizens. Pakistan cannot be allowed to seek a solution of [sic] its political or other problems at the expense of India and on Indian soil."[78] As she frequently put it: "One cannot but be perturbed when fire breaks out in a neighbour's house."[79]

From the start, the administration pleaded with the international community to hold Pakistan accountable for the crisis. In a unanimous assertion, India passed a parliamentary resolution that Pakistan's actions amounted to "calculated genocide" that was inimical to the norms underwriting the community of states in the international system.[80] By using language around genocide and pogroms in its rhetorical strategy to hierarchize norms around human rights, the Indira Gandhi administration aimed to persuade audiences to sideline the norms of nonintervention in this case. This rhetorical strategy was meant to expose contradictions between the norms of human rights and nonintervention and to press on the former. Gandhi wrote to Nixon: "Would the League of Nations Observers have succeeded in persuading the refugees who fled from Hitler's tyranny to return even whilst the pogroms against the Jews and political opponents of Nazism continued unabated?"[81] Thus, hierarchizing norms of human rights was the cudgel that reinforced India's preferred policy option that refugees must go back.

Hierarchizing human rights norms also allowed the Indian administration to point out that the crisis was not an India-Pakistan problem either. Although it was Hindus in East Pakistan who were systematically persecuted and expelled to India, the administration emphasized that the crisis was not an India-Pakistan problem. Indians were swift to show that the Bengalis settled in squalid camps in India not out of their own choice but as "victims of war who have sought refuge from military terror"[82] that had "nothing to do with the communal problem" between India and Pakistan.[83] As Hindu refugees swelled in number, indicating the Pakistani military regime's aggressive action against this population in the East, Foreign Minister Swaran Singh told Indian envoys, "In India we have tried to cover that up, lest it may inflame communal feelings but we have no hesitation in stating the figure to foreigners."[84]

Third, the Indira Gandhi administration refused the UN observers at the East Pakistan border as participants in a worthless bureaucratic endeavor. Gandhi asked, "What is the purpose of their [UN personnel] coming here? It is said that they will come and see why the refugees are not returning." We know why they are not returning. And "it is because of the atrocities of the Pakistani military regime."[85] This was a crucial innovation meant to challenge the UN. In the postindependence period, Indian policymakers experienced a bitter truth about impartial UN mediation as Jawaharlal Nehru took the Kashmir problem to the international body. The distrust of the UN also became part of the improvisation of its repertoire of statecraft evident in the rejection of the Treaty on the Non-Proliferation of Nuclear Weapons, commonly known as the Nuclear Non-Proliferation Treaty (NPT). In this incrementally evolving repertoire that squarely challenged the UN, the Indira Gandhi administration understood that its support for guerilla operations in East Pakistan might be exposed or, worse, the UN relief agencies might be institutionalized in such a way that the return of refugees would be delayed. The rejection of the UN, in other words, represented a transition from an anti-imperial rhetoric that reached out to global institutions for impartial judgments (such as in the commitments to the League of Nations or UN mediation in the Nehruvian period) to one that saw these institutions as sites of power politics.

Fourth, the Indira Gandhi administration rejected third-party mediation by several different actors because the problem was not between two rivals.[86] Gandhi's counterclaim was vociferous: "On what subject will any country mediate? . . . There is a liberation struggle in Bangla Desh. What is the point of mediating with us? That problem has to be solved there."[87]

This led to worries about India's reputation as a nonaligned state. On August 8, 1971, the Indira Gandhi administration signed the Indo-Soviet Treaty of Peace, Friendship and Cooperation. Gandhi shrewdly asserted that "it will discourage adventurism on the part of countries which have shown a pathological hostility towards us [India]."[88] Rejection of mediation and signing a treaty with the Soviet Union required justification, and the administration returned to its anticolonial rhetoric. Gandhi frequently emphasized that the treaty was a continuation of its nonaligned position. "While staying out of power blocs, we have sought the friendship of governments of different persuasions. Peaceful co-existence and conviction that war should be ruled out as a means of settling issues have been the basic guiding principles of our policy. Simultaneously, we have also opposed colonialism and racialism. Many other nations of Asia and Africa have pursued a similar policy. The Soviet Union has extended unreserved respect and support to our policy of non-alignment. This has been incorporated in the Treaty itself."[89]

Despite these claims, India's rhetorical innovations using its anticolonial scripts did not persuade principal audiences from the United States,[90] Pakistan,[91] China,[92] and the UN. The Nixon administration continued to emphasize that the crisis was a domestic issue in Pakistan.[93] Kissinger viewed the Indira Gandhi administration's rhetorical strategy of protecting oppressed people as a decoy to dismember the Pakistani state. Kissinger offered a counter rhetorical flourish to Indian Ambassador Lakshmi Kant Jha in August 1971: "It is a pity" to "quarrel over a problem whose solution was preordained in history" because "East Bengal would be gaining autonomy even without Indian intervention." He added, "India was a potential world power; Pakistan would always be a regional power. For all these reasons, the problem would sort itself out if we separated the issue of relief from that of refugees and the issue of refugees from that of political accommodation."[94] American policymakers viewed its reputation and credibility in relations with friends and allies such as Pakistan as the fulcrum on which its pivot to China depended.[95]

The UN also remained unmoved by India's rhetorical politics and would continue to rebuff India's assertions in the crisis.[96] Even though India's claims about "genocide" in East Pakistan gained international traction in media reports,[97] most audiences sought to compel India to work within the UN for addressing the genocide and refugee crisis. But with a weak UN led by U Thant and buffeted by two superpowers, Indian political actors felt they could stand their ground against the UN's role in helping refugees. Many Western interlocutors viewed India's refusal of UN observers on the East Pakistan border, its support for guerrilla forces, and its rejection of mediation as problematic and a demonstration of its incompetence in managing regional order. It reinforced a general suspicion of India's legitimate concerns in the crisis.[98] The different assessments of audiences of the East Pakistan crisis provided an important baseline for the Indira Gandhi administration to delineate the types of audiences. The administration used its rhetoric to probe audiences in meetings with different policymakers. This offered another opportunity to adapt the administration's anticolonial rhetorical repertoire.

PROBING THE AUDIENCES

The Indian administration faced three salient groups of audiences in the East Pakistan crisis. First were the opponents who continued to emphasize the norms of nonintervention in the crisis. Second were sympathetic audiences who endorsed India's emphasis on refugee resettlement. Third were audiences who vacillated between any other forms of intervention in the internal affairs of Pakistan. For the Indira Gandhi administration, the claims of Pakistan, the United States, and China came from unsympathetic audiences who had to be sidelined to solve the East Pakistan crisis. Friends like the Soviet Union, Awami League, members of India's domestic public, and segments of the global media covering genocide acknowledged India's hierarchizing of human rights norms. Their endorsements were not perpetual and were always under challenge by the counterclaims and reactions of elites in the international system. All others, including Britain, France, and the UN, were vacillators because their evaluation of India's legitimation changed several times as events unfolded. If Indian political actors could not potentially persuade them, at least they could impress upon them not to join the side of the enemies.

The Indira Gandhi administration's assessments of audiences were based on audiences' evaluations of India's rhetorical claims. "Friends" were those who endorsed India's claims and counterclaims and remained concerned about the crisis. "Vacillators" were those who could be persuaded eventually. It was important to keep enemies closer but distinct, and friends and vacillators must not be malleable to the counterclaims from enemies. The administration now further deployed its rhetorical claims to engage in a divide-and-rule strategy but used familiar rhetorical scripts based on anti-imperialism and anticolonialism for exploiting the contradictions in the legitimating principles, norms, and rules of the international system. The Indira Gandhi administration made two creative rhetorical moves in relation to different audiences.

First, to audiences endorsing the validity of human rights norms in the crisis, the Indira Gandhi administration argued that the states supplying arms to the Pakistani military regime—especially the United States—directly contributed to its killing campaign in East Pakistan. Thus, states concerned about the death of millions of Bengalis should immediately stop supplying arms to Pakistan. However, Indira Gandhi couched this appeal with such diplomatic finesse that it appealed to all other audiences that their economic support of Pakistan had moral consequences because of the perpetration of the killing of Bengalis in East Pakistan. Second, for the audiences hierarchizing the norms of nonintervention in Pakistan's internal affairs, the Indira Gandhi administration's rhetoric now explicitly called for the release of the imprisoned leader of the Awami League, Sheikh Mujibur Rahman. The Pakistani military regime put Rahman through a secret trial, and India exploited this situation to appeal to global audiences. Indira Gandhi suggested, "If Sheikh Mujibur Rahman could be released and he would be willing to talk over these matters we would certainly not stand in the way."[99] These two rhetorical moves exploited the contradictions in legitimating principles of the international system: appeals against arms supplies to Pakistan targeted audiences focused on human rights norm and appeals to release Sheikh Mujibur Rahman focused on a proper understanding of democracy and self-determination norms.

But India's rhetoric on stopping arms supplies to Pakistan to end the genocide was a careful innovation of its anti-imperial repertoire appealing to morality in the court of public opinion against war. As Srinath Raghavan shows, Canada, Japan, Britain, France, and "the governments of Austria, Belgium, and the Netherlands also bowed to public opinion that had grown censorious of Pakistan, and they suspended further economic aid."[100] The Soviets, as we saw, called on Pakistan to uphold the Universal Declaration of Human Rights.[101] In response to India's rhetoric concerning the continued U.S. arms shipments to Pakistan, Soviet Air

Marshal P. S. Koutakhov negotiated a shipment of arms requested by the Indian army on October 28, 1971.[102] India's innovations to its anti-imperial and anticolonial rhetoric resonated with the Soviet Union because of its own ideological battles against the United States and China. From the end of September through mid-October, Moscow endorsed India's claims both publicly and privately.

However, the United States did not stop its arms shipments.[103] Kissinger secretly continued to deliver arms to Pakistan. Aware of the repercussions in global public opinion, the Nixon administration was afraid that U.S. senator Edward Kennedy would discover the arms shipments and disclose to the American people that the administration has "been trying to sneak arms to Pakistan behind the back of Congress."[104] Other actors, such as China and members of the Non-Aligned Movement (NAM), did not acknowledge India's rhetorical moves on arms shipments or endorse its claims on the perpetration of genocide in East Pakistan, so much for India's leadership in the NAM. But more than anything, India's rhetoric drove a wedge between different audiences by exploiting the meaning and scope of human rights norms.

India's rhetoric on releasing Rahman worked with some audiences but not others. Couched in anticolonial rhetoric, however, the call to release Rahman spoke to the legitimating principles of democracy and self-determination. British prime minister Edward Heath was deeply concerned that Pakistan was violating the results of free and fair elections in the east and assured Indira Gandhi that he would try to dissuade Pakistan's Yahya Khan from taking "any irrevocable step."[105] Heath wrote to Yahya Khan seeking the release of Rahman, and Britain later withheld its development aid to Pakistan. French president Georges Pompidou urged Yahya Khan both to release Rahman and to negotiate with the Awami League.[106] Both Britain and France stood against the United States on this issue because of their interpretation of the norms of democracy in the international system.

But the United States, China, and Pakistan rejected India's rhetoric on the secret trial of Rahman and questioned whether India truly intended to steer clear of the crisis even if Pakistan released Rahman. Hierarchizing norms of sovereignty and nonintervention and implicitly referencing India, Chinese delegate Fu Hao argued at the UN that "[India] continued to exploit the question of refugees in order to interfere in the internal affairs of Pakistan, to carry out subversive activities against it and to obstruct the return of refugees to their homeland."[107] In a public interview, Pakistani president Yahya Khan warned, "If the Indians imagine they will be able to take one morsel of my territory without provoking war, they are making a serious mistake. Let me warn you and warn the world that it would mean out-and-out war, which I hate. But to defend my country I will not hesitate."[108] With these attitudes of the different audiences, India's rhetoric putting the contradictions of democratic norms on full display drove a wedge between them. Already by late October to mid-November 1971, the Indira Gandhi administration believed that the best response to the East Pakistan crisis was a limited military intervention. Such a position was not predetermined but emerged as a practical necessity through the evaluations and assessments of its audiences.

BOUNDED DIALOGUE

In the period between November 15, 1971, and December 22, 1971, the Indira Gandhi administration drew on these evaluations to engage in a *bounded* dialogue with sympathetic audiences. Using multiple norms that should have resonated with different scorekeepers, Indian political actors further improvised their rhetorical repertoire. Thus, for anti-Indian audiences delineated as enemies—Pakistan, the United States, and China—India's strategic anticolonial rhetoric hierarchized the norms of national security and self-defense against Pakistan that culminated in the claim of "refugee aggression."[109] In November 1971, Indira Gandhi stated rather explicitly, "I must make it clear that we cannot depend on the international community, or even the countries which I visited, to solve the problem for us . . . the brunt of the burden has to be borne by us and by the people of Bangla Desh who have our fullest sympathy and support. So far as the threat to our security is concerned, we must be prepared—and we are prepared—to the last man and woman, to safeguard our freedom and territorial integrity."[110] The use of self-defense norms by India did not impress these audiences.

With such a rhetorical move, however, Indian policymakers refused any form of interaction through claims and counterclaims. In an early November visit to the White House, Prime Minister Gandhi, having exposed the contradictions of the international system in continuous arms sales to Pakistan and in the imprisonment of Rahman, grew pessimistic about the inability of the United States to hold the Pakistani regime accountable for both human rights and self-determination norms. In the meeting, Indira Gandhi felt obliged to set the record straight, but the Americans refused to endorse India's strategic interests and still insisted that Pakistan was reaching a peaceful solution to the crisis. As Raghavan shows, "In the meeting that afternoon, it was Indira Gandhi who assumed her iciest air of aloofness. She made no reference at all to the subcontinental crisis . . . [that] brought out all of Nixon's insecurities . . . [leading him to claim that] . . . she was playing us."[111] The Indira Gandhi administration refused any meaningful form of communication, meetings, or summits with Pakistan or China.[112] The act of not engaging in rhetoric is itself a form of rhetorical performance in politics.

At this point in the East Pakistan crisis, many undecided audiences occupied multiple positions that offered the opportunity for the Indira Gandhi administration to exploit the contradictions of the international system in a multivocal manner. For audiences who endorsed the gravity of the East Pakistan crisis and the contradictions in the legitimating principles of the international system such as democracy, human rights, and self-determination norms—in this case, the Soviet Union, Britain, France, and those who stopped military aid to Pakistan—India's rhetoric hierarchized the norms of refugee resettlement to Pakistan. Its rhetorical repertoire looked back to fighting for the oppressed and innovated its statecraft to legitimating refugee resettlement, even if it entailed a limited military intervention. Soviet leadership pushed for a political solution to the problem rather than a technical or procedural one through UN mediation. Soviet premier Kosygin wrote to U.S. president Nixon on December 3, 1971, when India started its military intervention in East Pakistan that Yahya Khan should "immediately release Mujibur Rahman"[113] and "resume negotiations with him and with other leaders of the people's party."[114] The Soviets vetoed the UN Security Council (UNSC) resolution tabled by the United States on December 4, for the cessation of hostilities and to bring in UN mediation to broker a settlement. Both Britain and France abstained on this vote, thereby isolating the United States. A *New York Times* editorial wrote, "In responding to the crisis, it is essential that the Council go beyond a simple call for a cease-fire and address itself simultaneously to the root cause of the conflict—*the repression in East*

Pakistan which has placed intolerable strains on the economic, social and political fabric of neighboring India [emphasis added]."[115]

In continuing a limited dialogue with audiences, the Indira Gandhi administration reinforced its affective performances that refugees from East Pakistan resulted from calculated genocide, and refugees must go back to a safe place without fear of death or extermination. In the middle of the war, on December 12, 1971, Indira Gandhi publicly reinforced this view and asserted: "We are facing this danger not because it is a sport, not because we want the territory of another nation or we want to destroy any nation. We do not want anybody's territory. We never wanted that any nation which is our neighbour, or any other, should be destroyed. But we knew fully well that what had happened in Bangla Desh—the voice of freedom of its people . . . could not be suppressed. We also knew that if that voice of freedom was suppressed, our own independence would be seriously threatened and this blow to our freedom would mean a blow to our basic principles."[116]

At the same time, the Indira Gandhi administration rhetorically emphasized refugee safety, dignity, and honor to appeal to audiences. Britain and France did not endorse any military intervention. India's rhetoric thus secured only a tacit recognition that the refugee crisis posed a problem and that the United States was failing to help find a solution. Recognizing that these audiences were concerned about their own self-interests, the administration emphasized India's own economic and political burden of managing refugees to focus indirectly on the problems that would arise in seeking development aid from rich nations.

> Taking care of the refugees means cutting a lot of our programmes, it means a certain austerity in living, cutting government spending and re-orienting various schemes and programmes. . . . It is indeed a very, very heavy (burden) . . . of social and political tensions which are growing out of this problem. And, we feel that there is even a very real threat to our security.[117]

Even audiences who opposed India's legitimation politics found that its selective dialogue with friends on the presence of refugees on its soil and the importance of the release of Rahman proved difficult to overcome. Prince Sadruddin Aga Khan, UN High Commissioner for Refugees who favored Pakistan, discussed with Yahya Khan that India did "gain a certain political leverage by the presence of refugees on its soil" and Pakistan must "grant the outside world access to Mujib," which will bring interlocutors back to the negotiating table rather than turn them towards war.[118] Pakistan had always countered India's rhetoric on refugee influx as an exaggeration and as an excuse to dismember the state. But the Indian government brought Senator Kennedy directly to the border to show him the conditions of the suffering refugees. Kennedy publicly remarked that it was a "travesty" and "the only crimes Mujib is guilty of is winning an election."[119] Thus, many audiences now endorsed the "heroic" role of India in managing the refugee burden.[120] India's rhetorical innovation was effective in stopping the flow of European military supplies to Pakistan and splitting Britain and France from their alignment with the United States. As Raghavan puts it, "India had precluded the possibility of an Atlantic entente on the Bangladesh crisis."[121]

Thus, the Indira Gandhi administration used its anticolonial repertoire to frame the crisis as a problem of the oppressed and used this rhetoric to exploit the contradictions of the system by engaging with the norms of self-defense, refugee protection, and refugee resettlement through safety, dignity, and honor. It enabled India to legitimize a military intervention to sympathetic audiences and then rhetorically impress upon unsympathetic audiences that India's decision to intervene stemmed from a commitment to protecting India's national integrity and security.[122] This selective dialogue with delineated audiences led Nixon to quip that Indira Gandhi "was playing us . . . this woman suckered us."[123]

INDIA'S RHETORIC REPERTOIRE IN HIERARCHY VERSUS ALTERNATIVE EXPLANATIONS

As I showed in chapter 1, two competing theories aim to illuminate power politics between states. Realists focus on the material dimensions of relations between states and the dynamics of military hierarchy in the anarchical international system. Social constructivists focus on the language and symbolic dynamics among political actors and their legitimacy battles using norms, rules, and principles. From a realist perspective, India's realpolitik in the East Pakistan crisis of 1971 might seem simple: India's power politics resulted from its superior military and material capabilities vis-à-vis Pakistan, or India was a regional hegemonic power, and the Indira Gandhi administration started the war to improve its standing in South Asia. When one adds to this fact that any pursuit of power is a costly enterprise, rhetoric serves a strategic legitimating purpose even if it is deceptive, as realists argue, to offset the cost. From a realist view then, we have seen Indira Gandhi's power maximization strategy in the crisis.

However, realist explanations infer causes based on the consequence of India's successful prosecution of war. Indian political actors certainly pursued power politics, but their rhetorical realpolitik was different in principle and practice because of the social hierarchy and inequalities between superpowers and the third world states. Interlocutors more often viewed the claims of non-Europeans, such as from the Indira Gandhi administration, as incompetent and inimical to international and regional order. The racial and gendered aspects of the social hierarchy, where East Pakistani people were treated as "inferior" by the West Pakistani army and the elites, and Indira Gandhi was treated with gendered expletives by the Nixon administration, were structural features of epistemic silencing. Political realism that does not take this social hierarchy into account does not offer a clear explanation of India's strategy in the crisis. My account of India realpolitik could be understood as a theory informed by realism that takes social hierarchy into account.

Three considerations matter for a better view of power politics. First, the mere numerical tally of the military power of India vis-à-vis Pakistan, including any "objective" measurements of military balance, is unhelpful in making sense of the political processes of the event. India, even with the support of the Soviet Union, was militarily and materially weak in the face of the alliance between Pakistan and the United States. If military consideration was the prime factor in India's legitimation, the Indira Gandhi administration need not have gone to such lengths to engage with multiple audiences. India could have launched an early and less costly military showdown in April 1971. Second, the Indira Gandhi administration, even with its authoritarian tendencies, relied on and improvised on anti-imperial and anticolonial rhetoric throughout the East Pakistan crisis. Policymakers rely on established scripts and improvise them creatively rather than calculate payoffs like automatic machines. In this sense, the

Indira Gandhi administration demonstrated linguistic dexterity from lessons learned in the anti-imperial struggles and improvised for new conditions under the continuing hierarchical structure. Third, as we saw above, the rhetorical strategy of the administration was not ex ante focused on achieving regional hegemony in the crisis.

Elites wield rhetorical instruments to preserve order and the status quo. Underdogs wield this rhetoric to highlight contradictions and problems that plague the international system. They also do it strategically so that policymakers can improvise the established tool kits and scripts in translating such strategies into action. Bringing a postcolonial sensibility to rhetorical power politics shows that Indian political actors were not engaged in a rhetorical entrapment strategy either. The Indira Gandhi administration could not simply corner opponents with principled claims and trap audiences into "publicly endorsing positions they may, or may not, find anathema."[124] The structural burdens of incompetence worked against India's ability to secure reciprocity on its claims and counterclaims in the hierarchical international system. Thus, Indian political actors looked back to their rhetorical repertoire and carefully orchestrated their performance in the social hierarchical system and frequently changed their content—and sometimes disregarded content and returned to anticolonial rhetoric solely with emotional performances—based on the assessments and evaluations of their audiences.

Despite the enormous burdens on the impoverished Indian state, it is also incomplete to treat the Indira Gandhi administration as a mere victim of the hierarchical system as most postcolonial and ontological security accounts based on stigma argue in IR. In response to the Nixon administration's attempts at disempowerment, the Gandhi administration pushed back using rhetorical innovation. As we saw in the above account, the Gandhi administration exploited the contradictions in the principles and norms of the system by interpreting human rights, self-defense, genocide prevention, regional conventions, and norms on order versus nonintervention in multiple ways. Realist accounts dismiss norms, institutions, and audience appraisals as epiphenomenal to power politics. But rhetorical entrapment scholarship treats the principled content derived from these norms as a vehicle through which actors can change the conduct of other actors. As is clear from the discussion in this chapter, however, the Indira Gandhi administration pointedly interrogated global norms, rules, and institutions in the hierarchical world. Without norms and rules, India's power politics becomes mysterious, but without a robust understanding of the anticolonial and anti-imperial rhetorical repertoire through which the administration challenged these norms—through emotional performances—the realist accounts of power politics becomes trivial.

India's engagement in East Pakistan cannot be viewed as a principled commitment to the norms of human rights or values. Jawaharlal Nehru, with grand liberal cosmopolitan values, rejected nonviolence in the management of India's territorial integrity through geopolitics and parted ways with Mohandas Gandhi. He stated that there was "no question of the doctrine of non-violence coming in the way of armed conflict for defense or against aggression."[125] The Indira Gandhi administration did not lose sight of geopolitics in international politics. In the fluid boundaries of normative discourse during the Cold War, Indian political actors were strategic and used multiple norms on human rights, mass atrocities, refugee resettlement, territorial integrity, and humanitarian crises to pursue political projects. Even in the post–Cold War period, we cannot assume that India's democratic and humanitarian values guided its international conduct. India compromised its "humanitarian values" in dealing with other mass atrocity crimes in Kosovo (1999), Libya (2011), and Syria (2011–2020).[126] Closer to home, Sri Lanka massacred thousands of Tamil kin in 2009, yet India aligned with Sri Lanka in the UN Human Rights Council (UNHRC). Liberal IR accounts that ostensibly emphasize values as drivers of political action are not enough to study the power politics of states in the hierarchy.

Strategic actors are strategic precisely because they work through the fluid boundaries of discourse to establish their rhetorical strategy with multiple audiences to achieve their goals. By rhetorically portraying certain norms as urgent, important, and meaningful, strategic actors wrestle and impose a dominant meaning—even if temporarily—in the public sphere. By engaging in a bounded dialogue with some audiences and not others, India devised a rhetorical strategy that was selectively anti-imperial, appropriating the instrumental norms and rules that dominate the heterarchical arrangement of scorekeeping audiences. The dark side of power politics through this form of rhetorical wedging thrives in the fluid boundaries of discursive structures. In the absence of a thorough institutionalization of equality between Western and non-Western powers in international politics, the boundaries of discursive practices are waiting to be appropriated by the powerful. Here non-Western actors on the lower rungs of the hierarchy are not very different.

SHOWCASING INDIA'S RHETORICAL MASTERY ACROSS AUDIENCES

It would be tempting to view India's power politics in 1971 as a local South Asian affair between two rivals in the region. Given the history and context, however, it would be a mistake to view the entire situation as sui generis. India's rhetorical power politics in the East Pakistan crisis stemmed from the administration's desire to demonstrate competence in managing both South Asian regional order and international order.

The historical reconstruction in chapter 2 showed how Indian actors transformed rhetoric into an instrument of power. Indian political actors took their well-rehearsed anticolonial and anti-imperial arguments and flipped them to achieve their goals starting in the twentieth century. Rhetoric was necessary for Indian policymakers to reclaim their voice from lower rungs in the hierarchy, but shrewd actors knew how to use this instrument to shape the regional and international order. The East Pakistan crisis and the refugee problem became another opportunity for Indian policymakers to do just that.

This chapter showed the continuation of Indian policymakers' resort to rhetorical repertoire for pursuing power politics and how the Indira Gandhi administration played this game in the East Pakistan crisis. It occurred in different stages. Such a strategy emerged within the instrumental position of audiences throughout the East Pakistan crisis against which the Indian policymakers carefully maneuvered. Audiences such as the Awami League representing the Bangladesh liberation movement, the Pakistani military regime, the United States, the Soviet Union, China, the UN, and the global public evaluated India's rhetoric to reinforce the incompetence of a third world state to manage order, a stance that further fueled the engine of power politics. Indian political actors wrestled with and against the claims of multiple audiences; divided the audiences into types based on their evaluations of India's rhetoric; and delineated them as friends, enemies, or vacillators. The chapter showed how Indira Gandhi plowed through a shifting terrain of superpower rivalry and Sino-Pakistan friendship by innovating; changing tack; and spinning new solutions such as a treaty with the Soviet Union, which was anathema to India's purported nonaligned position. Indian policymakers engaged in a selective dialogue with a sympathetic audience to isolate some enemies and confound others.

The chapter showed that the Indira Gandhi administration improvised established repertoire based on anticolonial and anti-imperial rhetoric and responded to the uncertainties in the crisis in novel ways. The Indira Gandhi administration demonstrated the art of improvising the rhetorical repertoire for power politics, not seen until Narendra Modi's use of Mahatma Gandhi style today. In all such games, as Friedrich Kratochwil puts it, "Potentially there are innumerable moves, and no two games are identical since moves at different times will have different consequences. On the other hand, no move of them is free in the sense that 'anything goes.' But none could have been predicted by the 'view from nowhere.'"[127]

In other words, the ways in which other Indian policymakers might improve upon the established anticolonial and anti-imperial scripts might not be able to replicate Indira Gandhi. But a similar quest to demonstrate competence and policymakers' continued reliance on different lessons learned in the age of Western imperialism and colonialism must not be underestimated. Such rhetorical power politics has important consequences for the future of regional and international order. The conclusion will reflect on this problem in some detail.

4

BRAZIL'S RHETORICAL POWER POLITICS
IN THE HAITIAN CRISIS, 2004

I n 2003, *O Estado de Sao Paulo*, a prominent newspaper in Brazil, interviewed the new president Luiz Inácio Lula da Silva (Lula), who pressed a progressive left-liberal agenda for Brazil. Lula stated, "When I had dinner with the American ambassador she asked me: 'What can I tell the American government for them not to be afraid of Lula?' Tell them there is no reason to fear me, I said. All I want to do is the same thing they do for the American people. I will defend the interests of the Brazilian people first and foremost. Only then we can talk about other people's interests. This is what the Germans, the Italians, the British, and the Americans do."[1] In the months and years thereafter, Lula relentlessly pushed to place Brazil at the heart of the most crucial debates on the international order. And the administration saw an opportunity in Haiti.

In the early 2000s, Haiti convulsed in the throes of political, economic, and security crises. On February 28, 2004, Haitian president Jean-Bertrand Aristide was ousted from power. Haiti became a "failed state," and the United States, France, and Canada took an undue interest in overthrowing the regime and fixing the problem. Latin America was once again under the machinations of Great Power politics. Brazil, under the leadership of Lula, stepped in to construct "a new paradigm" of regional order in Latin America.[2] Brazil set foot in Port-au-Prince on May 29, 2004, as part of UN *Mission des Nations Unies pour la Stabilisation en Haïti* (MINUSTAH); its military engagement swelled from 1,200 troops to 37,500 soldiers by the time the mission ended in 2017.[3] This was Brazil's biggest military deployment abroad since World War II. The intervention appeared to be a reasonable political action by a regional leader. In 2008, Condoleezza Rice, U.S. secretary of state under George Bush, included Brazil as a "stakeholder of international order" and defined "Brazil as a regional leader and global partner."[4] Brazil under Lula thus came of age, and the Haitian crisis became a fulcrum for the country to seek international recognition and voice.

Brazil's intervention in Haiti was not inevitable for this "regional leader," however, and required work. In the post–Cold War period, Brazil's position in the international system was precarious because of its transition from military dictatorship to democracy (1964–1989). Many international political actors viewed Brazil as too incompetent to manage regional and international order and, in the early years of the Lula administration, such prejudices in the hierarchy were explicit. For example, when Lula engaged in electoral campaigning at the end of 2002, some members of the U.S. establishment treated Brazil as an "axis of evil" along with the communist leaders of Cuba and Venezuela. U.S. Representative Henry J. Hyde claimed Lula was part of this axis because of Lula's long association with "terrorist organizations" in silent partnership with Fidel Castro, the Cuban revolutionary.[5] Constantine Menges of the Hudson Institute worried that "if the United States should lose Brazil to a 'Marxist like da Silva,' one of the issues of the 2004 presidential election might well be 'Who lost South America?' "[6] Lula's vehement denunciation of the U.S.-led war on Iraq only reinforced American prejudices about Brazil's incompetence in the management of the international order. American pundits advocated for the Bush administration to tolerate "divergent interests" and avoid unnecessary conflicts and disagreements against a reluctant Brazilian state.[7] At that point, no one would have imagined that Brazil might take up a prominent role in the management of the Haitian crisis in the Western Hemisphere, much less articulate novel views about international order.

Yet the Lula administration skillfully used the Haitian crisis as a forum to debate explicitly the legitimating principles, rules, and norms of the international order and lay the foundations for its central role in regional and global politics. Today, many academics and policymakers view Brazil's intervention in Haiti in 2004 as a mistake.[8] But a retrospective reading should not color our understanding of Brazil's power politics to mobilize support and demobilize opposition. All this was accomplished by maneu-vering within the hierarchical international system that was structured to silence non-European actors on matters relating to international order. Even as the United States acknowledged Brazil's role as a regional leader and global partner, many North American and Latin American political administrations were not oblivious to the shrewd statecraft of the Lula administration.

How did Brazil under the Lula administration pursue power in the context of the hierarchical international system? For some, Brazil is a principled and progressive state in terms of its integration within the lib-eral international order.[9] In this light, Haitian intervention to promote democracy is a progressive or a "noble" step.[10] Some accounts emphasize Brazil's "middle-power position" or its role as a "rising power," and its quest for international status in taking on the responsibilities for peace-keeping operations.[11] But Brazil pursued these goals within the institu-tions, both formal and informal. Institutions are "explicit arrangements, negotiated among international actors, that prescribe, proscribe, and/or authorize behavior."[12] The Lula administration worked with Latin Ameri-can conventions and improved relations with South American neighbors to stand up diplomatically against American hegemony. Brazilian poli-cymakers also worked within the institutional principles of the United Nations. Formal institutions and informal conventions do not supplant or eliminate power politics but are avenues to practice it in creative ways.[13] Thus, accounts of status or Brazil's progressive integration into the liberal order do not study its power politics within the unwritten rules of Latin American regional institutions and its conventions. Others view Brazil's politics as emanating from an identity crisis of the state.[14] Such views rightly focus on the shrewd politics of its Brazilian policymakers as works that emphasize the instrumental nature of Brazil's engagement in regional and international politics.[15]

Yet these accounts ignore the fact that in the post–Cold War period, Brazil maneuvered within a hierarchical international system that silenced Asia, Africa, and Latin American states on international order. Taking Brazil's position in the international hierarchy forged in imperialism and colonialism, the Lula administration came to rhetorically defend its inter-ests in Haiti as a state that has constantly experienced the oppressive form of liberal hegemony and American power in the Western Hemisphere.

Using the conventional international relations (IR) scholarship and resorting to realism cannot explain this concern with epistemic silencing and the intricate power politics that followed in the hierarchy. The Lula administration took on a huge social cost in undertaking an intervention and asserted a costly "Brazilian way" of enforcing peace through the reconstruction and development of Haiti. Constructivist IR accounts that resort to the view that political actors make arguments to corner opponents cannot explain Brazil's rhetorical power politics in the deeply racial and imperial hierarchies of international politics manifest in the Haitian crisis and Brazil as the "savior" of the Black population in Haiti.

The central argument of this chapter is that the Lula administration leveraged Brazil's rhetorical repertoire of anti-imperialism and anti-Yankee colonialism forged in the hierarchical international system and flipped it to exercise power. In 2005, Lula declared, "In Haiti, we do not want to impose political solutions. We reject the arrogance and hubris of those who are nostalgic for colonial adventures. We know that it is up to Haitians alone to decide their future."[16] This follows the established rhetorical repertoire of anti-Yankee sentiment and anti-imperialism in Brazilian foreign policy practices. Building on this repertoire, the Lula administration used rhetoric to expose the contradictions in the legitimating principles of the hierarchical system, exploit the anti-American conventions of Latin America, and problematize UN-based institutionalized peace enforcement operations.

In particular, Brazilian political actors used the established anti-imperial rhetorical repertoire by working with other institutional players in South America and adapted the rhetoric to frame its intervention to avoid other great powers meddling in the region. In the dynamics of rhetorical power politics, the Lula administration also reinforced its commitment to the conventions of the Latin American community, changing its rhetorical claims about Brazilian exceptionalism in the region to accommodate the perspective of other states in the management of the crisis.

The structure of the chapter is as follows. The next section offers a brief background of the Haitian crisis in 2004. The subsequent section shows Brazil's position in the hierarchical international system and elaborates on how Western powers engaged in a continuous reproduction of silencing practices while portraying the state as incompetent in managing regional and international order. The third section shows how the Lula administration used familiar anti-imperial and anticolonial scripts and amended its rhetoric to fit within the demands of the institutional environment and to maneuver against silencing practices. The final section examines Brazil's rhetorical power politics against alternative explanations based on realism and rhetorical entrapment scholarship and shows the payoff of taking social hierarchies and colonial legacies seriously in international politics.

HAITI AND THE CONTEXT OF CRISIS, 2004

Haiti has been in the throes of political instability since the nineteenth century. Only seven of its forty-four presidents have served their terms, and there have been just a few peaceful transitions of power in the state since the beginning of the republic in 1801.[17] The U.S. occupation of Haiti between 1915 and 1934 provided no meaningful governance system in the country, and the subsequent economic fragility of the state offered a political window for dictators. François Duvalier, popularly known as Papa Doc, came to power in Haiti in 1957 based on an election platform of economic equality and improvement of the devastated infrastructure.[18] The heart of Papa Doc's politics, however, was repression, and he often used brutal violence to keep the dictatorship in power. He slowly built up a relationship with the United States based on the Anti-Communist Law of April 28, 1969. While anticommunism delighted the Americans, it further reinforced torture, killings, and massive human rights violence to fight rebels in the state. When Papa Doc died in 1971, his nineteen-year-old son Jean-Claude Duvalier, popularly known as Baby Doc, took over the dynasty and continued the mass atrocities.[19] However, some groups within Haiti began to resist authoritarianism and mass violence in the state.

This political mobilization coalesced around a charismatic young Catholic priest, Jean-Bertrand Aristide. Through a network of social resistance movements, Aristide engaged in a public critique of Baby Doc and stood up against the violence of the dictatorship. A church-based civil society movement under Aristide gathered further steam and organized into a strong political group called *Lavalas*—the Haitian Creole word for "flood"—aiming to stop violence, ensure economic reform, and create space for democratic governance.[20] Aristide's efforts ended twenty-nine years of Duvalier rule in Haiti, and Baby Doc fled the country and secured asylum in France on February 7, 1986.[21] For a brief period beginning on December 16, 1990, Aristide and his *Lavalas* party legitimately ruled Haiti. After a coup orchestrated by General Raoul Cedras, however, another repressive regime took power for three years and undertook more violence in the state.

During the wave of liberal humanitarianism in the post–Cold War period, the United States, along with other powers such as France and Canada, took an active interest in restoring democracy in Haiti. These countries laid the groundwork for peacekeeping operations.[22] After a series of failed political negotiations with the military regime, prodded by these powers, the UN Security Council (UNSC) adopted Resolution 940, which authorized a U.S.-led multinational force (MNF) under Chapter VII of the UN Charter to undertake a peace enforcement mission and create a "secure and stable environment" in Haiti. Brazil abstained from Resolution 940 because its political actors argued that intervention in Haiti should be a UN Chapter VI peacekeeping, not a UN Chapter VII peace enforcement, operation.[23] Yet the MNF deployed smoothly under Operation Restore Democracy, and Aristide returned to power in Haiti on October 17, 1994.[24] Aristide governed the country with reasonable stability, reduced and disbanded the capabilities of the Haitian armed forces, and negotiated with the opposition political parties in good faith to reduce violence. The subsequent election in February 1996 was thus an opportunity for improvement.

Aristide's successor, René Préval, worked to further the country's democratic progress. The regime still witnessed a massive violation of human rights from independent gangs and death squads, including disbanded soldiers who engaged in brutal killings in the streets. When Haitian prime minister Rosny Smarth resigned in June 1997, it created a constitutional crisis in the state. Unable to find a negotiated compromise, Préval dissolved the legislature in January 1999 to rule by decree. "The achievements of 'Operation Restore Democracy' seemed to be lying in ruins."[25] In January 2000, U.S. soldiers withdrew from Haiti and left nation building to Haitians, even though the state was in disarray. A new election was called for, which took place in May 2000, but it led to a troubled transition of power. Aristide won reelection for a second time in November 2000. Yet many viewed Aristide's electoral victories as the result of a flawed method of calculating the election results.[26] The United States called immediately for an aid freeze, and the Bush administration pressured the Inter-American Development Bank to cancel more than $650 million in development assistance. This money, as activist and professor Justin Podur put it, was slated "to pay for safe drinking water, literacy programmes and health services, and had serious economic consequences."[27]

By this time, the Haitian state had lost its monopoly on the use of force, and the period between 2000 and 2004 witnessed horrific murders and indiscriminate killings in the streets. It looked as though the *Tontons Macoutes*, the death squads under the Duvalier dictatorship, had appeared in new forms to terrorize the population. Aristide worked to stem popular discontent. Using populist diversionary tactics, he upped the ante by appealing to France seeking compensation for the reparations extracted by France from Haiti. After the Haitian revolution and independence (1791–1804), the French King, Charles X, in 1825, made Haiti pay the dispossessed French colonists and put Haiti in 122 years of indemnity debt.[28] Aristide's anti-imperial rhetoric that discussed this history touched a nerve in France. Jacques Chirac worked with the United States, despite disagreements over the Iraq War, to concoct plans to overthrow Aristide. Although Aristide and his party won a democratic election in Haiti in 2000 with 89 of 115 mayoral positions, 72 of 83 seats in the legislature, and 18 of the 19 Senate seats, the United States and France forced Aristide to step down on February 29, 2004. The Bush administration stated, "This long-simmering crisis is largely of Mr. Aristide's making" and his "failure to adhere to democratic principles" "is why Aristide must go."[29] The administration forcefully exiled him to the Central African Republic.[30] Haiti was once again in a severe crisis with large-scale kidnapping and killing of the local population by competing gangs and death squads. With the force of liberal humanitarianism, calls for "sustainable peace" in Haiti increased. The Lula administration was obsessed with demonstrating competence under the pressure of hierarchy.[31] This crisis presented an opportunity to assert its unique role in the management of regional order.

BRAZIL'S POSITION IN THE HIERARCHICAL INTERNATIONAL SYSTEM

In the 2000s, Brazil was reeling from the pressures of the capitalist market economy, poverty and underdevelopment, and a precarious transition from military dictatorship to democracy (1964–1989). Under the

Henrique Cardoso administration (1995–2002), Brazil endorsed the dominant neoliberal regime and the core norms of the post–Cold War period, such as missile technology, arms control, and nuclear proliferation. Yet the Cardoso administration did not completely embrace free market liberalism. Cardoso also emphasized protecting Brazil's strategic interests in trade through Mercosur (the Southern Common Market) and pursued pragmatic diplomatic relations with the United States.[32] In the spirit of pragmatism, Cardoso viewed South America as Brazil's "historic-geographic space" and Mercosur as "strategic pawn" for broader integration in the region.[33] The rhetoric of autonomy meant avoiding American pressures in Brazil's foreign policy. As Foreign Minister Luiz Felipe Lampreia argued in 1999:

> For a few days, or maybe weeks, at the beginning of the year [1999], Brazil was dubbed by some "the sick man of Latin America." . . . President Fernando Henrique Cardoso will not flinch in his determination to lay the groundwork for our country to become modern, economically fit and dynamic, as well as socially more just and politically mature. . . . Democracy has made it possible for the countries of Latin America to provide mutual assistance—without undue and unsolicited foreign interference and in a spirit of collaboration—whenever there is a jointly perceived threat to the institutional stability of one of them. Thanks to democracy, the countries of our region have successfully solved disputes that for long disturbed the harmony of the more peaceful and stable of continents. At the end of last year, Ecuador and Peru, with the diplomatic support of Brazil, Argentina, Chile and the United States, signed in Brasília the agreements that put an end to their long running boundary dispute. Thus, despite all manner of difficulties, Latin America is transforming itself into a tightly knit entity that is politically, economically and socially integrated.[34]

However, the global shock of 9/11 reinforced American hegemony in Brazil and Latin America. Washington evaluated Brazil's foreign policy and trade strategies in Mercosur and Free Trade Areas of the Americas (FTAA) as "discreet in its appearance, dangerous in its tendency."[35] The United States also ousted Brazilian ambassador José Maurício Bustani, the director-general of the Organization for the Prohibition of Chemical Weapons (OPCW), in order to pursue its false narrative on Iraq's alleged

weapons of mass destruction. Brazil was not new to American machinations in regional and global politics. After 9/11, these machinations, led
by the Bush administration, were carried out through an uncompromising diplomatic campaign within regional and global institutions to build
a coalition on an expansive understanding of self-defense. The United
States manipulated the customary legal norms and legitimating principles
of the international system and put all formal institutions, such as the UN,
the North Atlantic Treaty Organization (NATO), and the Organization
of American States (OAS), in service of American hegemony. As George
Bush put it in September 2001, "Every nation, in every region, now has a
decision to make. Either you are with us, or you are with the terrorists."[36]

When a left-wing stalwart, Lula, came to power in January 2003, the
force of American hegemony was a defining feature in regional and global
institutions. The structural problem of the hierarchical international system is the enduring silencing of Asia, Africa, and Latin American states
in managing international order. The terrorist attacks of 9/11 further reinforced this silencing. As we saw in the chapter's introduction section, Brazil under the Lula administration was largely viewed as an incompetent
Marxist, and for some American (and Latin American) conservatives, it
was, at least implicitly, part of the "axis of evil." Brazil was not the first
choice to address the humanitarian crisis in Haiti. The West, specifically
the United States, France, and Canada, worked within the UN to overthrow the "illegitimate" Aristide.[37] UN Secretary-General Kofi Annan
endorsed this interventionist approach to resolve the Haiti crisis as a
duty to secure liberal peace. As he put it, "Haiti is clearly unable to sort
itself out, and the effect of leaving it alone would be continued or wors-
ening chaos. Our globalized world cannot afford such a political vacuum,
whether in the mountains of Afghanistan or on the very doorstep of the
sole remaining superpower."[38]

Many members of the OAS also endorsed the institutional hegemony
of the United States and reinforced the language of the new world order
and democratization. For example, Chile endorsed the American position on Haiti in order to mend relations after its refusal to support the
American-sponsored UNSC Resolution 1441, which authorized the use
of force in Iraq.[39] Chile acknowledged a normative commitment to liberal
peace and deployed a sizable military force to the Multilateral Interim Force
(MIF) for mopping up operations in Haiti.[40] The Argentine administration,

with a long history of participation in UN peacekeeping operations in Haiti (1993–1996, 1997–2000) acknowledged its own role in restoring order in Haiti.[41] Argentina was now a member of the Group of Friends of Haiti established by the UN and OAS, which justified its commitment in terms of its responsibility to the principles of the United Nations.[42]

Brazil's Lula's administration was in a severe predicament in this unequal hierarchical system. In Haiti, Aristide challenged the claims of liberal internationalism and its commitment to human rights by calling his overthrow a coup. As Aristide himself put it, "During the night of the 28th February 2004, here was a coup d'état. One could say that it was a geo-political kidnapping. I can clearly say that it was terrorism disguised as diplomacy."[43] The Caribbean Community (CARICOM),[44] Brazil's domestic public,[45] and some media reports[46] also challenged the overthrow of Aristide and the reigning spirit of liberal interventionism in the region.[47] These interlocutors opposed the imposition of peace from outside prima facie and broadly endorsed the norm of nonintervention in the internal affairs of Haiti.

To advance these claims and counterclaims, multiple audiences worked within the formal institutional structure of the UN. This is an extraordinary evolution in "liberal statecraft" in the post–Cold War period, when states increasingly turned to the UN and other formal institutions to champion their views and obstruct those of their rivals. As Paul MacDonald puts it, "Liberal statecraft is not necessarily incompatible with self-interest, but for powerful liberal states, it can be a way to construct a stable and mutually beneficial 'constitutional' international order."[48] As we saw above, the United States invoked UNSC Resolution 940, which first authorized a military force in Haiti in 1994, and the mandate for further intervention in Haiti ten years later also came from the authority of the UNSC.[49] UNSC Resolutions 1529 and 1542, which established the MIF and MINUSTAH, respectively, had the UN's institutional legitimacy for military intervention. Other interlocutors such as Chile, France, and Canada—as well as those who challenged the rules and norms of intervention, such as Argentina and CARICOM—accepted the authority of the UN, resolved to work within its institutional mandate, debated with other institutional members, and rejected any possibility of unilateral humanitarian intervention in Haiti.[50] CARICOM relied on the institutional support of the OAS and submitted a formal request to the UN to end the violence in Haiti,[51] and restore the political position of Aristide.[52] The administration in Brazil deferred to the UN Secretary-General Reports on MINUSTAH issued on April 16 and August 30, 2004 for a legitimate engagement in Haitian reconstruction.[53] Brazil's endorsement of the UN as *the* significant body for the collective legitimization of major political functions in international society after the Cold War was in line with how other interlocutors deferred to the legitimacy of the UN during the crisis.

In addition, most regional audiences aimed to find a negotiated solution to the political crises in Haiti through established conventions in Latin America. Even those, like Argentina, who opposed the intervention did not proceed in a beggar-thy-neighbor fashion to worsen the relative situation of Brazil.[54] This institutional commitment came through both past shared practices between Brazil and Argentina to promote "a sense of regional awareness or community." Brazil viewed its principal focus as being on the South American community, and Argentina looked to both South America and Latin America. Despite differences, South American states aimed to resolve economic or political crises peacefully.[55] By committing to the South American common market Mercosul (*Mercosur* in Spanish), which was established in the Treaty of Asuncion in 1991, Brazilian policymakers worked with Argentina, Paraguay, and Uruguay to focus on economic stability. Brazilian policymakers also showed leadership in the Brasilia Summit in late August 2000 to strengthen Mercosul through a stronger regional integration plan. They deepened relations with Argentina, Brazil, and Chile (ABC) to address challenges in Mercosul against regional trade disputes. These interactions established important ties between actors based on the common concern for economic and political stability in South America. Brazilian policymakers established a predictable environment in which members held discussions for cooperative pursuit of collective goals. Thus, Brazil's role in stabilizing regional security issues during the Ecuador-Peru peace process (1995–1998) and Paraguay's democratic transition (1997) offered institutionalized opportunities for political agreements among states despite their differences.

The regular interactions between members in the OAS and the joint endorsement among Latin American, Caribbean, and North American states of the June 1991 OAS declaration, the "Santiago Commitment to Democracy and the Renewal of the Inter-American System," put these institutionalized interactions—and negotiations of prescriptions, proscriptions, and authorizations in these arrangements—among members at the forefront.[56] Shared conventions created incentives for weaker and secondary states in Latin America to articulate views on foreign policy and economic issues as bona fide members and without fear of reprisals. All regional members stood by the accepted convention to reject arbitrary domination by any one state. This institutional arrangement stood as a background when the Haitian crisis erupted. Thus, even the United States, France, and Canada did not work unilaterally but worked within existing institutional structures such as the UN and OAS, and they negotiated with Latin American countries for the first time in the UN and not as a unilateral American military operation in the Western Hemisphere.

Many works focus on the formal and informal institutional dynamics underwriting the Haitian crisis in international politics and its influence on Brazilian practices.[57] However, the regional conventions and formal institutional arrangement did not make Brazilian political choices easier. They only established the baseline for how other audiences as members would evaluate the rhetoric of the Lula administration, what inferences followed, and what were good reasons in this institutional environment for crisis management. Brazil pursued its rhetorical power politics within this institutional environment to manage the Haitian crisis, albeit with an understanding of the hierarchy and prejudiced silencing of its voices in this network.

BRAZIL'S RHETORICAL POWER POLITICS IN THE HAITIAN CRISIS, 2004

In chapter 1, I argued that political actors on the lower rungs in the hierarchical international system speak up against silencing practices by using rhetoric as a weapon of the weak. In this regard, anti-imperialism and anticolonialism were important rhetorical instruments that enabled these states to be heard. Some political actors in the hierarchy have developed a rhetorical repertoire over time by improvising and adapting this rhetoric, which has then become part of their statecraft for making claims, mobilizing support, and demobilizing opposition to their preferred policies. The rhetorical repertoire of power politics involves exposing and exploiting the contradictions in the principles, norms, and rules of the international system. In the inter-imperial network, many Brazilian political actors improvised this anti-imperial and anti-Yankee repertoire and experimented and innovated in a variety of ways to push back against the West's tendency to sow doubt about Brazil's capabilities, judgment, and authority in managing international order.

In 2004, the Lula administration deployed this rhetoric and engaged in an innovation to its repertoire in statecraft. In particular, political actors used the rhetorical repertoire of anti-imperialism and anti-Yankee claims and worked with other institutional members to innovate upon this rhetoric in the pursuit of power. Merely deploying arguments about liberal internationalism or claims based on ideas of sovereign equality in its rhetoric would lead nowhere because of the enormous power differentials between the West and the rest. The affective and emotional performances that make up Brazil's anti-Yankee rhetorical repertoire and the country's ability to maneuver strategically against the fears of left-wing radicalism mark the most innovative aspects of Brazilian power politics.

ANTI-IMPERIALISM AS BRAZILIAN EXCEPTIONALISM

Within the institutional context, the Lula administration deployed its first volley of rhetorical firepower between January 1, 2003, and February 29, 2004. Brazil's rhetoric on solidarity, humanism, and poverty alleviation relied on antihegemony but emphasized ideas of exceptionalism based on its political and economic stability in the region. Brazil sought to exercise responsible leadership in South America.[58] To that end, the newly elected Lula deployed his anti-imperial and antihegemonic rhetorical repertoire:

> Several of our neighbors are today facing difficult situations. If called up, and with the means that are available to us, we will contribute towards finding peaceful solutions to resolve these situations of crises, based on dialogue, democratic principles and on the constitutional precepts of each country. . . . The democratization of international relations without *hegemonies of any kind* is as important for the future of Humanity as the consolidation and development of democracy within each state. . . . Today we are beginning a new chapter in the history of *Brazil, not as a*

submissive Nation, giving up its sovereignty, not as an unjust Nation, pas-
sively watching the suffering of the poorest, but as a proud, noble Nation,
courageously asserting itself in the world as a Nation for all, without distinction of class, ethnicity, sex, and belief [emphasis added].[59]

The core of the Lula administration's rhetoric leveraged ideas about
political exceptionalism to draw a sharp contrast with its unstable and
crisis-prone neighbors. Minister of Foreign Affairs Celso Amorim also
argued, "Several of our neighbors are experiencing difficult situations or
even moments of crisis. The democratic process of change that Brazil is
presently going through under the Lula Government may serve as an element of inspiration and stability to the whole of South America."[60] Thus,
the rhetoric is that Brazil's political stability was an inspiration for those
unstable states in the region, and the administration would help engineer
a stable South America.

Brazil's rhetoric flipped anticolonialism on its head by arguing that
Brazil could engage in conflict resolution in the region. Again, as Amorim
put it, "We earnestly respect the principle of non-intervention, in the
same way that we defend our right to be respected by others. But we will
not balk at making our contribution towards finding solutions of conflict,
provided that we are invited to do so and only when we believe that we
may play a useful role, taking into account the primacy of democracy and
constitutional principles."[61] A mix of antihegemonic solidarity and multilateralism with assertive rhetoric each formed part of Brazil's power political repertoire.[62] As Maria Regina Soares De Lima and Mônica Hirst put
it, "The government's fight against poverty and unequal income distribution at home and its assertive and activist foreign policy can be viewed as
two sides of the same coin."[63]

Brazil's claims and counterclaims of the past found resilience in new
vocabularies under the Lula administration. In 2003, Lula looked back
to the country's diplomatic forefathers, such as Rio Branco and Ruy Barbosa, and used the ideas of *grandeza* to assert that Brazil "was ready to
assume its greatness." Secretary-general of the ministry of external affairs,
Samuel Pinheiro Guimarães, who consistently embraced developmental nationalism, argued that Lula's election was a moment of extraordinary historical importance because it could position Brazil as a new pole
of power in the international system.[64] An ardent nationalist, Foreign

Minister Amorim told a journalist during a 2004 press conference with U.S. Secretary of State Colin Powell that the international community's participation in Iraqi reconstruction through the UN was important for Iraq's future: "You did not ask, but I also mentioned our willingness, if it so happens, for us to somehow contribute. We have no illusions about our power, but sometimes countries with less power can do things that more powerful countries can't."[65] In other words, the Lula administration used its established rhetorical scripts about Brazil's size and importance in Latin America to articulate a grand role for the state in international politics.

The Lula administration's rhetoric about Brazilian exceptionalism was followed by concrete foreign and security policy practices. Brazil slowly shored up its military capabilities and used surveillance of the Amazon (Sistema de Vigilancia da Amazonia [SIVAM]), launched by Fernando Cardoso, for regional stability against the war on drugs.[66] Yet this was also an attempt to "civilize" its Indigenous tribes in the Amazon. Brazilian armed forces talked in geopolitical terms about nuclear submarine projects for a blue-water navy. This development led the chief of staff of Brazil's navy to later declare: "Those who have nuclear submarines sit on the United Nations Security Council. . . . We have to develop our own."[67] Brazilian exceptionalism under the Lula administration was moving full throttle to spearhead change in the region.

INSTITUTIONAL ACCOUNTABILITY AND AUDIENCE CHALLENGE

In the formal and informal institutional arrangements of Latin America, other members kept track of Brazil's rhetoric and evaluated Brazil's constitutive obligations in the management of the Haitian crisis. They assessed whether Brazil had followed established patterns of institutionalized solutions to regional problems and evaluated the consequences of Brazil's rhetoric for institutional solidarity. In particular, Latin American states rejected Brazil's rhetoric about its exceptionalism in the Haitian crisis.

During the Haitian crisis, multiple audiences exposed the fundamental normative incompatibilities between Brazil's political rhetoric of exceptionalism and its desire to resolve the issue through institutional cooperation and coordination. First, some members of the regional community, like Argentina, Chile, and CARICOM, challenged Lula's implicit arguments in his rhetoric that Brazil was entitled to regional leadership because of its political and economic power. In the late 1990s already, President Carlos Menem of Argentina, a close regional contender of Brazil's, challenged Brazil's quest for a UNSC seat, saying this would upset the "regional balance of power."[68] In the 2000s, Argentina implicitly rejected Brazil's regional leadership initiatives by looking to the United States as the core partner of Argentina's foreign policy. The relation with Brazil is instead one of the equals.[69] By rejecting Brazil's exceptionalist rhetoric, Argentinian political actors rejected Brazil's attempt to use the Haitian crisis to strengthen its case for a permanent seat on the UNSC.[70] In 2004, the Argentine ambassador to the UN, César Mayoral, "promoted the idea of a regional Latin American seat as an alternative to an upgrading of Brazil."[71] In the debates on trade in Mercosur, Argentina often sought to counteract its trade imbalance and asymmetry with Brazil. As Roberto Russell and Juan Gabriel Tokatlian argue, Argentine political actors aimed to tame Brazilian protectionism because it "ignores certain rules" or does not "accept limits to the autonomous management of its foreign policy." Thus, "the pro-Brazilian episodic euphoria of the years of Duhalde (Brazil as a 'great strategic ally') turned into doubt and criticism in the second phase, which goes from the beginning of 2004 to the end of 2006."[72] The administration of Argentina's president Cristina Elisabet Fernández de Kirchner (CFK) showed its own commitment to human rights as a regional and international responsibility, particularly after the Dirty War, the infamous campaign of the military dictatorship between 1976 and 1983 that killed more than thirty thousand left-wing citizens. Argentinian senators emphasized that the new state must rectify this mistake by standing in international society for human rights protection and the maintenance of regional order.[73] All this shows that Brazil did not get automatic support from Argentina to exercise its leadership on the Haitian crisis.

Under the Ricardo Lagos administration, Chile pressed for equality in the regional institutional environment. Although Chile contributed troops to multilateral intervention force to overthrow Aristide, the Lagos administration was focused on mending Chilean-American relations through existing institutions. As President Lagos put it later, "When we said no within the United Nations about [the United States] going to war [in Iraq] without the agreement of the Security Council, we were trying to strengthen that [UN] institution that exists for us. It's really important."[74] In this light, Brazil's rhetoric of exceptionalism sparked concerns about unilateralism, which might have weakened existing regional conventions and institutions against unilateralism. Chile's foreign policy itself rested on an exceptionalist discourse based on its position behind the Andes and beneath the Atacama that was isolated from the rest of the continent: "*una Buena casa en un mal barrio*" (a beautiful house in a bad neighborhood).[75] But Lagos, in solidarity with Lula, minimized his exceptionalist rhetoric. Lagos recognized that it was important for regionally powerful actors to foreground cooperative partnerships that strengthened regional conventions of solidarity rather than challenged them.

The solidarity narrative became central in the region's bourgeoning progressive social movements. Talk of exceptionalism through the strong arm of the state, even from progressive leftist governments, was being challenged by these social movements. For example, the Movimento Sem Terra (MST) in Brazil, peace communities in Colombia, the Piquetero ("unemployed") movement in Argentina, the Mapuche movement in Chile, the Zapatistas in Mexico, and Indigenous social movements in Bolivia rejected arguments about exceptional nation-states and state-led progress. They anticipated the problems in Brazil's securitization of development in Haiti, meaning the view that lack of development is an existential threat and thus requires emergency measures based on neoliberalism to bring development, even if it involves loss of life, liberty, and values.[76]

Some of these audiences also exposed the incompatibility between the Lula administration's antihegemonic rhetoric, on the one hand, and its commitments to solidarity and equality in engineering South American stability, on the other.[77] With its exceptionalist rhetoric, they asked if the administration would "abide" by institutionalized norms of solidarity.[78] Within Brazil, diplomat and special representative of OAS in Haiti between 2009 and 2011, Ricardo Seitenfus, advocated for solidarity—with no claims of Brazilian exceptionalism—as the only way to resolve problems in Haiti.[79] Through solidarity, Seitenfus called for the development and reconstruction of Haiti rather than mere peace enforcement operations.[80]

The fiercest challenge to Brazil's rhetoric about the Haitian crisis came from the members of CARICOM. They questioned the conditions under which Aristide was forced to leave and planned their own peacekeeping mission to deal with refugees.[81] They affirmed that Haiti was a member of

CARICOM, and thus the chair of CARICOM, prime minister of Antigua and Barbuda Baldwin Spencer, had a central role to play. Jamaica offered temporary accommodations to the Aristide family, reinforcing the view that Brazil was not part of the Caribbean region and thus not entitled to intervene in Haiti. Venezuela claimed that Brazil was displaying pro-U.S. sentiments and that Haiti would transform into an American military foothold after Ecuador rescinded its lease for the U.S. military base at Manta.[82] This followed the general consensus in Latin America against U.S. interventionism in the region, which was spearheaded by activists and political entrepreneurs in Argentina.[83] Neither the UN nor the population of Haiti extended any public invitation to Brazil to respond to the crisis in the Caribbean.

Thus, multiple audiences who evaluated the Lula administration's rhetoric found Brazil's assertive claims about anti-imperialism and anti-hegemony mixed with solidarity and humanism as incompatible with the Latin American institutional norms underwriting the crisis. When the Lula administration emphasized that "several of our neighbors are experiencing difficult situations" and "if invited Brazil will contribute to finding peaceful solutions," Brazil put the onus on itself to identify which countries in the neighborhood were facing a crisis, what constituted its regional ambit, whose invitation it might respond to, how it would respond to crises, what constituted their resolution, and how to define the meaning of political stability. In other words, the institutional environment compelled the Lula administration to make its normative commitments explicit in the region.

Against this backdrop, the international community began to call for Brazil to make its commitment to institutional norms explicit. Hugo Fernandez Araoz, Bolivia's vice chancellor under Evo Morales, said: "Brazil cannot be a regional leader without accepting the 'costs' of promoting a more just situation for the other countries in South America. . . . The big countries [such as Brazil] cannot look upon this price as a cost, but must see it as an investment." The former Uruguayan ambassador to the World Trade Organization (WTO), Carlos Péres del Castillo, noted, "Brazil was simply not playing the leader's role: 'If a country wants to be a leader, it must involve itself in regional problems.'"[84] Such calls were expressions of discontentment "with Brazil's leadership in the continent during the first three years of Lula's presidency." During the presential Summits in

2005, Argentina's Kirchner complained about "Brazilian hegemonism," Ricardo Lagos complained about "few substantive opportunities for the participants" in the summit, and Hugo Cháves later claimed there was a "neoliberal model embedded in Mercosul and CAN [Andean Community]."[85] Thus, Latin American states did not unanimously endorse Brazil as a follower of regional conventions and solidarity.

Under these conditions of uncertainty and opposition from regional members, Brazil adapted its rhetorical repertoire of power politics. Brazil's first step was to commission internal studies about Brazilian operations in Haiti that were carried out by Itamaraty (Brazil's ministry of external affairs), on the one hand, and the Brazilian armed forces, on the other.[86] This led to a greater "rapprochement with the United States" and "an intense dialogue with the US Southern Command." As Lieutenant General Floriano Peixoto Vieira Neto put it, "The immediate effect of this *rapprochement* was a two-week inter-force reconnaissance mission to Haiti organised by the MD [Ministry of Defense] in March of the same year. The efforts of the officers participating in that mission resulted in a consistent Strategic Area Study (SAS) based on which the planning of a potential deployment of Brazilian troops began, in parallel with the efforts jointly undertaken at home with the Ministry of Foreign Affairs (Itamaraty) and the National Congress to analyse the situation and, if such deployment was deemed justified, approve it. This is, indeed, what eventually happened."[87]

Thus, by late January and early February 2004, the Lula administration had already decided on intervention in Haiti. The Lula administration aimed to persuade its Latin American members by voting for UNSC Resolution 1529 on February 29, 2004, which authorized the deployment of a three-thousand-strong MIF in Haiti. Brazil did not contribute troops to this operation. The vote for MIF was the Lula administration's attempt to show that it could play by the institutional rules in the region. This also allowed Brazil a window for formal interaction with the U.S. Southern Command about the logistics of the military operations in Haiti.

Despite the vote, Brazil's rhetoric did not persuade other members of the Latin American regional community that the Lula administration was entitled to play an important role in the Haitian crisis. Like Argentina, Chile, and CARICOM, many regional members attributed Lula's rhetoric to a quest for a permanent seat for Brazil on the UNSC, which, if sustained, could derail regional cooperation.[88] Such a view was consistent among many of Brazil's regional neighbors, like Chile and Venezuela, and as an Argentine diplomat put it later, "We want a powerful Brazil that benefits all of us, but we see sometimes Brazil wanting to benefit only itself when it wants a permanent seat in the UNSC."[89] In the Haitian crisis, the Lula administration justified its nonparticipation in the MIF because it was a Chapter VII peace enforcement and not a Chapter VI peacekeeping operation of the UN Charter.[90] Brazilian policymakers recognized that a shift in rhetoric and affective performances was important to secure the support of Latin American members for its political project in Haiti.

The window of opportunity was open only for a short period (ninety days) in which Brazilian political actors moved many levers in closed-door sessions to establish the conditions to persuade audiences to support its plan for leading a UN-led peace enforcement in Haiti.[91] In March 2004, Brazil's undersecretary for political affairs, Vera Pedorsa, spoke with U.S. ambassador to Brazil Donna Hrinak to assuage concerns about the UN peacekeeping versus peace enforcement (Chapters VI and VII of the UN Charter) dilemma. The dilemma was that UN peacekeeping operations (Chapter VI) were acceptable but UN peace enforcement operations (Chapter VII) would contravene the Brazilian constitutional principle of nonintervention. The White House special envoy for the Western Hemisphere, Otto Reich, met with the Brazilian president's chief of staff, Jose Dirceu, to discuss Brazilian constitutional obligations to pursue a peace enforcement operation in Haiti. It was also important for Brazil to weave a narrative about the country's Haitian operations that resonated with the domestic public. The MIF vote, however, set the stage for further evaluations by Latin American members and the onset of innovations to Brazil's rhetorical repertoire by the Lula administration.

RHETORICAL POWER ADJUSTED THROUGH AFFECTIVE PERFORMANCES

The formal institutional arrangements in the form of UN principles and rules and the informal Latin American conventions on regional community put Brazilian political actors in a bounded environment to pursue power politics. Institutional members require explicit public justifications for political projects. In the period after February 20, 2004, the Lula administration engaged in a novel affective performance in the meeting of the Comissão de Relaçoes Exteriores e Defensa Nacional (CREDN).[92] Brazilian policymakers' reasoning here was important because the National Congress retains the right to authorize military intervention abroad. By taking the administration's rhetorical justifications seriously, we can better understand the workings of its power politics to intervene in Haiti.

The Lula administration deployed two important rhetorical moves: (1) arguing that the principle of nonintervention did not mean one must be indifferent to the mass atrocities and suffering of the people in the region (this was emotional and performative posturing based on so-called non-indifference), and (2) arguing that diplomacy of solidarity was the pathway for Haitian reconstruction through the UN. Such deployments were aimed at specifying the conditions under which Brazil would intervene in Haiti within the institutional rules of the game, setting the stage for Brazil's next moves.

On March 17, 2004, Celso Amorim asserted that "a spirit in which our traditional attachment to non-interference in the internal affairs of others is [now] tempered by what I like to call 'non-indifference.'"[93] Brazil's rhetoric around nonindifference and solidarity were innovations to its anti-Yankee and antihegemony rhetoric that moved away from its assertions of exceptionalism. The rhetoric of nonindifference was itself borrowed from the African Union (AU) and remained relevant within the so-called responsibility-to-protect discourse spearheaded by Canada (a member of the Group of Friends of Haiti). This rhetorical ammunition aimed to persuade audiences that Brazil could push back against Western liberal interventionism in internal affairs while addressing the root causes of instability without remaining indifferent to regional issues. Brazilian policymakers, including Lula himself, repeated this rhetoric of nonindifference on many different platforms.[94] Assertions of nonindifference sought to impress on Chile and Argentina that this unique way of state building based on a Latin American vision required staying in Haiti for a long time to bring about a new form of development.

The rhetoric of solidarity translated into a concrete form of institutional solidarity. At this time, Brazil and Chile joined as nonpermanent members of the UNSC. Their election was orchestrated by the United States, France, and Canada to bring a façade of regional participation to regional problems. Brazil's institutional position allowed it an opportunity to show good faith to interlocutors by deferring to the United Nations. In a debate in the Brazilian domestic legislature, Amorim relied on this institutional legitimacy and flatly declared: "From both a political and a legal point of view, I do not know where [else] to seek more legitimacy for an action."[95] Using the institution as an instrument for statecraft enabled the Lula administration to make Brazilian participation in Haiti predictable within the existing UN rules on peace enforcement operations.

Through closed-door power politics, Brazilian policymakers negotiated a change in the language of Chapter VII intervention from the preamble as it was in UNSC Resolution 1529 to a brief mention in paragraph 7 so that an eventual UNSC Resolution 1549 could be sold to the domestic public. This was important, as we saw, because a straightforward peace enforcement operation would contravene the Brazilian constitutional principle of nonintervention. As the astute scholar and observer of Brazilian politics, Eugenio Diniz, put it, this allowed the Lula administration to claim that only paragraph 7 of Resolution 1542 was based on Chapter VII and therefore "MINUSTAH would not be based on Chapter VII and would be a peacekeeping operation."[96]

Brazil's closed-door power politics and its semantic juggling over Chapter VI versus Chapter VII required a shift in public justificatory rhetoric so the state would not be perceived as hypocritical. To that end, Brazilian political actors engaged in two creative rhetorical strategies. First, the Lula administration asserted a form of "we-reasoning"—incorporating the role of Argentina, Chile, members of Latin America, and the UN as a team in helping Haiti. As the minister of defense in the Lula administration, José Viegas Filho, put it:

After the idea circulated and the news that Brazil would lead the UN peacekeeping force, there was a flood of adherence by South American countries—Latin Americans, Mexico joined too; Argentina, with 500 men; the Chileans, with about 300 men; the Paraguayans wanted to integrate directly into our force; Peruvians, Uruguayans and some as yet unconfirmed signs of Bolivians and Colombians. It is the cooperation that much distinguishes us, [from those] decisions by countries, [and] our neighbors, to send military contingents to act specifically under the command of the Armed Forces of Brazil.[97]

The core of this team's rhetoric rested on the joint commitment that intervention in Haiti was a cooperative pursuit toward a collective goal by Latin

American states, not because of Brazilian exceptionalism but because of the mutual responsibility of states in the region. Thus, during the Haitian crisis, Brazilian policymakers asserted, "If we do not exercise our responsibility, others will,"[98] essentially reasoning that the "we" ought to be Latin Americans as opposed to Western liberal interventionist states, particularly the United States, defining solutions for regional humanitarian problems. Amorim echoed this stance in the following way: "So, the first question that I mention is this: the spirit in which Brazil participates in it [Haiti]. It is a spirit to answer a call to a military security emergency not only *to serve the interests of this or that country*, but to serve, above all, an interest to participate effectively in Haiti's reconstruction process, the first independent country in Latin America with a history of suffering, of great political crises, and for which little has been done effectively [emphasis added]."[99]

The Lula administration now resorted to rhetorical performances about race in the region. Brazil invoked its cultural ties and "egalitarian" values toward Black communities to help the Haitian population. As Amorim put it, "In Brazil it has been often said, and frequently reiterated by the Government of President Lula, that we have to reach out to Africa [because of our strong cultural links with Africa]. It would be strange, then, if we do not extend our hands for a country with the secondary largest black population in Latin America and the third largest black population in the Continent—it is Haiti that searches for a chance to rebuild."[100] Brazil's innovations to its anti-imperial rhetoric emphasized Latin American cooperation because Haiti has the largest Black population, it was part of "our" region, and Brazil is ready to offer help to a "sister country" because of its racial connections with Africa.[101] Lula's rhetoric added that any indifference by members sharing the same socio-institutional status might lead to liberal interventionist states defining solutions for "our" regional problems.

This innovative rhetorical performance now represented a powerful demonstration of Brazil's obligations to Latin American conventions by disowning its exceptionalism and appealing to other states, foregrounding joint commitments, and emphasizing collective regional goals. Thus, Brazil presented its attitude as one of nonindifference toward Haiti, not exceptionalism; national reconstruction through Latin American experience rather than purely Brazilian experience; and a duty to help Haitians because of an inclusive commitment to the Black population.

AUDIENCE ENDORSEMENTS OF BRAZILIAN RHETORIC

The Lula administration's adaptation of its rhetorical repertoire and its affective performances moved many Latin American community members. As we saw above, Chile, along with Brazil, now occupied the UN Security Council as a nonpermanent member. Chilean foreign minister Juan Gabriel Valdés, appointed as the UN special representative for Haiti, claimed that "concerns of officials in Chile and other Latin American countries is legitimate [sic] regarding the deterioration in the situation in the Caribbean island nation."[102] Thus, when Lula deployed the idea of nonindifference in the Latin American region, Chile endorsed the rhetoric as consistent with the institutional norms in the region and acknowledged "joint commitment" with shared intentions to help Haiti.[103] Argentina's defense minister Jose Pampuro would later claim that the MINUSTAH operation was "a remarkable example of regional responsibility."[104] As Mônica Hirst points out:

> The ABC countries have perceived the MINUSTAH as an opportunity to deepen inter-state diplomatic and military coordination. To pursue this goal the Chilean Juan Gabrial Valdes head of the UN Mission in Haiti collaborated closely with the Brazilian military command who relied upon an Argentinean official, the second military command and a Chilean official as Chief of Operations. Convergent foreign policy perceptions regarding the Haitian reconstruction process strengthened this team-spirit.[105]

Such cooperation and endorsements by Argentina and Chile remained crucial because they came from members occupying the same institutional status. Their endorsements established nonindifference and exercise of solidarity as viable justifications for an institutional member concerned about the Haitian crisis. In an agreement between the ABC states (Argentina, Brazil, and Chile's pact that goes back to 1915), these policymakers worked together to endorse each other's justifications as reflections of institutional solidarity. The Kirchner administration in Argentina faced severe domestic opposition to U.S. interventionism in Haiti, and its endorsements of Brazil's rhetoric allowed the administration to justify its support of sending food and medicine to Haiti after UN Resolution 1529 in February 2004.[106] Endorsing Brazil's rhetoric of nonindifference along-side Chile also enabled Argentina to demonstrate its joint commitment to multilateralism in the region. Chile endorsed Brazil's rhetoric and coop-erated with ABC to avoid any criticism of its military participation in MIF under a U.S. aegis to overthrow Aristide.

The fact that Chile and Argentina endorsed Brazil's rhetoric of non-indifference with regard to the suffering Haitian population and the diplomacy of solidarity based on Latin American cooperation were both strategic. Both members saw siding with Brazil as the best way to improve their standing in the hierarchical international system. Brazil's rhetoric in the context of this ABC pact also allowed for further institutionalization of their participation through the creation of a 2 × 9 mechanism, under which ministers of defense and foreign affairs of nine Latin American countries with troops in Haiti (Argentina, Bolivia, Brazil, Chile, Ecua-dor, Guatemala, Paraguay, Peru, and Uruguay) would meet regularly to discuss "security and development cooperation matters" on Haitian reconstruction.[107]

The United States, which was deeply involved in the controversial Iraq War, eagerly and strategically endorsed Brazil's bona fide status in Latin America and its responsibility in Haiti. In early 2004, Brazil's role in Haiti was important for the Bush administration to free its material and highly stretched bureaucratic expertise from Latin America and direct both toward the Middle East. As one top U.S. official stated, "Brazil really did take a leadership role at a crucial moment, and that's a big deal."[108] Presi-dent Bush, on a later occasion, appreciated Brazil's leadership in the Hai-tian crisis.[109] In the hierarchical system, the endorsements of the United States (one done for its own strategic geopolitical goals) led to a chain reaction of acknowledgments from the United Nations and other West-ern liberal interventionist states. After the "we" claim in Brazil's rhetoric on Latin American responsibility, other interlocutors evaluated the Lula administration's claim of solidarity with the Haitians not as a moral value but as one that came from a bona fide player in the game.

Brazil's rhetoric and its invocation of Black values showed Latin Amer-ican members that Brazil has a credible ability to work with Black com-munities. As Brazilian critical theorist Maíra Gomes puts it, there are "little Haitis" in Brazil that formed part of Brazil's rhetoric about its ability to engage in peace enforcement operations in the way it pacifies favelas.[110]

Such claims gave other regional members an assurance that one did not have to fear Brazil's leadership and its command of MINUSTAH troops in Haiti under a UN Chapter VII peace enforcement mission.

However, the Black Movement (*Movimento Negro*) showed that Afro-Brazilians comprised nearly half of the Brazilian population but suffered discrimination and underrepresentation in the Brazilian state. The Lula administration created a special secretariat to promote racial equality (Special Secretariat for Policies to Promote Racial Equality/Secretaria de Gestão do Sistema Nacional de Promoção da Igualdade Racial [SEP-PIR]) and in 2003 appointed the charismatic militant Black feminist leader Matilde Ribeiro as its head. These choices demonstrated Brazil's seriousness in addressing racial inequalities to audiences both at the domestic and regional levels. In this light, Brazil's engagement in Haiti could demonstrate reliably to regional members that the Lula administration was bound to a larger obligation of racial equality and would *not* change its preferences to exercise hegemony or dominate its cooperative partners. Despite initial contestation, domestic opponents deferred to the administration's claim that one could not be indifferent to the suffering of a "Brother country" in the region.[111] The rhetorical flipping of the racial problems in Brazil as opportunities for peace enforcement operations in Haiti was realpolitik.

Once other South American members associated with the same socio-institutional status came on board, however, Brazil's role, value claims on Latin American responsibility, nonindifference, solidarity with the Haitians, and other rhetorical deployments of the Lula administration were deemed acceptable rhetoric. Making explicit Brazil's commitment to Latin American institutional solutions also sidelined challenges from other audiences such as CARICOM, members of Brazil's domestic public, and supporters of the Aristide administration in Haiti. Minister of Foreign Affairs Celso Amorim stated in unequivocal terms that support of Latin American countries (even if Venezuela and Cuba differed) provided institutional legitimacy to Brazil's intervention in Haiti. He also stressed that the intervention would work very differently from the model proposed by the United States.[112]

To summarize, for audiences such as Argentina, Chile, Western liberal interventionist states, and the UN, Brazil's shift in rhetoric demonstrated its bona fide status within the regional institutional rules and its commitments to work jointly toward Haitian reconstruction. Brazil's rhetorical claims to nonindifference and its diplomacy of solidarity became institutionally acceptable reasons for a Chapter VII military intervention in Haiti. In this way, the shrewd innovations of its anti-Yankee and anti-imperial rhetoric enabled the Lula administration to pursue its intervention in Haiti. At a ceremony marking the departure of the Brazilian military to Haiti, Lula summed up the position of his administration: "Maintaining peace has its price, and this price is participation. When we express ourselves in the face of a crisis such as is occurring in Haiti, we are exercising our responsibility in an international context."[113]

RHETORICAL POWER POLITICS VERSUS ALTERNATIVE EXPLANATIONS

Brazil's humanitarian military intervention in Haiti in 2004 as a Chapter VII UN peace enforcement operation is an important foreign and security policy event in international politics. IR scholarships tend to see Brazil's action as a "new era" of regional cooperation with liberal concern to address the sufferings of the Haitian people and promote democracy and justice in the Latin American region without relying on the United States.[114] The diffusion of global human rights norms to the "developing world" in the post–Cold War period enabled Brazilian policymakers to play the role of a "humanitarian superpower" in Haiti in 2004.[115] Others view Brazil as a rising power that offered a "constructive engagement" in Haiti and its "coming of age" in peace operations that addressed the sufferings of the Black population in the country.[116] As Brazilian political actors talked about Responsibility to Protect (R2P) and Responsibility While Protecting (RwP), many scholars view Brazil as a norm maker rather than a norm taker in international politics.[117] However, liberal explanations of Brazil's intervention in Haiti underplays Brazil's power politics. What is overlooked in these studies is that the Lula administration stood up, resisted, and challenged the hierarchical international system and U.S. hegemony and, in the process, pursued the most ambitious foreign policy in its history.

From 2003, the Lula administration adopted a policy to challenge Brazil's secondary status and the silencing of its voice in managing regional and international order. Many historians rightly point out that for the first time, Brazil "began to think of itself as a regional power," which was a "necessary condition for global power."[118] Existing IR explanations fail to see, however, that this ambition was situated under the inability to voice its views in managing regional and international order. Rhetoric was a necessity for policymakers to be heard in the hierarchy. Building on anti-Yankee rhetorical repertoire, the Lula administration pursued its power politics, exploiting the contradictions in the international system. To explain the progressive aspect of Brazil's engagement in UN peacekeeping operations in a teleological way, most liberal accounts whitewash the histories of contentious performances and how Brazilian policymakers challenged the rules and norms to pursue power.

The rhetorical strategies of the Lula administration were thus power politics under hierarchy. Its policymakers engaged in affective performances focused on regional conventions, formal institutional norms, and the prescriptions and proscriptions of regional community members. In this light, Brazil did not progressively embrace global humanitarian norms (contrary to the liberal-constructivist perspective) but adjusted its concerns based on what its institutional audiences considered as appropriate reasons for taking part in the game. The Lula administration engaged with ongoing social transactions and how the Western liberal states "made" the situation and, subsequently through its rhetoric, made its own situation by maneuvering within institutional norms. Working with and against the normative pull of the institutional social world is power politics, but the adaptation of the repertoire to reorient the institutional world toward novel objectives, such as what Brazil did in convincing South American states to support its intervention, is rhetorical power politics under hierarchy. In this light, Brazil's practical choices were about the validity and applicability of liberal norms, not their "truth values" or their "fit" to the Haitian crisis or UN peacekeeping.[119]

However, sophisticated realist accounts recognize the rhetoric but dismiss the centrality of epistemic violence that drives its power politics. Randall Schweller writes that Brazil is a spoiler in international politics. "Indeed, Brazilian elites do not describe the Western global order in terms of multilateralism and inclusion, but rather as an imposed order ruled by powerful Anglo-Saxon states, which use international institutions and arbitrarily enforced rules to control weaker, non-Western states. Global hierarchy, in their eyes, is less a function of material power than of race. Little wonder, at the height of the 2008 global financial crisis, Brazilian president, Luiz Inacio Lua da Silva declared: 'This crisis was created by white men with blue eyes.' He went on to say that he had never met a black banker.'"[120]

Such a view rightly recognizes power politics and the challenges offered by Brazilian elites in the international system. Nevertheless, it also underplays the pressure of racial and material inequalities between the West and the rest in the hierarchical international system and the reigning silencing practices against Brazil in managing the international order. The Lula administration enacts such anti-imperial rhetorical scripts because it does not have the opportunities to voice its views politely without being ignored. The assumption that any policymakers in the so-called rules-based international order could voice their views and secure a response from audiences is one of the continuing myths of the ordering practices. Some members from Asia, Africa, and Latin America are treated as incompetent, and other Indigenous and stateless actors are plainly ignored. Rhetorical performances are thus a necessity in order to be heard, and ambitious states like Brazil have a rhetorical repertoire of power politics in statecraft.

Through rhetoric, Brazilian policymakers worked against these pressures of the hierarchical system to demonstrate competence in managing order. On Brazil's competent ways of managing the Haitian crisis, Foreign Minister Amorim later noted:

> Since 2004, Brazil has had the responsibility of leading the military component of the United Nations Mission in Haiti (MINUSTAH), committing herself to the stabilisation of the Caribbean country after a period of turmoil and political instability. At the same time as our military achieved the demobilization of armed gangs, bringing peace to Port-au-Prince shantytowns, the Brazilian Government has been carrying out a series of civilian activities aimed at tackling problems related to poverty, infrastructure and development. In addition to the activities of our military engineers stationed in Haiti, a great number of projects of technical cooperation were set in motion. Along with the other IBSA [India,

Brazil, and South Africa Dialogue Forum] Fund partners (India and South Africa), Brazil has financed a solid residues [sic] recycling plant in Port-au-Prince, which creates jobs and helps clean the environment. This "cash for work" project was considered a model of South-South cooperation by the United Nations Development Programme, from which it earned two special prizes, including one in the context of the Millennium Development Goals.[121]

The fact that the Lula administration focused on poverty and social justice for an engagement in Haiti, along with concerns over equitable development, must not belie the fact that this was a strategic project.

Existing accounts that deploy attributes such as identity,[122] culture,[123] and norms that distinguish between strategic and communicative action[124] to explain Brazil's engagement in the Haitian crisis are relevant but insufficient without attention to rhetoric and the social hierarchies that drive politics. Claims about Brazil's identity as a pacifist nation, its racial identity based on the role of the Black population in the state, and the Latin American culture of cooperation were all rhetorical performances in the social hierarchy, which enabled Brazilian policymakers to be heard among interlocutors in the South American community. In the specific Haitian crisis game, appraisal among interlocutors did not allow Brazil to exercise exceptionalist or hegemonic projects in Haiti, including the realization of a permanent seat on the UNSC. Instead, institutional members tamed Brazil and made it coherent within the regional conventions. Absent consideration of these sociorelational adjustments among regional members, any alternative explanations based on Brazil's unique "regional leadership project" fail to offer a complex account of Brazil's engagement in Haiti.[125]

PUTTING BRAZIL'S RHETORICAL REPERTOIRE IN PERSPECTIVE

The chapter showed the continuities and changes in Brazil's rhetorical repertoire based on anti-imperialism and anticolonialism and how these changes manifested in its power politics during the UN-led humanitarian intervention in Haiti in 2004. For Brazil, rhetoric is a learned product of struggle. Chapter 2 showed that Brazilian political actors perfected the rhetorical repertoire of anti-imperialism and anti-Yankee discourse during its struggle against U.S. interventionism in the Western Hemisphere and in the world. Many Brazilian elites developed a rhetorical way of confronting U.S. hegemony. Without rhetoric, the voices of Brazilian political actors were seldom heard in the hierarchical system. Political actors frequently innovated on this rhetorical repertoire to achieve their objectives.

The Haitian crisis in 2004 became another opportunity for Brazilian policymakers to update the repertoire and exercise power. Within the ongoing arrangement of audiences as scorekeepers, patterns of institutional rules, and their social transactions, Brazilian policymakers returned to the established rhetorical repertoire to cut across these dynamics and legitimize their engagement in the Haitian crisis. Such a rhetorical strategy involved making adjustments to audiences' appraisals, eliminating fear about Brazilian exceptionalism, and demonstrating Brazil's bona fide status among Latin American community members. These are power politic moves packaged in a rhetorical strategy to maneuver within the institutional norms of the region. In chapter 5, we will see the rhetorical power politics of China in the Syrian crisis, where its political actors similarly activated anti-imperial and anticolonial rhetoric for a more ambitious reordering of the world.

5

CHINA'S RHETORICAL POWER POLITICS
IN THE SYRIAN CRISIS, 2011-2020

I n 2011, antigovernment protests and uprisings spread across the Arab world and hit Syria like a thunderclap. The protests escalated into a civil war with widespread violence. The Syrian civil war had global consequences that continue to haunt the international community today. The massive exodus of Syrian refugees, the rise of explicitly radical right-wing parties and anti-Islamic movements in Europe, the advent of the Islamic State in Iraq and Syria (ISIS) and its allegiance to Al-Qaeda with grotesque videos of beheadings, the central role of special forces and mercenaries in the rivalry between the United States and Russia in the Arab World—all are consequences of the Syrian civil war.[1]

As a permanent member of the UN Security Council (UNSC), China faced political, economic, and ethical challenges throughout the crisis unfolding in the Middle East. In international politics as well as in the Middle East and Asia, China has been a vocal defender of sovereignty and territorial integrity and consistently resisted the idea of military intervention for regime change. Against the backdrop of the humanitarian crisis in Syria, China also officially sought a "political settlement" in the form of "peace talks between the Syrian government and oppositions in a balanced way."[2] Chinese political actors were opposed to the recent episode of the North Atlantic Treaty Organization's (NATO) "imperial overreach" in the overthrow of Muammar Gaddafi in the Libyan civil war of 2011.[3]

In the Syrian crisis, Chinese political actors were worried about the activism of Western democracies in the UNSC about plans to discipline local governance; plans of foreign-imposed regime change and violations of sovereignty; economic consequences, especially the loss of oil imports; and the growing exclusion of China from "Western-led" international ordering. Such predicaments were compounded by China's uneven position in the hierarchical international system. China is a permanent member of the UNSC, but other Western powers—the United States, the United Kingdom, and France—form the so-called P3. This P3 is increasingly used in discussion of the UNSC's working method, particularly the penholder system representing the like-mindedness of three permanent members creating an implicit hierarchy in relation to China and Russia in the opposite camp. Western states' also frequently see China as incompetent in managing humanitarian crises and protecting human rights. The evaluation of China's incompetence, like that of India and Brazil in chapters 3 and 4, respectively, has two sources: one inherited historically from the mid- to the late nineteenth century as Western empires silenced the country's claims and counterclaims on the international stage, and the other acquired in response to China's successive vetoes of the Western-led UNSC resolutions to address humanitarian crises and human rights violations.

After a veto by the Chinese and the Russians in the UNSC in 2012, Hillary Clinton famously called China's and Russia's actions a travesty: "It's quite distressing to see two permanent members of the Security Council using their veto while people are being murdered, women, children, brave young men, houses are being destroyed. It is just despicable, and I ask whose side are they on? They are clearly not on the side of the Syrian people."[4] Barack Obama called China a "free rider."[5] Susan Rice argued in the UNSC, "The United States is disgusted that a couple of members of this Council continue to prevent us from fulfilling our sole purpose here, which is to address an ever-deepening crisis in Syria and a growing threat to regional peace and security. For months, this Council has been held hostage by a couple of members."[6] The Western powers explicitly stated that China (and Russia) "failed in its responsibility" and that they were appalled, disgusted, or ashamed because permanent members of the UNSC had disobeyed the rules of the liberal international order.[7] Such reprobation continued throughout the decade of the Syrian crisis. In 2019, France explicitly stated that the Chinese and Russian vetoes are "irresponsible and sinister . . . politicizing and exploiting humanitarian aid must end. We must not hold the Syrian people hostage and let us get back to work."[8]

Despite these assessments of China's conduct in the Syrian civil war, Chinese political actors pursued power politics on two fronts. China cast multiple successive vetoes on UN resolutions and steadfastly condemned plans for military interventions for regime change in Syria. The Xi Jinping administration cooperated with Russia and protected Syria's Bashar al-Assad regime from collapse, wearing down the West. The Xi Jinping administration specifically leveraged anticolonial and anti-imperial rhetoric in pursuing this power politics. Chinese political actors improvised and innovated on old anti-imperial scripts and made a mark in the Middle East, a space outside its traditional spheres of influence. China's rhetorical engagement in the Syrian crisis reduced the diplomatic and military options available to the West and awakened the world to a new order.

China's use of anticolonial and anti-imperial rhetoric might be surprising when its objective military and economic capabilities could easily have translated into a confident role in managing international order and leveraging its role as a permanent member of the UNSC, casting its vetoes to protect the Assad regime without fear of Western military threats or economic sanctions. Instead, Chinese political actors used rhetorical tools in response to the Syrian crisis. As China's foreign minister Wang Yi argued in talking about the UN during the peak of the Syrian crisis:

> In the more than 100 years after the Opium War, *colonialism and imperialism inflicted untold sufferings on China.* . . . The Chinese people fought indomitably and tenaciously to uphold China's sovereignty, independence, and territorial integrity and founded New China. . . . Seeing the contrast between China's past and present, the Chinese people fully recognize how valuable sovereignty, independence and peace are. China ardently hopes for the rule of law in international relations against hegemony and power politics, and rules-based equity and justice, and *hopes that the humiliation and sufferings it was subjected to will not happen to others* [emphasis added].[9]

Through such rhetoric, China achieved several objectives. It challenged the West and the changing norms of military intervention for regime change, avoided direct military confrontation with the West by sending its special forces to Syria as Russia did, maintained the stability of the Chinese Communist Party (CCP), delegitimized the global authority of the United States and Europe by successfully showcasing the hypocrisies of the liberal order, and demonstrated that China was not shirking responsibilities as a permanent member of the UNSC but meeting the expectations of the Global South. Such power politics of the Xi Jinping administration in the Syrian crisis awakened the United States, the United Kingdom, and France—the P3 states—to their inability to arm-twist China into submission on managing humanitarian crises abroad.

This chapter will put the conceptual framework of this book into motion. Recall that in hierarchical international politics, rhetoric is a tool that underdogs use to push back against systematic silencing. Rhetoric is a weapon of the weak that policymakers use to challenge their silencing in the hierarchy, and ambitious states develop a rhetorical repertoire of power politics to exploit the contradictions in the principles, norms, and rules of the international system. Chapters 3 and 4 showed how Indian and Brazilian political actors pursued rhetorical power politics in the East Pakistan crisis of 1971 and the Haitian crisis of 2004, respectively. This chapter will focus on how the Xi Jinping administration activated its anti-imperial and anticolonial rhetoric and adapted established scripts of its power political games in managing the Syrian crisis. By examining how China's rhetoric unfolded against multiple audiences during the crisis, we can understand how policymakers interrogated the contradictions in the system to assert competence in international ordering.

By focusing on China's rhetorical power politics this way, the chapter will offer a corrective to alternative accounts in international relations (IR) scholarship. Most IR scholars fail to examine the rhetoric through which China's power politics unfolded during the Syrian crisis.[10] Some accounts suffer from a confirmation bias of the "China threat theory"—the idea that China cannot rise peacefully, it seeks to subvert the West, and the West must restrict China to preserve order.[11] Many IR accounts concentrate on the inevitability of Beijing's rise to overturn the U.S.-dominated international order.[12] These accounts overlook the fact that even the same outcomes predicted by realist soft balancing, for example, often result from different strategies and can rely on entirely different political projects.[13] Scholarship based on the idea of democracy versus autocracy likewise views Beijing and Moscow as an evolving "alliance" or treats China as a second fiddle to the machinations of Russian military engagement in the Middle East.[14] Such views on the authoritarian solidarity of China and Russia might be right, yet they miss the far more complex power politics at work when China responds to a humanitarian crisis. Taking China's rhetoric into account allows us to see that China's engagement in the Syrian crisis was not merely an outlier to its broader engagement with international peacekeeping,[15] or that it was only an opportunistic and profit-oriented player with a sudden concern for energy security.[16] China's sharpening of its anti-imperial rhetorical repertoire sought to upend the unequal and hegemonic framework of the international order, which was consistent with its power political practices in statecraft.

The chapter is organized as follows: The first section will offer a brief background on the Syrian crisis between 2011 and 2020. The second section will show China's dilemma in the Syrian crisis. It will elaborate on the continuous reproduction of silencing practices in the hierarchy and the incompetence attributed to China in managing the crisis and international order. The third section will demonstrate how Chinese political actors used familiar anti-imperial and anticolonial scripts and flipped this rhetoric to maneuver against the silencing practices in the system. The final section will examine China's rhetorical power politics against alternative explanations based on realism and rhetorical entrapment scholarship in IR. From a rhetorical repertoire of power politics perspective offered in this chapter, we can understand a much deeper and more intricate form of China's statecraft to challenge the international order. Managing global disorder requires that Western policymakers acknowledge the imperial and colonial legacies of international ordering and restrict the ability of Chinese policymakers to flip those scripts in statecraft.

SYRIAN CIVIL WAR, 2011–2020: BACKGROUND AND CONTEXT

Syria has witnessed myriad conflicts and crises since the early twentieth century. It started with European imperialism, which interfered in the domestic affairs of the Ottoman Empire. Such interference was justified to manage the so-called barbarism of Muslims against Christians and non-Muslims. After the end of World War I and the defeat of the Ottoman Empire, such machinations turned into a mandate authorized by the League of Nations in the 1920s. In the so-called Middle East region, Britain took on the mandate of rule over Palestine, Iraq, and the coastal strip between the Mediterranean Sea and the Jordan River. France took over the mandate for Syria and Lebanon to prepare the states ostensibly for eventual independence.

In the interwar years, Syria, like other states in the region, was profoundly influenced by multiple global debates on rights, responsibilities, and sovereignty.[17] Many Syrians began to articulate their visions of nationalism, autonomy, and independence to challenge the mandate-colonialism of France. Some Syrian nationalists called for a Greater Syria that encompassed Lebanon and Palestine into one unit; Pan-Arab nationalists expressed grievances against the Western empires along with their anxieties over a Jewish state in Palestine; and Syrian republican nationalists and communists spoke out against all forms of monarchies. The Sunni Islamist movement in Syria took inspiration from the Muslim Brotherhood in Egypt. Syria witnessed fierce debates on the right forms of governance within its polity because Syria also had Druze, Armenian and Greek Orthodox Christians, Jews, and a whole host of diverse minorities. Under these diverse groups, the French mandate system viewed Syria as "not yet ready" for mature governance. An independent Syria was born at the end of World War II; however, many Western states continued to interfere in Syria's internal affairs.[18] Under such conditions, anti-Westernism, anti-imperialism, and anti-Zionism became rallying cries among domestic actors who wished to engineer political autonomy in Syria.[19]

Against this background, the Ba'ath Party came to power in 1963. The party advanced a platform of anti-Western Syrian nationalism and a pan-Arab socialist doctrine to consolidate Arab identity in the Middle East. This created several factions and divisions within the Ba'ath Party. Hafiz al-Assad capitalized on these divisions and took power in Syria through a coup in 1970. At that time, Arab nationalism was already in a slow decline. Thus, he mixed the older nonconformist anti-Zionism with new pragmatism to consolidate his autocratic regime. He leveraged the status of his minority Alawite sect at the domestic level against different factions at the regional and international level by engaging with Iran, keeping diplomatic channels open with Lebanon, and playing a central role in the management of intra-Arab relations. In this way, Hafiz al-Assad positioned Syria as the lynchpin of the Middle East. He also supported the U.S.-led coalition to expel Iraq from Kuwait in the 1990–1991 Gulf crisis and thus engaged with several rivals in the region, such as Iraq, Israel, and Saudi Arabia. The death of Hafiz al-Assad in June 2000 set the stage for his second son, Bashar al-Assad, to assume power in July 2000.

Between taking office in 2000 and the onset of civil war in 2011, Bashar al-Assad's approach mirrored his father's custom of practicing statecraft. He manipulated the domestic political system by offering office positions to loyal senior political and military personnel to sustain his autocratic regime. He also aimed to secure Syria in a threatening regional environment that was the result of problems of multiple religious fighters who crossed sectarian lines alongside the growing consolidation of power by Israel and Iran. With fierce pan-Arab and anti-Western rhetoric, Bashar al-Assad managed different domestic factions, including the majority Sunni groups, Druze, Arab nationalists, and anti-Israel groups against regional elites from Aleppo and Damascus.[20] Syrian troops that moved into Lebanon in 1976 also exited the country in 2005, yet Syria treated Lebanon as its sphere of influence. The Assad regime came to terms with the U.S. invasion of Iraq in March 2003 by signaling its readiness to cooperate with the temporary Iraqi administration established by the United States.[21] Assad also agreed to police the porous Iraq-Syria border, consolidated diplomatic and military relations with Iran, and was invited by the George W. Bush administration to the Middle Eastern peace process in Annapolis, Maryland, in 2007 to find a solution to Israel-Palestine conflict. It looked as if the Assad's regime was poised to survive, but another major event took over: the Arab uprising.

In early March 2011, only a few protestors marched in the streets of Damascus and Aleppo and demanded political reform. Yet it was the arrest and torture of teenage children for painting antiregime graffiti in the southern city of Deraa that became the lightning rod for controversy. The repressive reaction by the Syrian regime through its secret service *Mukhabarat* and Bashar al-Assad's violent speech in the Syrian parliament on March 30, 2011, led to a serious uprising in the streets. The diversity of Syrian domestic society meant that many groups saw this unrest as an opportunity to challenge the minority rule of the Alawites. The ruthless suppression of the revolt by the government gave rise to further demonstrations in which protestors called for the overthrow of the Assad regime. Protests and violent uprisings also spread across several cities in Syria, unleashing atrocities on both sides and leading to further cycles of bloody violence and immeasurable destruction.[22]

Over this period, violence in Syria and calls to overthrow Assad became increasingly sectarian, funded by several external networks such as states and religious groups, which had regional and international implications through a proxy war that was supported by Turkey, Hezbollah, Iran, Russia, Britain, and the United States. As researchers Frank Hoffman and Andrew Orner, and also Daniel Byman show, "just about everyone backed proxies in Syria."[23] This is also because sectarian strife came into being in Syria after Arab uprisings.[24] Some religious sectarians of the Sunni Islamists challenged the secular politics of Assad. They supported radical projects such as the Jabhat al-Nusra, an Al-Qaida affiliate, and later ISIS, as we shall see below. Hezbollah and Iraqi Shia militias supported the regime. Defection among the Syrian armed forces contributed to a weak but prominent Free Syrian Army (FSA) and a coalition of political opposition in the form of the National Coalition for Syrian Revolutionary and Opposition Forces, commonly known as Syrian National Coalition (SNC). At the regional and international levels, the supporters of the regime, such as Russia, Iran, and Hezbollah, were working against the opponents of the regime, such as the United States, the United Kingdom, France, Israel, Turkey, Saudi Arabia, and Qatar.

The UN took an immediate role in the crisis.[25] The UN appointed Kofi Annan as the joint special envoy for the United Nations and the League of Arab States to mediate different local and regional factions and bring an end to the violence. These efforts were futile, however, and Annan resigned after less than six months in his role. By July 2012, the International Committee of the Red Cross (ICRC) had determined that the fighting in Syria had become a full-scale civil war. By early 2013, High Commissioner for Human Rights Navi Pillay and Under-Secretary-General and Emergency Relief Coordinator Valerie Amos reported that there were 4 million people in need in Syria, 2 million internally displaced persons (IDPs), and 650,000 Syrian refugees.[26] Switzerland, supported by more than fifty countries, alleged crimes against humanity and asked the UNSC to refer Syria to the International Criminal Court (ICC). After the Assad regime used chemical weapons in 2013 in the Ghouta area of Damascus,[27] the United States and Russia agreed to a framework for the elimination of chemical weapons.[28] Russian air campaigns eliminated many stockpiles of chemical weapons but "did not include the destruction of all chloride gas."[29] Multiple factions within Syria used this oversight to engage in several hundred punitive chemical attacks.

Under the rapidly deteriorating situation in Syria, ISIS found opportunities to seize oilfields and pipelines and declared its own state.[30] Abu Bakr al-Baghdadi, an Iraqi, and his radical cohorts took the northeastern city of Raqqa in 2014, declared a "caliphate," and lured foreign fighters to engage in jihad. The beheadings of U.S. journalist James Foley by ISIS and many others sent shock waves around the world. The Syrian crisis took on greater international significance.[31]

The Syrian crisis that ignited the Middle East also manifested as a serious refugee crisis across Europe, and Turkey bore the brunt of the exodus of Syrian refugees. However, anti-immigration and xenophobia became defining issues in Europe, bringing into the open radical right-wing parties such as the anti-Islamic demonstrators of Pegida in Germany, the neo-Nazis of Golden Dawn in Greece, Fidesz led by Viktor Orban in Hungary, the People's Party in Switzerland, and the Law and Justice Party of Poland. By 2019, Syria was experiencing a widespread humanitarian crisis, "including 6.6 million refugees, 6.2 million internally displaced people (IDPs) and 140,000 asylum-seekers,"[32] and about 350,000 people killed in ten years. The UNSC came under fierce ideological conflict between P3 states that sought regime change, on the one hand, and China and Russia, on the other, that rejected liberal interventionist projects. The United States, France, and Britain called for economic sanctions from the very beginning and debated "humanitarian intervention," and Russia and China, among other members, held that "council action on Syria" must not "escalate into muscular military action."[33] While Susan Rice, U.S. ambassador to the UN, argued for sanctions backed by plans for humanitarian intervention, Sergey Lavrov, Russian foreign minister, "commented that advancing democracy with iron and blood just does not work."[34] In the UN, China expressed its concern for the "humanitarian situation in Syria" but argued that "the effort to abate the humanitarian crisis in Syria must be based on strict compliance with the humanitarian principles of neutrality and impartiality and respect for Syria's sovereignty, independence, unity and territorial integrity. Politicization of humanitarian issues must be avoided."[35]

CHINA'S PREDICAMENT IN THE HIERARCHICAL ORDER REGARDING THE SYRIAN CRISIS

In 2010, China was a formidable great power in international politics and had recorded a double-digit growth average of 10.9 percent, "roughly five times that of the West," for the past decade.[36] The United States under Barack Obama thus shifted its foreign policy to "pivot to Asia" and thus manage China, which was now "the only plausible long-term rival to America as a global superpower."[37] Many pundits and academics believed that China's statecraft would resemble Otto von Bismarck's Germany: as Charles Kupchan put it, just as Bismarck made Germany Europe's diplomatic pivot, China today is the diplomatic pivot of East Asia, and just as Bismarck pursued muscular statecraft but also pulled back to forestall a balancing coalition, Chinese political actors seek stability, fully aware of the threats of countervailing coalition. Kupchan adds, "Just as Bismarck's Germany took advantage of the stability provided by British hegemony to expand its trade and influence, China is reaping the benefits, but not sharing the costs, of the global public goods provided by the United States."[38]

As a permanent member of the UNSC, however, Chinese political actors viewed that at the onset of the Syrian crisis in 2011, its material and economic power were secondary to the Western-led understandings of managing the rules-based international order. In other words, Chinese political actors could not pursue the strategies of Bismarck under the pressures of international social hierarchy. First, on the political front, China defended the sovereignty and territorial integrity of states and opposed any form of military intervention for regime change. But by May 2011, there were explicit calls in the West to overthrow Bashar al-Assad's regime in Syria. As Obama put it, "First, it will be the policy of the United States to promote reform across the region, and to support transitions to democracy." In this light, "President Assad now has a choice: He can lead that transition, or get out of the way."[39] David Cameron of Great Britain, Nicolas Sarkozy of France, and Angela Merkel of Germany, in a joint statement, asserted, "Our three countries believe that President Assad . . . has lost all legitimacy and can no longer claim to lead the country. . . . We call on him to face the reality of the complete rejection of his regime by the Syrian people and to step aside."[40] Such calls came in the immediate aftermath of UNSC Resolution 1973 of March 2011 on the Libyan crisis, which authorized a no-fly zone over Libya and ended up overthrowing Muammar Gaddafi in October 2011. China's position, led by state councilor Dai Bingguo and Permanent Representative of China to the UN Li Baodong, opposed coercive regime change and the extension of liberal interventionist projects to Syria.

China's political position against regime change in Syria was at odds with the West but also with several regional actors. For example, Qatar supported the radical Muslim Brotherhood and sought regime change in Syria. Qatar had previously played an active role in NATO-led intervention in the overthrow of the Gaddafi regime in Libya.[41] Now, Qatar aimed to serve as a mediator between the Sunni Arab world and the West. Saudi Arabia, in its own geopolitical rivalry with Iran, prioritized its focus on the Wahhabi group instead of the Muslim Brotherhood. It saw the crisis in Syria as a forum in which it could support *takfiri*-Wahhabi radicals such as Jaysh al-Islam and Ahrar al-Sham to counterbalance Iran's own *Basij* volunteer force and Shia militias in Syria.[42] Thus, Saudi Arabia actively backed political opposition to the Assad regime. Israel focused on the threat of Hamas and Hezbollah and sought regime change in Syria to prevent Iran from creating a stronghold in Syria or transferring advanced weaponry to that country. Turkey was focused on the massive refugee exodus into the country and on the strengthened Kurdish community on the border that received U.S. support for the fight against ISIS. In its proxy war in Syria, Turkey trained defectors of SNC, from whom emerged the FSA, which hosted political opposition and rallied against the Assad regime. Regional organizations such as the Gulf Cooperation Council (GCC) and the Arab League opposed the Assad regime, but they sought "an Arab solution rather than any foreign intervention."[43]

However, many other external political actors opposed regime change in Syria. Russia played an important strategic role in Syria and the Middle East, safeguarding the Assad regime with military and mercenary support. India rejected regime change in Syria, and Foreign Minister Salman Khurshid said at the 2014 Geneva II peace conference that Syria cannot be reordered from the outside.[44] At the same time, India was also firmly focused on its fight against global jihad. It has the third largest Muslim population in the world and is one of the top ten terrorism-affected countries, with more than two hundred militant groups and about ten thousand terrorism-related causalities since 2001.[45] The arrival of the Bharatiya Janata Party (BJP) in 2014 coincided with the creation of the South Asian

wing of Al-Qaeda, which in turn led to an active Indian intelligence operation (Operation Chakravyuh) to thwart Indian foreign fighters joining
ISIS. It was in India's strategic interest to focus on Syrian sovereignty and
territorial integrity to avoid any foreign fighters landing in Kashmir.[46]

As a unit, Brazil, Russia, India, China, and South Africa (BRICS) took
a conservative position of nonintervention without anti-Westernism.
BRICS issued a joint statement in March 2013: "A Syrian-led political process leading to a transition can be achieved only through broad national
dialogue that meets the legitimate aspirations of all sections of Syrian society and respect for Syrian independence, territorial integrity, and sovereignty."[47] BRICS stood steadfastly opposed to what they viewed as NATO's
imperial overreach in the overthrow of Gaddafi in the Libyan civil war
of 2011. With many prominent regional actors supporting regime change
in Syria and external actors rejecting such moves, China increasingly
found that its established views about sovereignty and territorial integrity
needed a stronger argumentative defense than a mere demonstration of
its economic capabilities and importance in trade would provide.

In the aftermath of the global financial crisis of 2008–2009, many members of the CCP pursued vigorous state-led capitalism and also emphasized
China's commitment to the world, preserving the path of peaceful development and an independent foreign policy of peace and building a prosper-
ous country and a strong military.[48] The arrival of Xi Jinping as president
in 2013 increased these commitments on a grander scale. The Xi Jinping
administration championed *fenfa youwei* ("striving for achievement") in
foreign affairs, signaling a more assertive stance.[49] It also launched the Belt
and Road Initiative (BRI) in 2013 with the plan of integrating Arab states
into its vast economic and trade network. The promise of trade and development pulled multiple regional interlocutors in the Middle East toward
economic cooperation with Beijing. Thus, despite Turkey's past references
to China's treatment of Uighurs in Xinjiang as "genocide,"[50] and Arab
states' criticisms of China's intransigence against regime change in Syria,
many regional interlocutors took an instrumentalist position to increase
trade with China through the BRI. Saudi Arabia, along with thirty-seven
other states, backed China's Xinjiang policy and "commended China's
remarkable achievements in the field of human rights."[51]

Despite these developments and the grand framing of peace and economic prosperity, Chinese political actors faced inordinate pressure from
Western policymakers to toe their line on the Syrian crisis. As China's

UN ambassador Li Baodong put it rather explicitly: "During the consultations on this draft resolution [on Syria on July 19, 2012], the sponsoring countries failed to show any political will of cooperation. They adopted a rigid and arrogant approach to the reasonable core concerns of the relevant countries, and refused to make revisions . . . a few countries made statements that confused right and wrong, and made unfounded accusations against China. This is utterly wrong. It is out of ulterior motives, and firmly opposed by China . . . a few countries have been intent on interfering in other countries' internal affairs, fanning the flames and driving wedges among countries. They are eager to see tumult in the world."[52]

However, China also used the Syrian crisis to increase its import of crude oil. Chinese political actors focused on trade and emphasized peace talks between the Syrian government and its opposition groups while simultaneously opposing regime change. As Courtney Fung shows, China's National Petroleum Corporation has shares in "Syria's two largest oil firms, and Sinochem, through a subsidiary, has a 50 percent stake in Syrian oil fields. China rounded out the purchases of Syrian crude oil after the European Union's embargo in 2011. That year, China was Syria's biggest trading partner, with exports of $2.4 billion shepherded by closer state-to-state coordination through the Syrian-Chinese Business Council."[53] Chinese political actors believed that this policy of running with the hare and hunting with the hounds required skillful maneuvering under the hierarchical system.

Chinese political actors also faced ethical predicaments in the Syrian crisis. The P3 states (the United States, the United Kingdom, and France) took an ethical high ground when addressing the gross violations of human rights in Syria. Several other audiences, such as the UN, followed suit. Secretary-General Ban Ki-moon, Special Representative Lakhdar Brahimi, and UN High Commissioners for Human Rights Navanethem Pillay (2008–2014) and Zeid Ra'ad Al Hussein (2014–2018) acknowledged gross human rights violations in Syria and criticized China and Russia. The UN Human Rights Council (UNHRC) established an independent inquiry and stated that the Syrian government failed "in its responsibility to protect its people" and maintained this position throughout the crisis.[54] High Commissioner for Human Rights Zeid Ra'ad explicitly stated that the "responsibility for the continuation of so much pain lies with the five permanent members of the U.N. Security Council. So long as the veto is used by them . . . it is they—the permanent members—who must answer before the victims."[55] When the UNHRC found that the Syrian government forces and state-sponsored militias (*Shabiha*) committed crimes against humanity, ethical concerns explicitly took center stage.[56] As Ra'ad put it: "For the love of mercy [please put an end to] the pernicious use of the veto."[57]

In the past, Chinese political actors accepted humanitarian intervention and cast aside their iron-clad commitments to sovereignty when other political actors emphasized grave ethical and moral emergencies. For example, in the Rwandan genocide of 1994 and the mass killings of civilians in the Darfur region of Sudan in 2003, Chinese policymakers recognized the need for humanitarian intervention and endorsed the so-called responsibility to protect (R2P) in 2005 at the UN World Summit. Many Western political actors believed that the Syrian crisis and the crimes against humanity could put similar moral pressure on China to respond in kind. In the Syrian crisis, moral framing of multiple interlocutors took center stage.

For example, many policymakers feared "moral obscenity" in the use of chemical weapons;[58] "moral panic" in the rise of ISIS;[59] and brutal violence of ISIS in the public murdering of victims along with systematic looting and destruction of antiquities, specifically at Palmyra. Europe's "erosion of moral authority"[60] in the refugee crisis in the moving images of the death by drowning of infamous two-year-old Syrian boy Alan Kurdi and in the deaths of thousands of refugees and children fleeing the crisis showed the "moral dilemma" and the ugly side of fortress Europa. The decimation of cities like Aleppo with burned bodies shook the "moral conscience" of the world. Thus, there was no lack of moral concern among multiple interlocutors as horror followed horror not seen since World War II. And different moral positions of various actors translated into mutual antagonisms and "reproduced themselves into a complicated dialogue of moral claim and counter-claim."[61] Chinese political actors felt the moral pressure to take a stand with the West to demonstrate its commitment to addressing mass atrocity crimes.

But for Chinese political actors, the moral predicaments and multiple factions in the Syrian crisis meant that external intervention and regime change would worsen and not resolve the problems of suffering and the humanitarian crisis in Syria. As UN Ambassador Li Baodong put it, "No external parties should engage in military intervention in Syria or push for regime change."[62] China focused on providing humanitarian assistance to Syrian civilians. Chinese political actors frequently reminded the audiences of the absolute moral commitment of the UN Charter (Article 2, paragraph 4) concerning the use of force against the territorial integrity or political independence of any state.[63] But a more serious problem, from the perspective of China, Russia, and many of the BRICS, was their experience with the NATO-led overthrow of Gaddafi in Libya, which perpetuated moral problems and humanitarian crises in the Middle East. UN Resolution 1973 authorized the no-fly zone, which in turn led to the overthrow of Gaddafi based on R2P. With this in mind, Li Baodong asserted in the UN debates on Syria that "the Security Council resolutions must be strictly and comprehensively implemented. No party is to interpret them in any way it wants, let alone take action that exceeds Council mandates."[64] In this way, Chinese political actors stood squarely against the challenge of Western policymakers fixated on regime change in Syria. However, that was not enough.

Against the political, economic, and moral challenges in the Syrian crisis compounded by assessments of China's incompetence in managing international order to protect human rights and mass atrocity crimes, Chinese political actors resorted to power politics to defend their views on international order. They returned to their anti-imperial and anticolonial rhetorical repertoire and adapted it in novel ways.

CHINA'S RHETORICAL POWER POLITICS IN THE SYRIAN CRISIS, 2011–2020

In chapter 1, I argued that international hierarchy rests on fundamental structural inequality between the West and the rest and that it is sustained by silencing Asia, Africa, and Latin American states. Rhetoric under this structural condition of silencing is a necessity to be heard and thus a weapon of the weak in the hierarchy. Anti-imperial and anticolonial rhetoric and their affective performances not only enabled political actors to challenge the hierarchical system but also brought revolutionary transformation to end imperialism with the onset of decolonization. However, some ambitious policymakers often found rhetoric more than a simple weapon of the weak. As chapter 2 showed, they developed a rhetorical repertoire of power politics to expose and exploit the contradictions in the principles, rules, and norms of the international system. Enacting their anti-imperial and anticolonial rhetoric and innovating and improvising the repertoire are power politics under hierarchy. In the Syrian crisis, the Xi Jinping administration engaged in ruthless rhetorical power politics while at the same time shielding itself from any form of direct involvement in the Middle East crisis.

For the Xi Jinping administration, the Syrian crisis served as an opportunity to articulate China's competence in managing the international order. Xi's statecraft returned to the established rhetorical repertoire of power politics that looked back to the lessons learned from the struggles against Western empires. As Xing Lu, the scholar who studies Mao's rhetoric and its influence, puts it, Xi frequently builds on Mao Zedong: "As Xi said in his speech commemorating Mao's 120th birthday, 'Once the fate of China is in the hands of its people, China will be like the sun rising from the east that shines throughout the earth with its radiance.' He said, 'We Chinese have the spirit of fighting with our enemy until the end,' and 'We have the determination to be independent; we have the ability to stand high in the world.' Just as Mao once predicted, so Xi says that the 'Chinese people have the will and competence to catch up and surpass the advanced countries in the world.'"[65] In the Syrian crisis, the Xi Jinping administration engaged in far more intricate adaptations to its anti-imperial rhetoric, and its power politics came into sharp relief.

QUESTIONING THE SINCERITY OF THE WEST

In chapter 2, we saw the evolution of China's rhetorical repertoire. During the Syrian civil war, China's policymakers further adapted this repertoire in statecraft to expose the contradictions in the system. The People's Republic of China (PRC) did not dismiss the problems of humanitarian crises in Syria. Chinese policymaker argued instead that they would exercise judgment based on equity and justice on a "case-by-case basis."[66]

In February 2012, China and Russia vetoed a draft UN resolution that condemned the violence in Syria and called for a "Syrian-led political transition," which, in other words, meant Assad had to leave.[67] U.S. Secretary of State Hillary Clinton called out China and Russia's veto as "despicable." The Communist Party mouthpiece, the *People's Daily*, wrote immediately: "The United States' motive in parading as a 'protector' of the Arab peoples is not difficult to imagine. The problem is, what *moral basis* does it have for this patronizing and egotistical super-arrogance and self-confidence? [The Iraq invasion in 2003] alone is enough for us to draw a huge question mark over the sincerity and efficacy of U.S. policy."[68] The rhetoric questioning the sincerity of the West continued. In July 2012, Li Baodong argued that China seeks consensus in the UNSC, "but the United Kingdom, the United States and France completely contradicts such aims." He went on to lambast the West because this time they invoked "Chapter VII of the Charter [for humanitarian intervention] and the threat of sanctions, in an attempt to change or even repudiate the hard-won consensus."[69] Given that the West selectively acknowledged the problems of grave humanitarian crises in the world, such as in Palestine, Yemen, or Haiti, and frequently used the pretext of a humanitarian crisis to engage in regime change, such as in Kosovo, Afghanistan, or Libya, Chinese policymakers' rhetorical performances played against these contradictions in ordering practices.

PRC deployed this rhetoric through two moves that were an innovation of its anti-imperial and anticolonial rhetorical repertoire. One, China's policymakers ethically positioned China as a *spiritus rector* for the protection of sovereignty and territorial integrity of small and developing states.[70] When UK representative Sir Mark Grant lambasted China and Russia for refusing Chapter VII military support to the UN Supervision Mission in Syria (UNSMIS) and failing to protect the people of Syria,[71] Chinese representative Li Baodong said, "China has no self-interest in the Syrian issue" as it only stands for small countries to protect the basic standards of international relations.[72] Beijing hedged that the West did not have the standing to blame China for its irresponsible vetoes. When Xi Jinping came to power, his foreign minister Wang Yi continued this rhetoric and argued that China was only working to "safeguard norms governing international relations [to] protect the legitimate interests of developing countries, especially small and medium-sized countries."[73] The claim that China stands for small and weak countries was a trademark rhetorical strategy of Mao Zedong. Appealing to this morality became ammunition for opposing sanctions, travel bans, and arms embargoes in Syria.

That this rhetorical performance is strategic is evident in the way China reversed such ideals about the equality of small states in its own region. Foreign Minister Yang Jeichi had told leaders of the Association of Southeast Asian Nations (ASEAN) in 2010 that China was "a big country and [these] countries are small countries and that is just a fact."[74] When Xi Jinping came to power, this rhetoric became filled with anti-imperial claims based on Asia for Asians. In May 2014, Xi told an international audience, "Certain non-Asian powers, through forming alliances and cliques with some Asian countries, have constantly interfered in the balance and cooperation of Asia, [but] security in Asia should be maintained by Asian themselves."[75] This use of anti-imperial claims in novel ways also signaled the centrality of China in Asia. In the midst of the Syrian crisis in the Middle East, Foreign Minister Wang Yi categorically stated that in Asia, China would "never bully smaller countries, yet [it will] never accept unreasonable demands from smaller countries."[76] In other words, Beijing morally positioned itself as a *spiritus rector* for respecting small and developing states in the Syrian crisis while at the same time asserting the importance of its size in its own region.

Second, in keeping with its repertoire of anti-imperial and anticolonial rhetoric, the PRC morally repositioned itself within the debates on the appropriate forms of maintaining the rule of law and international justice. The case in point is the international clamor to refer the Syrian regime to the ICC for the prosecution of war crimes.[77] The big concern for Chinese policymakers with the ICC was that Article 12 grants the ICC automatic jurisdiction without the consent of state parties of the crime. Chinese political actors believe the ICC's jurisdiction over certain crimes must be based on a democratic "opt-in" based on the consent of national states rather than "automatic" jurisdiction. Chinese policymakers believe that the ICC can act only when the national court systems fail to act. In other words, the ICC or any international body cannot override national criminal jurisdictions. These considerations follow from China's rhetoric on its past struggles with foreign invasion and bullying. Immediately after taking power in 2013, Xi Jinping followed Mao's claims and asserted that "Chinese history is a history of imperialist oppression, humiliation, and suffering. Almost all the imperialist countries in the world had invaded and bullied China."[78] But Xi also emphasized that "China will take an active part in reforming and developing the global governance system, keep contributing Chinese wisdom and strength to global governance."[79] Reconciling these two positions led to China's renewed anti-imperial rhetoric in the Syrian crisis to reform the ICC to serve international justice properly.

In May 2014, the UNSC submitted a draft resolution to refer the situation in Syria to the ICC.[80] A few years later, in December 2016, the UN General Assembly adopted Resolution 71/248 and called for an international, impartial, and independent mechanism to investigate crimes committed by the Syrian regime since March 2011. Chinese representative Wu Haitao asserted the importance of the "judicial sovereignty of the host country" and vetoed the UNSC proposal.[81] The recrimination by deputy representative Wang Min was that for "the UNSC to forcibly refer the situation in Syria to the ICC is not conducive either to building trust among all parties in Syria or to an early resumption of the negotiations in Geneva. It will only jeopardize the efforts made by the international community to push for a political settlement."[82]

Even when many other Western audiences condemned China's (and Russia's) veto for enabling the Syrian regime to continue its violence with impunity, China's rhetoric appealed to the Global South by emphasizing human rights norms based on the democratic principle of contestation. In Syria, China called for a democratic inquiry into war crimes and human rights violations of antigovernment armed groups, such as the Syrian Democratic Forces (SDF),[83] People's Protection Units, which is a Kurdish militant group supported by the United States,[84] and Turkey's violation of humanitarian law in Operation Olive Branch.[85] By showing that the Syrian regime alone did not engage in human rights violations but were complemented by other groups, including those supported by the West, China led a severe charge against Western complicity in human rights violations in the Middle East.[86]

Through these rhetorical performances, Chinese political actors exploited the contradiction in the norms and rules of enforcing international justice and flipped established anti-imperial scripts to defend their position. This form of power politics is not dissimilar to the U.S. position on international justice to protect Israel against ICC referrals in the UNSC. By batting for Syria, Chinese political actors used rhetoric to inflect universally recognized human rights norms. Flipping democratic inquiry of international justice to shield Syria from the ICC also allowed Chinese political actors to question the sincerity of the West in managing humanitarian crises and in punishing mass atrocity crimes.

COUNTERSHAMING

Chinese political actors leveraged their anti-imperial and anticolonial rhetorical repertoire to shame Western interlocutors. Through the Syrian crisis, multiple audiences focused on pressuring the Assad regime to stop indiscriminate bombing and the use of heavy weapons in populated areas. They also pressed for negotiations through Kofi Annan's six-point plan of mediation. Yet it was the regime's use of chemical weapons that shook the moral conscience of the world.[87] Subsequent plans for Western military intervention came to naught, and a brief cooperation between Moscow and Washington to dismantle Syrian chemical weapons was on the table. The permanent representative of France, Gérard Araud, argued for referring Syria to the ICC, which was in line with "similar provisions in resolutions 1593(2005), on the situation in Darfur, and in resolution 1970 (2011), on Libya, against which no Member state voted against [therefore] it is not a political gesture [but] it is quite simply a *moral* act [emphasis added]."[88]

Yet China and Russia issued their fourth vetoes that led to a fierce shaming game in the UN. Russian representative Vitaly Churkin countered that the past referral of Libya to the ICC was a mistake, but more important was that "the United States frequently indicates the ICC option for others, but is reluctant to accede to the Rome Statute itself. . . . Great Britain is part of the ICC, but for some reason is unenthusiastic about the exploration in the Court of crimes committed by British nationals during the Iraq war."[89] Against such shaming, Samantha Power, the U.S. ambassador to the UN, retorted, "Aleppo will join the ranks of those events in world history that define modern evil, that stain our conscience decades later. Halabja, Rwanda, Srebrenica, and now, Aleppo." And she pointedly asked the Assad regime, Russia, and Iran: "Are you truly incapable of shame? Is there literally nothing that can shame you? Is there no act of barbarism against civilians, no execution of a child that gets under your skin?"[90]

Against this backdrop of shaming and countershaming, the PRC moved beyond ICC debates to pursue its own countershaming in the Syrian crisis. Chinese political actors engaged in two rhetorical innovations that focused less on content and more on emotional appeals from the social constraints of the hierarchical system. First, Beijing morally positioned itself as a major responsible country that can exercise its own independent judgment and authority for managing international crises. As Foreign Minister Wang Yi put it, "We must also have backbone [sic]. The backbone comes from our national pride. Gone is the century of humiliation in China's modern history. We feel passionately [sic] about our sovereignty and national dignity. We have our own judgment about international affairs."[91] As such, China supported UNSC Resolution 2118 to destroy Syria's chemical weapons in 2013, and in 2015 it supported the investigation of chlorine gas use in Syria through the UN Resolutions 2209 and 2235. It also sent escort missions to help with the destruction of chemical weapons in Syria.[92] Yet China argued that the moral shock of chemical weapons use was ideologically focused against the Assad regime without investigating rebels and terrorists who had also used these weapons in Syria. Through emotional rhetorical performances, the PRC shamed P3 states by pointing out their hypocrisy, shielding the Syrian regime in its violation of a moral norm.

To that end, Chinese representative Liu Jieyi engaged in fierce rhetoric: "As we all recall, the purported existence of weapons of mass destruction was used in the past to unleash a war [the Iraq War] that has brought untold suffering to the people in the Middle East. Countries in the Middle East remain beset today by the legacy of that war. The lessons of history must be learned. Only in that way can mistakes be avoided in the future."[93] References to the U.S. invasion of Iraq under the false pretext of weapons of mass destruction offered rhetorical ammunition to justify China's moral position. Thereafter, Chinese policymakers blocked the resolution sanctioning Syria for chemical weapons.[94] Multiple audiences worked to shame China and Russia by suggesting that one cannot dilute the a priori validity of some moral norms through tu quoque justifications or ad hominem attacks. The PRC began to abstain from debates on chemical weapons use.[95] China emphasized that it did not always endorse a blanket condemnation of the West like Russia did, but the PRC also stood clear of supporting military intervention against the Assad regime for its violation of the chemical weapons use taboo. By countershaming, China's rhetorical moves exposed and exploited the contradictions of Western practices of international ordering.

In taking a position on the Syrian crisis, China's political actors also adapted their rhetoric to position their state as vulnerable to transnational jihadist networks. In keeping with the debates on China's colonial relations with Uyghurs, the Chinese policymakers flipped the colonial rhetoric and stated that China has a moral role in the protection of its Uyghur population—of which China is often accused as a colonizer—against the rise of ISIS terrorism in the Syrian crisis.

As we saw earlier in this chapter, the ruthless actions of ISIS terrorists in Syria shocked the moral conscience of the world. Since the 1990s, however, PRC treated the "three evil forces" of terrorism, separatism, and extremism as a moral problem for the Chinese state.[96] With at least seven terrorist attacks and two riots in Xinjiang in 2013, the Xi Jinping administration relied on a new strategic plan (*zhanlue bushu*) that culminated in a Strike Hard Against Violent Terrorist Activity campaign in 2014.[97] At this time, ISIS leader Abu Bakr al-Baghdadi vowed revenge against China because of its treatment of Muslims in the state.[98] China's countershaming used the antiterrorism principle in the Syrian crisis. As Foreign Minister Wang Yi put it, "China has also suffered at the hands of terrorism. The 'Eastern Turkestan Islamic Movement' is a clear and present threat to our security. We would like to work with other countries in the spirit of mutual respect and equal-footed cooperation to jointly address the new threats and new challenges brought by terrorism."[99]

Such a concern was not unfounded: Israeli intelligence estimated in 2017 that there were three thousand Uyghur fighters in Syria who might return to China and threaten its internal security.[100] Through countershaming rhetoric, China called for an alternative resolution (S/2019/757) to tackle the problem of terrorism in Syria comprehensively, but it failed to elicit support from P3 states. But it deepened China's involvement in the proxy war in Syria and in an increasingly repressive counterterrorism campaign in Xinjiang.[101]

Flipping anticolonial rhetoric through countershaming enabled China to pursue imperial projects in the name of counterterrorism to defend its interests against terror attacks. The objective of such rhetorical moves was to secure endorsements among some audiences from the Middle East and the Global South on China's concerns against Islamic radicalism in the Syrian crisis. As we saw above, China's success in securing Saudi Arabia's support for its treatment of Muslims in Xinjiang is a case in point. Thus, PRC's permanent representative for the UN, Zhang Jun, boldly admonished the United States for politicizing humanitarian issues and accused the United States of the "crime it has committed in Syria."[102]

DEFENDING MORAL PLURALISM

China deployed its rhetoric against P3 states to defend moral pluralism in managing the Syrian crisis. It endorsed a diplomatic middle ground through mediation and accommodation and suggested reconciliation of opposing factions as the path forward to resolving the crisis. In the 2014 Geneva Conference, Beijing argued that Syrian actors must learn from the experiences of other countries in resolving internal conflict and find a "middle way" in keeping with Syria's domestic conditions and the interests of different parties. Such rhetorical suggestions came from its anti-imperial repertoire focused on autonomy and opposed to externally imposed political solutions.[103] In the Syrian crisis, the PRC accused the international community, particularly the P3 states, of seeking to impose one-size-fits-all solutions on other states. Building on its rhetorical repertoire, Beijing strategically positioned itself as a paragon of pluralism. China's UN diplomat, Li Baodong, unequivocally stated that China's policy focused on nonviolent ways of addressing the humanitarian crisis, but many countries who could not see the importance of pluralism "refused to heed the calls for further consultation made by China" and remained steadfast on military interventions "in complete disregard of the possible consequence."[104]

Chinese political actors stepped up their game by claiming that "China has never exercised its veto other than to check the instinct of war and resist power politics."[105] The Xi Jinping administration invited the Syrian government and the opposition for peace discussions in Beijing, appointed Xie Xiaoyan as its first special envoy for Syria in 2016, and provided personnel training and humanitarian aid to the al-Assad regime.[106] The Syrian regime retook large swaths of lost territories in the civil war, and in August 2016, Rear Admiral Guan Youfei from the People's Liberation Army met Syrian officials and "promised increased military aid and training for government forces."[107] China's rhetorical engagement in the Syrian crisis was the way to advance its geopolitical engagement outside its Asian region since the end of the Cold War.

Here again, China's political actors made two creative innovations to its anti-imperial and anticolonial rhetoric to manage international order. First, Beijing emphasized dialogue among multiple groups and, in contrast to the P3 states, it showed that the concerns of every party, including rebels and opposition groups, must be balanced to accommodate each other. By taking such a moral high ground on the crisis, China claimed to be attentive to legitimate factional struggles and not the interests of any single party. Li Baodong stated that the draft resolution put forth by the United States, the United Kingdom, and France, along with others, which gave the Syrian regime ten days to stop the use of heavy weapons or face sanctions, was one-sided and unfair.[108] In China's political rhetoric, thus the draft resolution must be rejected because of "its unbalanced content [that] seeks to put pressure on only one party [the Assad regime]."[109]

If pluralism is a priority, then all parties must come to the negotiating table, which became a constant counterclaim in China's appeal to "all parties" in the Geneva communique for dialogue and negotiations, in the ICC referral to respect international humanitarian law, in ceasefire debates, and in the postconflict reconstruction process. As Foreign Minister Wang Yi put it, implicitly referencing the United States, "Some countries follow a pragmatist or a double-standard approach to international law, using whatever that suits their interests and abandoning whatever that does not."[110] But he argued that China is principled and objective. Such affective performances were central to communicate the PRC's responsible engagement in world politics to the domestic audience as its long-understood position of a kingly way (*wang dao*) or rule by virtue rather than tyrant way (*ba dao*) or rule by force.[111]

Foreign policymakers from the PRC improvised on anticolonial rhetoric and flipped it to emphasize the role of regional actors in shaping regional order. Such rhetoric allowed Chinese actors to call for moral pluralism in the sense that each region has a different order, and thus the only overarching criterion to manage international order must be the UN Charter that respects the principles of sovereignty. As Foreign Minister Wang Yi put it, "Regional order should be shaped by countries in the region on the basis of the UN Charter and in light of the circumstances on the ground and the needs of the people there."[112] Such rhetoric also allowed Chinese political actors to reinforce their ideas on the "Asian way" in the management of the Asian order, dilute the U.S. influence in its Asian region, and admonish the United States for interfering in areas outside its own region. With such innovations in its anti-imperial rhetorical repertoire, China's policymakers shrewdly framed China as a responsible actor that prioritized agency among the Middle Eastern states.

Yet the tension was that most regional actors in the Middle East sought to shape the regional order by removing Assad from power. As we saw above, many Middle East countries were critical of the Assad regime. China's rhetoric on pluralism enabled its leaders to reprimand the League of Arab States (LAS) for not following the unanimity principle and blindly following Western lines in Syria on regime change. As Courtney Fung's interview with officials from the Chinese mission shows, "Chinese officials were able to dismiss the LAS's stance [on sanctions] as a guide or standard for Chinese action, as the rules and procedures have all been disregarded (by the League) . . . they don't follow their own (rules)."[113] Through such rhetorical politics, China positioned itself as a responsible actor in the management of global order to its domestic audiences. Foreign Minister Wang Yi claimed, "We have taken an active part in seeking solutions to issues as diverse as Afghanistan, the Iranian nuclear issue, Syria and South Sudan and worked with other countries to tackle global challenges such as terrorism, climate change, cyber security, and refugees. By so doing, China has demonstrated its sense of responsibility as a major country."[114] The strategy of using anti-imperial rhetoric to reprimand regional groups such as the LAS and pronouncing a victory in its negotiations to its domestic audience is an innovation in China's repertoire of power politics.

RHETORICAL POWER POLITICS UNDER HIERARCHY VERSUS ALTERNATIVE EXPLANATIONS

Despite China and Russia's concerted efforts to save the Assad regime, it succumbed to overwhelming internal and external pressures, collapsing on December 8, 2024. China's power politics in the Syrian crisis between 2011 and 2020 augmented its rivalry with the West in general and the United States in particular. Many view China's assertiveness in general as a consequence of its increasing military and economic capabilities. Or as a product of the CCP maintaining its domestic legitimacy.[115] To be sure, China has witnessed impressive growth in its economic and military capabilities and the CCP plays an important role in ensuring economic growth and prosperity to maintain its domestic legitimacy. However, such realist explanations treat rhetoric as a cover for China's ambitions rather than treating rhetoric itself as power politics.

It is unclear if Chinese political actors pursued power politics challenged the United States in the peak of the Syrian crisis (2011–2020) purely because of their perception of the relative decline of the United States.[116] Alistair Johnston says that "there is no evidence that the core decision-making [sic] group on foreign policy in this period—Hu Jintao, Xi Jinping, and Dai Bingguo—accepted the claim that a major shift in the distribution of power had occurred or had given China new opportunities to push its interests."[117] The same observation applies to the Xi Jinping administration, which did not treat the Syrian crisis as an opportunity because of the relative decline of the United States. Instead, political actors adapted familiar anti-imperial and anticolonial scripts to achieve their objectives. In 2014, Barack Obama asserted that the United States would lead the world in the next century and "if the US does not, then nobody will." It was also a claim against China's incompetence in international ordering.[118] Obama's comment created a backlash among Chinese political actors who deployed their rhetoric that "America retains its Cold War mentality for hegemony."[119] The West's insistence on China's incompetence created an imperative for the CCP to demonstrate competence. The Xi Jinping administration pushed its anti-imperial rhetoric to pry open the contradictions of the system.

It would be tempting to see China's partnership with Russia to safeguard the Assad regime as a case of autocratic countries blindly cooperating against the liberal-democratic West. From a liberal position, China's intransigence against military intervention might seem like an attempt to stymie humanitarian progress or plainly a spoiler game.[120] There is no doubt that between 2011 and 2020, China played a spoiler game. Its systematic and multiple vetoes on the same crisis mark a "significant change" from a carefully calibrated opposition or abstention to intervention in other cases of mass atrocity crimes such as in Rwanda, Srebrenica, or Darfur.[121] However, accounts that articulate authoritarian solidarity to explain China's politics in the Syrian crisis are problematic. They conflate China's realpolitik choice to associate with Russia to amplify its voice in the international system with the view that China lacks political judgment in managing the international order. Such silencing is precisely why rhetorical power politics became a mainstay of China's conduct in international politics.

Explanations focusing on China's image and reputational concerns do not go far enough to understand its repertoire of power politics. Catherine Gegout and Shogo Suzuki, for example, argue that China aims to uphold its image as a responsible power. "In the case of Syria, China's stance can be seen to be related to important questions of what policies should be adopted by the international community to solve a humanitarian crisis, rather than simply opposing the West to prove its 'assertiveness.' The Chinese have not necessarily merely offered critiques of the current arrangements, but also have suggested a number of proposals to overcome these shortcomings."[122] As we saw above, however, all proposals to overcome the problems in the governance of humanitarian crises abroad involved policymakers working with deep-rooted power political repertoires to shape global governance and the innovations in anti-imperial and anticolonial rhetoric through which Chinese political actors suggested changes. Chinese policymakers claim to portray the state as a "responsible power" is itself a rhetorical strategy in relation to the United States.

As we saw in this chapter, China's rhetorical strategies aimed to show its principled positions toward sovereignty and territorial integrity alone. Against the backdrop of disastrous military interventions in Iraq, Afghanistan, Libya, and other countries, holding the West accountable has become part of China's power politics. But China's rhetorical strategy in the Syrian crisis did not rely on merely articulating the content of international law or legitimating principles and norms of the system. Political actors exploited the contradictions in the liberal international system. They flipped anti-imperial and anticolonial scripts and adapted its rhetorical repertoire that the country learned from past engagements against the West.

Political rhetoric under the hierarchy of international politics is a creative project in which actors constantly work to change the hierarchy of audiences. In the Syrian crisis, China's power politics functioned only in relation to how other audiences assessed and evaluated the situation and placed an emphasis on a *moral* solution for which regime change or humanitarian military intervention seemed necessary. The point of the Chinese experiment was to enter this moral conversation, use its learned anti-imperial and anticolonial rhetorical repertoire, and assert its role in the management of international order. China's power politics in Syria does *not* represent a dramatic shift in its engagement with questions of international order as an inevitable consequence of balancing in the anarchical system; it is a continuation of its colonial scripts and rhetorical repertoires.[123]

TAKING CHINA'S RHETORICAL POWER SERIOUSLY IN THE LIBERAL INTERNATIONAL ORDER

The hierarchical international system has an established practice of silencing the international ordering claims and counterclaims of political actors from Asia, Africa, and Latin America. Under these power hierarchies, rhetoric is a fundamental instrument of statecraft that enables the silenced to be heard. In this sense, rhetoric is a weapon of the weak and a product of the pressures of the modern international system forged in Western imperialism and colonialism. The conceptual framework of this book shows, however, that shrewd political actors develop a rhetorical repertoire in statecraft. They flip standard rhetorical engagement on its head by paying serious attention to the contradictions in the legitimating principles, norms, and rules of the international system. Rhetorical power politics of political actors from the lower rungs of the hierarchical system accumulate learned lessons from past struggles but use and exploit the stratified social system and its constraints to achieve their strategic objectives. This chapter put this conceptual framework to work by looking at China's power politics in the Syrian crisis between 2011 and 2020.

Political actors from the Xi Jinping administration faced the silencing pressures of the hierarchical international system throughout the Syrian crisis. To push back, they activated their rhetorical repertoire by looking back to anticolonial and anti-imperial scripts and systematically innovated their rhetoric against the opposition. The chapter showed that, by flipping colonial scripts, Chinese political actors deployed their rhetoric to question the sincerity of the West, engaged in countershaming, and argued for moral pluralism for managing the Syrian crisis. It was realpolitik but done through the constraints of power hierarchies to establish competence in international ordering. For a brief but consequential time, Chinese policymakers were central in saving Bashar al-Assad's regime from collapse. China's rhetorical choices in the process—despite mass atrocities in the state—can therefore be understood as power politics meant to demonstrate Beijing's competency in managing international order. As we will see in the next chapter, such games were short-lived in the hierarchical international system.

6

RHETORICAL POWERS, FLIPPED SCRIPTS,
AND GLOBAL DISORDER

This book aims to study the rhetorical power politics of states in hierarchical international politics. Rhetoric is an instrumental use of language and argument by policymakers with emotions and affective performances to persuade audiences, articulate symbolic connections, or coerce audiences into submission to a political project. It is an art of persuasion, as Aristotle showed: a "counterpart of dialectic" that actors often use to "conduct investigations and to furnish explanations, both to defend and to prosecute [emphasis deleted from the original]."[1] Along these lines, Bryan Garsten argues, "The moment in which politicians face citizens' everyday opinions, the rhetorical moment, cannot be avoided in democratic politics."[2] In the world of international politics, there is a frequent misunderstanding of rhetoric as empty and cheap. However, if one looks into the dynamics of rhetoric and not beyond it then rhetoric is power politics.

The fundamental reality of hierarchy in international politics affects the rhetorical force that policymakers bring to bear in their attempts to change the world. Against the history of Western empire, imperialism, and colonialism, rhetoric was a weapon of the weak for non-European states. In this book, I have argued that rhetoric belongs to a venerable tradition of practicing politics to be heard under oppressive conditions of silencing. There are different variants of rhetorical deployments in world politics. My focus on anti-imperial and anticolonial rhetoric showed that it allowed policymakers from Asia, Africa, and Latin America to challenge many exclusionary practices in international ordering.

For ambitious states in lower rungs of hierarchy, this rhetorical strategy also became part of their statecraft as a repertoire, which is a set of routines learned, shared, and acted out as products of struggle.[3] One of the central rhetorical repertoires of power politics is to expose and exploit the contradictions in the legitimating principles, norms, and rules of the international system. These repertoires allowed non-Western policymakers to maneuver within the hierarchy to achieve political objectives. Many of these policymakers also learned to flip the anti-imperial and anticolonial scripts and frequently put their rhetorical repertoire to creative use when pursuing power. Such rhetorical power politics is very much alive today and continues to define geopolitical problems. Before presenting a detailed critique of such power politics, it is useful to see the broad spectrum of this repertoire.

On October 2, 2019, the sun was rising over Raj Ghat, the memorial to Mahatma Gandhi, in New Delhi. Indian prime minister Narendra Modi was there to pay homage to the 150th anniversary of Gandhi's birth. Modi's rhetoric often mentions India's duty and belonging to humanity, and he repeatedly asserts that Indian civilization figured these things out three thousand years ago.[4] On that day in October, he cleverly used Gandhi's idea that "it is impossible for one to be internationalist without being a nationalist."[5] On that day, the sun was setting over the Sabarmati Ashram in Ahmedabad, which had once been the site of Gandhi's residence and has now become one of the temples of the anti-imperial mass movement in India. Calling for collective mobilization for a New India, Modi roared, "People mobilized for Satyagraha (non-violent anti-imperial resistance) on Mahatma Gandhi's call," and now people must "do the same to bring about a mass movement for Swachhagraha (Clean India)."[6]

Modi's return to anti-imperial and anticolonial rhetoric using Mahatma Gandhi's thought is a familiar strategy that works within the established repertoire of power politics. He is not the first to engage in such innovations. Jawaharlal Nehru, a charismatic leader in the Indian independence movement and later India's first prime minister, made exactly the same remarks in the meeting of the League Against Imperialism (LAI) in 1927. Nehru asserted, "The Indian National Congress is necessarily national and has nationalism as its basis, but as our great leader Gandhi has said, our nationalism is based on the most intense internationalism."[7] Both Nehru and Modi were working within an intricate repertoire of anti-imperial and anticolonial rhetoric. Both cleverly flipped the repertoire in their own way to exercise a distinct form of power politics. However, there is a danger in Modi's return to familiar rhetorical scripts for rising India when the world is heading toward geopolitical peril from forever wars, predatory capitalism, ideological polarization, climate change, economic inequalities, food insecurity, injustice for religious minorities, challenges to LGBTQIA+ rights, disinformation, and the rise of artificial intelligence (AI). Familiar anti-imperial and anticolonial rhetorical scripts are state-centric, focused on elite-led statecraft and narrowly defined national interests, and in today's world of transnational challenges and weaponized interdependence, such rhetoric is also out of place.

Nevertheless, several political actors resort to this form of rhetorical power politics. As we saw in the introduction to this book, the shrewd anti-imperial rhetoric against liberal internationalism is very much part of the arguments from the newly elected administration of Donald Trump in 2024. In a masterclass of rhetorical power, the Trump administration has cleverly flipped the antiestablishment, anti-imperial, and antielite scripts in the United States and has created the most polarized form of domestic politics against all opponents—veering straight into fascism—and is pursuing the most aggressive form of foreign policy in the form of continuous wars, aggression, and geoeconomics in the form of tariffs.

More than anything, such rhetorical politics is also evident among diverse state policymakers who have flipped anti-imperial and anticolonial rhetoric in recent years. Since 2014, Russia's Vladimir Putin has explicitly used anti-imperial rhetoric to wage war against Ukraine, and his anticolonial rhetoric in 2022 has secured a significant following from the Global South. In 2003 and 2012, Brazilian president Luis Inácio Lula da Silva (Lula) engaged in anti-imperial rhetoric. He headed to Mozambique and other African countries to secure mineral resources for an exploitative Brazilian-based transnational mining corporation, Vale, all in the name of South-South solidarity.[8] China's "wolf warriors" engage in anti-imperial and anticolonial rhetoric against the West. The European Union led by President Ursula von der Leyen called for "self-reliant Europe in the face of 'imperial ambitions,'" pointing to Russia's invasion of Ukraine. The EU also made a deal for obtaining critical minerals from Rwanda which many critics have accused as part of a new "inter-imperial competition" to acquire resources from Africa to fuel the AI revolution in Europe. Also from Azerbaijan to Hungary, Venezuela, Iran, and North Korea, but also Sri Lanka, Cambodia, and Myanmar, policymakers worldwide resort to anti-imperial and anticolonial rhetoric in international politics.[9]

Some of our academic and media pundits recognize the problems of flipped scripts in such rhetorical politics. Matthew Duss, executive vice president at the Center for International Policy, wrote, "Calling Trump an anti-imperialist is nonsense. The anti-war left shouldn't fall for this dishonest pitch."[10] William Robinson, a leading professor of transnational capitalism and an activist, writes that the "self-declared anti-imperialist left deploys its rhetoric and clings to a singular view of the U.S. empire and defends repressive, authoritarian and dictatorial states simply because these states face hostility from Washington." He rightly calls attention instead to the "politics of capitalist exploitation and social control around the world [that is] fundamentally shaped by the contradictions between a globally-integrated economy and a nation-state-based system of political domination."[11]

Before discussing an anticapitalist critique, we must also recognize that anti-imperial rhetoric is also the mainstay of conservative and right-wing radical members to spread hate in international politics. Anti-anti-imperialism and anti-anticolonialism in the West glorify British or U.S. imperialism as a force for good in the world. Such rhetoric from radical groups in the United States offers the lever for cultural subversion and rejection of diversity. Many conservative British academics and politicians call for rehabilitating British colonialism as a cause for admiration and pride.[12] To be sure, "anti-imperial imperialism" is not new in the United States.[13] But the calls to Make America Great Again look back to the imperial days of American power that rested on white supremacy, proselytizing Christian identity, gender-critical feminism, and exclusion and disenfranchisement of the "unfit." In this logic, any critique of Israel's settler-colonialism and brutal killings in Gaza is also deemed unacceptable. Rhetoric using imperial and colonial scripts is a double-edged sword and will unfortunately remain central in our world.

Critically examining rhetorical power politics enables us to understand the nature of deeper transformations in the ordering dynamics of our world. Rhetoric about the imperial roots of the liberal international order was the mainstay of non-European states in hierarchical international politics. Their affective performances, as this book has showed, were a product of the silencing practices of centuries of international ordering that excluded members on the lower rungs of hierarchy. Today, anti-imperial rhetoric is part of both progressive and conservative foreign and security policy. And the rhetorical power politics of elites that borrows from the playbooks of underdogs is certainly new. The lessons from the non-Western world can perhaps help us understand the nature of global disorder. Thus, the theoretical approach developed here is not limited to the so-called non-Western world. Grasping the changing dynamics of rhetorical power politics under hierarchy has implications for understanding global order.

In the remainder of this chapter, I will first summarize the central theoretical arguments and empirical findings offered in this book. Then I will take up two implications of my argument. First, focusing on repertoires of power struggles under international hierarchy offers a way to rethink some established international relations (IR) theories on power. Second, I will present implications for studying the dynamics of global disorder, especially when rhetoric slips into demagoguery and progressives aim to hold conservative projects accountable. The core problem of rhetorical repertoire in statecraft is its contribution to global disorder. At the same time, continuous silencing thrives in the hierarchy structured by the liberal international order. The coming changes in world politics are in the form of U.S.-China competition, regional reordering and disordering starting with Europe and the Middle East, radicalization and polarization of society fed by social media, and public and private demand for critical minerals from both Africa and Latin America, to mention just a few. These systemwide changes have imperial, expansionist, and colonial undertones, which are perilous. For this reason, one must recognize rhetorical power politics and urgently address its problems.

SUMMARY AND FINDINGS

Hierarchy is a fundamental feature of international politics. Throughout the history of the Western empire, imperialism, and colonialism—supported by industrial modernity from the late eighteenth century onward—the hierarchical world became more unequal, unjust, and humiliating for underdogs. Modern international order was created and maintained by the West, even when there were several non-European contributions and labor of Asia, Africa, and Latin American actors. The West played a key role in the formal ordering moments in the form of the Concert of Europe after the Napoleonic Wars, the League of Nations after World War I, and the United Nations after World War II, as well as multiple informal and unwritten practices. All these ordering dynamics established and refined the legitimating principles, rules, and norms used to govern the world. But it also reproduced the material and ideational inequalities between the West and the rest. In all ordering practices, non-Europeans were effectively prevented from having a voice in so-called high politics, the arena of diplomacy, security, war, and peace. All ordering practices have long-term structural effects. In this book, I have argued that a fundamental structural dynamic in international politics arising from two centuries of West-led world-ordering practices was epistemic violence, which refers to the practice of silencing speakers because they belong to a group perceived as unworthy of a hearing. In other words, non-Europeans were considered incompetent in the high politics of managing international order. Such a hierarchical world continues today.

This book theorized that attributing incompetence and thus silencing non-Europeans in international ordering rested on three practices. It involved Western policymakers asking non-Europeans, first, if they had the material capabilities to manage international or regional orders; second, if non-Europeans had the authority, and, third, if they could exercise objective judgment in managing order. As I explained in chapter 1, the rhetorical force of attributing incompetence in this way meant that no matter how policymakers on the lower rungs of the hierarchy demonstrated that they held the requisite capabilities, authority, and judgment, their responses ended up reinforcing their incompetence in managing the international order. The curse is that the more these non-Europeans communicated their competence, the more their behavior supported Western judgments of their incompetence, which involved silencing to preserve order. Deep structures such as epistemic violence that form the background of international political life rest on intentional and unintentional agential activities, from deciding who is a penholder in the UN to addressing humanitarian crises, to everyday diplomatic activities such as the assessment of testimony of actors from Asia, Africa, and Latin America.

Despite the pernicious features of hierarchical international politics, non-Western agents were not always silent victims or spectators. They challenged, stood up, resisted, and fought back. Rhetoric is a weapon of the weak, and actors' emotional rhetorical performances were designed, as the historian Christopher Bayly puts it, "to subvert the contemporary self-confidence of colonial elites by emphasizing their moral failure as colonial rulers and the degeneracy of British and European domestic society."[14]

As I have aimed to theorize in this book, anti-imperial and anticolonial rhetoric became part of the non-Western foreign and security policy repertoire in international politics: a reliable tool kit in statecraft.[15] A rhetorical repertoire is not a static inventory but rather an expansive and dynamic set of practices that actors adapt over years of struggle. The book argued that rhetorical repertoire has involved exposing and exploiting the contradictions in the legitimating principles and norms of the international system. The rhetorical repertoire of power politics aims to pry open the order to achieve political objectives. For non-European policymakers, the anti-imperial and anticolonial rhetorical repertoire resonated with their community of policymakers and broke the barriers of silencing. In this sense, anti-imperialism and anticolonialism were creative performances in international politics—like jazz musicians who know the song and, most important, know how to riff on it.

Chapter 2 demonstrated the historical development of this rhetorical repertoire in India, Brazil, and China, where policymakers systematically learned and built a tool kit of statecraft to exploit the contradictions of the modern international system. Chapter 3 examined the rhetorical performances of Indira Gandhi's administration in India during the East Pakistan crisis of 1971. It showed how the administration used anti-imperial rhetoric to create a wedge between audiences to achieve its objective of resettling Bengali refugees and also cutting its archenemy Pakistan down to size. Chapter 4 looked at Lula's administration in Brazil and the Haitian crisis of 2004. It showed how the Lula administration used rhetoric to signal inclusivity among regional audiences by incorporating anti-Yankee and anticolonial scripts and engaged in a humanitarian military intervention in Haiti. Chapter 5 studied the rhetoric of Xi Jinping's administration in China during the Syrian crisis between 2011 and 2020. It showed how

Xi Jinping used anti-imperial rhetoric to defend ruthlessly the principles of sovereignty, nonintervention, and territorial integrity in the crisis to confront the West and hedge its role in international ordering.

All these policymakers saw opportunity in crisis, returned to their rhetorical repertoire, and flipped their anti-imperial rhetorical repertoire to change the course of regional and international ordering. They exploited the contradictions in the legitimating principles, norms, and rules of the international system in their rhetorical performances in the interests of pursuing power. The performative posturing and emotional ways of engaging with and against interlocutors were not merely add-ons to their conduct. They formed their power politics.

In each of the cases studied here, the ruthless power politics of Indian, Brazilian, and Chinese policymakers under the hierarchy worked around or bypassed silencing practices. Power politics is vile, and it is more so when it comes from actors conventionally understood as "incompetent" in international ordering. This ruthlessness is not accidental or fluid and contingent. On the contrary, leaders worked within the structural constraints of hierarchy that "made" each of the crises in one way rather than another, and subsequently, through exploiting anti-imperial and anticolonial rhetoric, the policymakers in India, Brazil, and China remade their situation in novel ways. The framework here joins many others that have focused on structured agency: "Leaders are important, but they do not operate in a world of their own making."[16] As Karl Marx memorably put it: "Men make their own history, but they do not make it just as they please; they do not make it under circumstances chosen by themselves, but under circumstances directly encountered, given and transmitted from the past."[17]

IMPLICATIONS FOR IR THEORY

When policymakers deploy anti-imperial and anticolonial rhetoric, analysts often dismiss it as a crude form of anti-Western and anti-American policy and diagnose the problem from a normative assessment of saving "the West." Many others take anti-imperial and anticolonial rhetoric seriously and suggest ways to pursue progressive politics.[18] Focusing on progressive politics is important. In keeping with these views, it is also important to focus on rhetorical power politics in the context of enduring silencing practices in the international hierarchy, without which progressive politics cannot be realized. This means we cannot relegate rhetoric as a product of left- or right-wing populism and then equate it with authoritarianism, even fascism.[19] Populism is only a convenient shortcut to avoid explaining far more deeply intricate power political moves in flipping anti-imperial rhetoric.

The brief but consequential period of Western imperialism and colonialism and its continuing legacy remain tangential to most IR scholarship on international order.[20] This is because a significant portion of Anglo-American IR scholarship and its European counterparts want to theorize from the experience of Great Power diplomacy in Europe and the United States, ignoring its connection to imperial expansion. One cannot theorize about the world from European-American experience alone when the West was tightly interconnected with "the history of colonial and imperial expansion."[21]

More than anything, ignoring the interconnected world produces grand theories that reproduce a parochial worldview. And Daniel Levine, IR theorist, argues that the scholarly theoretical idiom of IR borrowed from ideas that created catastrophe and is now expected to avert catastrophe: "Realism had ties to realpolitik nationalism and hypernationalism; laissez-faire liberalism had ties to social upheaval at home and imperialism abroad; and the humanism of early Marxist thought did not undo its complicity, even as a perversion of itself, in the terrors of Stalin."[22] He suggests "sustainable critique" as a scholarly ethos to check partisan agenda and ideological assumptions in any theoretical enterprise in international studies. Despite such pleas, our IR scholarship remains Anglo-American and Eurocentric. It treats Asia, Africa, and Latin America as laboratories for testing theories formulated with historical amnesia about imperialism and colonialism. Our IR theories are increasingly unhelpful for understanding the proliferation of anti-imperial and anticolonial rhetoric across the political spectrum or for making sense of the power dynamics in these language games in the hierarchical system.

However, we must not commit to the view of postcolonial victimhood in the study of the geopolitics of our world. To be sure, in the hierarchical international system, many people suffer from the politics of exploitation, resource extraction, and control. Many Indigenous people fail to secure recognition of their rights and liberties. However, the skilled repertoire in the power politics of many ambitious postcolonial states challenges the international order in the pursuit of their own imperial projects. Our postcolonial IR scholarship too often ignores this power politics from below. It treats postcolonial states as subaltern victims of empire and imperialism whose only option is to embrace "bare-life," biological life stripped of political character.[23]

The conceptual framework offered here for studying the dynamics of power politics offers a useful corrective. It brings together the siloed conversations on realpolitik, the construction of social reality through argumentation and discourse, and postcolonial sensibilities on the hierarchical international system in one thread. It prioritizes connections, arrangements, networks and ties, and the different repertoires of power politics among actors who are positioned differently in the hierarchical international system.[24]

Through case studies, I showed that multiple audiences have come together and created different arrangements within the hierarchy to turn a crisis into an opportunity. In the East Pakistan crisis, the network that audiences formed was dog-eat-dog instrumentalism in the Cold War ideological clash between the two superpowers. In contrast, in the Haitian crisis, the arrangement of audiences created a different game that prioritized conventions and institutional rule structures of the UN. Many Western audiences were appalled by the Syrian crisis, and the network they formed focused on the morality and ethics of intervening against a mass atrocity. We cannot offer a covering law to show how audiences come together in various ways or predict how different audiences authoritatively fix the type of international norms necessary to deal with a practical problem. Yet the rhetorical power of political actors and their performative posturing remains attentive to this attitude and the ensuing arrangement of audiences, and cuts across these dynamics that can also be violent and exclusionary. The repertoire of power politics of Indian, Brazilian, and Chinese political actors worked within these audience networks to achieve their political objectives.

In other words, norms and rules are not "good things," and power is not a "bad thing" that must be kept separate. Instead, norms are constitutive of making a move in the language game through clusters of normative attitudes and appraisals of interlocutors who then work with and against the field of what is possible. However, IR's reigning "efficient causality" view establishes cause and effect antecedently and independently of each other.[25] It does not appreciate these constitutive connections between appraisals of audiences and the exercise of power in hierarchy.[26]

The conceptualization offered in this book can create a useful conversation about the dynamics of international ordering beyond mainstream theories such as realism or liberal-constructivism. Chapter 1 offered detailed analysis of my conceptual argument. The analysis does not require repetition here. Thus, I will focus on the implication of my framework for two new advancements in IR scholarship: ontological security studies and new materialism.

Ontological security studies refer to "security as being."[27] Subjects fend off the anxiety that affects the security and stability of the self through routines, rituals, identification patterns, or through mobilization of emotions such as anger or shame. Others with debilitating anxiety suffer from ontological insecurity. Within this school of thought, IR scholars have recently turned to existentialist philosophy and discuss the importance of authenticity of the self to address anxiety. Authenticity allows subjects to exercise choice through integrity. To put it boldly, this focus on existentialist philosophy relies on the view that "subjectivity is the truth," as Søren Kierkegaard puts it in terms of singular authenticity.[28]

Such a view is at odds with life in the sociopolitical world, however, where interlocutors must engage in pluralistic ways by keeping track of each other. Ontological security scholars recognize the problem. As Bahar Rumelili, the foremost scholar on ontological security studies, puts it, "Yet, while pointing to the potential, existentialism, as a normative theory on meaningful and authentic existence, does not explain the conditions under which this radical agency materializes."[29] From the rhetorical repertoire of power politics perspective, we can zoom in on rhetoric as a cause and consequence of anxiety without subjectivizing and psychologizing the phenomenon. It also then steps outside the view that ontologically insecure actors are stigmatized actors unable to exercise agency in international politics. A focus on rhetorical repertoire allows us to see how authenticity itself is a rhetorical performance for exercising power by weaponizing anxiety.

Some advancements in "new materialism" in the assemblage scholarship argue that humans are not the only agents with intentionality and purpose.[30] An agency can be found in machines, artifacts, and networks that humans have created. Using assemblage as a concept, many IR scholars focus on how heterogeneous material and symbolic elements "come together and are made to cohere and hence form a distinct type of order."[31] This approach has been useful in allowing us to decenter and dethrone humanistic ideas of self, agent, and subject that seem ill suited for addressing collective challenges like anthropogenic climate change.

However, we cannot simply focus on how heterogenous things cohere to form an assemblage and ignore the central import of social hierarchy and exclusion in the enterprise. From the perspective of epistemic violence in Western imperialism and the imperial practices of attributing incompetence offered in this book, it is racial and gendered silencing that has decentered some humans in the imperial context. An assemblage's perspective that sidesteps the ethical problem of silencing by further decentering humans and thus the possibilities of political critique could benefit from the rhetorical power struggle conceptualization offered here. The anti-imperial and anticolonial rhetorical repertoire of political actors seems to revert old statist habits and fails to see new materiality like climate change or AI. The sociology of association that treats the materiality of climate change as something that defies mediation or something that is not amenable to mediation ignores the voices and worldviews from alternative cosmologies, including the ideas of mediation from Indigenous thinkers who face the problem on a different scale. As Arjun Appadurai rightly asks, "If the only sociology left is the sociology of association, then will the only guilt left be guilt by association?"[32]

The implication is that this book allows an opening to investigate and change the core concepts of IR using evidence from the non-Western world. However, the book cautions against treating the behavior of non-Western actors as paralyzed subjects that arise from their ontological insecurity and against theories that reject the normativity inherent in their status as incompetent actors. If we know the patterns of their realpolitik, concerned academics could offer a grounded criticism of their foreign and security policy behavior instead of ideological critiques from the left or the liberal perspective.

RHETORICAL POWERS AND
IMPLICATIONS IN PRACTICE

This book started with the anti-imperial and anticolonial rhetoric of policymakers from India, Brazil, and China in the Russian invasion of Ukraine in 2022. The *Financial Times* called such performances "the hour of the global south."[33] This assessment is not surprising, but it ignores the deep-rooted rhetorical repertoire that is part of the tool kit of these states and the innovation that policymakers brought to bear to pursue power. I submit that such innovations to the anti-imperial and anticolonial scripts are ill suited for addressing today's political, economic, justice, and climate crises.

Although the cases in the book showed the awesome working of rhetorical power politics, these were also violent enterprises by hubristic governments led by Indira Gandhi, Lula da Silva, and Xi Jinping. The creative processes in their rhetorical campaigns certainly secured strategic successes and put the imperialist West in its place. They cut across the assessment of incompetence through innovation, practical judgment, and skillful maneuvering. Yet their power politics did not create a plural world. It did not undermine the imperial powers or persuade them to change their assessments of incompetence. Instead, it restarted the cyclical process of incompetence-competence relations.

In the aftermath of India's power politics, the dismembered nation of Pakistan licked its wounds with a hyper-anti-India stance and strongly aligned itself with China. That India could not drive a wedge in the Sino-Pakistan alliance is a direct consequence of its rhetorical wedging strategy in 1971. In the transactions between India's rhetorical strategy and Western audiences, Indira Gandhi developed a fear of foreign machinations in domestic politics. In a few years, she declared a state of emergency (1975–1977) and undermined democracy at home. Brazil's power politics in an institutionalized environment led to heightened confidence among the military and its peacekeeping contingents. This led to numerous instances of sexual exploitation of women and girls in Haiti.[34] Brazilian peacekeepers replicated operational lessons on pacification in Haiti through systematic killings in the favelas back home.[35] And China's moral rhetoric in the Syrian crisis embraced mass atrocity crimes in the Middle East for geopolitical ends. Yet the objective of China's rhetorical hedging in the Syrian crisis was arguably to advance its Belt and Road Initiative (BRI). The COVID-19 pandemic derailed its grand strategic BRI plans. Instead, its power politics in Syria protected a dictatorial regime. China's actions brought its worst nightmare of a unified alliance of the divided West that was suspicious of the infrastructure and other investments of China in the developing world. The United States made its challenge to China a bipartisan geopolitical goal and reoriented its European allies to balance China. Policymakers from Beijing moved close to Moscow. However, Beijing has been unable to drive a wedge in this Euro-American consensus on "China threat" until today, despite the vagaries of Trump that threaten the traditional Euro-Atlantic relations. Furthermore, on December 8, 2024, the Bashar al-Assad regime collapsed. The fall of the Assad regime in Syria in 2024 showed the limits of China's rhetorical power politics. The Sino-Russian partnership further increased the distrust of China. From this vantage point, the rhetorical power politics of India, Brazil, and China were only small victories that evaporated quickly.

The Russian invasion of Ukraine in 2022 came as a shock to the world. The silencing of the voices and concerns of the Global South by the United States and the United Kingdom in the Ukraine crisis, not the least the rejection of Brazilian or Indian mediation for a ceasefire, repeated similar patterns of the hierarchical ordering of the world. And it led to hubristic leaders in India, Brazil, and China offering their solutions to the war, which divided supporters and opposers of Russia in their domestic societies and led to further polarization and radicalization of actors in the public space. In this way, Modi, Lula, and Xi became part of the larger demagogic discourse. As Patricia Roberts-Miller shows, demagogues take part in the larger demagogic cultural discourse "that promises stability, certainty, and escape from the responsibilities of rhetoric by framing public policy in terms of the degree to which and the means by which (not whether) the out-group should be scapegoated for the current problems of the in-group."[36]

Instead of focusing on the problems of the people, rhetorical power politics that relies on the rough script of anticolonialism and anti-imperialism returns to an outdated form of identity politics and a nation-state-centric model of order management. In the past, struggles against Western empires, the central focus of anti-imperialism and anticolonialism, was to assert an identity as a nation. Today, the problem is the transnational capitalist class—a global elite with a hegemonic fraction of capital on a world scale that is not tethered to territory but has to contend with nation-states as they appropriate resources, exploit people to accumulate capital, and reorder the world.[37] The power of the transnational capitalist class cuts across the South and North. As the leading theorist of this phenomenon, William Robinson, reminds us, the expansion of transnational capital often integrates into national bourgeoisies and into global circuits of accumulation and exploitation. Robinson puts it this way: "A multipolar inter-state system remains part of a brutal, exploitative, global capitalist world in which the BRICS [Brazil, Russia, India, China, and South Africa] capitalists and states are as much committed to control and exploitation of the global working and popular classes as are their Northern counterparts."[38] The rhetorical repertoire of power politics deployed by Modi, Lula, and Xi works within the capitalist order rather than moving beyond it to solve global crises.

RETURN TO NON-WESTERN POWER POLITICS

We need a new power politics that challenges the exploitation of global capitalism. Against the continuous structural burdens of incompetence, non-Western rhetoric is here to stay. The most significant power politics performances that non-Western states could deploy involves resolving their differences. The rhetorical performances of India and China that could fix the territorial tensions between them (even if they cannot resolve all strategic problems at once) rather than augment their differences by giving opportunities to the West to divide them would be the first step toward forging new forms of power politics to tame global capitalism. Brazil's performance, which leverages its sovereignty over the Amazon and forces interlocutors worldwide to immediately change their conservative policies to address the problem of anthropogenic climate change, will similarly require rhetorical power politics. Global South states that deploy rhetoric to address the fundamental structural problem of superordinate states attributing incompetence but without the urge to demonstrate competence is a novel form of power politics. This sometimes requires playing rhetorical power like Mohandas Mahatma Gandhi.[39]

In December 1931, Mohandas Gandhi spent five days in Switzerland to attend a roundtable meeting on the future of colonial India. On the invitation of the Women's International League for Peace and Freedom, he gave two public lectures: one on December 8 at the *Maison du Peuple* in Lausanne and the second on December 10 at Victoria Hall in Geneva.[40] Eminent Romanian poet and philosopher Lucian Blaga was present at the Lausanne lecture. He explained his encounter with Gandhi in the following way:

> Then Gandhi started to speak in such a way that everybody was astonished: it was the concise, unadorned style characteristic only of the spirits who could see the ultimate essence. No gestures used by an orator, no rhetorical modulation of the voice, nothing sought for to captivate the audience, nothing of that unbearable pose of a speaker. . . . Jesus of Nazareth might have had the same tone when he spoke on the Lilies hill about God's heaven. After that, Gandhi reminded us that he had to leave us as he must pray. That was the signal for everybody's departure. Back to Berne, I told Marti: "The feeling cannot be described; to describe it would be a sacrilege. *But be sure that I, who have always despised oratory, have now a real hatred for this shallow art.* This is going to be my thirty years' war [emphasis added]."[41]

Claims made through prophetic language for humanity, such as that deployed by Gandhi, display a form of authenticity through performance.[42] They involve rhetoric against rhetoric, including the appearance of not cultivating appearances, as a form of persuasion.[43] Blaga could not even spot this strategy. Gandhi was not outside the linguistic realm of politics as he was deploying rhetoric and preaching politics outside capitalist modernity. Some remember this when a journalist asked Gandhi what he thought of Western civilization: "I think it would be a good idea."[44] Today, the age of disorder requires this form of Gandhian power politics in international politics.

NOTES

INTRODUCTION

1. Emily Tamkin, "India Is Struck in a New World Disorder," *Foreign Policy*, June 1, 2023.
2. Lauren Frayer, "A Year into the Ukraine War, the World's Biggest Democracy Still Won't Condemn Russia," NPR News, February 20, 2023. See also Ashley Tellis, "'What Is in Our Interest': India and the Ukraine War," *Carnegie Report*, April 25, 2022; Sharinee Jagtiani and Sophia Wellek, "In the Shadow of Ukraine: India's Choices and Challenges," *Survival* 62, no. 3 (2022): 29–48.
3. United Nations Security Council draft resolution S/2022/155, February 25, 2022.
4. See Chirayu Thakkar, "Russia-Ukraine War, India, and US Grand Strategy: Punishing or Leveraging Neutrality," *Policy Studies* 45, no. 3–4 (2024): 595–613.
5. Jan Gellemi, "India's Balancing Act in the Ukraine War: Implications for EU-India Relations," Center for Global Affairs and Strategic Studies, Universidad de Navarra, November 29, 2022, https://www.unav.edu/en/web/global-affairs/india-s-balancing-act-in-the-ukraine-war-implications-for-eu-india-relations.
6. See India's External Affairs Minister's remark at the seventeenth edition of the Bratislava Forum, June 2–4, 2022. See also Associated News Agency (ANI), "Jaishankar's Europe Remark Echoes in German Chancellor's Statement in Munich," *The Hindu*, February 20, 2023.
7. See the press statement by External Affairs Minister Dr. S. Jaishankar during his meeting with Foreign Minister of the Russian Federation Mr. Sergey Lavrov, November 8, 2022, https://www.mea.gov.in/Speeches-Statements.htm?dtl/35864.
8. India under Modi has frequently challenged colonial-era laws, from the education system to legal and criminal justice, to renaming streets and boulevards. See Sanya Dhingra, "How Hindu Nationalists Redefined Decolonization in India," *New Lines Magazine*, August 14, 2023.

9. Stuart Lau and Saim Saeed, "India's Modi Tells Putin: This Is 'Not the Era for War,'" *Politico*, September 16, 2022.

10. See the quote in Associated News Agency (ANI), "Rajnath Singh Reiterates India's Commitment to Freedom of Navigation, Overflight and Unimpeded Lawful Commerce in International Waters," *ANI*, November 16, 2023, https://www.aninews.in/news/world /asia/rajnath-singh-reiterates-indias-commitment-to-freedom-of-navigation-overflight -and-unimpeded-lawful-commerce-in-international-waters20231116125753/.

11. Prime Minister Modi's remarks at the Opening Session of the Voice of Global South Summit 2023, Prime Minister's Office News, January 12, 2023, https://www.pmindia.gov.in/en /news_updates/pms-remarks-at-opening-session-of-voice-of-global-south-summit-2023/.

12. Janiz Lazda, "India's Stance on the Ukraine War Makes Little Sense," *Politico*, October 17, 2022, https://www.politico.eu/article/indias-stance-on-the-ukraine-war-makes-little-sense/.

13. Sumit Ganguly, "India Must Take a Stand on Russia's War in Ukraine," *Foreign Policy*, March 3, 2022, https://foreignpolicy.com/2022/03/03/india-ukraine-russia-war-putin -weapons-un/.

14. See Ramachandra Guha, "How Modi Is Trying to Use Gandhi's Name to Whitewash His Dark Record," *Scroll*, July 18, 2021, https://scroll.in/article/1000459/ramachandra-guha -how-modi-is-trying-to-use-gandhis-name-to-whitewash-his-dark-record. See also Ramachandra Guha, "India Against Gandhi—a Legacy Rewritten," *Financial Times*, January 27, 2023.

15. "Brazil Condemns 'Violation' of Ukraine's Territory Amid Criticism," *Al Jazeera*, April 19, 2023, https://www.aljazeera.com/news/2023/4/19/brazil-condemns-violation-of-ukraines -territory-amid-criticism.

16. Ciara Nugent, "Lula Talks to TIME About Ukraine, Bolsonaro and Brazil's Fragile Democracy," *Time*, May 23–30, 2022, https://time.com/6173232/lula-da-silva-transcript/.

17. See report from *O Globo*, March 2, 2023, https://oglobo.globo.com/mundo/assembleia -geral-da-onu-condena-russia-por-141-votos-so-cinco-contra-brasil-apoia-condenacao -1-25415843.

18. Barney Jopson, Henry Foy, and Bryan Harris, "Lula's Stance on Ukraine War Mars His Iberian Trip," *Financial Times*, April 23, 2023.

19. Nugent, "Lula Talks to TIME About Ukraine."

20. Nugent, "Lula Talks to TIME About Ukraine."

21. "Brazil's Foreign Policy Is Hyperactive, Ambitious, and Naïve," *The Economist*, April 10, 2023, https://www.economist.com/the-americas/2023/04/10/brazils-foreign-policy-is -hyperactive-ambitious-and-naive.

22. See Sean Burges, "How to Stay a Leader Without Followers: Brazil's Foreign Policy Under Lula III," *CEBRI: Brazilian Center for International Relations* 3, no. 9 (January–March 2024): 50, https://cebri.org/revista/en/artigo/136/how-to-stay-a-leader-without-followers -brazils-foreign-policy-under-lula-iii; Felipe Krause, "Explaining Brazil's Stance on the Ukraine War," *Bulletin of Latin American Research*, 2024, https://doi.org/10.1111/blar.13575.

23. Burges, "How to Stay a Leader Without Followers," 50.

24. Gulherme Casarões, "Lula and the World: What to Expect from the New Brazilian Foreign Policy," *The Conversation*, March 31, 2023, https://theconversation.com/lula -and-the-world-what-to-expect-from-the-new-brazilian-foreign-policy-202645.

25. "Joint Statement of the Russian Federation and the People's Republic of China on the International Relations Entering a New Era and the Global Sustainable Development," February 4, 2022, http://www.en.kremlin.ru/supplement/5770.

26. Series of commentaries in *People's Liberation Army* (*PLA*) *Daily* titled "Fanning the Flames, the Initiator of Tension in Ukraine," focused on the United States as the cause of the crisis. Jun Sheng [pen name], "Examining America's Despicable Role on the International Stage Through the Ukraine Crisis," *PLA Daily*, https://www.uscc.gov/research/chinas-position-russias-invasion-ukraine.

27. This is China's position on the Russia-Ukraine War made by President Xi Jinping in a virtual summit with French president Emmanuel Macron and German chancellor Olaf Scholz on March 8, 2022. See Embassy of the People's Republic of China in Jamaica, "Falsehoods Spread by the U.S. on the Ukraine Issue: A Reality Check," *China News*, May 4, 2022, http://jm.china-embassy.gov.cn/eng/zgxw/202205/t20220504_10681527.htm. See also "China Supports Holding Conference on Ukraine with Participation of Moscow, Kiev," *Russian News Agency*, April 9, 2022, https://tass.com/world/1772369.

28. Statements on China's basic position on Ukraine issue made by foreign minister Wang Yi on February 25, 2022, in a phone conversation with UK's foreign secretary Elizabeth Truss, high representative of the European Union for foreign affairs Josep Borrell, and French diplomatic advisor to the president Emmanuel Bonne. See Ministry of Foreign Affairs, People's Republic of China, "Wang Yi Expounds China's Five-Point Position on the Current Ukraine Issue," February 26, 2022, https://www.mfa.gov.cn/eng/wjbzhd/202202/t20220226_10645855.html.

29. See remarks by China's Permanent Representative to the UN Ambassador Zhang Jun at the UN Security Council Briefing on Ukraine, February 17, 2023, https://www.fmprc.gov.cn/mfa_eng/wjb_663304/zwjg_665342/zwbd_665378/202302/t20230223_11030077.html.

30. Ministry of Foreign Affairs, People's Republic of China, "Ma Zhaoxu Attends UN Security Council High-Level Open Debate on Ukraine Issue," September 21, 2023, https://www.fmprc.gov.cn/mfa_eng/xw/wjbxw/202405/t20240530_11343665.html, accessed on June 19, 2025.

31. "Foreign Minister Wang Yi Talks About China's Five-Pronged Perseverance on Ukraine Issue," March 31, 2022, https://www.fmprc.gov.cn/mfa_eng/zxxx_662805/202204/t20220401_10663132.html, accessed on February 26, 2024.

32. Global Engagement Center Special Report, "How the People's Republic of China Seeks to Reshape the Global Information," U.S. Department of State, 2023, page 25, https://www.state.gov/wp-content/uploads/2023/10/HOW-THE-PEOPLES-REPUBLIC-OF-CHINA-SEEKS-TO-RESHAPE-THE-GLOBAL-INFORMATION-ENVIRONMENT_508.pdf.

33. U.S. Department of State Press Releases, "Secretary Antony J. Blinken at a Press Availability," Bali, Indonesia, July 9, 2022, https://www.state.gov/secretary-antony-j-blinken-at-a-press-availability-21/.

34. Quoted in Katherine Walla, "Inside the United States' Plan to Compete with China in the Global South," *New Atlanticist*, February 23, 2024, https://www.atlanticcouncil.org/blogs/new-atlanticist/inside-the-united-states-plan-to-compete-with-china-in-the-global-south/.

35. See, for example, G. John Ikenberry, "Why American Power Endures: The U.S.-Led Liberal Order Isn't in Decline," *Foreign Affairs*, November 1, 2022, https://www.foreignaffairs

.com/united-states/why-american-power-endures-us-led-order-isnt-in-decline-g-john
-ikenberry; Tanja Borzel and Micheal Zurn, "Contestations of the Liberal International
Order: From Liberal Multilateralism to Postnationalism Liberalism," *International
Organization* 75, no. 2 (2021): 282–305; Daniel Deudney, John Ikenberry, and Karoline
Postel-Vinay, eds., *Debating Worlds: Contested Narratives of Global Modernity and World
Order* (Oxford University Press, 2023).

36. Charles Kupchan, *No One's World: The West, The Rising Rest, and the Coming Global
Turn* (Oxford University Press, 2012).

37. Kupchan, *No One's World*, 5.

38. G. John Ikenberry, "Three Worlds: The West, East and South and the Competition to
Shape Global Order," *International Affairs* 100, no.1 (2024): 137–38.

39. See Jade McGlynn, "Why Russia Markets Itself as an Anti-Colonial Power to Africans,"
Foreign Policy, February 8, 2023. For specific comments of Vladimir Putin, see "Article
by Vladimir Putin in Rodong Sinmun Newspapers, Russia and the DPRK: Traditions of
Friendship and Cooperation Through the Years," Kremlin Events, June 18, 2024, http://
en.kremlin.ru/events/president/news/74317. For the wave of support from the non-Western
world, see Benjamin Young, "Russia Is Riding an Anti-Colonial Wave Across Africa,"
RAND Commentary, September 16, 2024, https://www.rand.org/pubs/commentary/2024
/09/russia-is-riding-an-anti-colonial-wave-across-africa.html, accessed June 19, 2025.

40. Seb Starcevic, "What JD Vance Really Thinks About Europe," *Politico*, July 16, 2024,
https://www.politico.eu/article/j-d-vance-donald-trump-mate-us-isolationism-brussels
-europe-relations/, accessed June 19, 2025.

41. Jeet Heer, "The Surprisingly Durable Myth of Donald Trump, Anti-Imperialist," *The
Nation*, April 17, 2023, https://www.thenation.com/article/politics/trump-anti-imperialist/,
accessed June 19, 2025.

42. Heer, "The Surprisingly Durable Myth of Donald Trump." See also Christian Parenti,
"Trump Against Empire: Is That Why They Hate Him?," *The Grayzone*, February 15, 2023,
https://thegrayzone.com/2023/02/15/trump-empire-they-hated-him/, accessed June 19, 2025.

43. The literature is extensive, and I will engage with some debates in chapter 1. For important
accounts, see Uday Mehta, *Liberalism and Empire* (University of Chicago Press, 1999);
Antony Anghie, *Imperialism, Sovereignty, and the Making of International Law* (Cam-
bridge University Press, 2005); David Harvey, *The 'New' Imperialism: Accumulation by
Dispossession* (Routledge, 2012); Jeanne Morefield, *Empires Without Imperialism: Anglo–
American Decline and the Politics of Deflection* (Oxford University Press, 2014); Ann Laura
Stoler, *Duress: Imperial Durabilities in Our Times* (Duke University Press, 2016); Sam
Moyn, *Liberalism Against Itself: Cold War Intellectuals and the Making of Our Times* (Yale
University Press, 2023).

44. The literature on the meaning and unity of the Global South is extensive. For some,
these states can be understood from their materially disadvantaged and marginalized
conditions, which is also ideological. Immanuel Wallerstein, *World-Systems Analysis: An
Introduction* (Duke University Press, 2004); Arturo Escobar, *Encountering Development:
The Making and Unmaking of the Third World* (Princeton University Press, 2011); Nour
Dados and Raewyn Connell, "The Global South," *Contexts* 11, no. 1 (2012): 12–13. For

others, the Global South is a distinct even if overlapping space to voice alternative views. Jacqueline Braveboy-Wagner, ed., *Diplomatic Strategies of Nations in the Global South: The Search for Leadership* (Springer, 2016); Vijay Prashad, *The Poorer Nations: A Possible History of the Global South* (Verso, 2012); Arlene Tickner and Karen Smith, *International Relations from the Global South: Worlds of Difference* (Routledge, 2020). Others view the Global South as spaces of resistance and thus as a network of actors that challenge and exist as radical spaces within the Global North. Anne Mahler, *From the Tricontinental to the Global South: Race, Radicalism, and Transnational Solidarity* (Duke University Press, 2018); Anne Mahler, "The Global South in the Belly of the Beast: Viewing African-American Civil Rights Through a Tricontinental Lens," *Latin American Research Review* 50, no. 1 (2015): 95–116. Other important and combined perspectives on the Global South are Siba Grovogui, "A Revolution Nonetheless: The Global South in International Relations," *Global South* 5, no. 1 (2011): 175–90; Caroline Levander and Walter Mignolo, "Introduction: The Global South and World Dis/Order," *Global South* 5, no. 1 (2011): 1–11; Robbie Shilliam, ed., *International Relations and Non-Western Thought: Imperialism, Colonialism and Investigations of Global Modernity* (Routledge, 2011); Nicholas Guyatt, *Bind Us Apart: How Enlightened Americans Invented Racial Segregation* (Oxford University Press, 2016); Inderjeet Parmar, "Transnational Elite Knowledge Networks: Managing American Hegemony in Turbulent Times," *Security Studies* 28, no. 3 (2019): 532–64.

45. Hans Henrik Bruun, *Science, Values and Politics in Max Weber's Methodology: New Expanded Edition* (Ashgate, 2012), 264. Max Weber's conception of power politics is developed clearly by Stacie E. Goddard and Daniel H. Nexon, "The Dynamics of Global Power Politics: A Framework for Analysis," *Journal of Global Security Studies* 1, no. 1 (February 1, 2016): 4–18. On general understandings of power and its workings, see Peter J. Katzenstein and Lucia A. Seybert, eds., *Protean Power: Exploring the Uncertain and Unexpected in World Politics* (Cambridge University Press, 2018); Peter J. Katzenstein, "Protean Power: A Second Look," *International Theory* 12, no. 3 (November 2020): 481–99.

46. Martin Thomas and Richard Toye, eds., *Rhetorics of Empire: Languages of Colonial Conflict After 1900* (Manchester University Press, 2017), 13. For a detailed account of rhetoric along the lines I have defined, see Chaim Perelman, *The Realm of Rhetoric* (University of Notre Dame Press, 1982); Bryan Garsten, *Saving Persuasion: A Defense of Rhetoric and Judgement* (Harvard University Press, 2006); Ronald Krebs and Patrick Thaddeus Jackson, "Twisting Tongues and Twisting Arms: The Power of Political Rhetoric," *European Journal of International Relations* 13, no. 1 (2007): 35–66; Richard Toye, *Rhetoric: A Very Short Introduction* (Oxford University Press, 2013); Sasikumar Sundaram, "Varieties of Political Rhetorical Reasoning: Norm Types, Scorekeepers, and Political Projects," *International Theory* 12, no. 3 (2020): 358–86.

47. Strategic narrative literature misses an important role of rhetoric within narratives to provoke action. See, for example, Alister Miskimmon, Ben O'Loughlin, and Laura Roselle, *Strategic Narratives: Communication Power and the New World Order* (Routledge, 2013). See also Daniel Deudney, John Ikenberry, and Karoline Postel-Vinay, eds., *Debating Worlds: Contested Narratives of Global Modernity and World Order* (Oxford University Press, 2023).

48. Aristotle, *The Art of Rhetoric* (Penguin Classics, 1991), 66.

49. The literature on hierarchy is extensive and growing in international relations. See, for example, John M. Hobson and Jason C. Sharman, "The Enduring Place of Hierarchy in World Politics: Tracing the Social Logics of Hierarchy and Political Change," *European Journal of International Relations* 11, no. 1 (March 2005): 63–98; Ann E. Towns, *Women and States: Norms and Hierarchies in International Society* (Cambridge University Press, 2010); Edward Keene, "International Hierarchy and the Origins of the Modern Practice of Intervention," *Review of International Studies* 39, no. 5 (2013): 1077–90; Evelyn Goh, *The Struggle for Order: Hegemony, Hierarchy, and Transition in Post-Cold War East Asia*, repr. ed. (Oxford University Press, 2015); Alexander D. Barder, *Empire Within: International Hierarchy and Its Imperial Laboratories of Governance* (Routledge, 2017); Paul K. MacDonald, "Embedded Authority: A Relational Network Approach to Hierarchy in World Politics," *Review of International Studies* 44, no. 1 (January 2018): 128–50; Ayse Zarakol, ed., *Hierarchies in World Politics* (Cambridge University Press, 2017); Vincent Pouliot, *International Pecking Orders: The Politics and Practice of Multilateral Diplomacy* (Cambridge University Press, 2016); Jack Donnelly, "Levels, Centers, and Peripheries: The Spatio-Political Structure of Political Systems," *International Theory* 13, no. 1 (March 2021): 1–35; Alexander D. Barder, *Global Race War: International Politics and Racial Hierarchy* (Oxford University Press, 2021).

50. On military hierarchy, see Alexander Cooley and Daniel Nexon, "'The Empire Will Compensate You': The Structural Dynamics of U.S. Overseas Basing Network," *Perspectives on Politics* 11, no. 4 (2013): 1034–50; David Vine, *Base Nation: How U.S. Military Bases Abroad Harm America and the World* (Henry Holt, 2015). On economic hierarchy, see Immanuel Wallerstein, *The Modern World-System I: Capitalist Agriculture and the Origins of the European World-Economy in the Sixteenth Century* (University of California Press, 2011); Alexander Anievas and Kerem Nişancıoğlu, *How the West Came to Rule: The Geopolitical Origins of Capitalism* (Pluto, 2015). On racial hierarchy, see Robbie Shilliam, *Black Pacific: Anticolonial Struggles and Oceanic Connections* (Bloomsbury, 2015); Alexander Anievas, Nivi Manchanda, and Robbie Shilliam, *Race and Racism in International Relations: Confronting the Global Colour Line* (Routledge, 2014); Alexander D. Barder, *Global Race War: International Politics and Racial Hierarchy* (Oxford University Press, 2021). On gender hierarchy, see Laura J. Shepherd, *Gender Matters in Global Politics* (Routledge, 2010); Cynthia Weber, *Queer International Relations: Sovereignty, Sexuality and the Will to Knowledge* (Oxford University Press, 2016); Valerie M. Hudson, Donna Lee Bowen, and Perpetua Lynne Nielsen, *The First Political Order: How Sex Shapes Governance and National Security Worldwide* (Columbia University Press, 2020).

51. Gerrit W. Gong, *The Standard of "Civilization" in International Society* (Oxford University Press, 1984); Gerry Simpson, *Great Powers and Outlaw States: Unequal Sovereigns in the International Legal Order* (Cambridge University Press, 2004); Anghie, *Imperialism, Sovereignty and the Making of International Law*; Siba Grovogui, *Sovereigns, Quasi Sovereigns, and Africans: Race and Self-Determination in International Law* (University of Minnesota Press, 2006); Ayse Zarakol, *After Defeat: How the East Learned to Live with the West* (Cambridge University Press, 2011); Shilliam, *Black Pacific*; Jennifer Pitts, *Boundaries of the International: Law and Empire* (Harvard University Press, 2018).

52. Anghie, *Imperialism, Sovereignty and the Making of International Law*, 6.

53. Stoler, *Duress*, 25.

54. See Jutta Weldes, "High Politics and Low Data," in *Interpretation and Method*, ed. Dvora Yanow and Peregrine Schwartz-Shea, 178 (M. E. Sharpe, 2006).

55. James Scott, *Weapons of the Weak: Everyday Forms of Peasant Resistance* (Yale University Press, 1985).

56. Charles Tilly, "Contentious Repertoires in Great Britain, 1758–1834," *Social Science History* 17, no. 2 (1993): 264. See also Charles Tilly, *Regimes and Repertoires* (University of Chicago Press, 2010).

57. Imperialism and the study of colonialism is, of course, broad and diverse. For reference work, see Immanuel Ness and Zak Cope, *The Palgrave Encyclopedia of Imperialism and Anti-Imperialism* (Springer, 2021).

58. Matthew Craven, "Colonialism and Domination," in *The Oxford Handbook of the History of International Law*, ed. Bardo Fassbender and Anne Peter (Oxford University Press, 2012), https://doi.org/10.1093/law/9780199599752.003.0037.

59. Julian Go, *Patterns of Empire: The British and American Empires, 1688 to the Present* (Cambridge University Press, 2012), 35, 55.

60. J. A. Hobson, *Imperialism* (London, 1902), 11. See also Duncan Bell, *Reordering the World: Essays on Liberalism and Empire* (Princeton University Press, 2016). Hobson's work on imperialism influenced Vladimir Lenin, "Imperialism: The Highest Stage of Capitalism" (Marxist Internet Archive, 1917), https://www.marxists.org/archive/lenin/works/1916/imp-hsc/; Carl Schmit, *The Concept of the Political*, trans. Georg Schwab (Rutgers University Press, 1976).

61. Tony Ballantyne and Antoinette Burton, *Empires and the Reach of the Global, 1870–1945* (Harvard University Press, 2014), 1.

62. Gong, *The Standard of "Civilization" in International Society*; Edward Keene, *Beyond the Anarchical Society: Grotius, Colonialism and Order in World Politics* (Cambridge University Press, 2002); Grovogui, *Sovereigns, Quasi Sovereigns, and Africans*; Zarakol, *After Defeat*; Adom Getachew, *Worldmaking After Empire: The Rise and Fall of Self-Determination* (Princeton University Press, 2019).

63. Getachew, *Worldmaking After Empire*, 10.

64. The idea of imperial formations that captures the multiple ways of the rule of empires is from Stoler, *Duress*.

65. Article 22 of the Covenant of the League of Nations. See Susan Pedersen, *The Guardians: The League of Nations and the Crisis of Empire* (Oxford University Press, 2015).

66. See William G. Grewe, *Epochs of International Law*, trans. and rev. Michael Byers (Walter de Gruyters, 2000). See also Carl Schmitt, *Nomos of the Earth in the International Law of Jus Publicum Europacum*, trans. G. L. Ulmen (Telos, 2003); Anghie, *Imperialism, Sovereignty and the Making of International Law*.

67. Hobson and Sharman, "The Enduring Place of Hierarchy in World Politics."

68. See Ballantyne and Burton, *Empires and the Reach of the Global*. See also Erez Manela and Heather Streets-Salter, eds., *The Anticolonial Transnational: Imaginaries, and Networks in the Struggle Against Empire* (Cambridge University Press, 2023).

69. Christopher Bayly, "European Political Thought and the Wider World During the Nineteenth Century," in *The Cambridge History of Nineteenth-Century Political Thought*, ed. Gareth Stedman Jones and Gregory Claeys, 835 (Cambridge University Press, 2011).

70. On epistemic violence, see Gayatri Chakravorty Spivak, *A Critique of Postcolonial Reason: Toward a History of the Vanishing Present* (Harvard University Press, 1999); Rosalind C. Morris, ed., *Can the Subaltern Speak? Reflections on the History of an Idea* (Columbia University Press, 2010); Boaventura Santos, *The End of the Cognitive Empire: The Coming Age of Epistemologies of the South* (Duke University Press, 2018). For epistemic violence in general in international relations, see Siba Grovougui, *Beyond Eurocentrism and Anarchy: Memories of International Order and Institutions* (Springer, 2006); Shilliam, *International Relations and Non-Western Thought*. Epistemic violence is also an important topic in feminist international relations. For important treatments along these lines, see R. W. Connell, *Gender and Power* (Blackwell, 1987); Christine Sylvester, *Feminist Theory and International Relations in a Postmodern Era* (Cambridge University Press, 1994); Carolyn Nordstrum, "Visible Wars and Invisible Girls, Shadow Industries, and the Politics of Not-Knowing," *International Feminist Journal of Politics* 1, no. 1 (1999): 14–33; Kristie Dotson, "Tracking Epistemic Violence, Tracking Practices of Silencing," *Hypatia* 26, no. 2 (Spring 2011): 236–57. See also Claudia Brunner, "Conceptualizing Epistemic Violence: An Interdisciplinary Assemblage for IR," *International Politics Review* 9 (2021):193–212.

71. Such a focus on competence goes back to John Locke, *Two Treatises of Government* (Cambridge University Press, 1988).

72. Winston S. Churchill, "To the Council of the West Essex Unionist Association," in *His Complete Speeches, 1897–1963*, ed. Robert Rhodes James (Chelsea House, 1974), vol. IV: 4985. See also https://www.mkgandhi.org/thiswasbapu/144halfnakedfakir.php for Gandhi's response.

73. Along the lines theorized by Dotson, "Tracking Epistemic Violence."

74. See Matthew Craven, "Colonialism and Domination," in *The Oxford Handbook of the History of International Law*, ed. Bardo Fassbender and Anne Peters (Oxford University Press, 2012).

75. See *Report of the American Section of the International Commission on Mandates in Turkey*, August 28, 1919, https://history.state.gov/historicaldocuments/frus1919Parisv12/d380. See also Henry N. Howard, *The King-Crane Commission: An American Inquiry in the Middle East* (Khayats, 1963).

76. Simpson, *Great Powers and Outlaw States*, 336.

77. Edward Said, *Orientalism: Western Conceptions of the Orient* (Penguin, 1991); Edward Said, "Representing the Colonized: Anthropology's Interlocutors," *Critical Inquiry* 15, no. 2 (1989): 207.

78. Ballantyne and Burton, *Empires and the Reach of the Global*, 171.

79. Ballantyne and Burton, *Empires and the Reach of the Global*, 139.

80. See Pankaj Mishra, *From the Ruins of the Empire: The Revolt Against the West and the Remaking of Asia* (Allen Lane, 2010).

81. W. E. B. Du Bois, "To the Nations of the World," in *W. E. B. Du Bois: A Reader*, ed. David Levering Lewis, 639 (Henry Holt, 1995).

82. Ballantyne and Burton, *Empires and the Reach of the Global*, 158.

83. Quoted in Ramachandra Guha, *Gandhi Before India* (Vintage, 2013), 367.

84. Ssu-yü Teng and John King Fairbank, *China's Response to the West: A Documentary Survey, 1839–1923* (Harvard University Press, 1979), 328.

85. C. A. Bayly, *Recovering Liberties: Indian Thought in the Age of Liberalism and Empire* (Cambridge University Press, 2012).

86. Bayly, *Recovering Liberties*, 105.

87. Asish Nandy, *The Intimate Enemy: Loss and Recovery of Self Under Colonialism* (Oxford University Press, 1983), 56.

88. See Adom Getachew and Karuna Mantena, "Anticolonialism and the Decolonization of Political Theory," *Critical Times* 4, no. 3 (2021): 359–88.

89. Ballantyne and Burton, *Empires and the Reach of the Global*, 141.

90. On repertoires, see Doug McAdam, Sidney Tarrow, and Charles Tilly, *Dynamics of Contention* (Cambridge University Press, 1991); Tilly, "Contentious Repertoires in Great Britain"; Tilly, *Regimes and Repertoires*. For statecraft as repertoires, see Stacie Goddard, Paul MacDonald, and Daniel Nexon, "Repertoires of Statecraft: Instruments and Logics of Power Politics," *International Relations* 33, no. 2 (2019): 304–21; Paul MacDonald, "Parliament of Man, Federation of the World: Repertoires of Statecraft, the Hague Conferences, and the Making of the Liberal Order," *Diplomacy and Statecraft* 32, no. 4 (2021): 648–73.

91. Rachel A. Ankeny and Sabina Leonelli, "Repertoires: A Post-Kuhnian Perspective on Scientific Change and Collaborative Research," *Studies in History and Philosophy of Science Part A* 60 (December 2016): 20.

92. McAdam, Tarrow, and Tilly, *Dynamics of Contention*; Tilly, "Contentious Repertoires in Great Britain"; Tilly, *Regimes and Repertoires*. For statecraft as repertoires, see Goddard, MacDonald, and Nexon, "Repertoires of Statecraft"; Elana Rowe, "Analyzing Frenemies: An Artic Repertoire of Cooperation and Rivalry," *Political Geography* 76 (2020): 1–10; MacDonald, "Parliament of Man, Federation of the World."

93. Goddard, MacDonald, and Nexon, "Repertoires of Statecraft"; McAdam, Tarrow, and Tilly, *Dynamics of Contention*, 138.

94. Patrick Thaddeus Jackson and Daniel H. Nexon, "Paradigmatic Faults in International-Relations Theory," *International Studies Quarterly* 53, no. 4 (2009): 921. See also Patrick Thaddeus Jackson, *The Conduct of Inquiry in International Relations: Philosophy of Science and Its Implications for the Study of World Politics* (Routledge, 2011), 142–55.

95. The postcolonial studies literature in international relations is also extensive. For important works, see Partha Chatterjee, *Nationalist Thought and the Colonial World: A Derivative Discourse* (University of Minnesota Press, 1993); Ranajit Guha, *Dominance Without Hegemony: History and Power in Colonial India* (Harvard University Press, 1998); Lily H. M. Ling, *Postcolonial International Relations* (Palgrave Macmillan, 2002); Naeem Inayatullah and Daved L. Blaney, *International Relations and the Problem of Difference* (Routledge, 2004); Geeta Chowdhry and Shiela Nair, *Power, Postcolonialism and International Relations* (Routledge, 2004); John M. Hobson, *The Eastern Origins of Western Civilization* (Cambridge University Press, 2004); Anghie, *Imperialism, Sovereignty, and the Making of International Law*; Tarak Barkawi and Mark Laffey, "The Postcolonial Moment

in Security Studies," *Review of International Studies* 32, no. 2 (2006): 329–52; David Slater, *Geopolitics and the Post-Colonial: Rethinking North-South Relations* (Wiley, 2008); John Hawley and Revathi Krishnaswamy, *The Postcolonial and the Global* (University of Minnesota Press, 2008); David Blaney and Naeem Inayatullah, *Savage Economics: Wealth, Poverty, and the Temporal Walls of Capitalism* (Routledge, 2010); Himadeep Muppidi, *The Colonial Signs of International Relations* (Columbia University Press, 2012); Sanjay Seth, "Postcolonial Theory and the Critique of International Relations," in *Postcolonial Theory and International Relations*, ed. Sanjay Seth (Routledge, 2013); Vivienne Jabri, *The Postcolonial Subject: Claiming Politics/Governing Others in Late Modernity* (Routledge, 2013); Robbie Shilliam, Alexander Anievas, and Nivi Manchanda, *In Confronting the Global Color Line* (Routledge, 2014); Hamid Dabashi and Walter Mignolo, *Can Non-Europeans Think?* (Zed, 2015); Olivia Rutazibwa and Robbie Shilliam, *Routledge Handbook of Postcolonial Politics* (Routledge, 2018); Walter D. Mignolo, *The Politics of Decolonial Investigations* (Duke University Press, 2021).

96. For example, A. F. K. Organski, *World Politics* (Knopf, 1958); Robert Gilpin, *War and Change in World Politics* (Cambridge University Press, 1981); Robert Ross and Zhu Feng, eds., *China's Ascent: Power, Security, and the Future of International Politics* (Cornell University Press, 2008); Jack Levy and William Thompson, *Causes of War* (Wiley-Blackwell, 2010); Matthew David Hamilton and Mark Fisher, "Opening the Thucydides Trap: A Genealogy of Rise-and-Fall Theory," *International Affairs* 100, no. 3 (2024): 1189–1206.

97. See Zygmunt Bauman, "Modernity, Racism, Extermination," in *Theories of Race and Racism*, ed. Les Black and John Solomos (Routledge, 2020). See also Guyatt, *Bind Us Apart*. For a recent systemic critique of neorealism, see Jack Donnelly, *Systems, Relations, and Structures of International Societies* (Cambridge University Press, 2023).

98. For a general theory of neoclassical realism on these lines see Jack L. Snyder, *Myths of Empire: Domestic Politics and International Ambition* (Cornell University Press, 1991); Randall L. Schweller, *Unanswered Threats: Political Constraints on the Balance of Power* (Princeton University Press, 2006); Norrin M. Ripsman, Jeffrey W. Taliaferro, and Steven E. Lobell, *Neoclassical Realist Theory of International Politics* (Oxford University Press, 2016).

99. Stefano Guzzini, *Power, Realism and Constructivism* (Taylor and Francis, 2013). The foundation of these arguments goes back to Friedrich V. Kratochwil, *Rules, Norms, and Decisions: On the Conditions of Practical and Legal Reasoning in International Relations and Domestic Affairs* (Cambridge University Press, 1989); Nicholas Onuf, *World of Our Making: Rules and Rule in Social Theory and International Relations* (University of South Carolina Press, 1989); Nicholas Onuf, *Making Sense, Making Worlds: Constructivism in Social Theory and International Relations* (Routledge, 2013); K. M. Fierke, *Changing Games, Changing Strategies: Critical Investigations in Security* (Manchester University Press, 1998); Neta C. Crawford, *Argument and Change in World Politics: Ethics, Decolonization, and Humanitarian Intervention* (Cambridge University Press, 2002). See also Patrick Thaddeus Jackson, *Civilizing the Enemy: German Reconstruction and the Invention of the West* (University of Michigan Press, 2006); Friedrich Kratochwil, *Praxis: On Acting and Knowing* (Cambridge University Press, 2018).

100. Martha Finnemore and Kathryn Sikkink, "International Norm Dynamics and Political Change," *International Organization* 52, no. 4 (1998): 887–917. For a detailed constructivist position, see Antje Wiener, *A Theory of Contestation* (Springer, 2014); Antje Wiener, *Contestation and Constitution of Norms in Global International Relations* (Cambridge University Press, 2018).

101. Critical works on rhetorical politics in international politics are many and diverse. They focus on actors' meaning making and interpretation rather than on neopositivist methods to test rhetoric through content analysis. On rhetoric as a strategy from a bargaining perspective, see Frank Schimmelfennig, "The Community Trap: Liberal Norms, Rhetorical Action, and the Eastern Enlargement of the European Union," *International Organization* 55, no. 1 (2001): 47–80; Frank Schimmelfennig, *The EU, NATO, and the Integration of Europe* (Cambridge University Press, 2003); Tine Hanrieder, "The False Promise of the Better Argument," *International Theory* 3, no. 3 (2011): 390–415; Courtney J. Fung, "Rhetorical Adaptation, Normative Resistance and International Order-Making," *Cooperation and Conflict* 55, no. 2 (2020): 193–215. For works that approach rhetoric from a relational and contentious performance perspective, see Jackson, *Civilizing the Enemy*; Krebs and Jackson, "Twisting Tongues and Twisting Arms"; Ronald R. Krebs and Jennifer K. Lobasz, "Fixing the Meaning of 9/11: Hegemony, Coercion, and the Road to War in Iraq," *Security Studies* 16, no. 3 (2007): 409–51; Stacie E. Goddard, *Indivisible Territory and the Politics of Legitimacy* (Cambridge University Press, 2009); Stacie E. Goddard and Ronald R. Krebs, "Rhetoric, Legitimation, and Grand Strategy," *Security Studies* 24, no. 1 (2015): 5–36; Markus Kornprobst, *Irredentism in European Politics: Argumentation, Compromise and Norms* (Cambridge University Press, 2009); Ronald R. Krebs, *Narrative and the Making of US National Security* (Cambridge University Press, 2015); Stacie E. Goddard, *When Right Makes Might: Rising Powers and World Order* (Cornell University Press, 2018).

102. Goddard, *When Right Makes Might*, 25.

103. Ian Hurd, "The Strategic Use of Liberal Internationalism: Libya and the UN Sanctions, 1992–2003," *International Organization* 59, no. 3 (2005): 495–526; Ian Hurd, *How to Do Things with International Law* (Princeton University Press, 2017).

104. Leela Gandhi, *Postcolonial Theory: A Critical Introduction* (Columbia University Press, 2019), 188.

105. Rhetorical politics scholarship in international relations has not fully grasped the implications of race, inequality, gender, and postcolonial perspectives. This book aims to address this gap.

106. Rutazibwa and Shilliam, *Routledge Handbook of Postcolonial Politics*; Mignolo, *The Politics of Decolonial Investigations*.

107. See, for example, Jenny Edkins, Michael J. Shapiro, and Veronique Pin-Fat, eds., *Sovereign Lives: Power in Global Politics* (Routledge, 2004); Jenny Edkins, *Trauma and the Memory of Politics* (Cambridge University Press, 2003); Jabri, *The Postcolonial Subject*; Diane Enns, *The Violence of Victimhood* (Pennsylvania State University Press, 2012). For a good critique, see Chandra Talpade Mohanty, Ann Russo, and Lourdes Torres, eds., *Third World Women and the Politics of Feminism* (Indiana University Press, 1991); John

M. Hobson and Alina Sajed, "Navigating Beyond the Eurofetishist Frontier of Critical IR Theory: Exploring the Complex Landscapes of Non-Western Agency," *International Studies Review* 19, no. 4 (2017): 547–72.

108. For a superb critique, see Hobson and Sajed, "Navigating Beyond the Eurofetishist Frontier of Critical IR Theory," 548.

109. See, for example, Tony Ballantyne, Lachy Paterson, and Angela Wanhalla, eds., *Indigenous Textual Cultures: Reading and Writing in the Age of Global Empire* (Duke University Press, 2020).

110. See Zarakol, *After Defeat*; Manjari Chatterjee Miller, *Post-Imperial Ideology and Foreign Policy in India and China* (Stanford University Press, 2013), 7.

111. Raz Segal, "Israel Must Stop Weaponising the Holocaust," *The Guardian*, October 24, 2023, https://www.theguardian.com/commentisfree/2023/oct/24/israel-gaza-palestinians -holocaust.

112. See *Times of Israel* (*TOI*) Staff, "Netanyahu Ad Copies Trump, Who Ripped Off Modi," *The Times of Israel*, December 22, 2019, https://www.timesofisrael.com/netanyahu-ad-copies-trump-who-ripped-off-modi/. See also Yasmeen Serhan, "The Trump-Modi Playbook," *The Atlantic*, February 25, 2020, https://www.theatlantic.com/international /archive/2020/02/donald-trump-narendra-modi-autocrats/607042/. Russia's appropriation of rhetoric from China is evident in cybersecurity debates where Moscow follows the "Great Firewall of China" model and censors internet traffic to maintain a strictly conformist domestic society. See Mika Kerttunen and Eneken Tikk, "The Politics of Stability: Cement and Change in Cyber Affairs," in *Routledge Handbook of Cyber Security*, ed. Eneken Tikk and Mika Kerttuen, 56 (Routledge, 2022).

113. See Lizz Truss's attack on Michael Foucault: Lizz Truss, "Fight for Fairness," December 17, 2020, https://web.archive.org/web/20201217144124/https://www.gov.uk/government /speeches/fight-for-fairness. The term "alternative fact" was coined by Kellyanne Conway, an adviser to President Trump, during a *Meet the Press* interview in January 2017 to defend Sean Spicer's inflated numbers of people attending President Donald Trump's inauguration. Rudy Giuliani asserted that truth isn't truth. The prolife movement appropriated the language of women's empowerment to reject abortion. Michiko Kakutani blamed all of it on academics promoting postmodernism, and philosopher Daniel Dennett concurred that the problem was postmodernism and relativism. See Aaron Hanlon, "Postmodernism Didn't Cause Trump. It Explains Him," *Washington Post*, August 31, 2018, https://www.washingtonpost.com/outlook/postmodernism-didnt-cause-trump-it -explains-him/2018/08/30/0939f7c4-9b12-11e8-843b-36e177f3081c_story.html.

1. RHETORICAL POWER POLITICS: A FRAMEWORK

1. Mainstream international relations (IR) views of cheap talk rest on microeconomic foundations. Joseph Farrell and Matthew Rabin, "Cheap Talk," *Journal of Economic Perspectives* 10 (1996): 103–18. Farrell and Rabin (p. 116) define cheap talk as "costless, nonbinding, nonverifiable messages that may affect the listener's beliefs."

2. The literature on silencing is extensive. See, for example, Gayatri Chakravorty Spivak, "Can the Subaltern Speak?," in *Marxism and the Interpretation of Culture*, ed. Cary Nelson and Lawrence Grossberg, 271–313, repr. ed. (University of Illinois Press, 1987); Kristie Dotson, "Tracking Epistemic Violence, Tracking Practices of Silencing," *Hypatia* 26, no. 2 (2011): 236–57; Boaventura de Sousa Santos, *The End of the Cognitive Empire: The Coming of Age of Epistemologies of the South* (Duke University Press, 2018); Sabelo J. Ndlovu-Gatsheni, "The Cognitive Empire, Politics of Knowledge and African Intellectual Productions: Reflections on Struggles for Epistemic Freedom and Resurgence of Decolonisation in the Twenty-First Century," *Third World Quarterly* 42, no. 5 (May 4, 2021): 882–901; Claudia Brunner, "Conceptualizing Epistemic Violence: An Interdisciplinary Assemblage for IR," *International Politics Reviews* 9, no. 1 (June 1, 2021): 193–212.

3. Classic text is Walter Bryce Gallie, "Essentially Contested Concepts," *Proceedings of the Aristotelian Society* 56 (1956): 167–98; David Collier, Fernando Daniel Hidalgo, and Andra Olivia Maciuceanu, "Essentially Contested Concepts: Debates and Applications," *Journal of Political Ideologies* 11 (2006): 211–46. For a recent study, see Gary Goertz, *Social Science Concepts and Measurement: New and Completely Revised Edition* (Princeton University Press, 2020); John Gerring and Lee Cojocaru, "Conceptual Contestation: An Empirical Approach," *Polity* 56, no. 1 (2024), https://doi.org/10.1086/727976.

4. Stefano Guzzini, "Power in World Politics," Oxford Research Encyclopedia of Politics Online, April 20, 2022, https://oxfordre.com/politics/display/10.1093/acrefore/9780190228637.001.0001/acrefore-9780190228637-e-118, accessed June 24, 2025. See also Felix Berenskoetter and Micheal Williams, eds., *Power in World Politics* (Routledge, 2007); Stefano Guzzini, *Power, Realism and Constructivism* (Routledge, 2013).

5. See David Baldwin, *Power and International Relations: A Conceptual Approach* (Princeton University Press, 2016).

6. Rebecca Adler-Nissen and Vincent Pouliot, "Power in Practice: Negotiating the International Intervention in Libya," *European Journal of International Relations* 20, no. 4 (2014): 893.

7. Hans Henrik Bruun, *Science, Values and Politics in Max Weber's Methodology: New Expanded Edition* (Ashgate, 2012), 264. For advancements along these lines, see Stacie E. Goddard and Daniel H. Nexon, "The Dynamics of Global Power Politics: A Framework for Analysis," *Journal of Global Security Studies* 1, no. 1 (February 1, 2016): 4–18.

8. For the tragic aspect of classical realism, see Richard Ned Lebow, *The Tragic Vision of Politics* (Cambridge University Press, 2009); Jonathan Kirshner, *An Unwritten Future: Realism and Uncertainty in World Politics* (Princeton University Press, 2022). For a challenge, see Richard Ned Lebow, "What Is Classical Realism?," *Analyse & Kritik* 46, no. 1 (2024): 215–28. For a debate on "protean power," see Peter J. Katzenstein and Lucia A. Seybert, eds., *Protean Power: Exploring the Uncertain and Unexpected in World Politics* (Cambridge University Press, 2018); Peter J. Katzenstein, "Protean Power: A Second Look," *International Theory* 12, no. 3 (November 2020): 481–99.

9. For a postcolonial perspective, I largely follow Ann Laura Stoler, *Duress: Imperial Durabilities in Our Times* (Duke University Press, 2016). The postcolonial literature is multidisciplinary and extensive, and I draw on the works of Partha Chatterjee, *Nationalist*

Thought and the Colonial World: A Derivative Discourse (University of Minnesota Press, 1993); Ranajit Guha, *Dominance Without Hegemony: History and Power in Colonial India* (Harvard University Press, 1998); Lily H. M. Ling, *Postcolonial International Relations* (Palgrave Macmillan, 2002); Naeem Inayatullah and Daved L. Blaney, *International Relations and the Problem of Difference* (Routledge, 2004); Geeta Chowdhry and Shiela Nair, *Power, Postcolonialism and International Relations* (Routledge, 2004); John M. Hobson, *The Eastern Origins of Western Civilization* (Cambridge University Press, 2004); Anthony Anghie, *Imperialism, Sovereignty, and the Making of International Law* (Cambridge University Press, 2005); Tarak Barkawi and Mark Laffey, "The Postcolonial Moment in Security Studies," *Review of International Studies* 32, no. 2 (2006): 329–52; David Slater, *Geopolitics and the Post-Colonial: Rethinking North-South Relations* (Wiley, 2008); John Hawley and Revathi Krishnaswamy, *The Postcolonial and the Global* (University of Minnesota Press, 2008); David Blaney and Naeem Inayatullah, *Savage Economics: Wealth, Poverty, and the Temporal Walls of Capitalism* (Routledge, 2010); Himadeep Muppidi, *The Colonial Signs of International Relations* (Columbia University Press, 2012); Sanjay Seth, "Postcolonial Theory and the Critique of International Relations," in *Postcolonial Theory and International Relations*, ed. Sanjay Seth (Routledge, 2013); Vivienne Jabri, *The Postcolonial Subject: Claiming Politics/Governing Others in Late Modernity* (Routledge, 2013); Robbie Shilliam, Alexander Anievas, and Nivi Manchanda, *In Confronting the Global Color Line* (Routledge, 2014); Hamid Dabashi and Walter Mignolo, *Can Non-Europeans Think?* (Zed, 2015); Olivia Rutazibwa and Robbie Shilliam, *Routledge Handbook of Postcolonial Politics* (Routledge, 2018); Walter D. Mignolo, *The Politics of Decolonial Investigations* (Duke University Press, 2021).

10. Hans Morgenthau, *Politics Among Nations* (Knopf, 1965), 150.

11. Morgenthau, *Politics Among Nations*, 151–52; Lebow, *The Tragic Vision of Politics*.

12. Kenneth N. Waltz, *Theory of International Politics* (Addison-Wesley, 1979), 195.

13. Waltz, *Theory of International Politics*, 131.

14. John Mearsheimer, *The Tragedy of Great Power Politics* (Norton, 2001), 34.

15. The classic work is Paul Kennedy, *The Rise and Fall of the Great Powers* (Vintage, 1989).

16. For a general theory of the problems caused by domestic politics, see Jack Snyder, *Myths of Empire: Domestic Politics and International Ambition* (Cornell University Press, 1993). Recent advancements in neoclassical realism include, but are not limited to, Randall L. Schweller, *Unanswered Threats: Political Constraints on the Balance of Power* (Princeton University, 2006); Norrin M. Ripsman, Jeffrey W. Taliaferro, and Steven E. Lobell, *Neoclassical Realist Theory of International Politics* (Oxford University Press, 2016); Norris Ripsman, "A Neoclassical Realist Explanation of International Institutions," in *International Institutions and Power Politics*, ed. Andres Wivel and T. V. Paul, 53–72 (Georgetown University Press, 2019).

17. Baldwin, *Power and International Relations*, 50.

18. Thomas Schelling, "An Essay on Bargaining," *American Economic Review* 46, no. 3 (1956): 281–82; Thomas Schelling, *The Strategy of Conflict* (1960; Harvard University Press, 1980).

19. For example, James Fearon, "Domestic Political Audiences and the Escalation of International Disputes," *American Political Science Review* 88, no. 3 (1994): 577–92. For a superb

work on audience cost, see Jack Levy, "Coercive Threats, Audience Cost and Case Studies," *Security Studies* 21, no. 3 (2012): 383–90.

20. The literature is extensive. See, for example, Robert Jervis, *Perception and Misperception in International Politics* (1976; Princeton University Press, 2017); Josuha Kertzer, *Resolve in International Politics* (Princeton University Press, 2016); Keren Yarhi-Milo, *Who Fights for Reputation: The Psychology of Leaders in International Conflict* (Princeton University Press, 2018).

21. Jack Goldsmith and Eric Posner, "Moral and Legal Rhetoric in International Relations: A Rational Choice Perspective," *Journal of Legal Studies* 31, no. S1 (2002): S132–S133.

22. Goldsmith and Posner, "Moral and Legal Rhetoric," S134.

23. Frantz Fanon, *The Wretched of the Earth* (Grove, 1961), 58, 72.

24. Karuna Mantena, "Another Realism: The Politics of Gandhian Nonviolence," *American Political Science Review* 106, no. 2 (2012): 455–70. See also Adom Getachew and Karuna Mantena, "Anticolonialism and the Decolonization of Political Theory," *Critical Times* 4, no. 3 (2021): 365.

25. John M. Hobson and Jason C. Sharman, "The Enduring Place of Hierarchy in World Politics: Tracing the Social Logics of Hierarchy and Political Change," *European Journal of International Relations* 11, no. 1 (2005): 69–70; Alexander Anievas, Nivi Manchanda, and Robbie Shilliam, *Race and Racism in International Relations: Confronting the Global Colour Line* (Routledge, 2014); Ayse Zarakol, ed., *Hierarchies in World Politics* (Cambridge University Press, 2017); Alexander D. Barder, *Global Race War: International Politics and Racial Hierarchy* (Oxford University Press, 2021).

26. Adler-Nissen and Pouliot, "Power in Practice," 893.

27. Guzzini, *Power, Realism and Constructivism*, 5.

28. The foundational text for such a focus on language is Friedrich Kratochwil, *Rules, Norms, and Decisions: On the Conditions of Practical and Legal Reasoning in International Relations and Domestic Affairs* (Cambridge University Press, 1989). See also Friedrich Kratochwil, *Praxis: On Acting and Knowing* (Cambridge University Press, 2018). For interesting engagement, see Gunther Hellmann and Jens Steffek, *Praxis as a Perspective on International Politics* (Bristol University Press, 2022). I have also tried to engage with Friedrich Kratochwil's thinking about linguistic rules and practical reasoning: Sasikumar S. Sundaram, "Varieties of Political Rhetorical Reasoning: Norm Types, Scorekeepers, and Political Projects," *International Theory* 12, no. 3 (2019): 358–86. Other important relational-constructivist approaches are Patrick Thaddeus Jackson, *Civilizing the Enemy: German Reconstruction and the Invention of the West* (University of Michigan Press, 2006); Ronald R. Krebs and Patrick Thaddeus Jackson, "Twisting Tongues and Twisting Arms: The Power of Political Rhetoric," *European Journal of International Relations* 13, no. 1 (March 1, 2007): 35–66; Ronald R. Krebs and Jennifer K. Lobasz, "Fixing the Meaning of 9/11: Hegemony, Coercion, and the Road to War in Iraq," *Security Studies* 16, no. 3 (August 24, 2007): 409–51; Stacie E. Goddard, *Indivisible Territory and the Politics of Legitimacy: Jerusalem and Northern Ireland* (Cambridge University Press, 2009); Stacie E. Goddard and Ronald R. Krebs, "Rhetoric, Legitimation, and Grand Strategy," *Security Studies* 24, no. 1 (2015): 5–36; Ronald R. Krebs, *Narrative and the Making of US*

National Security (Cambridge University Press, 2015); Stacie E. Goddard, *When Right Makes Might: Rising Powers and World Order* (Cornell University Press, 2018).

29. It is based on speech act, that is, to say something is to do something. For example, demanding, appointing, apologizing, asserting, and threatening are all speech acts in language that are constituted by norms. John Searle, *Speech Acts* (Cambridge University Press, 1969).

30. Krebs, *Narrative and the Making of US National Security*, 2.

31. Strategic narrative literature misses an important role of rhetoric within narratives to provoke action. See, for example, Alister Miskimmon, Ben O'Loughlin, and Laura Roselle, *Strategic Narratives: Communication Power and the New World Order* (Routledge, 2013). See also Daniel Deudney, John Ikenberry, and Karoline Postel-Vinay, eds., *Debating Worlds: Contested Narratives of Global Modernity and World Order* (Oxford University Press, 2023).

32. Chaim Perelman, *The Realm of Rhetoric* (University of Notre Dame Press, 1982), 19.

33. Aristotle, *The Art of Rhetoric* (Penguin Classics, 1991), 75.

34. Partha Chatterjee, *Nationalist Thought and the Colonial World: A Derivative Discourse* (University of Minnesota Press, 1993), 52.

35. Matthew Spector warns, "The similarities between the geopolitical discourses of the 1890s and the ideas labeled 'classical realism' associated with thinkers of the mid-twentieth century were too compelling to ignore." See Matthew Specter, *The Atlantic Realists: Empire and International Political Thought Between Germany and the United States* (Stanford University Press, 2022), 203.

36. Waltz, *Theory of International Politics*, 103, 89.

37. John Mearsheimer, "Bound to Fail: The Rise and Fall of the Liberal International Order," *International Security* 43, no. 4 (2019): 47–48.

38. Goddard, *When Right Makes Might*, 18.

39. Alexander Wendt, *Social Theory of International Politics* (Cambridge University Press, 1999), 43.

40. Wendt, *Social Theory of International Politics*, 263.

41. The socialization literature in IR is vast. See Ayse Zarakol, *After Defeat: How the East Learned to Live with the West* (Cambridge University Press, 2011). See also Ayse Zarakol, "What Made the Modern World Hang Together: Socialization or Stigmatization," *International Theory* 6, no. 2 (2014): 311–32.

42. As Kratochwil puts it, social facts are those where "the underlying normative underpinnings that establish the practice in the first place, and that is not the result of any individual plans or subjective ideas but antecedent to any of them." Kratochwi, *Praxis*, 40.

43. Frank Schimmelfennig, "Strategic Calculation and International Socialization: Membership Incentives, Party Constellations, and Sustained Compliance in Central and Eastern Europe," *International Organization* 59, no. 4 (2005): 830; Frank Schimmelfennig, *The EU, NATO, and the Integration of Europe: Rules and Rhetoric* (Cambridge University Press, 2004).

44. Peter Katzenstein, *The Culture of National Security: Norms and Identity in World Politics* (Columbia University Press, 1996) 5.

45. See Martha Finnemore, *The Purpose of Intervention: Changing Beliefs About the Use of Force* (Cornell University Press, 2004); Martha Finnemore, *National Interest in International Society* (Cornell University Press, 1996).

46. Nicholas Onuf, *World of Our Making: Rules and Rule in Social Theory and International Relations* (University of South Carolina Press, 1989); Nicholas Onuf, *Making Sense, Making Worlds: Constructivism in Social Theory and International Relations* (Routledge, 2013); Neta C. Crawford, *Argument and Change in World Politics: Ethics, Decolonization, and Humanitarian Intervention* (Cambridge University Press, 2002). Other works also talk of social construction of reality drawing from different theories. For a classic work that uses Louis Althusser's interpellation to study the social construction of reality, see Jutta Weldes, *Constructing National Interests: The United States and the Cuban Missile Crisis* (University of Minnesota Press, 1999). For classic works that use poststructuralism to study the world making, see Jenny Edkins, *Poststructuralism and International Relations: Bringing the Political Back In* (Lynne Rienner, 1999); Lene Hansen, *Security as Practice: Discourse Analysis and the Bosnian War* (Routledge, 2006); Charlotte Epstein, *The Power of Words in International Relations: Birth of an Anti-Whaling Discourse* (MIT Press, 2008). For further novel advancements, see Einar Wigen, *State of Translation: Turkey in Interlingual Relations* (University of Michigan Press, 2018).

47. Vladimir Putin, "On the Historical Unity of Russians and Ukrainians," July 2021, https://en.wikisource.org/wiki/On_the_Historical_Unity_of_Russians_and_Ukrainians.

48. The best work on thick constructivism is Kratochwil, *Praxis*. Recent research on reputation costs and strategic bargaining retain what is called methodological individualism and treat "reputation cost" as costs largely in actors' heads. For a mainstream view see Ryan Brutger and Joshua Kertzer, "A Dispositional Theory of Reputation Costs," *International Organization* 72, no. 3 (2018): 693–724. For an alternative view, see Sasikumar Sundaram, "The Practices of Evaluating Entitlements: Rethinking 'Reputation' in International Politics," *International Studies Quarterly* 64, no. 3 (2020): 657–68.

49. K. M. Fierke, "Multiple Identities, Interfacing Games: The Social Construction of Western Action in Bosnia," *European Journal of International Relations* 2, no. 4 (December 1, 1996): 467–97; K. M. Fierke, *Changing Games, Changing Strategies: Critical Investigations in Security* (Manchester University Press, 1998). "In the context of war in former Yugoslavia (1991–2001), how actors fixed the meaning of war, whether it resembled—World War I or II, Vietnam, the Gulf War, etc.—was significant in establishing the parameters of how to go on" and the significance of "identities of different players involved." Fierke, *Changing Games, Changing Strategies*, 473.

50. Antje Wiener, *The Invisible Constitution of Politics: Contested Norms and International Encounters* (Cambridge University Press, 2008); Antje Wiener, *A Theory of Contestation* (Springer, 2014); Antje Wiener, *Constitution and Contestation of Norms in Global International Relations* (Cambridge University Press, 2018).

51. This emphasis on language and meaning is different from that of poststructuralist and that of Michel Foucault or Jacques Derrida, where shared meanings of actors are constituted by broader discursive structures, or Louis Althusser's view that actors engaged in

arguing over shared meaning are subjects of ideology because it is ideology that allows them to act that way in the first place.

52. Jennifer Mitzen, "Ontological Security in World Politics: State Identity and the Security Dilemma," *European Journal of International Relations* 12, no. 3 (2006): 342–43. See also Brent Steele, *Ontological Security in International Relations: Self-Identity, and the IR State* (Routledge, 2008); Bahar Rumelili, ed., *Conflict Resolution and Ontological Security* (Routledge, 2015); Christopher Browning, Pertti Joenniemi, and Brent Steele, *Vicarious Identity in International Relations* (Oxford University Press, 2021).

53. Brent Steele, *Defacing Power: The Aesthetics of Insecurity in Global Politics* (University of Michigan Press, 2010).

54. Jackson, *Civilizing the Enemy*; Krebs and Jackson, "Twisting Tongues and Twisting Arms"; Goddard, *Indivisible Territory and the Politics of Legitimacy*; Goddard and Krebs, "Rhetoric, Legitimation, and Grand Strategy"; Krebs, *Narrative and the Making of US National Security*; Goddard, *When Right Makes Might*.

55. Ian Hurd, "The Strategic Use of Liberal Internationalism: Libya and the UN Sanctions, 1992–2003," *International Organization* 59, no. 3 (2005): 495–526; Ian Hurd, *How to Do Things with International Law* (Princeton University Press, 2017).

56. Krebs and Jackson, "Twisting Tongues and Twisting Arms," 44–45.

57. As Stacie Goddard argues, it is not the cost that makes public rhetoric meaningful, as rationalists assume, but "it is the *meaning* of the signal that imbues it with cost. It was because the invasion of Manchuria in 1931 was framed as a challenge to the Western order that it became costly. It was because the American invasion of Florida in 1819 was justified as self-defense that it was costless. In these cases, talk was costly, but for reasons that conventional signal models do not explain." Goddard, *When Right Makes Might*, 28.

58. Goddard, *When Right Makes Might*, 15.

59. Zarakol, *After Defeat*; Hobson, *The Eastern Origins of Western Civilisation*; Ann E. Towns and Bahar Rumelili, "Taking the Pressure: Unpacking the Relation Between Norms, Social Hierarchies, and Social Pressures on States," *European Journal of International Relations* 23, no. 4 (December 1, 2017): 756–79; Valerie M. Hudson, Donna Lee Bowen, and Perpetua Lynne Nielsen, *The First Political Order: How Sex Shapes Governance and National Security Worldwide* (Columbia University Press, 2020). Barder, *Global Race War*; Anievas, Manchanda, and Shilliam, *Race and Racism in International Relations*. For recent critics of hierarchical scholarship on similar lines, see Meera Sabaratnam, "Bring Up the Bodies: International Order, Empire, and Re-Thinking the Great War (1914–1918) from Below," *European Journal of International Relations* (2023): 1–23.

60. Edward Said, *Culture and Imperialism* (Chatto & Windus, 1993), 8.

61. Zarakol, *Hierarchies in World Politics*, 10.

62. On blame, see Toni Erskine, "'Blood on the UN's Hands'? Assigning Duties and Apportioning Blame to an Intergovernmental Organisation," *Global Society* 18, no. 1 (January 1, 2004): 21–42; Liam Clegg, "Benchmarking and Blame Games: Exploring the Contestation of the Millennium Development Goals," *Review of International Studies* 41, no. 5 (2015): 947–67. On shame, see Margaret E. Keck and Kathryn Sikkink, *Activists*

Beyond Borders: Advocacy Networks in International Politics (Cornell University Press, 1998); Rebecca Adler-Nissen, *Opting Out of the European Union: Diplomacy, Sovereignty and European Integration* (Cambridge University Press, 2014); Rebecca Adler-Nissen, "Stigma Management in International Relations: Transgressive Identities, Norms, and Order in International Society," *International Organization* 68, no. 1 (2014): 143–76; Steven Ward, *Status and the Challenge of Rising Powers* (Cambridge University Press, 2017).

63. John M. Hobson and Alina Sajed, "Navigating Beyond the Eurofetishist Frontier of Critical IR Theory: Exploring the Complex Landscapes of Non-Western Agency," *International Studies Review* 19, no. 4 (2017): 559. The charge is against postcolonial subjectivity scholarship, which is also largely shared in recent years by ontological (in)security scholarship. See Jabri, *The Postcolonial Subject*; Jenny Edkins, Michael J. Shapiro, and Veronique Pin-Fat, eds., "Introduction: Life, Power, Resistance," in *Sovereign Lives: Power in Global Politics* (Routledge, 2004), 1–21; Jenny Edkins, *Trauma and the Memory of Politics* (Cambridge University Press, 2003). See Nina Krickel-Choi, "The Concept of Anxiety in Ontological Security Studies," *International Studies Review* 23, no. 3 (2022): 1–20. For a critique of ontological security models, see Richard Ned Lebow, *National Identities and International Relations* (Cambridge University Press, 2016).

64. The focus on practices has generated extensive scholarship in IR. For formative texts, see Emanuel Adler and Vincent Pouliot, "International Practices," *International Theory* 3, no. 1 (February 2011): 1–36; Emanuel Adler and Vincent Pouliot, *International Practice* (Cambridge University Press, 2011). For critique of the Bourdieu-inspired practice turn in IR, see Sasikumar Sundaram and Vineet Thakur, "A Pragmatic Methodology for Studying International Practices," *Journal of International Political Theory* 17, no. 3 (2019): 337–55.

65. Andrew Phillips, *How the East Was Won: Barbarian Conquerors, Universal Conquest and the Making of Modern Asia* (Cambridge University Press, 2021), 22.

66. Jürgen Osterhammel, *The Transformation of the World: A Global History of the Nineteenth Century*, trans. Patrick Camiller (Princeton University Press, 2014), 432.

67. Goddard, *When Right Makes Might*, 17.

68. Edward Keene, "International Hierarchy and the Origins of the Modern Practice of Intervention," *Review of International Studies* 39, no. 5 (2013): 1090.

69. Goddard, *When Right Makes Might*, 19. On legitimating principles, see Ian Clark, *Legitimacy in International Society* (Oxford University Press, 2005); Friedrich Kratochwil, "On Legitimacy," *International Relations* 20, no. 3 (2006): 302–8; Ian Clark, *International Legitimacy and World Society* (Oxford University Press, 2007).

70. There are multiple ways of understanding world ordering. See Wiener, *Constitution and Contestation of Norms*; Emanuel Adler, *World Ordering: A Social Theory of Cognitive Evolution* (Cambridge University Press, 2019); Ayşe Zarakol, *Before the West: The Rise and Fall of Eastern World Orders* (Cambridge University Press, 2022).

71. Gerrit W. Gong, *The Standard of "Civilization" in International Society* (Oxford University Press, 1984); Gerry Simpson, *Great Powers and Outlaw States: Unequal Sovereigns in the International Legal Order* (Cambridge University Press, 2004); Anghie, *Imperialism, Sovereignty and the Making of International Law*; Siba Grovogui, *Sovereigns, Quasi Sovereigns, and Africans: Race and Self-Determination in International Law* (University of

Minnesota Press, 2006); Robbie Shilliam, *Black Pacific: Anticolonial Struggles and Oceanic Connections* (Bloomsbury, 2015); Jennifer Pitts, *Boundaries of the International: Law and Empire* (Harvard University Press, 2018).

72.   Getachew, *Worldmaking After Empire*, 20.

73.   Zarakol, *Hierarchies in World Politics*. See also Barder, *Global Race War*. For an improvement from the previous version of hierarchy scholarship, see Towns and Rumelili, "Taking the Pressure"; Sabaratnam "Bring Up the Bodies."

74.   David A. Lake, "Escape from the State of Nature: Authority and Hierarchy in World Politics," *International Security* 32, no. 1 (July 1, 2007): 47–79, https://doi.org/10.1162/isec.2007.32.1.47; Alexander Cooley and Daniel H. Nexon, "'The Empire Will Compensate You': The Structural Dynamics of the U.S. Overseas Basing Network," *Perspectives on Politics* 11, no. 4 (2013): 1034–50; David Vine, *Base Nation: How U.S. Military Bases Abroad Harm America and the World* (Henry Holt, 2015); Sebastian Schmidt, *Armed Guests: Territorial Sovereignty and Foreign Military Basing* (Oxford University Press, 2020).

75.   Immanuel Wallerstein, *The Modern World-System I: Capitalist Agriculture and the Origins of the European World-Economy in the Sixteenth Century* (University of California Press, 2011); Alexander Anievas and Kerem Nişancıoğlu, *How the West Came to Rule: The Geopolitical Origins of Capitalism* (Pluto, 2015); Chris King-Chi Chan and Elaine Sio-Ieng Hui, "Bringing Class Struggles Back: A Marxian Analysis of the State and Class Relations in China," *Globalizations* 14, no. 2 (2017): 232–44; David Blaney and Naeem Inayatullah, *Within, Against, and Beyond Liberalism: A Critique of Liberal IPE and Global Capitalism* (Rowman & Littlefield, 2021).

76.   T. V. Paul, Deborah Welch Larson, and William C. Wohlforth, *Status in World Politics* (Cambridge University Press, 2014). Rohan Mukherjee, *Ascending Orders: Rising Powers and the Politics of Status in International Institutions* (Cambridge University Press, 2022).

77.   Robbie Shilliam, *Black Pacific: Anticolonial Struggles and Oceanic Connections* (Bloomsbury, 2015); Anievas, Manchanda, and Shilliam, *Race and Racism in International Relations*; Barder, *Global Race War*.

78.   Laura J. Shepherd, *Gender Matters in Global Politics* (Routledge, 2010); Cynthia Weber, *Queer International Relations: Sovereignty, Sexuality and the Will to Knowledge* (Oxford University Press, 2016); Marie E. Berry, *War, Women, and Power: From Violence to Mobilization in Rwanda and Bosnia-Herzegovina* (Cambridge University Press, 2018); Valerie M. Hudson, Donna Lee Bowen, and Perpetua Lynne Nielsen, *The First Political Order: How Sex Shapes Governance and National Security Worldwide* (Columbia University Press, 2020).

79.   Towns and Rumelili, "Taking the Pressure."

80.   Spivak, "Can the Subaltern Speak?"; Phillip Darby, *Postcolonizing the International: Working to Change the Way We Are* (University of Hawai'i Press, 2006); Dotson, "Tracking Epistemic Violence"; de Sousa Santos, *The End of the Cognitive Empire*; Brunner, "Conceptualizing Epistemic Violence."

81.   From the theoretical view of silencing established by Gayatri Chakravorty Spivak, *A Critique of Postcolonial Reason* (Harvard University Press, 1999); Dotson, "Tracking Epistemic Violence"; de Sousa Santos, *The End of the Cognitive Empire*.

82. Dotson, "Tracking Epistemic Violence," 242.

83. See Patricia Hill Collins, *Black Feminist Thought: Knowledge, Consciousness, and the Politics of Empowerment*, 30th anniversary ed. (Routledge, 2022).

84. Dotson, "Tracking Epistemic Violence."

85. Sujit Sivasundaram, *Waves Across the South: A New History of Revolution and Empire* (University of Chicago Press, 2021); Gyan Prakash and Jeremy Adelman, "Imagining the Third World: Genealogies of Alternative Global Histories," in *Inventing the Third World*, ed. Gyan Prakash and Jeremy Adelman, 8 (Bloomsbury, 2023).

86. David Spurr, *The Rhetoric of Empire: Colonial Discourse in Journalism, Travel Writing, and Imperial Administration* (Duke University Press, 1993). See also Martin Thomas and Richard Toye, eds., *Rhetorics of Empire Languages of Colonial Conflict After 1900* (Manchester University Press, 2017).

87. Uday Singh Mehta, *Liberalism and Empire: A Study in Nineteenth-Century British Liberal Thought* (University of Chicago Press, 1999), 48.

88. Martin Wight, *Power Politics* (Penguin, 1986); Edward Keene, "The Naming of Powers," *Cooperation and Conflict* 48, no. 2 (June 2013): 268–82. See also Keene, "International Hierarchy." For an interesting scientific and cosmological view, see Bentley Allan, *Scientific Cosmology and International Orders* (Cambridge University Press, 2018).

89. Spurr, *The Rhetoric of Empire*, 105.

90. Osterhammel, *The Transformation of the World*, 485.

91. Ali Hamoudi, "Iraq, Imperialism, Political Economy, and International Law," in *The Palgrave Encyclopedia of Imperialism and Anti-Imperialism*, ed. Immanuel Ness and Zak Cope, 1372 (Springer, 2021). See also Susan Pedersen, *The Guardians: The League of Nations and the Crisis of Empire* (Oxford University Press, 2015).

92. Mohammed Bedjaoui, *Towards a New International Economic Order* (Lynne Rienner, 1979). See also Mohammed Bedjaoui, "The Right to Development," in *International Law: Achievement and Prospects*, ed. Federick Mayor and Mohammed Bedjaoui, 1177–1203 (Brill, 1992).

93. Sundhya Pahuja, *Decolonizing International Law: Development, Economic Growth and the Politics of Universality* (Cambridge University Press, 2011).

94. UN Doc A/C.3/41/SR.46 (1986), Statement of Ms Clark, cited in Philip Alston, "Making Space for New Human Rights: The Case of the Right to Development," *Harvard Human Rights Yearbook* 1 (1988): 3–40.

95. United Nations, "General Assembly Resolution 3201 (S-VI): Declaration on the Establishment of a New International Economic Order," and "General Assembly Resolution 3202 (S-VI): Programme of Action on the Establishment of a New International Economic Order," *Official Records of the General Assembly: Sixth Special Session*, supplement no. 1 (A/9559) (United Nations): 3–12.

96. Anthony Anghie, "Legal Aspects of the New International Economic Order," *Humanity: An International Journal of Human Rights, Humanitarianism, and Development* 6, no. 1 (2015): 146.

97. A classical work is Leo Panitch and Sam Gindin, *The Making of Global Capitalism: The Political Economy of American Empire* (Verso, 2013). For traditional understanding of

material capabilities, see Barry Eichengreen, *Exorbitant Privilege: The Rise and Fall of the Dollar* (Oxford University Press, 2011); Eric Helleiner, *Forgotten Foundations of Bretton Woods: International Development and the Making of the Postwar Order* (Cornell University Press, 2014); Eric Helleiner and Jonathan Kirshner, eds., *The Future of the Dollar* (Cornell University Press, 2019). For a critical understanding of the incompetence based on capabilities, see David Blaney and Naeem Inayatullah, "Liberal International Political Economy as Colonial Science," in *The Sage Handbook of the History, Philosophy and Sociology of International Relations*, ed. Andreas Gofas, Inanna Hamati-Ataya, and Nicholas Onuf, 60–74 (Sage, 2018).

98.   Dianne Otto, "Subalternity and International Law: The Problems of Global Community and the Incommensurability of Difference," *Social & Legal Studies* 5, no. 3 (September 1996): 337–64; Kevin Jon Heller, "Retreat from Nuremberg: The Leadership Requirement in the Crime of Aggression," *European Journal of International Law* 18, no. 3 (2007): 477–97; Kevin Jon Heller, "Deconstructing International Criminal Law," *Michigan Law Review* 106 (2007–2008): 975; Obiora Chinedu Okafor, "Critical Third World Approaches to International Law (TWAIL): Theory, Methodology, or Both?," *International Community Law Review* 10, no. 4 (2008): 371–78. For a superb account of third world approaches to international law (TWAIL), see Antony Anghie, "Rethinking International Law: A TWAIL Retrospective," *European Journal of International Law* 34, no. 1 (February 1, 2023): 7–112.

99.   Martin Daniel Niemetz, *Reforming UN Decision-Making Procedures: Promoting a Deliberative System for Global Peace and Security* (Routledge, 2015); John Langmore and Ramesh Thakur, "The Elected but Neglected Security Council Members," *Washington Quarterly* 39, no. 2 (April 2, 2016): 99–114, https://doi.org/10.1080/0163660X.2016.1204412; Marie-Eve Loiselle, "The Penholder System and the Rule of Law in the Security Council Decision-Making: Setback or Improvement?," *Leiden Journal of International Law* 33, no. 1 (March 2020): 139–56, http://dx.doi.org/10.1017/S0922156519000621.

100.   Jill Lepore, *These Truths: A History of the United States* (Norton, 2018), 144, Kindle.

101.   Robin Blackburn, "Haiti, Slavery, and the Age of the Democratic Revolution," *William and Mary Quarterly* 63, no. 4 (2006): 657.

102.   Lepore, *These Truths*.

103.   Getachew, *Worldmaking After Empire*, 21.

104.   Karuna Mantena, *Alibis of Empire: Henry Maine and the Ends of Liberal Imperialism* (Princeton University Press, 2010), 9.

105.   Mantena, *Alibis of Empire*, 39–41.

106.   J. Fitzjames Stephen, *Liberty, Equality, Fraternity* (Holt & Williams, 1873).

107.   B. K. Shrivastava, "The United States and the Non-Aligned Movement," *International Studies* 20, no. 1–2 (January 1, 1981): 429–44, https://doi.org/10.1177/002088178102000132.

108.   Thomas Borstelmann, "Jim Crow's Coming Out: Race Relations and American Foreign Policy in the Truman Years," *Presidential Studies Quarterly* 29, no. 3 (1999): 552, https://doi.org/10.1111/ j.0268-2141.2003.00049.x.

109.   Odd Arne Westad, *The Global Cold War* (Cambridge University Press, 2012), 265.

110.   See, for example, Vijay Prashad, *Arab Spring, Libyan Winter* (LeftWord, 2012).

111. "UK Minister Says West Must Learn to Listen Better to Global South," *The Guardian*, September 20, 2023, https://www.theguardian.com/politics/2023/sep/20/uk-minister -james-cleverly-says-west-must-learn-to-listen-better-to-global-south.

112. Hannah Arendt, "What Is Authority?," in *Between Past and Future: Eight Essays in Political Thought* (Penguin, 2006), 92.

113. For an important account of the authority enactment of the British Empire, see Bernard Cohn, "Representing Authority in Victorian England," in *The Invention of Tradition*, ed. Eric Hobsbawm and Terence Ranger, 165–210 (Cambridge University Press, 2012).

114. William Mulligan, "Decisions for Empire: Revisiting the 1882 Occupation of Egypt," *English Historical Review* 135, no. 572 (2000): 117.

115. On intermediaries, see Colin Newbury, *Patrons, Clients, and Empire: Chieftancy and Over-Rule in Asia, Africa, and the Pacific* (Oxford University Press, 2003); Daniel H. Nexon and Thomas Wright, "What's at Stake in the American Empire Debate," *American Political Science Review* 1, no. 2 (May 2007): 253–71; Cooley and Nexon, "The Empire Will Compensate You"; Paul K. Macdonald, *Networks of Domination: The Social Foundations of Peripheral Conquest in International Politics* (Oxford University Press, 2014); Phillips, *How the East Was Won*.

116. Spurr, *The Rhetoric of Empire*, 69.

117. Pedersen, *The Guardians*, 112.

118. See Tara Zahra, *Against the World: Anti-Globalism and Mass Politics Between the World Wars* (Norton, 2023), 350. See also Mark Mazower, *No Enchanted Palace: The End of Empire and the Ideological Origins of the United Nations* (Princeton University Press, 2009).

119. Nicholas J. Wheeler, *Saving Strangers: Humanitarian Intervention in International Society* (Oxford University Press, 2001); Gary J. Bass, "The Indian Way of Humanitarian Intervention," *Yale Journal of International Law* 40, no. 2 (2015): 228–94.

120. See, for example, Anghie, *Imperialism, Sovereignty and the Making of International Law*; Anne Orford, *Reading Humanitarian Intervention: Human Rights and the Use of Force in International Law* (Cambridge University Press, 2003); Jochen von Bernstorff and Philipp Dann, eds., *The Battle for International Law: South-North Perspectives on the Decolonization Era* (Oxford University Press, 2019); Anghie "Rethinking International Law."

121. Anghie, "Rethinking International Law," 68.

122. See Victor Kattan, "Furthering the 'War on Terrorism' Through International Law: How the United States and the United Kingdom Resurrected the Bush Doctrine on Using Preventive Military Force to Combat Terrorism," *Journal on the Use of Force and International Law* 5, no. 1 (2018): 97–144; Chloe Goldthrope, "The Imbalanced Geography of the Law on Use of Force in Self-Defence," *International Community Law Review* 26 (2024): 434–75; Application of the Convention on the Prevention and Punishment of the Crime of Genocide in the Gaza Strip (South Africa v. Israel). On December 29, 2023, South Africa filed the proceedings in International Court of Justice (ICJ) against Israel under the Genocide Convention. The UN has reiterated Israel's genocide in Gaza. "Report of the Special Rapporteur on the Situation of Human Rights in the Palestinian Territories Occupied Since 1967, Francesca Albanese," Human Rights Council, 56th Session,

February 26 to April 5, 2024, Agenda item 7, *Human Rights Situation in Palestine and Other Occupied Arab Territories*, A/HRC/55/73, https://www.ohchr.org/sites/default /files/documents/hrbodies/hrcouncil/sessions-regular/session55/advance-versions/a -hrc-55-73-auv.pdf (advance unedited version, accessed on November 14, 2023). "It is Important to Call a Genocide a Genocide: Consider Suspending Israel's Credential as UN Member State, Experts Tell Palestinian Rights Committee," 419th Meeting, UNGA, GA/PAL/1473, October 31, 2024, https://press.un.org/en/2024/gapal1473.doc.htm.

123. The role of the United Kingdom in silencing the claims of others in elaborating a modern law of self-defense was evident in the speech of then attorney general Jeremy Wright in 2017, which presented the United Kingdom as authority and leader in customary international law on the use of force and self-defense. Jeremy Wright, *The Modern Law of Self-Defence* (EJIL: Talk, January 2017), https://www.ejiltalk.org/the-modern-law-of-self -defence/. For China and other non-Western actors who opposed the Western imposition on self-defense norm, see UNGA and UNSC Arria Formula Meeting of the Security Council on the Theme "Upholding the Collective Security System of the Charter of the United Nations: The Use of Force in International Law, Non-State Actors and Legitimate Self Defence," February 24, 2021 (March 16, 2021) UN Doc A/75/993-S/2021/247 30.

124. Ann E. Kent, *China, the United Nations, and Human Rights: The Limits of Compliance* (University of Pennsylvania Press, 1999). But see Randall Peerenboom, "Assessing Human Rights in China: Why the Double Standard?," *Cornell International Law Journal* 38, no. 1 (2005): 72–172; Samuel Moyn, "The Future of Human Rights," *Sur: International Journal on Human Rights* 11 (2014): 57.

125. Anghie, "Rethinking International Law."

126. Daniel Nexon, "International Order and Power Politics," in *International Institutions and Power Politics*, ed. Andres Wivel and T. V. Paul, 199 (Georgetown University Press, 2019). See also Goddard, *When Right Makes Might*.

127. The literature on performativity in IR is extensive and largely builds on feminist IR from the works of Judith Butler, *Excitable Speech: A Politics of Performative* (Psychology Press, 1997); Judith Butler, "Performative Agency," *Journal of Cultural Economy* 3, no. 2 (2010): 147–61. There are two distinctive even if overlapping debates on performance. Some treat performers as prior to their performances. An important work is Erik Ringmar, "How the World State Makes Its Subjects: An Embodied Critique of Constructivist IR Theory," *Journal of International Relations and Development* 19, no. 1 (2016): 101–25. Others do not make such distinctions because of the ontological effects of practices. See Cynthia Weber, "Performative States," *Millennium* 27, no. 1 (1998): 77–95. See also David McCourt, "Practice Theory and Relationalism as the New Constructivism," *International Studies Quarterly* 60, no. 3 (2016): 475–85; Benjamin Braun, Sebastian Schindler, and Tobias Wille, "Rethinking Agency in International Relations: Performativity, Performances, and Actor-Networks," *Journal of International Relations and Development* 22 (2018): 787–807; Iver Neumann and Ole Jacob Sending, "Performing Statehood Through Crises: Citizens, Strangers, Territory," *Journal of Global Security Studies* 6, no. 1 (2021): 1–16. Scholarship on affective performances in IR draws mostly from Gilles Deluze, William Connolly, and Henri Lefebvre, among others. See Gilles Deluze, *Spinoza: Practical Philosophy*, trans. R.

Hurley (City Lights, 1988). Important advancements in IR are discussed in Brent Steele, *Defacing Power: The Aesthetics of Insecurity in Global Politics* (University of Michigan Press, 2010); Karin Fierke, *Political Self-Sacrifice: Agency, Body and Emotion in International Relations* (Cambridge University Press, 2013); Emma Hutchinson, *Affective Communities in World Politics* (Cambridge University Press, 2016); Robin Markwica, *Emotional Choices: How the Logic of Affect Shapes Coercive Diplomacy* (Oxford University Press, 2018). These two strands of scholarship in IR have not clarified the role of affective performances in the rhetoric of non-Western states for realpolitik objectives.

128. Elizabeth Anderson, "Moral Bias and Corrective Practices: A Pragmatist Perspective," *Proceedings and Addresses of the American Philosophical Association* 89 (2015): 39.

129. See Clark, *International Legitimacy and World Society*. On contradictions, see David Harvey, *Seventeen Contradictions and the End of Capitalism* (Profile Books, 2014). See also Gisela Febel, Kerstin Knopf, and Martin Nonhoff, eds., *Contradiction Studies: Exploring the Field* (Springer, 2023).

130. George Lawson and Ayşe Zarakol, "Recognizing Injustice: The 'Hypocrisy Charge' and the Future of the Liberal International Order," *International Affairs* 99, no. 1 (January 9, 2023): 203.

131. Osterhammel, *The Transformation of the World*, 495.

132. Harvey, *Seventeen Contradictions and the End of Capitalism*, 23.

133. The norm contestation in IR scholarship, however, does not focus on the problem of contradictions between norms and its diverse contestation practices in the Global South, arguably because of its Eurocentrism in the analysis of norm contestations. See Wiener, *The Invisible Constitution of Politics*; Wiener, *A Theory of Contestation*.

134. This is what Homi Bhabha calls resistance in colonial discourse that is not merely opposition but ambivalence in the dominating discourse. See Spurr, *The Rhetoric of Empire*, 185.

135. Christopher Bayly, "European Political Thought and the Wider World During the Nineteenth Century," in *The Cambridge History of Nineteenth-Century Political Thought*, ed. Gareth Stedman Jones and Gregory Claeys, 845 (Cambridge University Press, 2011).

136. C. A. Bayly, *Recovering Liberties: Indian Thought in the Age of Liberalism and Empire* (Cambridge University Press, 2012).

137. Doug McAdam, Sidney G. Tarrow, and Charles Tilly, *Dynamics of Contention* (Cambridge University Press, 1991), 138.

138. Stacie Goddard, Paul MacDonald, and Daniel Nexon, "Repertoires of Statecraft: Instruments and Logics of Power Politics," *International Relations* 33, no. 2 (2019): 315.

139. Charles Tilly, *Durable Inequalities* (University of California Press, 1998), 155.

140. On conceiving practices in a static way, see Emanuel Adler and Vincent Pouliot, "International Practices," *International Theory* 3, no. 1 (February 2011): 1–36; Vincent Pouliot, *International Security in Practice: The Politics of NATO-Russia Diplomacy* (Cambridge University Press, 2010); Christian Bueger and Frank Gadinger, *International Practice Theory* (Palgrave Macmillan, 2014); Emanuel Adler, *World Ordering: A Social Theory of Cognitive Evolution* (Cambridge University Press, 2019). The best study on the problems of the practice turn in IR is Kratochwil, *Praxis*, chap. 10. Vineet Thakur and I made some reflections on the normative aspect of any practices. See Sundaram and Thakur,

"A Pragmatic Methodology for Studying International Practices." In challenging the static view of practices in many of Bourdieu-inspired practice turns in IR, I follow the works of Friedrich Kratochwil and other critical constructivists. For the role of normativity in practices, see Sundaram and Thakur, "A Pragmatic Methodology for Studying International Practices." For a normative view to improve community of practice approach, see Sasikumar Sundaram, "The Practices of Evaluating Entitlements: Rethinking 'Reputation' in International Politics," *International Studies Quarterly* 64, no. 3 (2020): 657–68.

141. Rachel A. Ankeny and Sabina Leonelli, "Repertoires: A Post-Kuhnian Perspective on Scientific Change and Collaborative Research," *Studies in History and Philosophy of Science Part A* 60 (December 2016): 21. For an important sociological study on the innovations in the repertoires of jazz music, see Robert Faulkner and Howard Becker, *"Do You Know . . ." The Jazz Repertoire in Action* (University of Chicago Press, 2009). Although Inayatullah's work is not framed as repertoire, see also Naeem Inayatullah, "Gigging on the World Stage: Bossa Nova and Afrobeat After De-Reification," *Contexo Internacional* 38, no. 2 (2016): 523–43.

142. Spurr, *The Rhetoric of Empire*, 190.

143. Patrick Thaddeus Jackson, *The Conduct of Inquiry: Philosophy of Science and Its Implications for the Study of World Politics* (Routledge, 2011), 142–55. For a similar ideal-typical treatment on revisionism, see Alexander Cooley, Daniel Nexon, and Steven Ward, "Revising Order or Challenging the Balance of Military Power? An Alternative Typology of Revisionist and Status-Quo States," *Review of International Studies* 45, no. 4 (2019): 689–708.

144. Barbara Koremenos, Charles Lipson, and Duncan Snidal, "The Rational Design of International Institutions," *International Organization* 55, no. 4 (2001): 761–99. See also Anders Wivel and T. V. Paul, eds., *International Institutions and Power Politics: Bridging the Divide* (Georgetown University Press, 2019).

145. As Margaret Gilbert puts it, what goes on in such reasoning is of joint commitment in the form: "We* accept [a principle], therefore in so far as I am one of us*, I ought to conform to [the principles]." Margaret Gilbert, *On Social Facts* (Princeton University Press, 1992), 374.

146. Translation is also an important theoretical idea in IR scholarship. Many draw influence from Jacques Derrida, *The Ear of the Other: Otobiography, Transference, Translation*, ed. Christie McDonald, trans. Peggy Kamuf (Schocken, 1985); Ernesto Laclau and Chantal Mouffe, *Hegemony and Socialist Strategy* (Verso, 1985); Pierre Bourdieu, *Language and Symbolic Power*, trans. Gino Raymond and Matthew Adamson (Harvard University Press, 1991); Slavoj Žižek, *How to Read Lacan* (Granta, 2006). In recent years in IR, see Reinhart Kosselleck, *Futures Past: On the Semantics of Historical Time*, trans. Keith Tribe (Columbia University Press, 2004). For some specific IR works that use and take these philosophical works in novel directions, see Edkins, *Poststructuralism and International Relations*; Lene Hansen, *Security as Practice: Discourse Analysis and the Bosnian War* (Routledge, 2006); Charlotte Epstein, *The Power of Words in International Relations: Birth of an Anti-Whaling Discourse* (MIT Press, 2008); Charlotte Epstein, "Constructivism or the Eternal Return of Universals in International Relations: Why Returning to Language Is Vital to Prolonging the Owl's Flight," *European Journal of International Relations* 19, no. 3 (2013): 499–519; Thomas Jacobs, "Poststructuralist Discourse Theory

as an Independent Paradigm for Studying Institutions: Towards a New Definition of 'Discursive Construction' in Institutional Analysis," *Contemporary Political Theory* 17 (2019): 1–22. For novel advancements, see Einar Wigen, *State of Translation: Turkey in Interlingual Relations* (University of Michigan Press, 2018).

147.   It is different from discourse analysis. See Kevin C. Dunn and Iver B. Neumann, *Undertaking Discourse Analysis for Social Research* (University of Michigan Press, 2016).

148.   Dvora Yanow and Peregrine Schwartz-Shea, eds., *Interpretation and Method: Empirical Research Methods and the Interpretive Turn* (M. E. Sharpe, 2006); Patrick Thaddeus Jackson, "Making Sense of Making Sense: Configurational Analysis and the Double Hermeneutic," in *Interpretation and Method*, ed. Dvora Yanow and Peregrine Schwartz-Shea, 264–80 (M. E. Sharpe, 2006); Peregrine Schwartz-Shea and Dvora Yanow, *Interpretive Research Design: Concepts and Processes* (Routledge, 2012); Cecelia Lynch, *Interpreting International Politics* (Routledge, 2014); David M. McCourt, "Practice Theory and Relationalism as the New Constructivism," *International Studies Quarterly* 60, no. 3 (2016): 475–85; Mark Bevir, *Routledge Handbook of Interpretive Political Science* (Routledge, 2016); R. A. W. Rhodes, *Interpretive Political Science: Selected Essays* (Oxford University Press, 2017); Mark Bevir, *Interpretive Social Science: An Anti-Naturalist Approach*, repr. ed. (Oxford University Press, 2019); Xymena Kurowska, "When Home Is Part of the Field: Experiencing Uncanniness of Home in Field Conversations," in *Tactical Constructivism, Method, and International Relations: Expression and Reflection*, ed. Brent J. Steele, Harry D. Gould, and Oliver Kessler (Routledge, 2020).

149.   Vijay Prashad, *Darker Nations: A People's History of the Third World* (New Press, 2008), 1.

150.   See United Nations Development Programme (UNDP), Human Development Report 2013: The Rise of the South: Human Progress in a Diverse World (2013), https://hdr.undp.org/content/human-development-report-2013.

151.   J. L. Holzgrefe, "The Humanitarian Intervention Debate," in *Humanitarian Intervention: Ethical, Legal, and Political Dilemmas*, ed. J. L. Holzgrefe and R. O. Keohane, 18 (Cambridge University Press, 2003).

152.   Keene, "International Hierarchy," 1090.

153.   Yanow and Schwartz-Shea, *Interpretation and Method*, xvii.

154.   Robert Brandom, *Making It Explicit: Reasoning, Representing, and Discursive Commitment* (Harvard University Press, 1994); Robert Brandom, *Reason in Philosophy: Animating Ideas* (Belknap Press of Harvard University Press, 2009); Steven Levine, "Norms and Habits: Brandom on the Sociality of Action," *European Journal of Philosophy* 23, no. 2 (June 1, 2015): 248–72; Sundaram, "Varieties of Political Rhetorical Reasoning."

155.   Sundaram and Thakur, "A Pragmatic Methodology for Studying International Practices."

2. REPERTOIRE OF POWER POLITICS IN INDIA, BRAZIL, AND CHINA

1.   Neil Genzlinger, "Immanuel Wallerstein, Sociologist with Global View, Dies at 88," *New York Times*, September 10, 2019.

2.   Immanuel Wallerstein, "Whose Interests Are Served by the BRICS?," in *Brazil, Russia, India, China, South Africa: An Anti-Capitalist Critique*, ed. Patrick Bond and Ana Garcia, 272 (Haymarket, 2015).

3.   Tony Ballantyne and Antoinette Burton, *Empires and the Reach of the Global, 1870–1945* (Harvard University Press, 2014), 131–32.

4.   Along the lines of contentious repertoire, see Charles Tilly, "Contentious Repertoires in Great Britain, 1758–1834," *Social Science History* 17, no. 2 (1993): 264; Charles Tilly, *Regimes and Repertoires* (University of Chicago Press, 2010).

5.   Sudipta Kaviraj, "Modernity and Politics in India," in *Multiple Modernities*, ed. Shmuel N. Eisenstadt, 140 (Routledge, 2002).

6.   For example, Himadeep Muppidi, *The Colonial Signs of International Relations* (Columbia University Press, 2012); Ballantyne and Burton, *Empires and the Reach of the Global*; Erez Manela and Heather Streets-Salter, eds., *The Anticolonial Transnational: Imaginaries, and Networks in the Struggle Against Empire* (Cambridge University Press, 2023).

7.   Sujit Sivasundaram, *Waves Across the South: A New History of Revolution and Empire* (Chicago University Press, 2021), chap. 2.

8.   Jane Burbank and Frederick Cooper, *Empires in World History: Power and the Politics of Difference* (Princeton University Press, 2010), 19.

9.   Christopher Bayly, "The First Age of Global Imperialism, c. 1760–1830," *Journal of Imperial and Commonwealth History* 26, no. 2 (May 1, 1998): 39–40.

10. John Darwin, "Imperialism and the Victorians: The Dynamics of Territorial Expansion," *English Historical Review* 112, no. 447 (1997): 614–42.

11. Christopher Bayly, *Recovering Liberties: Indian Thought in the Age of Liberalism and Empire* (Cambridge University Press, 2012), 10. See also C. A. Bayly, *The Origins of Nationality in South Asia: Patriotism and Ethical Government in the Making of Modern India* (Oxford University Press, 1998).

12. See Lynn Zastoupil, *Rammohun Roy and the Making of Victorian Britain* (Palgrave, 2010). See also Nazmul Sultan, *Waiting for the People: The Idea of Democracy in Indian Anticolonial Thought* (Harvard University Press, 2024).

13. Ram Raz, "On the Intellectual Character of the Hindus," *Asiatic Journal* 25 (1828), in Christopher Bayly, *Recovering Liberties: Indian Thought in the Age of Liberalism and Empire* (Cambridge University Press, 2012), 69.

14. Leslie Bethell, *Brazil: Essays on History and Politics* (Institute of Latin American Studies, School of Advanced Study, University of London, 2018), 71.

15. Bayly, *The Origins of Nationality in South Asia*, 8.

16. James N. Green, Victoria Langland, and Lilia Moritz Schwarcz, eds., *The Brazil Reader: History, Culture, and Politics* (Duke University Press, 2019), 175.

17. This survival strategy was largely successful. The Qing dynasty survived a series of rebellions: White Lotus Rebellion (1796–1804), Taiping Rebellion (1850–1864), Nien (1853–1868), and Muslim Rebellion (1855–1873). There were also a series of foreign wars against the British (1839–1842), Anglo-French (1856–1860), French (1883–1885), Japanese (1894–1895), Scramble for Concessions (1898), and the Boxer War of 1900.

18. Yen-P'ing Hao and Erh-min Wang, "Changing Chinese Views of Western Relations (1840–95)," in *The Cambridge History of China*, ed. Denis Twitchett and John Fairbank, 142–201 (Cambridge University Press, 1980).

19. John Fairbank, "The Far East," in Guy S. Métraux and François Crouzet, *The New Asia* (Mentor Books, 1965), 324–55. See also Li Man, "'To Change' or 'to Be Changed': The Dialectics of a Decaying Empire and the Political Philosophy of Wei Yuan (1794–1857)," *Global Intellectual History* 1, no. 3 (2016): 261–74; Peter Mitchell, "The Limits of Reformism: Wei Yuan's Reaction to Western Intrusion," *Modern Asian Studies* 6, no. 2 (1972): 175–204; Jane Leonard, *Wei Yuan and China's Rediscovery of the Maritime World* (Harvard University Press, 1984). For how Wei Yuan inspired imperial Japan, see Man, "'To Change' or 'to Be Changed.'"

20. Fairbank, "The Far East."

21. See Sivasundaram, *Waves Across the South*, chap. 6.

22. Hao and Wang, "Changing Chinese Views of Western Relations," 156.

23. On Bankim Chatterjee, see Sudipta Kaviraj, *The Unhappy Consciousness: Bankimchandra Chattopadhyay and the Formation of Nationalist Discourse in India* (Oxford University Press, 1995).

24. The best work is Manu Goswami, *Producing India: From Colonial Economy to National Space* (University of Chicago Press, 2010), chaps. 7–9. On Bankim Chatterjee, see Kaviraj, *The Unhappy Consciousness*. On Mahadev Ranade, see Mahadev Ranade, *Select Writings: The Late Hon'ble M.G. Ranade on Indian States*, ed. V. W. Thakur (Printing Works, 1942).

25. Goswami, *Producing India*, 214–15.

26. The republican revolution in the South of Brazil (Revolução Farroupinha) in 1835–1845 saw Ana Eurídice Eufrosina de Barandas' call for women's rights in light of the country's historical traditions, which also transformed into Francisa Senhorinha da Motta Diniz's call for women's education in 1873. See June Hahner, *Emancipação do sexo feminino: A Luta pelos direitos da mulher no Brasil 1850–1940* (Editora Mulheres, 2003).

27. Francisco Primo de Souza Aguiar, "The U.S. Civil War and Slave Rebellions in Brazil," in *The Brazil Reader: History, Culture, and Politics*, ed. James Green, Victoria Langland, and Lilia Moritz Schwarcz, 218 (Duke University Press, 2019).

28. Hao and Wang, "Changing Chinese Views of Western Relations," 164.

29. Gerrit W. Gong, *The Standard of "Civilization" in International Society* (Oxford University Press, 1984).

30. John King Fairbank and Merle Goldman, *China: A New History*, 2nd rev. and enlarged ed. (Belknap Press of Harvard University Press, 2006), 217.

31. Although on a smaller scale than the ones suggested by Liang Qichao and Kang Yuwei. See Liang Qichao and Kang Yuwei, "Sun Yet-Sen's Reform Proposal to Li Hongzhang, 1893," in *The Search for Modern China: A Documentary Study*, ed. Pei-Kai Cheng, Micheal Lestz, and Jonathan Spence, 168–72 (Norton, 2013).

32. Christopher Bayly, "European Political Thought and the Wider World During the Nineteenth Century," in *The Cambridge History of Nineteenth-Century Political Thought*, ed. Gareth Stedman Jones and Gregory Claeys, 848 (Cambridge University Press, 2011).

33. Jürgen Osterhammel, *The Transformation of the World: A Global History of the Nineteenth Century*, trans. Patrick Camiller (Princeton University Press, 2014), 432.

34. For recent elaborations, see Jeremy Black, *Geopolitics and the Quest for Dominance* (Indiana University Press, 2016); Or Rosenboim, *The Emergence of Globalism: Visions of World Order in Britain and the United States, 1939–1950* (Princeton University Press, 2016); Matthew Specter, *The Atlantic Realists: Empire and International Political Thought Between Germany and the United States* (Stanford University Press, 2022).

35. On British public goods, see Osterhammel, *The Transformation of the World*, 455. On Anglosphere as a geopolitical project of Greater Britain, see Duncan Bell, *The Idea of Greater Britain: Empire and the Future of World Order, 1860–1900* (Princeton University Press, 2007).

36. Karl Polyani, *The Great Transformation: The Politics and Economic Origins of Our Time* (Beacon, 1944).

37. Osterhammel, *The Transformation of the World*, 472. See also Paul Kennedy, *The Rise and Fall of the Great Powers* (Vintage, 1989); Thomas Christensen, "Perceptions and Alliances in Europe, 1865–1940," *International Organization* 51, no. 1 (1997): 65–97; Robert Jervis, *Perception and Misperception in International Politics*, new rev. ed. (Princeton University Press, 2017).

38. Cemil Aydin, "Pan-Islamic Narratives of the Global Order, 1870–1980," in *Debating Worlds: Contested Narratives of Global Modernity and World Order*, ed. Daniel Deudney, John Ikenberry, and Karoline Postel-Vinay, 87 (Oxford University Press, 2023).

39. Aydin, "Pan-Islamic Narratives of the Global Order," 87.

40. Dadabhai Naoroji, "Expenses of the Abyssinian War," in *Essays, Speeches, Addresses and Writings of the Hon'ble Dadabhai Naoroji*, ed. Chunilal Lallubhai Parekh, 53 (Caxton, 1887). For collection, see Rahul Sagar, *To Raise a Fallen People: The Nineteenth-Century Origins of Indian Views on International Politics* (Columbia University Press, 2022).

41. "The Causes of Discontent," submitted by Dadabhai Naoroji to the Welby Commission, January 31, 1897, in Dadabhai Naoroji, *Speeches and Writings of Dadabhai Naoroji 1825–1917* (Natesan, 1909), 375–81.

42. Bayly, *Recovering Liberties*, 223.

43. Goswami, *Producing India*, 221.

44. Goswami, *Producing India*, 233.

45. Bipin Pal, *Nationality and Empire: A Running Study of Some Current Indian Problems* (Thacker, Spink, 1916); Rabindranath Tagore, *Nationalism* (1917; Greenwood, 1973). On the violent control exercised by these elites, see Ranajit Guha, "Discipline and Mobilize," in *Dominance Without Hegemony* (Harvard University Press, 1997), 100–150.

46. E. Bradford Burns, *The Unwritten Alliance: Rio-Branco and Brazilian-American Relations* (Columbia University Press, 1966), 49.

47. See Manoel Gomes Pereira, ed., *Barão do Rio Branco: 100 Anos de Memoria* (FUNAG, Ministério das relações exteriors, 2012). In the territory of the Missions (1895), in the French Question on Amapá, in the Petrópolis Treaty with Bolivia (1903), the Treaty of Limits with Peru in 1909, in a total of 893,622 square kilometers.

48. Quoted in Celso Amorim and Luiz Feldman, "O Brasil em um ciclo maior: a atualidade do Barão do Rio Branco," in Manoel Gomes Pereira, ed., *Barão do Rio Branco: 100 Anos de Memoria* (FUNAG, Ministério das relações exteriors, 2012), 215.

49. Liang Qichao, "On Rights Consciousness," *Contemporary Chinese Thought* 31, no. 1 (October 1999): 14–22, https://doi.org/10.2753/CSP1097-1467310114.

50. See Xiaobing Tang, *Global Space and the Nationalist Discourse of Modernity: The Historical Thinking of Liang Qichao* (Stanford University Press, 1996).

51. Fairbank and Goldman, *China*, 235.

52. Goswami, *Producing India*; C. Mackenzie Brown, *Hindu Perspectives on Evolution: Darwin, Dharma, and Design* (Routledge, 2012); Bayly, *Recovering Liberties*; Inder S. Marwah, "Darwin in India: Anticolonial Evolutionism at the Dawn of the Twentieth Century," *Perspectives on Politics* (2023): 1–16.

53. See Gyanendra Pandey, *The Construction of Communalism in Colonial North India* (Oxford University Press, 1990); Christophe Jaffrelot, *Hindu Nationalism: A Reader* (Princeton University Press, 2007). See also Christophe Jaffrelot, "India's Democracy at 70: Toward a Hindu State?," *Journal of Democracy* 28, no. 3 (2017): 52–63.

54. Quoted in Sugata Bose and Ayesha Jalal, *Modern South Asia: History, Culture, Political Economy*, 3rd ed. (Routledge, 2011), 259.

55. "Hind Swaraj, 1910," in M. K. Gandhi, *The Collected Works of Mahatma Gandhi (CWMG)* (Publications Division, Government of India, 1998), EPUB.

56. See Stalin Rajangam, *Athothithasar vazhum bowtham* (Kalachuvadu, 2016). For news coverage, see Pon Vasanth, "Iyothee Thass and His Emancipatory Vision to Create a Casteless Society," *The Hindu*, December 21, 2023.

57. See M. S. S. Pandian, *Brahmin and Non-Brahmin: Genealogies of the Tamil Political Present* (Orient Blackswan, 2007); V. Geetha and S. V. Rajadurai, *Towards a Non-Brahmin Millennium: From Iyothee Thass to Periyar* (Samya, 1998).

58. The focus on these elites alone is because of the limitations of space in this chapter. It does an injustice to the remarkable diversity and number of diplomatic thinkers in Brazil. Paulo Roberto de Amedia writes that Rui Barbosa and Joaquim Nabuco are "more eloquent than practical." But their eloquence (Ruy Barbosa as Verbosa in the Hague) sets the passage point for other diplomats. The way that Almedia groups these elite thinkers, however, is interesting, that is, very much relevant. "Some of the figures—such as Rui Barbosa and Joaquim Nabuco—were perhaps more eloquent than practical. Many of these were exclusively diplomats, such as Cabo Frio, Freitas Valle, Edmundo Barbosa da Silva and Araújo Castro. Others were basically pragmatic. This latter group includes men such as Domício da Gama, Macedo Soares, and Álvaro Alberto. Some of them were important professionals in their respective areas, such as the historians Francisco Adolfo de Varnhagen, Oliveira Lima, and José Honório Rodrigues, and the jurists Afrânio de Melo Franco and San Tiago Dantas. Still others seemed to be visionaries, maybe even ideologues (in the positive sense of the word); men such as Euclides da Cunha, Augusto Frederico Schmidt and Helio Jaguaribe." Paulo Roberto de Almeida, "Brazilian Diplomatic Thought: Methodological Introduction to the Ideas and Actions of Some of Its

Representatives," in *Brazilian Diplomatic Thought: Policymakers and Agents of Foreign Policy (1750–1964)*, vol. 1, ed. José Vicente de Sá Pimentel, 37 (FUNAG, 2016).

59. Angela Alonso, "Joaquim Nabuco: An Americanist Diplomat," in *Brazilian Diplomatic Thought: Policymakers and Agents of Foreign Policy (1750–1964)*, vol. 2, ed. José Vicente de Sá Pimentel, 393 (FUNAG, 2016).

60. Carlos Henrique Cardim, "The Root of the Matter—Rui Barbosa: Brazil in the World," in *Brazilian Diplomatic Thought: Policymakers and Agents of Foreign Policy (1750–1964)*, vol. 2, ed. José Vicente de Sá Pimentel, 469 (FUNAG, 2016).

61. Cardim, "The Root of the Matter," 495.

62. See Manoel de Oliveira Lima, *The Evolution of Brazil Compared with That of Spanish and Anglo-Saxon America* (1914; Russel & Russel, 1966).

63. Helder Gordim da Silveira, "Manoel de Oliveria Lima: The Reform of Diplomatic Service," in *Brazilian Diplomatic Thought: Policymakers and Agents of Foreign Policy (1750–1964)*, vol. 2, ed. José Vicente de Sá Pimentel, 561–62 (FUNAG, 2016).

64. Alonso, "Joaquim Nabuco," 404.

65. Alonso, "Joaquim Nabuco," 406.

66. "Japan's Twenty One Demands," in *The Search for Modern China: A Documentary Study*, ed. Pei-Kai Cheng, Micheal Lestz, and Jonathan Spence, 216–20 (Norton, 2013).

67. Rana Mitter, *A Bitter Revolution, China's Struggle with the Modern World* (Oxford University Press, 2004), 23.

68. For these two contrasting views, see Hu Shih, "The Civilizations of the East and the West," in *Whither Mankind: A Panorama of Modern Civilization*, ed. Charles Beard, 17–22 (Longmans, Green, 1929); Liang Shuming, *The Final Awakening of the Chinese People's Self-Salvation Movement*, 3rd ed. (Shangai, 1932); Edmund Fung, *In Search of Chinese Democracy: Civil Opposition in Nationalist China, 1929–1949* (Cambridge University Press, 2000).

69. Edmund Fung, *The Intellectual Foundations of Chinese Modernity: Cultural and Political Thought in the Republican Era* (Cambridge University Press, 2010).

70. Fung, *The Intellectual Foundations of Chinese Modernity*, 35.

71. See Hu Shi, Jiang Menglin, Tao Menghe et al., "Manifesto of the Struggle for Freedom 1920," in *The Chinese Human Rights Reader: Documents and Commentary, 1900–2000*, ed. Stephen C. Angle and Marina Svensson (Routledge, 2015).

72. Jerome B. Grieder, *Hu Shi and the Chinese Renaissance: Liberalism in the Chinese Revolution, 1917–1983* (Harvard University Press, 1970).

73. Sun Yat-Sen, "Manifesto from the Republic of China to All Friendly Nations," reproduced in *Recent Events and Present Policies in China*, ed. John Otway Percy Bland, 52–55 (Lippincott, 1912).

74. Sun Yat-Sen, "The Principle of Nationalism: Lecture Four [February 17, 1924]," in *The Three Principles of the People*, ed. Tilman Aretz, 12–20 (Wonderful Taiwan Forum Publication, 2023). The entire speeches are available online from Wonderful Taiwan Forum, 2023. See https://www.taiwan-database.net/PDFs/WTFpdf21.pdf, accessed June 20, 2025. See also X. Y. Qin and Guofu Quanji Banji Weiyuanhui, eds., *Complete Works of the Founding Father* (Jindai Zhongguo Chuban She, 1989).

75. Much of the following discussion is based on Charlotte Furth, "Intellectual Change: From the Reform Movement to the May Fourth Movement, 1895–1920," in *The Cambridge History of China: Volume 12: Republican China, 1912–1949*, ed. John K. Fairbank, 322–405 (Cambridge University Press, 1983), https://doi.org/10.1017/CHOL9780521235419.008.

76. Fairbank, "The Far East."

77. Dong Wang, "The Discourse of Unequal Treaties in Modern China," *Pacific Affairs* 76, no. 3 (2003): 399–425; Dong Wang, *China's Unequal Treaties: Narrating National History* (Lexington, 2008).

78. Quoted in Erez Manela, *The Wilsonian Movement: Self-Determination and the International Origins of Anticolonial Nationalism* (Oxford University Press, 2009), 194.

79. Article 22 of The Covenant of the League of Nations. The entire document is available in the UN Document Database online: https://www.ungeneva.org/en/about/league-of -nations/overview. For Article 22 of the League of Nations, see https://www.un.org /unispal/document/auto-insert-185531/.

80. Itty Abraham, *How India Became Territorial: Foreign Policy, Diaspora, Geopolitics* (Stanford University Press, 2014), 83.

81. Bayly, *Recovering Liberties*, 230.

82. See Vanya Vaidehi Bhargav, "Letters to Sir Syed: Lajpat Rai's Response to the Muslim Refusal of Minorityhood," *Global Intellectual History* 7, no. 6 (2022): 987.

83. Susan Bayly, "Imagining 'Greater India': French and Indian Visions of Colonialism in the Indic Mode," *Modern Asian Studies* 38, no. 3 (July 1, 2004): 707. See also Caroline Stolte and Harold Fischer-Tine, "Imagining Asia in India: Nationalism and Internationalism (ca. 1905–1940)," *Comparative Studies in Society and History* 53, no. 1 (2012): 65–92.

84. Bayly, "Imagining 'Greater India,'" 711.

85. Bayly, "Imagining 'Greater India,'" 712.

86. For a brilliant discussion on the public debates on Kautilya's *Arthasastra*, see Prathama Banerjee, *Elementary Aspects of the Political: Histories from the Global South* (Duke University Press, 2020), chaps. 1 and 2.

87. Benoy Kumar Sarkar, "Hindu Theory of International Relations," *American Political Science Review* 13, no. 3 (August 1919): 400–14.

88. Sarkar, "Hindu Theory of International Relations," 404.

89. The point of reference here is Radhakumud Mookerji, *The Fundamental Unity of India: From Hindu Sources* (Longmans, Green, 1914).

90. M. K. Gandhi, *The Collected Works of Mahatma Gandhi (CWMG)* (Publications Division, Government of India, 1998), vol. 10, 255–26; vol. 23, 219; EPUB. See also Nazmul Sultan, "Moral Empire and Global Meaning of Gandhi's Anti-Imperialism," *Review of Politics* 84 (2022): 560.

91. For example, the Indian communist revolutionary Virendranath Chattopadhyaya ("Chatoo") played a central role in creating and taking bold anti-imperial positions in the League of Nations. And M. N. Roy founded the Communist Party of India.

92. Michele Louro, *Comrades Against Imperialism: Nehru, India and Interwar Internationalism* (Cambridge University Press, 2018); Michele Louro, Carolien Stolte, Heather

Streets-Salter, and Sana Tannoury-Karam, *The League Against Imperialism: Lives and Afterlives* (Leiden University Press, 2020).

93.   Quoted in Louro, *Comrades Against Imperialism*, 39.

94.   Gandhi had qualms about independence and for Nehru, Gandhi was not attentive to global anti-imperialism. Gandhi instead inaugurated Bharat Mata temple in the ancient pilgrimage city of Benares, United Provinces, in 1936.

95.   Quoted in Louro, *Comrades Against Imperialism*, 61.

96.   Louro, *Comrades Against Imperialism*, 154.

97.   Subhas Chandra Bose called for complete independence at the Calcutta session of Congress in December 1928. He asserted rhetorically, "If we want to make India really great," we need a "coalition between labour and nationalism" that can transform India "into an independent Federal Republic." Bose and Jalal, *Modern South Asia*, 118.

98.   Banerjee, *Elementary Aspects of the Political*, on Ambedkar burning the book.

99.   See Eugenio V. Garcia and Natalia B. R. Coelho, "A Seat at the Top? A Historical Appraisal of Brazil's Case for the UN Security Council," *Sage Open* 8, no. 3 (2018): 2.

100. See Garcia and Coelho, "A Seat at the Top?"

101. Stanley Hilton, "Afranio de Melo Franco: The Consolidation of Foreign Policy Strategy," in *Brazilian Diplomatic Thought: Policymakers and Agents of Foreign Policy (1750–1964)*, vol. 2, ed. José Vicente de Sá Pimentel, 625–70 (FUNAG, 2016).

102. W. Douglas McLain, "Alberto Torres, Ad Hoc Nationalist," *Luso-Brazilian Review* 4, no. 2 (1967): 32.

103. Everardo Backheuser, *A Estrutura Política Do Brasil: Notas Prévias* (Mendonça & Machado, 1926).

104. See Bethell, *Brazil*, 42; Stanley Hilton, "Brazil and the Post-Versailles World: Elite Images and Foreign Policy Strategy, 1919–1929," *Journal of Latin American Studies* 12, no. 2 (1980): 341–64.

105. Quoted in Bethell, *Brazil*, 33.

106. Stanley Hilton, "The Overthrow of Getulio Vargas in 1945: Diplomatic Intervention, Defense of Democracy, or Political Retribution?," *Hispanic American Historical Review* 67, no. 1 (1987): 1–37.

107. "Wn Ting-fang on China's Progress, 1908," in *The Search for Modern China: A Documentary Study*, ed. Pei-Kai Cheng, Micheal Lestz, and Jonathan Spence, 191 (Norton, 2013).

108. "Sun Yat-Sen Opening Speech at the Whampoa Academy, 1924," in *The Search for Modern China: A Documentary Study*, ed. Pei-Kai Cheng, Micheal Lestz, and Jonathan Spence, 252–54 (Norton, 2013).

109. Sun Yat-Sen, "The Principle of Nationalism: Lecture Four [February 17, 1924]," in *The Three Principles of the People*, ed. Tilman Aretz, 20 (Wonderful Taiwan Forum Publication, 2023).

110. League of Nations, "Fifth Meeting of the Second Committee," *Journal of the Fifth Assembly of the League of Nations*, no. 13 (September 14, 1924): 133. See also Alison Kaufman, "In Pursuit of Equality and Respect: China's Diplomacy and the League of Nations," *Modern China* 40, no. 6 (2014): 626.

111. See Anna Belogurova, "Networks, Parties, and the 'Oppressed Nations': The Comintern and Chinese Communists Overseas, 1926–1935," *Cross-Currents: East Asian History and Culture Review* 6, no. 2 (2017): 561.

112. Chiang Kai-shek, *China's Destiny* (Macmillan, 1947).

113. Fung, *The Intellectual Foundations of Chinese Modernity*, 105.

114. Fung, *The Intellectual Foundations of Chinese Modernity*, 43.

115. Fung, *The Intellectual Foundations of Chinese Modernity*, 55.

116. Quoted in "Editorial," *China Quarterly*, no. 12 (October–December 1962): 92–101.

117. For want of space, my presentation of the elites is also limited. Liang Shuming was a complex thinker who argued that "Westerners could understand themselves better by understanding 'authentic' Confucianism." The debate between Chen Duxiu (West is best) and Du Yaquan (capitalism is the problem) had a great impact on other socialists. Zhang Shizhao, a conservative who founded *The Tiger*, fled to Tokyo and emphasized continuity with the past as modernity. Then there was the New Confucianism movement led by Xiong Shili, Feng Youlan, He Lin, Ma Yifu, Tang Junyi, and Mou Zongsan, among others. Another group of elites talked of national reconstruction, salvation, and awakening. As Fung shows, a critic of the Kuomintang regime Zhang Junmai wrote *The Academic Basis of National Renaissance* (1935), *Chinese Culture Tomorrow* (1936), and *The Way to Build the State* (1938), which provided clear insights into the politics of his cultural conservatism. See Fung, *Intellectual Foundations of Chinese Modernity*, 103–18. As Fung shows, Qian Mu wrote *A General History of China* (1940), on China's culture that inspired Mao. And Zhanguoce writers emphasized state power that went beyond cultural conservativism. See Fung, *The Intellectual Foundations of Chinese Modernity*, 75, 108.

118. Pei-Kai Cheng, Micheal Lestz, and Jonathan Spence, eds., *The Search for Modern China: A Documentary Study* (Norton, 2013), 294.

119. "Li Dazaho Speech 1918," in *The Search for Modern China: A Documentary Study*, ed. Pei-Kai Cheng, Micheal Lestz, and Jonathan Spence, 241, 252–54 (Norton, 2013).

120. Cheng, Lestz, and Spence, *The Search for Modern China*, 263.

121. Nick Knight, *Marxist Philosophy in China: From Qu Qiubai to Mao Zedong, 1923–1945* (Springer, 2005).

122. Mao Zedong, "The League of Nations Is a League of Robbers!," excerpt from a telegram of the Chinese Soviet government, October 6, 1932, http://www.marxists.org/reference/archive/mao/selected-works/volume-6/mswv6_15.htm.

123. Mao Zedong, "The Chinese People Have Stood Up: Opening Address at the First Plenary Session of the Chinese People's Political Consultative Conference, 21 September 1949," *Selected Works of Mao Tse-tung*, http://www.marxists.org/reference/archive/mao/selected-works/volume-5/mswv5_01.htm. For the argument on Communist Revolution as a multiethnic national project, see Lin Chun, "China's Lost World of Internationalism," in *Chinese Visions of World Order: Tianxia, Culture, and World Politics*, ed. Ban Wang, 184 (Duke University Press, 2017).

124. John Lewis Gaddis, *We Now Know* (Clarendon, 1997), 284–86.

125. On geopolitical continuities in the Cold War period, see Gearóid Ó Tuathail, "Introduction: Thinking Critically About Geopolitics," in *The Geopolitics Reader*, ed. Gearóid Ó

Tuathail, Simon Dalby, and Paul Routledge (Routledge, 1998); Simon Dalby, "Recontextualizing Violence, Power and Nature: The Next Twenty Years of Critical Geopolitics?," *Political Geography* 29, no. 5 (2010): 282; Joanne Sharp, "Subaltern Geopolitics: Introduction," *Geoforum* 42, no. 3 (June 2011): 271–73; Sara Koopman et al., "Critical Geopolitics: 25 Years On," *Political Geography* 91 (2021):1–9.

126. See William Roger Louis, "Churchill and the Liquidation of the British Empire," Kemper Lecture, March 29, 1998, https://www.nationalchurchillmuseum.org/kemper-lecture-roger.html.

127. Garcia and Coelho, "A Seat at the Top?"

128. Odd Arne Westad, *The Global Cold War: Third World Interventions and the Making of Our Times* (Cambridge University Press, 2005), 20.

129. Sukarno, speech, April 18, 1955, at the Bandung Conference. Available in *Asia-Africa Speak from Bandung* (Ministry of Foreign Affairs, Indonesia, 1955) 19–29.

130. Jussi Hanhimaki and Odd Arne Westad, *The Cold War: A History in Documents and Eyewitness Accounts* (Oxford University Press, 2003), 355–56.

131. "Speech of Jawaharlal Nehru on World Peace and Cooperation," April 22, 1955, Asian-African Conference, Bandung.

132. C. S. Jha, "Statement by Indian Delegate C. S. Jha at the UN Security Council 987th Meeting," December 18, 1961, UN Security Council, UN Doc S/PV/987 (n 8) [40], https://digitallibrary.un.org/record/631425?ln=en&v=pdf.

133. See UN Doc S/PV/987 (n 80) [47], quoted in Tom Ruys, "The Indian Intervention in Goa-1961," in *The Use of Force in International Law: A Case-Based Approach*, ed. Tom Ruys, Oliver Corten, and Alexandra Hofer, online edition (Oxford University Press, 2018), https://doi.org/10.1093/law/9780198784357.003.0008, accessed June 20, 2025.

134. A. Varshney, "Contesting Meanings: India's National Identity, Hindu Nationalism, and the Politics of Anxiety," *Daedalus* 122, no. 3 (1993): 227–61. See also Sanjay Chaturvedi, "Indian Geopolitics: 'Nation-State and the Colonial Legacy,'" in *International Relations in India: Theorizing the Region and the Nation*, ed. Kanti Bajpai and Siddharth Mallavarapu, 238–83 (Orient Longman, 2004); Atul Mishra, *The Sovereign Lives of India: Post-Partition Statehood in South Asia* (Oxford University Press, 2021).

135. See C. Raja Mohan, "Beyond Geopolitics of the Nehru Raj," *Nehru Memorial Museum and Library Occasional Paper*, New Series 48 (2015). When Indian policymakers became aware that the British had plans to retain part of the northeast Indian states after independence, perhaps as a mandate, they put their rhetorical politics in motion. See David Syiemlieh, ed., *On the Edge of Empire: Four British Plans for North East India, 1941–1947* (Sage, 2014); Lydia Walker, *States-in-Waiting: A Counternarrative of Global Decolonization* (Cambridge University Press, 2024), 11.

136. Quoted in Andrew Hurrell, "The Quest for Autonomy: The Evolution of Brazil's Role in the International System, 1964–1985" (PhD diss., Oxford University, 1986).

137. Helio Sodre, *A eloqiuncia Juscelino Kubitschek (Orador moderno do Brasil futuro)* (Folha Carioca Editora, 1960); Ronald H. Chilcote, *National Identity in Twentieth Century Brazil* (Cambridge University Press, 2014).

138. Stanley Hilton, "The United States, Brazil, and the Cold War, 1945–1960: End of the Special Relationship," *Journal of American History* 68, no. 3 (1981): 618.

139. Quoted in Hurrell, "The Quest for Autonomy," 55.

140. These roots were established by diplomats such as Araújo Castro and Minister of Foreign Affairs San Tiago Dantas. See João A. C. Vargas, *Um mundo que também é nosso: o pensamento e a trajetória diplomática de Araujo Castro* (Funag, 2013); San Tiago Dantas, *Política Externa Independente*, updated ed. (FUNAG, 2011), 11; Gelson Fonseca, "Francisco Clementiono San Tiago Dantas: The East-West Conflict and the Limits of the Rational Argument" in *Brazilian Diplomatic Thought: Policymakers and Agents of Foreign Policy (1750–1964)*, vol. 2, ed. José Vicente de Sá Pimentel, 1001–43 (FUNAG, 2016).

141. Hurrell, "The Quest for Autonomy," 197.

142. "Report from the Brazilian Foreign Ministry to President Ernesto Giesel, Subject: The Indian Nuclear Test," May 21, 1974, Cold War International History Project (CWIHP), https://digitalarchive.wilsoncenter.org/document/report-brazilian-foreign-ministry -president-ernesto-geisel-subject-indian-nuclear-test.

143. Brazil-Argentine Agency for Accounting and Control of Nuclear Materials or Agencia Brasileño-Argentina de Contabilidad y Control de Materiales Nucleares (ABACC), July 18, 1991, https://www.abacc.org.br/es/a-abacc/sobre.

144. Zedong, "The Chinese People Have Stood Up." For the argument on Communist Revolution as a multiethnic national project see Chun, "China's Lost World of Internationalism."

145. John Garver, *China's Quest: The History of the Foreign Relations of the People's Republic of China* (Oxford University Press, 2016), 68.

146. Garver, *China's Quest*, 99.

147. Xing Lu, *The Rhetoric of Mao Zedong: Transforming China and Its People* (University of South Carolina, 2017), 167–69.

148. Lu, *The Rhetoric of Mao Zedong*, 636.

149. Garver, *China's Quest*, 56.

150. "The Shanghai Communique," February 28, 1972, in *The Search for Modern China: A Documentary Study*, ed. Pei-Kai Cheng, Micheal Lestz, and Jonathan Spence, 439 (Norton, 2013).

151. Deng Xiopoing, "Speech in UN, April 10, 1974," in *The Search for Modern China: A Documentary Study*, ed. Pei-Kai Cheng, Micheal Lestz, and Jonathan Spence, 444 (Norton, 2013).

152. "People's Daily: 'We Must Unequivocally Oppose Unrest,' April 26, 1989," in *The Search for Modern China: A Documentary Study*, ed. Pei-Kai Cheng, Micheal Lestz, and Jonathan Spence, 489 (Norton, 2013).

153. Lu, *The Rhetoric of Mao Zedong*, 191–92.

154. See Ann E. Towns and Bahar Rumelili, "Taking the Pressure: Unpacking the Relation Between Norms, Social Hierarchies, and Social Pressures on States," *European Journal of International Relations* 23, no. 4 (December 1, 2017): 756–79, https://doi.org /10.1177/1354066116682070.

155. Towns and Rumelili, "Taking the Pressure."

3. INDIA'S RHETORICAL POWER POLITICS IN
THE EAST PAKISTAN CRISIS, 1971

1. In the 1970s, many policymakers frequently used "Bangla Desh," which means land of the Bengali people. The reference to "Bangladesh" (without space) also means the same. In keeping with this convention, I use both ways interchangeably. See Indira Gandhi, "A Word to America," interview to the National Broadcasting Corporation of the USA, December 27, 1971, in *India and Bangla Desh: Selected Speeches and Statements March to December 1971*, 159–60 (Orient Longman, 1972) [hereafter Gandhi, *India and Bangla Desh*].

2. "Memorandum for the Record: Description of Kissinger-Haksar Talk," July 6, 1971, in U.S. Department of State, *Foreign Relations of the United States, 1969–1976*, vol. 11, Document 90, South Asia Crisis, 1971, ed. Louis Smith (United States Government Printing Office, 2005) [hereafter *FRUS year*, volume, document number], https://history.state .gov/historicaldocuments/frus1969-76v11/d90, accessed June 22, 2025; See also Srinath Raghavan, *1971: A Global History of the Creation of Bangladesh* (Harvard University Press, 2013), 104.

3. "Conversation Between President Nixon and the President's Assistant for National Security Affairs (Kissinger)," May 26, 1971, in *FRUS 1969–1972*, vol. E-7, Document 135, https:// history.state.gov/historicaldocuments/frus1969-76ve07/d135, accessed June 23, 2025.

4. "Minutes of Senior Review Group Meeting," July 23, 1971, in *FRUS 1971*, vol. 11, Document 105, https://history.state.gov/historicaldocuments/frus1969-76v11/d105, accessed June 23, 2025.

5. All quotes from Raghavan, *1971*, 124, 159, 166.

6. Raghavan, *1971*, 104.

7. Pratap Bhanu Mehta, "Reluctant India," *Journal of Democracy* 22, no. 4 (October 14, 2011): 97–109; Micheal Walzer, *Just and Unjust Wars: A Moral Argument with Historical Illustrations* (Basic Books, 2006), 90, 101–8.

8. Henry Kissinger, *White House Years* (Weidenfeld & Nicolson, 1979), 880.

9. Most studies offer multicausal explanations focused on the U.S. decision makers and their ideological habits in the crisis that worked alongside the failure of the UN. See A. Dirk Moses, "The United Nations, Humanitarianism, and Human Rights: War Crimes/ Genocide Trials for Pakistani Soldiers in Bangladesh, 1971–1974," in *Human Rights in the Twentieth Century*, ed. Stefan-Ludwig Hoffmann, 258–79 (Cambridge University Press, 2010); Gary J. Bass, *The Blood Telegram: Nixon, Kissinger, and a Forgotten Genocide* (Knopf, 2013); Ramachandra Guha, *Gandhi Before India* (Vintage, 2013), 453; Sonia Cordera, "India's Response to the 1971 East Pakistan Crisis: Hidden and Open Reasons for Intervention," *Journal of Genocide Research* 17, no. 1 (2015): 45–62; Joseph O'Mahoney, "Making the Real: Rhetorical Adduction and the Bangladesh Liberation War," *International Organization* 71, no. 2 (2017): 317–48.

10. Nicholas J. Wheeler, *Saving Strangers: Humanitarian Intervention in International Society* (Oxford University Press, 2001); Gary J. Bass, "The Indian Way of Humanitarian Intervention," *Yale Journal of International Law* 40, no. 2 (2015): 228–94.

11. Thomas Franck and Nigel Rodley, "After Bangladesh: The Law of Humanitarian Intervention by Military Force," *American Journal of International Law* 67, no. 2 (1973): 275–305. For an assessment, see Ryan Goodman, "Humanitarian Intervention and Pretexts for War," *American Journal of International Law* 100, no. 1 (2006): 107–41; Thomas G. Weiss, *Humanitarian Intervention: Ideas in Action*, 2nd ed. (Polity, 2012).

12. Doug McAdam, Sidney Tarrow, and Charles Tilly, *Dynamics of Contention* (Cambridge University Press, 1991); Charles Tilly, "Contentious Repertoires in Great Britain, 1758–1834," *Social Science History* 17, no. 2 (1993): 253–80; Charles Tilly, *Regimes and Repertoires* (University of Chicago Press, 2010).

13. "Prime Minister Indira Gandhi's Speech at a Luncheon Given by Chairman A. N. Kosygin in Moscow," September 28, 1971, in *Bangladesh Documents*, 2 vols. (Government of India, 1972), 2:239.

14. Important scholarship includes Richard Sisson and Leo Rose, *War and Session: Pakistan, India, and the Creation of Bangladesh* (University of California Press, 1991); Raghavan, *1971*; Bass, *The Blood Telegram*; Bass, "The Indian Way of Humanitarian Intervention"; Volker Prott, " 'We Have to Tread Warily': East Pakistan, India and the Pitfalls of Foreign Intervention in the Cold War," *Cold War History* 23, no. 1 (2023): 23–44.

15. Charles Tilly, *Durable Inequalities* (University of California Press, 1998), 155.

16. Ayesha Jalal, *The Sole Spokesman: Jinnah, the Muslim League and the Demand for Pakistan*, repr. ed. (Cambridge University Press, 1994), 277.

17. See Badruddin Umar, *The Emergence of Bangladesh*, 2 vols. (Oxford University Press, 2004).

18. Raghavan, *1971*, 18.

19. Umar, *The Emergence of Bangladesh*, 2:66–69.

20. "Awami League to Attend National Assembly Session if 4-Point Demand Is Accepted: Announcement of Sheikh Mujibur Rahman's Decision at a Public Meeting on March 7, 1971," *The Dawn*, March 8, 1971.

21. The details of the genocide were articulated by Antony Mascarenhas, "Genocide," *Sunday Times* (London), June 13, 1971.

22. Bass, *The Blood Telegram*, 53.

23. See Bass, *The Blood Telegram*.

24. Donald Beachler, "The Politics of Genocide Scholarship: The Case of Bangladesh," *Patterns of Prejudice* 41, no. 5 (December 1, 2007): 479.

25. R. J. Rummel, *Death by Government* (Transactions, 1994), 335.

26. The 1971 election established the Congress Party of Indira Gandhi with a massive majority in the Indian Parliament. With foreign affairs being an urban issue, the success of Indira Gandhi's Congress Party, with wins in thirty-three of the fifty-two urban constituencies effectively put Indian public opinion on her side. Indian publics in fact sought a more forceful action against Pakistan to ensure refugees could go back safely. As Myron Weiner put it, Indian public opinion in the East Pakistan crisis pressured the Indira Gandhi administration to take a more "forceful measure against Pakistan" and "Jan Sangh [opposition party,] with considerable support from other opposition parties, [were] organizing mass demonstrations for recognition of Bangla Desh." Myron Weiner, "The 1971 Elections and the Indian Party System," *Asian Survey* 11, no. 12 (1971): 1166.

27. Indira Gandhi, "The Refugee Influx," Speech in Lok Sabha (Lower House of the Indian Parliament), March 24, 1971; Gandhi, *India and Bangla Desh*, 15.

28. Raghavan, *1971*, 75, 206.

29. Indira Gandhi, "World's Tardy Response," in Reply to Discussion in Lok Sabha, May 26, 1971; Gandhi, *India and Bangla Desh*, 21.

30. See John Lewis, *India's Political Economy: Governance and Reform* (Oxford University Press, 1997); Pranab Bardhan, *The Political Economy of Development in India* (Basil Blackwell, 1984); Rahul Mukherji, "India's Aborted Liberalization-1966," *Pacific Affairs* 73, no. 3 (2000): 375–92; Rahul Mukherji, "India, Interests, and the Tipping Point: Economic Change in India," *Review of International Political Economy* 20, no. 2 (2013): 363–89.

31. Tanvi Madan, *Fateful Triangle: How China Shaped U.S.-India Relations During the Cold War* (Brooking Institution Press, 2020).

32. For contemporary accounts, see Lorne Kavic, *India's Quest for Security: Defence Policies 1947–1965* (University of California Press, 1962); Raju Thomas, "Nonalignment and Indian Security: Nehru's Rationale and Legacy," *Journal of Strategic Studies* 2, no. 2 (1979): 153–71; For recent accounts on nonalignment, see Harsh Pant and Julie Super, "India's 'Non-Alignment' Conundrum: A Twentieth-Century Policy," *International Affairs* 91, no. 4 (2015): 747–64; Shivshankar Menon, *India and Asian Geopolitics: The Past, Present* (Brookings Institution Press, 2021).

33. Jawaharlal Nehru, "Changing India," *Foreign Affairs* 41, no. 3 (1963): 453–65.

34. Raghavan, *1971*, 148.

35. See "White Paper on the Crisis in East Pakistan" (Government of Pakistan, August 1971).

36. "Mujib Is 'Enemy of Pakistani People,'" President Yahya Khan's interview, *Le Figaro* (Paris), September 1, 1971, in *Bangladesh Documents*, 2:23; "I Can't Speak with a Rebel," President Yahya Khan's interview, *Le Monde* (Paris), *The Dawn* (Karachi), October 20, 1971, in *Bangladesh Documents*, 2:24.

37. Geoffrey Warner, "Nixon, Kissinger and the Breakup of Pakistan, 1971," *International Affairs* 81, no. 5 (October 1, 2005): 1097–1118, https://doi.org/10.1111/j.1468-2346.2005 .00504.x.

38. On the origins of this all-weather friendship, see Rudra Chaudhuri, "The Making of an 'All Weather Friendship': Pakistan, China and the History of a Border Agreement," *International History Review* 40, no. 1 (2018): 41–64.

39. See Indira Gandhi, "Resolution on East Bengal," in both Houses of the Indian Parliament, March 31, 1971; Gandhi, *India and Bangla Desh*, 13.

40. See U Thant, *View from the UN* (David & Charles, 1978), 422; Wheeler, *Saving Strangers*, 59.

41. Bass, "The Indian Way of Humanitarian Intervention," 278.

42. Indira Gandhi, "The Refugee Influx," statement in Lok Sabha, March 24, 1971; Gandhi, *India and Bangla Desh*, 17.

43. Indira Gandhi, "World Opinion on Bangla Desh: Statement in Parliament," November 15, 1971; Gandhi, *India and Bangla Desh*, 105.

44. Bass, "The Indian Way of Humanitarian Intervention," 277.

45. See, for instance, Robert J. McMohan, *The Cold War on the Periphery* (Columbia University Press, 1994); David Malone, ed., *The UN Security Council: From the Cold War to*

the 21st Century (Lynne Rienner, 2004); Odd Arne Westad, *The Global Cold War: Third World Interventions and the Making of Our Times* (Cambridge University Press, 2005).

46. Bass, "The Indian Way of Humanitarian Intervention," 278.

47. Bass, *The Blood Telegram.*

48. Bass, "The Indian Way of Humanitarian Intervention," 250.

49. See Brigadier A. R. Siddiqi, *East Pakistan: The Endgame: An Onlooker's Journal 1969–1971* (Oxford University Press, 2004), 96–112; Bass, "The Indian Way of Humanitarian Intervention."

50. On India's plan for a guerrilla campaign, see Raghavan, *1971*, 70, based on the prime minister's Principal Secretary P. N. Haksar's note to Indira Gandhi on May 6–7, 1971 (transcript in Prime Ministers Museum and Library, formerly known as Nehru Memorial Museum and Library [NMML]), Teen Murti Bhavan, New Delhi, Subject File 227, III Installment. On Swaran Singh's statement, see T. N. Kaul Papers, I-III Installment, Subject File 19, Part II, NMML, Teen Murti Bhavan, New Delhi.

51. Umar, *The Emergence of Bangladesh*, 2:22. The communists called for armed revolution, 2:305–7.

52. Raghavan, *1971*, 215.

53. Raghavan, *1971*, 218.

54. Raghavan, *1971*, 66–67.

55. Raghavan, *1971*, 123.

56. Wheeler, *Saving Strangers*, 59.

57. Jack Donnelly, "The Heterarchic Structure of Twenty-First-Century International Governance," *Korean Journal of International Studies* 14, no. 1 (2016): 7; Jack Donnelly, *Systems, Relations, and the Structures of International Societies* (Cambridge University Press, 2023).

58. "P. N. Haksar, Policy Brief for Indira Gandhi," May 7, 1971, Haksar Papers, 166, III, Installment, II, Subject Files, NMML.

59. Doug McAdam, Sidney Tarrow, and Charles Tilly, *Dynamics of Contention* (Cambridge University Press, 1991); Charles Tilly, "Contentious Repertoires in Great Britain, 1758–1834," *Social Science History* 17, no. 2 (1993): 253–80; Charles Tilly, *Regimes and Repertoires* (University of Chicago Press, 2010). For statecraft as repertoires, see Stacie Goddard, Paul MacDonald, and Daniel Nexon, "Repertoires of Statecraft: Instruments and Logics of Power Politics," *International Relations* 33, no. 2 (2019): 304–21; Elana Rowe, "Analyzing Frenemies: An Artic Repertoire of Cooperation and Rivalry," *Political Geography* 76 (2020): 1–10; Paul MacDonald, "Parliament of Man, Federation of the World: Repertoires of Statecraft, the Hague Conferences, and the Making of the Liberal Order," *Diplomacy and Statecraft* 32, no. 4 (2021): 648–73.

60. MacDonald, "Parliament of Man, Federation of the World," 653–54.

61. "Mujib's Call for Emancipation of Bengalees: Talk with Pressmen After the Parliamentary Party Meeting at Hotel Purbani, March 1, 1971," *Bangladesh Documents*, 2:190.

62. "Bangla Desh PM's Plea for Aid, Recognition: Bangla Desh Prime Minister Mr. Tajuddin Ahmed's Appeal to Nations," June 13, 1971, *Bangladesh Documents*, 2:326.

63. Melvyn P. Leffler and Odd Arne Westad, *The Cambridge History of the Cold War*, vol. 2 (Cambridge University Press, 2011), 200.

64. Raghavan, *1971*, 75. See also J. N. Dixit, *Liberation and Beyond: Indo-Bangladesh Relations* (Konark, 1999), 49.

65. Indira Gandhi, "Resolution on East Bengal: Both Houses of the Indian Parliament," March 31, 1971; Gandhi, *India and Bangla Desh*, 13.

66. Bass, "The Indian Way of Humanitarian Intervention," 231.

67. Indira Gandhi, "Need for Immediate Action," at meeting with economic editors assembled in New Delhi, June 17, 1971; Gandhi, *India and Bangla Desh*, 31.

68. Indira Gandhi, "Refugee Influx," statement in Lok Sabha, March 24, 1971; Gandhi, *India and Bangla Desh*, 18.

69. Raghavan, *1971*, 122.

70. "Statement by Ambassador Sen, Permanent Representative of India to the UN in the Social Committee of the Economic and Social Council on Agenda Item 5(a): Report of the Commission on Human Rights on May 12, 1971," in *Bangladesh Documents*, 2:618.

71. Indira Gandhi, "Refugee Influx," statement in Lok Sabha, March 24, 1971; Gandhi, *India and Bangla Desh*, 17.

72. Indira Gandhi, "India's Strength Lies in Unity," August 9, 1971; Gandhi, *India and Bangla Desh*, 34.

73. "Prime Minister Indira Gandhi's Statement in the Indian Parliament, Lok Sabha," May 24, 1971, in *Bangladesh Documents*, 2:672–75.

74. Indira Gandhi, "India's Strength Lies in Unity," August 9, 1971; Gandhi, *India and Bangla Desh*, 34.

75. Bass, "The Indian Way of Humanitarian Intervention," 245.

76. India did not act because of the global norm of human rights. This view contrasts with the views put on human rights norm by Martha Finnemore, *The Purpose of Intervention: Changing Beliefs About the Use of Force* (Cornell University Press, 2003), 73–74.

77. Indira Gandhi, "World's Tardy Response," reply to discussions in Lok Sabha, May 26, 1971; Gandhi, *India and Bangla Desh*, 20.

78. Indira Gandhi, "Refugee Influx," statement in Lok Sabha, May 24, 1971; Gandhi, *India and Bangla Desh*, 17. For similar claims about India's entitlement to criticize Pakistan, see Indira Gandhi, "Call to Democratic Conscience," in the Federal Republic of Germany, November 11, 1971; Gandhi, *India and Bangla Desh*, 96.

79. "Prime Minister Indira Gandhi's Speech at a Luncheon Given by Chairman A. N. Kosygin in Moscow," September 28, 1971, in *Bangladesh Documents*, 2:239.

80. "Resolutions Passed in the Indian Parliament," May 26, 1971, in *Bangladesh Documents*, 2:223.

81. Bass, "The Indian Way of Humanitarian Intervention," 254.

82. Bass, "The Indian Way of Humanitarian Intervention," 254.

83. Indira Gandhi, "A National, Not Communal, Problem," July 2, 1971; Gandhi, *India and Bangla Desh*, 32.

84. Raghavan, *1971*, 76.

85. Indira Gandhi, "Duty of the United Nations," Press Conference at New Delhi, October 19, 1971; Gandhi, *India and Bangla Desh*, 44.

86. On the Yugoslavian mediation suggestion see "Indo-Yugoslav Joint Communique," October 20, 1971, in *Bangladesh Documents*, 2:169.

87. The clearest articulation of the challenge to mediation is in Indira Gandhi, "Duty of the United Nations," Press Conference at New Delhi, October 19, 1971; Gandhi, *India and Bangla Desh*, 45.

88. Indira Gandhi, "The Indo-Soviet Treaty: Replies to Questions from Shri Romesh Chandra, Secretary General of the World Peace Council," August 26, 1971; Gandhi, *India and Bangla Desh*, 40.

89. See also "Indira Gandhi's Replies to Questions on the Indo-Soviet Treaty," August 26, 1971, in *Bangladesh Documents*, 2:236.

90. For the U.S. assessment of India's strategy to split Pakistan, see "Minutes of the Senior Review Group Meeting," July 30, 1971, 292, in *FRUS 1971*, vol. 11, Document 111, 28–32.

91. See "Pakistan's Protest Note to the U.N. Secretary General, August 19, 1971," in *Bangladesh Documents*, 2:131; "President Yahya Khan's Broadcast to the Nation," October 12, 1971, in *Bangladesh Documents*, 2:131. On the position of the UN, see "UN Secretary General's Letters, and for Replies," in *Bangladesh Documents*, 2:319–23.

92. On China's opposition, see Raghavan, *1971*, 184–204.

93. See "Letter from President Nixon to Indian Prime Minister Gandhi," May 28, 1971, in *FRUS 1971*, Document 62. See also "Letter from President Nixon to Pakistani President Yahya," July 1, 1971, in *FRUS 1971*, Document 85.

94. See "Memorandum of Conversation" between Ambassador Lakshmi Kant Jha of India and Henry Kissinger, August 9, 1971, *FRUS 1971*, vol. 11, Document 117, https://history .state.gov/historicaldocuments/frus1969-76v11/d117, accessed June 24, 2025.

95. Raghavan, *1971*, 198.

96. On the position of the UN, see "UN Secretary General's Letters and Replies," in *Bangladesh Documents*, 2:319–23. See also "UN Secretary General U Thant Letters to President Yahya Khan," April 5 and 22, 1971, in Wheeler, *Saving Strangers*, 58. On the one-sided Indian criticism of U Thant's role, see K. P. Mishra, *The Role of the United Nations in the Indo-Pakistan Conflict*, 1971 (Vikas, 1973), 33–35.

97. Antony Mascarenhas, "Genocide," *Sunday Times* (London), June 13, 1971. See also Syndey H. Schanberg, "Kennedy, in India, Terms Pakistan Drive Genocide," *New York Times*, August 17, 1971.

98. Wheeler, *Saving Strangers*, 58.

99. Indira Gandhi, "Call to Democratic Conscience," from remarks at Britain-India Forum Meeting at Indian House, London, November 1, 1971; Gandhi, *India and Bangla Desh*, 54.

100. Raghavan, *1971*, 162.

101. Bass, "The Indian Way of Humanitarian Intervention," 250–51.

102. Soviet support became increasingly important for India to deter Chinese intervention on behalf of Pakistan. As John Garver wrote, "New Delhi calculated that the threat of Soviet intervention would deter Chinese intervention to counter India's planned action. The memory of China's threatened intervention in the 1965 India-Pakistan war was strong." John W. Garver, *China's Quest: The History of the Foreign Relations of the People's Republic, Revised and Updated* (Oxford University Press, 2016), 310.

103. Tad Szule, "U.S. Military Goods Sent to Pakistan Despite Ban," *New York Times*, June 22, 1971.

104. "Memorandum from Harold Saunders and Samuel Hoskinson of the National Security Council Staff to the President's Assistant for National Security Affairs (Kissinger)," October 29, 1971, in *FRUS 1971*, vol. 11, Document 173.

105. "Text of Edward Heath's Message to Indira Gandhi in Telegram 1214, Foreign and Common Wealth Office, New Delhi, August 14, 1971," in Angela Debnath, "British Perceptions of the East Pakistan Crisis 1971: 'Hideous Atrocities on Both Sides?,'" *Journal of Genocide Research* 13, no. 4 (2011): 74.

106. Raghavan, *1971*, 229.

107. On Pakistan, the United States, and China, see "Speech by Chinese Delegate, Mr. Fu Hao in the Third Committee of the UN Debate on Pakistani Refugees in India," November 19, 1971, in *Bangladesh Documents*, 2:298. On India's understanding of the pro-Pakistan stance of China, see "Statement by Indian Foreign Minister in the [Indian] Parliament," November 23, 1971, in *Bangladesh Documents*, 2:299.

108. Pierre Bois, "Yahya Khan Speaks," *New York Times Archives*, September 29, 1971.

109. UN Security Council Official Records, 1606th Meeting, December 4, 1971, 15. See also India's justifications during and after the war in a series of press conferences that engaged with "refugee aggression" rhetoric. *Bangladesh Documents*, 2:221–52.

110. Indira Gandhi, "World Opinion on Bangla Desh," statement in Parliament, November 15, 1971; Gandhi, *India and Bangla Desh*, 105.

111. Raghavan, *1971*, 228.

112. The Indira Gandhi administration's rhetoric on "refugee aggression" to its enemies compelled the United States to initiate a dialogue with China that India might attack *West* Pakistan, which required Chinese military pressure.

113. Avtar Singh Bhasin, ed., *India-Pakistan: 1947–2007: A Documentary Study*, vols. 1–10 (Geetika, 2012), 1521.

114. Raghavan, *1971*, 242.

115. Editorial, *New York Times*, "War on the Subcontinent," December 4, 1971, https://www.nytimes.com/1971/12/04/archives/war-on-the-subcontinent.html.

116. Indira Gandhi, "What We Are Fighting For," from translation delivered in Hindi at public rally at Ramlila Ground, Delhi, December 12, 1971; Gandhi, *India and Bangla Desh*, 136.

117. "Prime Minister Indira Gandhi's Interview to *Newsweek* Magazine," November 15, 1971, in *Bangladesh Documents*, 2:295.

118. David Myard, "Sadruddin Aga Khan and the 1971 East Pakistani Crisis," Global Migration Research Paper (Graduate Institute Geneva, 2010), 50, https://www.graduateinstitute.ch/sites/internet/files/2018-12/GMC%20-%20Global%20Migration%20Res-1.pdf, accessed June 22, 2025.

119. Bass, *The Blood Telegram*, chap. 15.

120. Myard, "Sadruddin Aga Khan and the 1971 East Pakistani Crisis," 49.

121. Raghavan, *1971*, 231.

122. UN Security Council Official Records, 1606th Meeting, December 4, 1971, 15.

123. See "Conversation Between President Nixon and His Assistant for National Security Affairs (Kissinger)," December 6, 1971, *FRUS 1969–1972*, vol. E-7, Document 162, https://2001-2009.state.gov/r/pa/ho/frus/nixon/e7/48535.htm, accessed June 24, 2025.

124. Ronald R. Krebs and Patrick Thaddeus Jackson, "Twisting Tongues and Twisting Arms: The Power of Political Rhetoric," *European Journal of International Relations* 13, no. 1 (January 3, 2007): 42.

125. Jawaharlal Nehru, *The Discovery of India*, new ed. (APH, 2004), 322.

126. Pratap Bhanu Mehta, "Do New Democracies Support Democracy? Reluctant India," *Journal of Democracy* 22, no. 4 (2011): 97–109.

127. Friedrich Kratochwil, "Constructing a New Orthodoxy? Wendt's 'Social Theory of International Politics' and the Constructivist Challenge," *Millennium—Journal of International Studies* 29, no. 1 (January 1, 2000): 47.

4. BRAZIL'S RHETORICAL POWER POLITICS IN THE HAITIAN CRISIS, 2004

1. "Brazil Wants Autonomy to Act," interview of Luiz Inácio Lula da Silva (Lula) for NPQ by the editors of *O Estado de Sao Paulo Brazil & Soft Anti-Globalization* (NPQ Winter 2003): 61–62.

2. The exact phrase that Lula used is "Foi assim que atendemos, o Brasil e outros países da América Latina, à convocação da ONU para contribuir na estabilização do Haiti. Quem defende novos paradigmas nas relações internacionais, não poderia omitir-se diante de uma situação concreta" ["This is how Brazil and other Latin American countries responded to the UN's call to contribute to the stabilization of Haiti. Those who defend new paradigms in international relations could not remain silent in the face of a concrete situation"] in Luiz Inácio Lula da Silva (Lula), "Discurso LIX Assembléia Geral da ONU," em *Discursos Selecionados do Presidente Luiz Inácio Lula da Silva*, ed. Ministério das Relações Exteriores, 37 (FUNAG, 2008).

3. Leticia Macedo, "Haiti: Missão de 13 anos do Exército brasileiro deixou legado questionável," *UOL*, July 11, 2021, https://noticias.uol.com.br/internacional/ultimas-noticias/2021/07/11/haiti-minustah-missao-de-paz-onu-exercito.htm?cmpid=copiaecola. See also Fabio Zanini, "Report Says Brazil's Army Wasn't Prepared for Human Rights Mission in Haiti," *Folha de Sao Paulo*, May 28, 2019.

4. Condoleezza Rice, "Rethinking the National Interest: American Realism for a New World," *Foreign Affairs* (July/August 2008): 2–14.

5. Moniz Banderia, "Brazil as a Regional Power and Its Relations with the United States," *Latin American Perspectives* 33, no. 3 (2006): 12–27.

6. Constantine C. Menges, "Blocking a New Axis of Evil," *Washington Times*, August 29, 2002.

7. Peter Hakim, "The Reluctant Partner," *Foreign Affairs* (January–February 2004): 114–23.

8. See Federico Neiburg, "The Brazilian Army in Haiti—Foreign Intervention and Domestic Politics," *OpinioJuris*, May 1, 2020, http://opiniojuris.org/2020/05/01/the-brazilian-army-in-haiti-foreign-intervention-and-domestic-politics/.

9. Tullo Vigevani and Gabriel Cepaluni, "Lula's Foreign Policy and the Quest for Autonomy Through Diversification," *Third World Quarterly* 28, no. 7 (2007): 1309–26; Monica Hirst, "Emerging Brazil: The Challenges of Liberal Peace and Global Governance," *Global Society* 29, no. 3 (2015): 1–14; Gian Luca Gardini, "Brazil: What Rise of What Power?," *Bulletin of Latin American Research* 35, no. 1 (2016): 5–19, https://doi.org/10.1111/blar.12417; Feliciano de Sá Guimarães and Maria Hermínia Tavares de Almeida, "From Middle Powers to Entrepreneurial Powers in World Politics: Brazil's Successes and Failures in International Crises," *Latin American Politics and Society* 59, no. 4 (2017): 26–46, https://doi.org/10.1111/laps.12032; Carlos R. S. Milani, Leticia Pinheiro, and Maria Regina Soares De Lima, "Brazil's Foreign Policy and the 'Graduation Dilemma,'" *International Affairs* 93, no. 3 (May 1, 2017): 585–605, https://doi.org/10.1093/ia/iix078; Feliciano de Sá Guimarães, "The Uneasy 'Well-Placed' State: Brazil Within Latin America and the West," *Cambridge Review of International Affairs* 33, no. 4 (July 3, 2020): 603–19.

10. Ricardo Seintefus, "Elementos para uma Diplomacia Solidária: a Crise Haitiana e os Desafios da Ordem Internacional Contemporânea," *Carta Internacional* 1, no. 1 (2006): 5–12.

11. Eugenio Diniz, "Brazil: Peacekeeping and the Evolution of Foreign Policy," in *Capacity Building for Peacekeeping: The Case of Haiti*, ed. John T. Fishel and Andrés Sáenz, 91–111 (National Defense University Press, 2007); Kai Michael Kenkel, "Five Generations of Peace Operations: From the 'Thin Blue Line' to 'Painting a Country Blue,'" *Revista Brasileira de Política Internacional* 56, no. 1 (2013): 122–43; Hirst, "Emerging Brazil"; Paulo Esteves, Maria Gabrielsen Jumbert, and Benjamin de Carvalho, eds., *Status and the Rise of Brazil: Global Ambitions, Humanitarian Engagement and International Challenges* (Palgrave Macmillan, 2019).

12. Barbara Koremenos, Charles Lipson, and Duncan Snidal, "The Rational Design of International Institutions," *International Organization* 55, no. 4 (2001): 762.

13. Anders Wivel and T. V. Paul, eds., *International Institutions and Power Politics: Bridging the Divide* (Georgetown University Press, 2019).

14. Maíra Siman Gomes, "Analysing Interventionism Beyond Conventional Foreign Policy Rationales: The Engagement of Brazil in the United Nations Stabilization Mission in Haiti (MINUSTAH)," *Cambridge Review of International Affairs* 29, no. 3 (July 2, 2016): 852–69.

15. Joao Paulo, "O Poder Militar como Instrumento da Política Externa Brasileira Contemporânea," *Revista Brasileira de Política Internacional* 52, no. 2 (2009): 173–91; Fernando Cavalcante, "Rendering Peacekeeping Instrumental? The Brazilian Approach to United Nations Peacekeeping During the Lula Da Silva Years (2003–2010)," *Revista Brasileira de Política Internacional* 53, no. 2 (2010): 142–59; Amelie Gautheir and Sarah John de Sousa, "Brasil en Haiti: El Debate Respecto a la Missión de Paz," November 2006, Fundación para las Relaciones Internacionales y el Diálogo Exterior (FRIDE). For a summary of different motives, see W. Alejandro Sanchez Nieto, "Brazil's Grand Design for Combining Global South Solidarity and National Interests: A Discussion of Peacekeeping Operations in Haiti and East Timor," *Globalizations* 9, no. 1 (2012): 161–78. For a useful instrumentalist account, see Markus-Michael Muller and Andrea Steinke, "The Geopolitics

of Brazilian Peacekeeping and the United Nations' Turn Towards Stabilization in Haiti," *Peacebuilding* 8, no. 1 (2020): 54–77.

16. Luiz Inácio Lula da Silva (Lula), "Discurso no Abertura da 1 Reunião de Chefes de Estado da Comunidade Sul-Americana de Nações," em *Discursos Selecionados do Presidente Luiz Inácio Lula da Silva*, ed. Ministério das Relações Exteriores, 60 (FUNAG, 2008).

17. Robert Fatton Jr., "The Fall of Aristide and Haiti's Current Predicament," in *Haiti: Hope for a Fragile State*, ed. Yasmine Shamsie and Andrew S Thompson, 15 (Wilfrid Laurier University Press, 2006).

18. Justin Podur, *Haiti's New Dictatorship: The Coup, the Earthquake and the UN Occupation* (Pluto, 2012), 15.

19. See James Ferguson, *Papa Doc, Baby Doc: Haiti and the Duvaliers* (Blackwell, 1987); Robert Fatton Jr., *The Roots of Haitian Despotism* (Lynne Rienner, 2007).

20. Peter Hallward, *Damning the Flood: Haiti, Aristide, and the Politics of Containment* (Verso, 2008).

21. Podur, *Haiti's New Dictatorship*, 16.

22. Paul Farmer, *Haiti After the Earthquake* (PublicAffairs, 2011), 150; Alex Dupuy, *Haiti in the New World Order* (Palgrave Macmillan, 1997).

23. Diniz, "Brazil: Peacekeeping and the Evolution of Foreign Policy," 101.

24. For a good summary, see Sebastian von Einsiedel and David M. Malone, "Peace and Democracy for Haiti: A UN Mission Impossible?," *International Relations* 20, no. 2 (2006): 156.

25. Einsiedel and Malone, "Peace and Democracy for Haiti," 158.

26. Cited in Hallward, *Damning the Flood*, 78.

27. Podur, *Haiti's New Dictatorship*, 25.

28. Michel-Rolph Trouillot, *Haiti: State Against Nation* (Monthly Review Press, 1990). For the origins of indemnity debt, see Liliana Obregón, "Empire, Racial Capitalism and International Law: The Case of Manumitted Haiti and the Recognition Debt," *Leiden Journal of International Law* 31 (2018): 597–615.

29. David E. Sanger and Eric Schmitt, "Bush Increases Pressure for Haitian to Leave Office," *New York Times*, February 29, 2004.

30. Podur, *Haiti's New Dictatorship*, 54–55.

31. Rubens Ricupero, "À Sombra de Charles de Gaulle: Uma Diplomacia Carismática e Intransferível. A Política Externa Do Governo Luiz Inácio Lula Da Silva (2003–2010)," *Novos Estudos—CEBRAP*, no. 87 (July 2010): 35–58.

32. Leticia Pinheiro, "Traídos Pelo Desejo: Um Ensaio Sobre a Teoria e a Prática Da Política Externa Brasileira Contemporânea," *Contexto Internacional* 22, no. 2 (2000): 305–35; Tullo Vigevani and Gabriel Cepaluni, *Brazilian Foreign Policy in Changing Times: The Quest for Autonomy from Sarney to Lula* (Lexington Books, 2009); Jeffrey W. Cason and Timothy J. Power, "Presidentialization, Pluralization, and the Rollback of Itamaraty: Explaining Change in Brazilian Foreign Policy Making in the Cardoso-Lula Era," *International Political Science Review* 30, no. 2 (March 1, 2009): 117–40, https://doi.org/10.1177/0192512109102432.

33. Tullo Vigevani and Marcelo Fernandes de Oliveira, "Brazilian Foreign Policy in the Cardoso Era: The Search for Autonomy Through Integration," *Latin American Perspectives* 34, no. 5 (September 1, 2007): 68.

34. Minister Luiz Felipe Lampreia, speech at the Regular Session of the General Assembly of the United Nations in 1999, in *Brazil in the United Nations (1946–2011)*, ed. Luiz Felipe de Seixas Corrêa, Ministry of External Relations, 777–78 (Alexandre de Gusmão Foundation, 2013).

35. Oliveiros Ferreira, *A Crise da politíca externa: Autonomia ou subordinação?* (Revan, 2001), quoted in Banderia, "Brazil as a Regional Power and Its Relations with the United States," 12–27.

36. George Bush, "Address to a Joint Session of Congress and the American People," September 20, 2001, White House Archives Online, https://georgewbush-whitehouse.archives .gov/news/releases/2001/09/20010920-8.html, accessed June 20, 2025.

37. See also Carol Williams, "Road to Democracy in Haiti Hits an Impasse," *Los Angeles Times*, June 26, 2003; Christopher Marquis, "Powell, Too, Hints Haitian Should Leave," *New York Times*, February 27, 2004. On the specific role of the United States, France, and Canada, see Podur, *Haiti's New Dictatorship*, 41–53; Farmer, *Haiti After the Earthquake*.

38. See Resolution Adopted by the General Assembly on International Civilian Support Mission in Haiti, UN General Assembly, Resolution A/RES/54/193, February 18, 2000; Kofi A. Annan, "Haiti: This Time We Must Get It Right," *Wall Street Journal*, March 16, 2004. See also Einsiedel and Malone, "Peace and Democracy for Haiti."

39. Andreas E. Feldmann and Juan Esteban Montes, "Learning to Be Likeminded: Chile's Involvement in Global Security and Peace Operations Since the End of the Cold War," in *South America and Peace Operations: Coming of Age*, ed. Kai Michael Kenkel, 156 (Routledge, 2013).

40. See Jorge Heine, "Between a Rock and a Hard Place: Latin America and Multilateralism After 9/11," in *Multilateralism Under Challenge? Power, International Order, and Structural Change*, ed. Edward Newman, Ramesh Thakur, and John Tirman, 481–503 (United Nations University Press, 2006).

41. Rut Diamint, "From Fear to Humanitarianism: Changing Patterns in Argentina's Involvement in Peace Operations," in *South American and Peace Operations: Coming of Age*, ed. Kai Michael Kenkel, 140 (Routledge, 2013).

42. Gilda Follietti, "La Participación Argentina en Haití: El Papel del Congreso," *Revista Fuerzas Armadas y Sociedad* 19, no. 1 (2005): 37–56.

43. Quoted in Podur, *Haiti's New Dictatorship*, 55–56.

44. On the role of Caribbean Community (CARICOM), see Bert Wilkinson, "Caribbean Won't Accept Haiti's New US Backed Government," *Associated Press*, March 26, 2004, https://www.globalpolicy.org/component/content/article/186/34379.html; J. G. Tokatlian, "Intervención En Haití, Misión Frustrada. Una Crítica de América Latina (Intervention in Haiti, Unsuccessful Mission. A Latin America Critique)," *FRIDE*, October 9, 2005.

45. Members of the Brazilian Social Democratic Party (PSDB) were the most vocal opponents of Brazil's intervention in Haiti.

46. Particularly important media that opposed liberal interventionism were Amy Goodman's *Democracy Now, Black Commentator*, and sections of the BBC.

47. Monica Hirst, "South American Intervention in Haiti," Fundación paralas Relaciones Internacionales y el Diálogo Exterior (FRIDE) Comment (FRIDE, 2007).

48. Paul MacDonald, "Parliament of Man, Federation of the World: Repertoire of Statecraft, the Hague Conferences, and the Making of the Liberal Order," *Diplomacy and Statecraft* 32, no. 4 (2021): 651.

49. Einsiedel and Malone, "Peace and Democracy for Haiti," 156.

50. Permanent Council of the OAS, "Report on OAS Activities Involving Haiti from November 11, 2003, to March 10, 2004," CP/doc.3849/04 corr. 1, March 17, 2004; "OAS Urges UN Efforts on Haiti Crisis," February 26, 2004, E-028/04; UN News Report, "CARICOM, Haiti Appeal to Security Council for Help as Haitian Security Worsens," February 26, 2004.

51. "Haiti's Interim Prime Minister Asks for OAS Election Support," *Caribbean Net News,* May 7, 2004.

52. Karen E. Bravo, "CARICOM, the Myth of Sovereignty, and Aspirational Economic Integration," *North Carolina Journal of International Law and Commercial Regulation* 31, no. 1 (2005): 146–206; Todd Howland, "Peacekeeping and Conformity with Human Rights Law: How MINUSTAH Falls Short in Haiti," *International Peacekeeping* 13, no. 4 (December 1, 2006): 470.

53. See UN Secretary General, Report on MINUSTAH, UN Doc. S/2004/300 (April 16, 2004); UN Secretary General, Report on Haiti, UN Doc. S.2004/698 (August 30, 2004). Brazilian policymakers made reference to this report in the domestic legislative debates as we will see below.

54. Hirst, "South American Intervention in Haiti," 2–3.

55. See Roberto Russell and Juan G. Tokatlian, "Contemporary Argentina and the Rise of Brazil," *Bulletin of Latin American Research* 35, no. 1 (2016): 23.

56. Stephen J. Schnably, "The Santiago Commitment as a Call to Democracy in the United States: Evaluating the OAS Role in Haiti, Peru, and Guatemala," *University of Miami Inter-American Law Review* (1994): 393–587.

57. Hirst, "South American Intervention in Haiti"; Kai Michael Kenkel, "South America's Emerging Power: Brazil as Peacekeeper," *International Peacekeeping* 17, no. 5 (November 1, 2010): 644–61; Kai Michael Kenkel, "Interest, Identity and Brazilian Peacekeeping Policy," *Perspectives of World Politics* 3, no. 2 (2011): 9–35; Ricardo Seitenfus, *Haiti: Dilemas e Fracassos Internacionais* (Editora Unijui, 2014).

58. For another interpretation of Brazil's focus on exceptionalism, see W. A. S. Nieto, "Brazil's Grand Design for Combining Global South Solidarity and National Interests: A Discussion of Peacekeeping Operations in Haiti and Timor," *Globalizations* 9, no. 1 (2012): 161–78.

59. President Luiz Inácio Lula da Silva, speech at his inaugural ceremony, National Congress, Brasilia, January 1, 2003, http://www.biblioteca.presidencia.gov.br/presidencia/ex-presidentes/luiz-inacio-lula-da-silva/discursos/10-mandato/2003/01-01-pronunciamento-a-nacao-do-presidente-da-republica-luiz-inacio-lula-da-silva-apos-a-cerimonia-de-posse.pdf/view. See also *Brazilian Foreign Policy Handbook of the Ministry of External Relations* (Alexandre de Gusmao Foundation, Ministry of External Relations, 2008), 43 [hereafter *Ministry of External Relations, 2008*].

60. Celso Amorim, speech given during the ceremony on taking office as Minister of External Relations, Brasilia, January 1, 2003. See *Ministry of External Relations, 2008*, 43–44.

61. Celso Amorim, speech given during the ceremony on taking office as Minister of External Relations, Brasilia, January 1, 2003. See *Ministry of External Relations*, 2008, 44.

62. Luiz Inácio Lula da Silva, speech in the National Congress, Brasilia, January 1, 2003. See *Ministry of External Relations*, 2008, 25.

63. Maria Regina Soares De Lima and Mônica Hirst, "Brazil as an Intermediate State and Regional Power: Action, Choice and Responsibilities," *International Affairs* 82, no. 1 (January 1, 2006): 21.

64. See Samuel Pinheiro Guimares, *Desafios brasileiros na era gigantes* (Contraponto, 2006).

65. See "Remarks with Brazilian Foreign Minister Celso Amorim," U.S. Department of State Archive, October 5, 2004, https://2001-2009.state.gov/secretary/former/powell/remarks/36801.htm.

66. Roberto Godoy, "World Events Makes Amazon a Priority of Military Refurbishment Plan," *O Estado de Sao Paulo*, October 17, 2001. For the assertive position of the Lula administration, see Rafael Villa and Manuela Viana, "Security Issues During Lula's Administration: From the Reactive to the Assertive Approach," *Revisita Brasiliera, Politica Internacional* 53, special ed. (2010): 91–114.

67. See Hal Brands, "Evaluating Brazilian Grand Strategy Under Lula," *Comparative Strategy* 30, no. 1 (2011): 32.

68. "Argentina and Brazil: Sweet Nothings?," *The Economist*, September 18, 1997, https://www.economist.com/the-americas/1997/09/18/sweet-nothings, accessed June 20, 2025.

69. R. Russell and J. G. Tokatlian, *El Lugar de Brasil en la Política Exterior Argentina* [*The Place of Brazil in the Foreign Policy of Argentina*] (Fondo de Cultura Económica, 2003).

70. Follietti, "La Participación Argentina en Haití."

71. See Stefan A. Schirm, "Leaders in Need of Followers: Emerging Powers in Global Governance," *European Journal of International Relations* 16, no. 2 (June 1, 2010): 203, https://doi.org/10.1177/1354066109342922.

72. Roberto Russell and Juan Gabriel Tokatlian, "Implications of the Global and Regional Changes for Argentina's Foreign Relations," *Journal of Iberian and Latin American Research* 19, no. 2 (December 1, 2013): 256.

73. Follietti, "La Participación Argentina en Haití," 47.

74. Alvaro Quezada-Hofflinger, "What Does the Left Do Right? An Interview with Ricardo Lagos," *Portal* 3 (2008): 13.

75. Martin Mullins, *In the Shadow of the Generals: Foreign Policy Making in Argentina, Brazil and Chile* (Routledge, 2017).

76. On Brazil's securitization in Haiti, see Thomaz Alexandre Mayer Napoleão and Mariana Alves da Cunha Kalil, "Stabilization as the Securitization of Peacebuilding? The Experience of Brazil and MINUSTAH in Haiti," *Brasiliana: Journal for Brazilian Studies* 3, no. 2 (2015): 87–112. Other works offer a deeper critique. "On the issue of agrarian reform, Lula is even vulnerable within his own government coalition, as a study revealed that 31 deputies from the Liberal Party (PL), the Labour Party (PTB) and the Social Democratic Party (PMDB) could be identified as defenders of the interests of large landowners. Whatever the case may be, this past June [2004], the MST decided to modify its position in respect

to the Lula government and initiated a series of land occupations in order to pressure the government to accelerate the pace of land distributions." See Leandro Vergara-Camus, "The Experience of the Landless Workers Movement and the Lula Government," *Revista Internacional Interdisciplinar Interthesis* 2, no. 1 (2005): 24.

77. Celso Lafer, "Governança e risco" ["Governance and Risk"], *O Estado de S. Paulo*, May 18, 2003; Celso Lafer, "Enthsiasmo no Itamaraty?" ["Enthusiasm in Itamaraty?"], *Valor Econômico*, July 23, 2003, A8; Marcelo de Paiva Abreu, "Alca por Nada?," *O Estado de S. Paulo*, August 11, 2003; Marcelo de Paiva Abreu, "Pobre Barão," *O Estado de S. Paulo*, October 27, 2003.

78. A. Sánchez, "Peacekeeping and Military Operation by Latin American Militaries: Between Being a Good Samaritan and Servicing the National Interest," *Washington: Council on Hemispheric Affairs*, www.coha.org, accessed July 1, 2016.

79. "Consultor da ONU diz essa é a última chance," *O Estado de S. Paulo*, January 14, 2004.

80. Seitenfus, *Haiti*, 50.

81. See "CARICOM Leaders to Hold Emergency Summit on Haiti," *Caribbean Net News*, March 2, 2004.

82. Julia D. Buxton, "Swimming Against the Tide: Venezuela and Peace Operations," in *South America and Peace Operations: Coming of Age*, ed. Kai Michael Kenkel, 180 (Routledge, 2013).

83. Academic criticism against Argentina's participation in the military operation in Haiti was consistent. See, for example, Luis Tibiletti, "Haiti en diez aciertos" ["Haiti in Ten Hits"], *Pagina/12* (Buenos Aires), June 16, 2004; Juan Gabriel Tokatlian, "El desacierto de enviar tropas a Haiti" ["The Misstep of Sending Troops to Haiti"], *Pagina/12*, June 13, 2004; Ernesto Lopez, "Diplomacia sin indiferencia" ["Diplomacy Without Indifference"], *Clarín*, August. 27, 2005. For detailed assessment on the legislative debates in Argentina about Haiti, see Follietti, "La Participación Argentina en Haití."

84. Quoted in Sean W. Burges, *Brazilian Foreign Policy After the Cold War* (University Press of Florida, 2009), 164.

85. Burges, *Brazilian Foreign Policy After the Cold War*, 164.

86. Eduardo Passarelli Hamann and Carlos Augusto Ramires Teixeira, eds., *Brazil's Participation in MINUSTAH (2004–2017): Perceptions, Lessons, and Practices for Future Missions* (Report Igarapé Institute, 2017).

87. Floriano Peixoto Vieira Neto, "The Brazilian Military Experience in Haiti," in *Brazil's Participation in MINUSTAH (2004–2017): Perceptions, Lessons, and Practices for Future Missions*, ed. Eduardo Passarelli Hamann and Carlos Augusto Ramires Teixeira, 17 (Report Igarapé Institute, 2017).

88. Andrés Malamud, "A Leader Without Followers? The Growing Divergence Between the Regional and Global Performance of Brazilian Foreign Policy," *Latin American Politics and Society* 53, no. 3 (2011): 1–24.

89. Argentine diplomat interviewed by Leslie Wehner in 2010. See the important study: Leslie Wehner, "Role Expectations as Foreign Policy: South American Secondary Powers' Expectations of Brazil as a Regional Power," *Foreign Policy Analysis* 11, no. 4 (2015): 435–55.

90.   Diniz, "Brazil: Peacekeeping and the Evolution of Foreign Policy," 101.

91.   See WikiLeaks, "Brazil: (Kind of) Making the World Safe for Democracy," January 9, 2008, 17:24 (Wednesday), https://wikileaks.org/plusd/cables/08BRASILIA57_a.html.

92.   Specifically in Comissão de Relaçoes Exteriores e Defensa Nacional [CREDN, Commission of External Relations and National Defense], 52nd Legislature, 2nd Session, May 12, 2004,   http://www.camara.leg.br/internet/ordemdodia/integras/216676.htm   [hereafter CREDN]. It is the Eighth Extraordinary Meeting of the Foreign Affairs Committee and National Defense of the Federal Senate and the Eighth Meeting of the Foreign Affairs Committee and National Defense of the Chamber of Deputies, the Second Session of the Legislative Meeting of the Fifty Second Legislature, held jointly on May 12, 2004. All translations from Portuguese to English are by the author.

93.   Celso Amorim, lecture by the Foreign Minister of Brazil, London School of Economics, March 17, 2004.

94.   See, for example, Luiz Inácio Lula da Silva, speech presented at the Brazilian Foreign Policy in the 21st Century and the Role of the Sino-Brazilian Strategic Partnership Conference, University of Beijing, May 25, 2004.

95.   CREDN, 19.

96.   Diniz, "Brazil: Peacekeeping and the Evolution of Foreign Policy," 92.

97.   CREDN, 13.

98.   CREDN, 11.

99.   Speech by Minister of Foreign Affairs, Celso Amorim, May 12, 2004, CREDN, 10.

100. CREDN, 10.

101. Reply by Minister of Foreign Affairs, Celso Amorim, May 12, 2004, CREDN, 52.

102. Inter Press Service (IPS) Correspondents, "Haiti: Latin America-Led Peacekeeping Operation—A 'Mission Impossible,'" November 5, 2004, http://www.ipsnews.net/2004/11/haiti-latin-america-led-peacekeeping-operation-a-mission-impossible/.

103. See Ignacio Walker, "Statement by H. E. Mr. Ignacio Walker, Minister of Foreign Affairs of the Republic of Chile," Sixtieth Session of the United Nations General Assembly, September 21, 2005, www.un.org/webcast/ga/60/statements/chile050921eng.pdf.

104. Marcela Valente, "Argentina: Rumsfeld Wants South American Troops to Remain in Haiti," Inter Press Service News Agency, March 22, 2005, http://www.ipsnews.net/2005/03/argentina-rumsfeld-wants-south-american-troops-to-remain-in-haiti/.

105. Hirst, "South American Intervention in Haiti," 6.

106. Monica Hirst and Elsa Llenderrozas, "La Dimensión Política de la Presencia en Haití: Los Desafíos para el ABC+U," Documento de Trabajo 3, Programa en Desarrollo, Innovación y Sociedad, Facultad Latinoamericana de Ciencias Sociales (IRDC/CRDI, 2008).

107. See Andreas Feldmann, Miguel Lengyel, Bernabé Malacalza, and Antonio Ramalho, "Lost in Translation: ABC Cooperation and Reconstruction in Haiti," Journal of Peacebuilding and Development 6, no. 3 (2011): 47.

108. Larry Rohter, "Brazil Is Leading a Largely South American Mission to Haiti," New York Times, August 1, 2004.

109. See George W. Bush, "President Bush Welcomes President Lula of Brazil to Camp David," White House Press Release, March 31, 2007, http://georgewbush-whitehouse.archives .gov/news/releases/2007/03/20070331-3.html.

110. Gomes, "Analysing Interventionism."

111. See the argumentation between Minister Celso Amorim and Senator Fernando Gabeira (S/Partido-RJ), CREDN, which relied on Brazil's changing race relations. According to the 2010 census, 7.6 percent of Brazilians said that they were Black, compared with 6.2 percent in 2000; 43.1 percent said that they were mixed race, up from 38.5 percent. For the first time, 97 million Brazilians, or 50.7 percent of the population, defined themselves as Black or mixed race, compared with 91 million, or 47.7 percent, who labeled themselves white. See Thomas Phillips, "Brazil Census Shows African-Brazilians in the Majority for the First Time," *The Guardian*, November 17, 2011.

112. Minister of Foreign Affairs, Celso Amorim, CREDN, 31–32.

113. *Ministry of External Relations*, 86.

114. Johanna Mendelson Forman, "Latin American Peacekeeping: A New Era of Regional Cooperation," in *Fixing Haiti: MINUSTAH and Beyond*, ed. Jorge Heine and Andrew S. Thompson, 139 (United Nations University Press, 2011).

115. Paul Amar, "Global South to the Rescue: Emerging Humanitarian Superpowers and Global Rescue Industries," *Globalizations* 9, no. 1 (2012): 11–15.

116. Kenkel, "South America's Emerging Power"; Kenkel, "Five Generations of Peace Operations."

117. See Felippe de Rosa and Kai Kenkel, "Localization and Subsidiarity in Brazil's Engagement with Responsibility to Protect," *Global Responsibility to Protect* 7 (2015): 325–49.

118. Leslie Bethell, *Brazil: Essays on History and Politics* (University of London, Institute of Latin American Studies, 2018), 53.

119. Kenkel, "South America's Emerging Power." For useful intervention, see Gomes, "Analysing Intervention."

120. Randall Schweller, "Emerging Powers in an Age of Disorder," *Global Governance* 17, no. 3 (2011): 293.

121. Celso Amorim, "Brazilian Foreign Policy Under President Lula (2003–2010): An Overview," *Revista Brasileira de Política Internacional* 53, no. SPE (December 2010): 225–26.

122. Oliver Stuenkel and Marcos Tourinho, "Regulating Intervention: Brazil and the Responsibility to Protect," *Conflict, Security & Development* 14, no. 4 (August 8, 2014): 379–402; Oliver Stuenkel, "Rising Powers and the Future of Democracy Promotion: The Case of Brazil and India," *Third World Quarterly* 34, no. 2 (2013): 339–55.

123. Carlos Chagas Vianna Braga, "MINUSTAH and the Security Environment in Haiti: Brazil and South American Cooperation in the Field," *International Peacekeeping* 17, no. 5 (November 1, 2010): 711–22.

124. Adriana Abdenur and Charles Call, "A 'Brazilian Way'? Brazil's Approach to Peacebuilding," in *Rising Powers and Peacebuilding: Rethinking Peace and Conflict Studies*, ed. Charles Call Cedric de Coning, 1–26 (Palgrave, 2017).

125. Diniz, "Brazil: Peacekeeping and the Evolution of Foreign Policy," 100.

5. CHINA'S RHETORICAL POWER POLITICS IN THE SYRIAN CRISIS, 2011-2020

1. On strategic competition, the U.S. National Security Strategy 2017 and 2018 defined a new era of interstate rivalry between states such as China and Russia with the United States. See White House, *National Security Strategy of the United States of America*, National Security Archive, December 1, 2017, 2, https://nsarchive.gwu.edu/document /16478-white-house-national-security-strategy. See also Jim Mattis, *Summary of the 2018 National Defense Strategy of the United States of America: Sharpening the American Military's Competitive Edge* (U.S. Department of Defense, 2018).

2. See "China and Syria," August 22, 2011, Ministry of Foreign Affairs of the People's Republic of China, https://www.mfa.gov.cn/irs-c-web/search_eng.shtml?code=18fe7c6489 d&dataTypeId=771&searchBy=title&searchWord=syria.

3. For a journalist's account of imperial overreach, see Katrina vanden Heuvel, "The 2010s Were a Decade of Imperial Overreach: Trump Is Making It Worse," *Washington Post*, January 7, 2020. For a critical scholarly account, see Somdeep Sen, "NATO and the Global Colour Line," *International Affairs* 100, no. 2 (March 2024): 491–507.

4. "Syria: Hillary Clinton Calls Russia and China 'despicable' for Opposing UN Resolution," *Telegraph*, February 25, 2012.

5. Bree Feng, "Obama's 'Free Rider' Comment Draws Chinese Criticism," *New York Times*, August 13, 2014.

6. UN Security Council, 6711th Meeting, "The Situation in the Middle East," February 4, 2012, New York, S/PV.6711, https://docs.un.org/en/S/PV.6711, accessed June 20, 2025.

7. UN Security Council, 6711th Meeting, "The Situation in the Middle East," February 4, 2012, New York, S/PV.6711, https://docs.un.org/en/S/PV.6711, accessed June 20, 2025.

8. UN Security Council, 8697th Meeting, "The Situation in the Middle East," December 20, 2019, New York, S/PV.8697, https://docs.un.org/en/S/PV.8697, accessed June 20, 2025.

9. Wang Yi, *China a Staunch Defender and Builder of International Rule of Law*, Ministry of Foreign Affairs, People's Republic of China, October 24, 2014, https://www.mfa.gov.cn /eng/wjb/zzjg_663340/xws_665282/xgxw_665284/202406/t20240606_11405665.html, accessed June 20, 2025.

10. For a useful corrective, see Courtney J. Fung, "Separating Intervention from Regime Change: China's Diplomatic Innovations at the UN Security Council Regarding the Syria Crisis," *China Quarterly* 235 (September 2018): 697, https://doi.org/10.1017 /S0305741018000851; Rosemary Foot, *China, the UN, and Human Protection: Beliefs, Power, Image* (Oxford University Press, 2020).

11. On details on the China "threat" theory in the media, see Kerry Liu, "The *Global Times* and the China Threat Narrative: An Empirical Analysis," *Journal of Chinese Political Science* 27, no. 1 (2022): 1–18.

12. Thomas Christensen views China as a high church of realpolitik. Thomas Christensen, "Chinese Realpolitik: Reading Beijing's World-View," *Foreign Affairs* 75, no. 5 (September/October 1996): 37; Richard Bernstein and Ross H. Munro, *The Coming Conflict with China* (Vintage, 1998); Edward Timperlake and William Triplett II, *Red Dragon Rising:*

Communist China's Military Threat to America (Regnery, 2001); Avery Goldstein, *Rising to the Challenge: China's Grand Strategy and International Security* (Stanford University Press, 2005); John Mearsheimer, "China's Unpeaceful Rise," *Current History* 105, no. 690 (2006); Camilla Sorensen, "Is China Becoming More Aggressive," *Asian Perspective* 37, no. 3 (2013): 363–85; Avery Goldstein, *Rising to the Challenge: China's Grand Strategy and International Security* (Stanford University Press, 2005); Wang Yuan-kang, *Harmony and War: Confucian Culture and Chinese Power Politics* (Columbia University Press, 2010). For a useful corrective, see Weiqing Song, "Securitization of the 'China Threat' Discourse: A Poststructuralist Account," *China Review* 15, no. 1 (2015): 145–69.

13. See this bias in Mordechai Chaziza, "Soft Balancing in the Middle East: Chinese and Russian Vetoes in the United Nations Council in the Syria Crisis," *China Report* 50, no. 3 (2014): 243–58.

14. Joseph Nye, "A New Sino-Russian Alliance?," *Project Syndicate*, January 12, 2015; G. Allison, "China and Russia: A Strategic Alliance in the Making," *National Interest*, December 14, 2018; A. Korolev and V. Portyakov, "China-Russia Relations in Times of Crisis: A Neoclassical Realist Explanation," *Asian Perspective* 42, no. 3 (2018): 411–43; A. Korolev, "On the Verge of an Alliance: Contemporary China-Russia Military Cooperation," *Asian Security* 15, no. 3 (2019): 233–52; S. Blank "The Unholy Russo-Chinese Alliance," *Defense & Security Analysis* 36, no. 3 (2020): 249–74; A. Lukin, "The Russia-China Entente and Its Future," *International Politics* 58 (2020): 363–80; Zhiqun Zhu, "Why Does China Still Play Second Fiddle?," *The Diplomat*, September 19, 2013, https://thediplomat.com/2013/09/why-does-china-play-second-fiddle-2/. See alternative views, Y. Fu, "How China Sees Russia," *Foreign Affairs* 95, no. 1 (2016): 96–105; Aglaya Snetkov and Marc Lanteigne, "The Loud Dissenter and Its Cautious Partner: Russia, China, Global Governance and Humanitarian Intervention," *International Affairs of the Asia-Pacific* 15, no. 1 (2015): 113–46; Elizabeth Wishnick, "In Search of the 'Other' in Asia: Russia-China Relations Revisited," *Pacific Review* 30, no. 1 (2017): 114–32.

15. Courtney Richardson, "A Responsible Power? China and the UN Peacekeeping Regime," *International Peacekeeping* 18, no. 3 (2011): 286–97.

16. See Danielle Cohen and Jonathan Kirshner, "The Cult of Energy Insecurity and Great Power Rivalry Across the Pacific," in *The Nexus of Economics, Security and International Relations in East Asia*, ed. Avery Goldstein and Edward D. Mansfield, 144–77 (Stanford University Press, 2012).

17. See Susan Pedersen, *The Guardians: The League of Nations and the Crisis of Empire* (Oxford University Press, 2015).

18. For example, Britain planned a regime change in Syria in the run up to the Suez Crisis in 1956, and the United States, embroiled in a Cold War ideological rivalry with the Soviet Union, planned to overthrow the pro-Communist Syrian regime in 1957.

19. For a comprehensive account, see David W. Lesch, *Syria: A Modern History* (Polity, 2019).

20. Eyal Zisser, "Bashar Al-Assad: In or Out of the New World Order," *Washington Quarterly* 28, no. 3 (2005): 122.

21. Zisser, "Bashar Al-Assad," 124.

22. Tim Castle and Tessa Unsworth, "Syrian Army Systematically Killing Civilians: Amnesty," *Reuters*, June 14, 2012, https://www.reuters.com/article/us-syria-amnesty /syrian-army-systematically-killing-civilians-amnesty-idUSBRE85D08520120614.

23. Frank G. Hoffman and Andrew Orner, "Proxy Wars and Strategic Competition," in *Routledge Handbook of Proxy Wars*, ed. Assaf Moghadam, Vladimir Rauta, and Michel Wyss, 428 (Routledge, 2023); Daniel Byman, "Are Proxy Wars Coming Back?," *Washington Quarterly* 46, no. 3 (2023): 149–64. In the context of Syria, see Nesrin Alrefaai, "Syria Between Civil and Proxy War: The Question of Terminology," *LSE Blog*, July 13, 2023, https://blogs.lse.ac.uk/mec/2023/07/13/syria-between-civil-and-proxy-war-the-question -of-terminology/, accessed June 20, 2025.

24. See Khaldoun Khashanah, "The Syrian Crisis," *Contemporary Arab Affairs* 7, no. 1 (2014): 1–21.

25. See UN Security Council, 6598th Meeting, "Statement by the President of the Security Council," August 3, 2011, UNSC, S/PRST/2011/16, https://docs.un.org/en/S/PRST/2011/16, accessed June 20, 2025.

26. See UN Security Council Report, "Syria Briefing," January 18, 2013, https://www .securitycouncilreport.org/whatsinblue/2013/01/syria-briefing-on-18-january.php, accessed June 20, 2025.

27. United Nations General Assembly, 67th Session, "Report of the United Nations Mission to Investigate Allegations of the Use of Chemical Weapons in the Syrian Arab Republic on the Alleged Use of Chemical Weapons in the Ghouta Area of Damascus on 21 August 2013," A/67/997-S/2013/553, September 16, 2013, https://documents.un.org/doc/undoc/gen /n13/476/14/pdf/n1347614.pdf, accessed June 20, 2025.

28. See White House, President Barack Obama, "Statement by the President on U.S.-Russian Agreement on Framework for Elimination of Syrian Chemical Weapons," White House Archives, September 14, 2013, https://obamawhitehouse.archives.gov/the-press-office/2013/09/14 /statement-president-us-russian-agreement-framework-elimination-syrian-ch.

29. Foot, *China, the UN, and Human Protection*, 165.

30. See United Nations Security Council, 7227th Meeting, "Statement by the President of the Security Council," S/PRST/2014/14, July 28, 2014, https://docs.un.org/en/S/PRST /2014/14, accessed June 20, 2025.

31. UN Secretary General Ban Ki-Moon Spokesman, "Secretary-General, on First Anniversary of Chemical Weapons Attack in Syria, says Conflict Remains Major Threat to International Peace and Security," UN Media Coverage and Press Releases, SG/SM/16095-HR/5208, August 21, 2014, https://press.un.org/en/2014/sgsm16095.doc.htm, accessed June 20, 2025.

32. United Nations High Commissioner for Refugees (UNHCR), "Global Trends: Forced Displacement in 2019," UNHCR, June 17, 2022, https://www.unhcr.org/flagship-reports /globaltrends/globaltrends2019/.

33. See UN Security Council, "Draft Resolution on Syria," *What's in Blue*, June 8, 2011, https:// www.securitycouncilreport.org/whatsinblue/2011/06/presidential-statement-on-syria .php.

34. Khashanah, "The Syrian Crisis," 2.

35. Li Baodong, "Remarks by Ambassador Li Baodong, Permanent Representative of China to the United Nations, at the Security Council Ministerial Meeting on the Humanitarian Situation in Syria," August 30, 2012, https://un.china-mission.gov.cn/eng/lmbf /gdxw/201208/t20120831_8405975.htm, accessed June 20, 2025.

36. Charles Kupchan, No One's World: The West, the Rising Rest, and the Coming Global Turn (Oxford University Press, 2012), 93.

37. See Gideon Rachman, "Obama's Asia Policy Is Distracted and Ambiguous," Financial Times, April 21, 2014, https://www.ft.com/content/bfe9c506-c4c7-11e3-8dd4-00144feabdc0, accessed June 20, 2025.

38. Kupchan, No One's World, 101–2. Note that, in Western parlance, sharing the costs of global public goods means partaking in advancing neoliberal capitalism at the expense of equality; liberal interventionism at the expense of sovereignty and the territorial integrity of states in Asia, Africa, and Latin America; and endorsing the moral high ground of militant democracy and Judeo-Christian ideas of secular nationalism.

39. Office of the Press Secretary of the White House, "Remarks by the President on the Middle East and North Africa," May 19, 2011, https://obamawhitehouse.archives.gov /the-press-office/2011/05/19/remarks-president-middle-east-and-north-africa.

40. Anna Fifield, "US and EU Call for Assad to Resign," Financial Times, August 19, 2011, https://www.ft.com/content/d93ee372-c963-11e0-9eb8-00144feabdc0.

41. Ian Black, "Qatar Admits Sending Hundreds of Troops to Support Libya Rebels," The Guardian, October 26, 2011, https://www.theguardian.com/world/2011/oct/26/qatar -troops-libya-rebels-support.

42. Ian Black, "Syria Crisis: Saudi Arabia to Spend Millions to Train New Rebel Force," The Guardian, November 7, 2013, https://www.theguardian.com/world/2013/nov/07/syria -crisis-saudi-arabia-spend-millions-new-rebel-force.

43. Neil MacFarquhar and Nada Bakri, "Isolating Syria, Arab League Imposes Broad Sanctions," New York Times, November 27, 2011.

44. External Affairs Minister's Statement at the International Conference on Syria (Geneva-II), United Nations Office at Geneva, January 22, 2014, https://mea.gov.in/Speeches -Statements.htm?dtl/22765/External+Affairs+Ministers+Statement+at+the+International +Conference+on+Syria+GenevaII.

45. GTD, Global Terrorism Index 2018: Measuring the Impact of Terrorism (Institute for Economics and Peace, 2018), https://www.visionofhumanity.org/maps/global-terrorism -index/#/.

46. Alan Bloomfield, "What Does New Delhi's Engagement with the War in Syria (and Iraq) Reveal About India as an International Actor?," India Review 17, no. 2 (2018): 209–41, https://doi.org/10.1080/14736489.2018.1452414.

47. "BRICS Summit Draws Clear Red Lines on Syria, Iran," The BRICS Post, April 3, 2013, https://thebricspost.com/brics-summit-draws-clear-red-lines-on-syria-iran/.

48. See China's White Paper, "China's National Defence in 2010," Information Office of the State Council of the People's Republic of China, March 31, 2011, http://www.china.org.cn /government/whitepaper/2011-03/31/content_22263357.htm.

49. See Charles Clover and Luna Lin, "China's Foreign Policy: Throwing out the Rule Book," *Financial Times*, September 5, 2016.

50. "Turkish Leader Calls Xinjiang Killings 'Genocide,'" *Reuters*, July 10, 2009, https://www .reuters.com/article/us-turkey-china-sb-idUSTRE56957D20090710.

51. Tom Miles, "Saudi Arabia and Russia Among 37 States Backing China's Xinjiang Policy," *Reuters*, July 12, 2019, https://www.reuters.com/article/us-china-xinjiang-rights -idUSKCN1U721X.

52. Explanation of Vote by Ambassador Li Baodong After Vote on Draft Resolution on Syria Tabled by the United Kingdom, Permanent Mission of the People's Republic of China to the UN, July 19, 2012, https://un.china-mission.gov.cn/eng/lmbf/gdxw/201207 /t20120720_8405973.htm, accessed June 21, 2025. See also Michael Swaine, "Chinese Views of the Syrian Conflict," *China Leadership Monitor*, 2012.

53. Fung, "Separating Intervention from Regime Change," 698.

54. UN Human Rights Council, *Report of the Independent International Commission of Inquiry on the Syrian Arab Republic*, A/HRC/S-17/2/Add.1, summary (November 23, 2011), https://www.ohchr.org/Documents/Countries/SY/A.HRC.S-17.2.Add.1_en.pdf; UN Human Rights Council, *Report of the Independent International Commission of Inquiry on the Syrian Arab Republic*, A/HRC/40/70, summary (January 31, 2019), https://perma .cc/8T88-X6AR, accessed June 21, 2025.

55. Zeid Ra'ad Al Hussein, "Opening Statement by UN High Commissioner for Human Rights," 37th session of the UN Human Rights Council, February 26, 2018, https://www .ohchr.org/en/statements-and-speeches/2018/02/37th-session-human-rights-council ?LangID=E&NewsID=22702, accessed June 21, 2025.

56. See United Nations General Assembly Human Rights Council, 21st Session, "Report of the Independent International Commission of Inquiry on the Syrian Arab Republic," A/ HRC/2150, August 16, 2012, https://www.ohchr.org/sites/default/files/Documents/HRBodies /HRCouncil/RegularSession/Session21/A-HRC-21-50_en.pdf, accessed June 21, 2025.

57. Zeid Ra'ad Al Hussein, "Opening Statement by UN High Commissioner for Human Rights," 37th session of the UN Human Rights Council, February 26, 2018, https://www .ohchr.org/en/statements-and-speeches/2018/02/37th-session-human-rights-council ?LangID=E&NewsID=22702, accessed June 21, 2025.

58. Micheal R. Gordon and Mark Landler, "Kerry Cites Clear Evidence of Chemical Weapon Use in Syria," *New York Times*, August 26, 2013, https://www.nytimes.com/2013/08/27 /world/middleeast/syria-assad.html.

59. Kris Boyle and Jordan Mower, "Framing Terror: A Content Analysis of Media Frames Used in Covering ISIS," *Newspaper Research Journal* 39, no. 2 (2018): 205–19.

60. Sultan Barakat and Steven A. Zyck, *The Syrian Refugee Crisis and the Erosion of Europe's Moral Authority*, Brookings Report, September 15, 2015, https://www.brookings .edu/blog/order-from-chaos/2015/09/15/the-syrian-refugee-crisis-and-the-erosion-of -europes-moral-authority/.

61. Tom Smith, Peter Lee, Vladimir Rauta, and Sammera Khalfey, "Understanding the Syria Babel: Moral Perspectives on the Syrian Conflict from Just War to *Jihad*," *Studies in Conflict & Terrorism* 43, no. 12 (2020): 1117.

62. UN Security Council, 6734th meeting, "The Situation in the Middle East," March 12, 2012, S.PV/6734, https://docs.un.org/en/S/PV.6734, accessed June 21, 2025.

63. Such absolute moral commitment against the use of force has only two exceptions in the form of authorization from the UN Security Council (Article 39) or when a state is acting under collective self-defense (Article 51).

64. UN Security Council, 6734th meeting, "The Situation in the Middle East," March 12, 2012, S.PV/6734, https://docs.un.org/en/S/PV.6734, accessed June 21, 2025. See also Fung "Separating Intervention from Regime Change"; Adrian Johnson and Saqeb Mueen, eds., *Short War, Long Shadow: The Political and Military Legacies of the 2011 Libya Campaign* (RUSI, Whitehall Report, 2012); Foot, *China, the UN, and Human Protection*, 176–78.

65. Xing Lu, *The Rhetoric of Mao Zedong: Transforming China and Its People* (University of South Carolina Press, 2017), 196.

66. Wang Yi, address at the Symposium, "New Starting Point, New Thinking and New Practice 2013: China and the World," *Embark of a New Journey of China's Diplomacy*, December 16, 2013, http://id.china-embassy.gov.cn/eng/sgdt/201312/t20131218_2048454.htm, accessed June 21, 2025. On a case-by-case approach, see Tiewa Liu and Haibin Zhang, "Debates in China About the Responsibility to Protect as a Developing International Norm: A General Assessment," *Conflict, Security and Development* 14, no. 4 (2014): 403–27.

67. See United Nations Security Council, "Draft Resolution," February 4, 2012, S/2012/77, https://www.securitycouncilreport.org/atf/cf/%7B65BFCF9B-6D27-4E9C-8CD3-CF6E4FF96FF9%7D/Syria%20S2012%2077.pdf, accessed June 21, 2025.

68. Chris Buckley, "China Calls U.S. Criticism over Syria 'Totally Unacceptable,'" *Reuters*, February 27, 2012, https://www.reuters.com/article/us-china-syria-idUSTRE81Q0AN20120227.

69. Li Boadong, "The Situation in the Middle East,"United Nations Security Council, 6810th Meeting, July 19, 2012, S/PV/6810, 9, 13, 14, https://docs.un.org/en/S/PV.6810, accessed June 21, 2025. See also Wang Min, "The Situation in the Middle East," United Nations Security Council, 7180th Meeting, May 22, 2014, S/PV.7180, 13, https://www.securitycouncilreport.org/atf/cf/%7B65BFCF9B-6D27-4E9C-8CD3-CF6E4FF96FF9%7D/s_pv_7180.pdf, accessed June 21, 2025.

70. For articulations of protecting small and medium states see discussions of China in Li Boadong, "The Situation in the Middle East," United Nations Security Council, 6627th Meeting, October 4, 2011, S/PV/6627, 5, https://www.securitycouncilreport.org/atf/cf/%7B65BFCF9B-6D27-4E9C-8CD3-CF6E4FF96FF9%7D/Golan%20Heights%20S%20PV%206627.pdf, accessed June 21, 2025. See also Li Boadong, "The Situation in the Middle East," United Nations Security Council, 6810th Meeting, July 19, 2012, S/PV/6810, 9, 13, 14, https://docs.un.org/en/S/PV.6810, accessed June 21, 2025; Wang Yi, "The Situation in the Middle East," United Nations Security Council, 7588th Meeting, December 18, 2015, S/PV/7588, 15-43795. See also Wang Yi, Speech at the Luncheon of the Fourth World Peace Forum, June 27, 2015, https://en.people.cn/n/2015/0628/c90883-8912267.html, accessed June 21, 2025.

71. See Mark Grant, "The Situation in the Middle East," United Nations Security Council, 6810th Meeting, July 19, 2012, S/PV/6810, 2, 3, https://docs.un.org/en/S/PV.6810, accessed June 21, 2025.

72. See Li Boadong, "The Situation in the Middle East," United Nations Security Council, 6810th Meeting, July 19, 2012, S/PV/6810, 9, 13, 14, https://docs.un.org/en/S/PV.6810, accessed June 21, 2025.

73. See, for example, China's similar claims in Wang Yi, "The Situation in the Middle East," United Nations Security Council, 7588th Meeting, December 18, 2015, S/PV/7588, 9, 10.

74. "The Dragon's New Teeth," *The Economist*, April 7, 2012, http://www.economist.com /node/21552193, accessed June 21, 2025.

75. Zhang Yu, "Xi Defined New Asian Security Vision at CICA," *Global Times*, May 22, 2014.

76. Edward Wong, "China's Hard Line: 'No Room for Compromise,'" *New York Times*, March 8, 2014, https://www.nytimes.com/2014/03/09/world/asia/china.html.

77. See United Nations Security Council, "Draft Resolution," S/2014/348, May 22, 2014.

78. Lu, *The Rhetoric of Mao Zedong*, 198.

79. China is not a state party to the International Criminal Court (ICC). But "as a permanent member of the Security Council, China *did not* seek to use its veto power to block the Council referrals of situations in Darfur or Libya to the ICC." United Nations Security Council, "Draft Resolution," S/Res/1593, March 31, 2005. See also United Nations Security Council, "Draft Resolution," S/Res/1970, February 26, 2011. Xi's speech on global governance was to the 19th Party Congress in 2017. See Dan Zhu, "China, the International Criminal Court, and Global Governance," *Australian Journal of International Affairs* 73, no. 6 (2019): 586.

80. United Nations Security Council, "Draft Resolution," S/2014/348, May 22, 2014.

81. Wu Haitao, "Official Statement," United Nations General Assembly, 71st session, 66th Plenary Meeting, December 21, 2016, A/71/PV.66, 36–37.

82. Wang Min, "The Situation in the Middle East," United Nations Security Council, 7180th Meeting, May 22, 2014, S/PV.7180, 18, https://www.securitycouncilreport.org/atf/cf /%7B65BFCF9B-6D27-4E9C-8CD3-CF6E4FF96FF9%7D/s_pv_7180.pdf, accessed June 21, 2025.

83. See *Report of the Independent International Commission of Inquiry on the Syrian Arab Republic*, UN Doc. A/HRC/40/70, January 31, 2019, 44–49.

84. Human Rights Council, *Report of the Independent International Commission of Inquiry on the Syrian Arab Republic*, UN General Assembly, 39th Session, August 9, 2018, UN Doc. A/HRC/39/65, https://docs.un.org/en/A/HRC/39/65, accessed June 21, 2025.

85. Human Rights Council, A/HRC/39/65, para 24.

86. See Human Rights Council, *Report of the Independent International Commission of Inquiry on the Syrian Arab Republic*, UN General Assembly, 34th Session, February 27–March 24, 2017, A/HRC/34/64, February 2, 2017, https://docs.un.org/en/A/HRC/34/64, accessed June 21, 2025.

87. See United Nations Security Council, "The Situation in the Middle East," UNSC, 7038th Meeting, September 27, 2013, S/PV/7038 and SC/11135, that unanimously adopted Resolution 2118, https://docs.un.org/en/S/PV.7038, accessed June 21, 2025.

88. Gérard Araud, "The Situation in the Middle East," United Nations Security Council, 7180th Meeting, May 22, 2014, S/PV.7180, 18, https://www.securitycouncilreport.org/atf

/cf/%7B65BFCF9B-6D27-4E9C-8CD3-CF6E4FF96FF9%7D/s_pv_7180.pdf, accessed June 21, 2025.

89. Vitaly Churkin, "The Situation in the Middle East," United Nations Security Council, 7180th Meeting, May 22, 2014, S/PV.7180, 22, https://www.securitycouncilreport.org /atf/cf/%7B65BFCF9B-6D27-4E9C-8CD3-CF6E4FF96FF9%7D/s_pv_7180.pdf, accessed June 21, 2025.

90. Lauren Said-Moorhouse, " 'Are You Truly Incapable of Shame?' Samantha Power Blasts Assad Regime, Allies," *CNN*, December 15, 2016, https://edition.cnn.com/2016/12/14 /middleeast/aleppo-samantha-power-speech/index.html.

91. Wang Yi, "Press Conference at the Second Session of the 12th National People's Congress," *Ministry of Foreign Affairs, People's Republic of China*, March 8, 2014, https://www .mfa.gov.cn/eng/wjb/wjbz/jh/202405/t20240527_11312091.html, accessed June 21, 2025.

92. See Wang Yi, remarks at the Second International Conference on Syria, Montreux, Switzerland, January 22, 2014, https://www.fmprc.gov.cn/mfa_eng/wjb_663304/wjbz_663308 /2461_663310/201401/t20140123_468496.html.

93. Liu Jieyi, "The Situation in the Middle East," United Nations Security Council, 7893rd Meeting, February 28, 2017, S/PV.7893, 17–18.

94. See United Nations Security Council, "The Situation in the Middle East," 7893rd Meeting, February 28, 2017, S/PV.7893, 18.

95. See United Nations Security Council, "The Situation in the Middle East," 7822nd Meeting, April 12, 2017, S/PV/7922; United Nations Security Council, "The Situation in the Middle East," 8228th Meeting, April 10, 2018, S/PV.8228.

96. "Xinjiang to Crack Down on 'Three Evil Forces,' " *Xinhua*, March 6, 2012, https://www .chinadaily.com.cn/china/2012-03/06/content_14766900.htm.

97. Yang Jingjie, "Xinjiang to See 'Major Strategy Shift,' " *Global Times*, January 9, 2014, http:// www.globaltimes.cn/content/836495.shtml#.UtS1ivaFZoQ.

98. Alexa Olesen, "China Sees Islamic State Inching Closer to Home," *Foreign Policy*, August 11, 2014, https://foreignpolicy.com/2014/08/11/china-sees-islamic-state-inching -closer-to-home/.

99. Wang Yi, press conference at the Third Session of the Twelfth National People's Congress, March 8, 2015, https://www.mfa.gov.cn/eng/wjb/wjbz/jh/202405/t20240527_11312109.html, accessed June 21, 2025.

100. Itamar Eichner, "Israeli Report: Thousands of Chinese Jihadists Are Fighting in Syria," *Ynet News*, March 27, 2017, https://www.ynetnews.com/articles/0,7340,L-4941411,00 .html. For a comprehensive treatment, see Sheena Chestnut Greitens, Myunghee Lee, and Emir Yazici, "Counterterrorism and Preventive Repression: China's Changing Strategy in Xinjiang," *International Security* 44, no. 3 (Winter 2019/2020): 9–47.

101. Mohanad Hage Ali, "China's Proxy War in Syria: Revealing the Role of Uighur Fighters," *Al-Arabiya*, March 2, 2016, https://english.alarabiya.net/en/perspective/analysis/2016/03 /02/China-s-proxy-war-in-Syria-Revealing-the-role-of-Uighur-aghters-.html.

102. Permanent Mission of the People's Republic of China to the UN, "Explanation of Vote by Ambassador Zhang Jun on the Security Council Draft Resolution Presented by Copenholders on the Mandate Renewal of Cross-Border Mechanisms in Syria," China Mission, July

2020, https://un.china-mission.gov.cn/eng/chinaandun/securitycouncil/regionalhotspots/mideast/202007/t20200711_8417292.htm, accessed June 21, 2025.

103.   Wang Yi, remarks at the Second International Conference on Syria, Montreux, Switzerland, January 22, 2014, https://www.fmprc.gov.cn/mfa_eng/xw/zyjh/202405/t20240530_11340682.html, accessed June 21, 2025.

104.   See S/PV.6810, July 19, 2012, 18.

105.   Wang Yi, "China's Role in the Global and Regional Order," Fourth World Peace Forum, June 27, 2015, https://en.people.cn/n/2015/0628/c90883-8912267.html, accessed June 21, 2025.

106.   Catherine Gegout and Shogo Suzuki, "China, Responsibility to Protect, and the Case of Syria: From Sovereignty Protection to Pragmatism," *Global Governance: A Review of Multilateralism and International Organizations* 26, no. 3 (September 17, 2020): 396, https://doi.org/10.1163/19426720-02603002.

107.   Charles Clover and Luna Lin, "China's Foreign Policy: Throwing Out the Rule Book," *Financial Times*, September 5, 2016.

108.   See the statement by Li Baodong, "The Situation in the Middle East," United Nations Security Council, 6810th Meeting, July 19, 2012, S/PV.6810, 13–14. China cast a negative vote in the final resolution. See United Nations Security Council, "Draft Resolution on Syria," July 19, 2012, S/2012/538.

109.   S/PV.6810, July 19, 2012, 14.

110.   Wang Yi, *China a Staunch Defender and Builder of International Rule of Law*, Ministry of Foreign Affairs, People's Republic of China, October 24, 2014, https://www.mfa.gov.cn/eng/wjb/zzjg_663340/xws_665282/xgxw_665284/202406/t20240606_11405665.html, accessed June 21, 2025.

111.   "China Saying 'No' on Syria Issue Is Responsible Move: FM Official," *Xinhua*, April 11, 2012, http://en.people.cn/90883/7783213.html; Li Qingsi, "Syria Another Western Power Move," *China Daily*, June 14, 2012, http://usa.chinadaily.com.cn/epaper/2012-06/14/content_15502548.htm.

112.   Wang Yi, "Settlement of Conflicts in the Middle East and North Africa and Countering the Terrorist Threat in the Region," United Nations Security Council Open Ministerial Meeting, 7525th meeting, September 30, 2015, S/PV.7527, https://www.mfa.gov.cn/eng/wjb/wjbz/jh/202405/t20240527_11312119.html, accessed June 21, 2025.

113.   Courtney J. Fung, "Global South Solidarity? China, Regional Organisations and Intervention in the Libyan and Syrian Civil Wars," *Third World Quarterly* 37, no. 1 (January 2, 2016): 42, https://doi.org/10.1080/01436597.2015.1078230.

114.   Wang Yi, "Forge Ahead Under the Guidance of General Secretary Xi Jinping's Thought on Diplomacy," September 1, 2017, https://www.fmprc.gov.cn/mfa_eng/xw/zyjh/202405/t20240530_11341188.html, accessed June 21, 2025.

115.   Camilla Sorensen, "Is China Becoming More Aggressive," *Asian Perspective* 37, no. 3 (2013): 363–85.

116.   The standard argument is from Randall L. Schweller and Xiaoyu Pu, "After Unipolarity: China's Visions of International Order in an Era of U.S. Decline," *International Security* 36, no. 1 (Summer 2011): 41–72. See also Gideon Rachman, *Easternisation: War and Peace in the Asian Century* (Random House, 2016); Riccardo Alcaro, John Peterson, and Ettore Greco, eds., *The West and the Global Power Shift: Transatlantic Relations and Global*

Governance (Palgrave Macmillan, 2016); Ian Bremmer, "It's Official: China Wants Its Share of Global Leadership," *Australian Financial Review*, January 15, 2018.

117. Alastair Iain Johnston, "How New and Assertive Is China's New Assertiveness?," *International Security* 37, no. 4 (April 1, 2013): 35.

118. Thomas J. Christensen, "Obama and Asia. Confronting the China Challenge," *Foreign Affairs* 5 (September/October 2015): 28–36.

119. Gu Jinglu, "Obama Says the U.S. Will Lead the World for the Next 100 Years; China Disagrees," *Washington Post*, May 30, 2014, https://www.washingtonpost.com/news /worldviews/wp/2014/05/30/ obama-says-the-u-s-will-lead-the-world-for-the-next-100 -years-china-disagrees/.

120. James Traud, "The World According to China," *New York Times Magazine*, September 3, 2006; M. D. Swaine, "Perceptions of an Assertive China," *China Leadership Monitor* (2010): 32; M. D Swaine, "Chinese Views of the Syrian Conflict," *China Leadership Monitor* (2012): 39; Will Piekos, "What China Loses for Its Support for Syria," *The Atlantic*, August 22, 2012.

121. Fung, "Separating Intervention from Regime Change," 694.

122. Gegout and Suzuki, "China, Responsibility to Protect, and the Case of Syria."

123. Chaziza, "Soft Balancing in the Middle East."

6. RHETORICAL POWERS, FLIPPED SCRIPTS, AND GLOBAL DISORDER

1. Aristotle, *The Art of Rhetoric* (Penguin Classics), 66.

2. Bryan Garsten, *Saving Persuasion: A Defense of Rhetoric and Judgement* (Harvard University Press, 2006), 5.

3. Charles Tilly, "Contentious Repertoires in Great Britain, 1758–1834," *Social Science History* 17, no. 2 (1993): 264. See also Charles Tilly, *Regimes and Repertoires* (University of Chicago Press, 2010).

4. Narendra Modi, address to the 74th session of the UN General Assembly, New York, September 27, 2019. For the full text, see https://pminewyork.gov.in/land.

5. Narendra Modi, "Why India and the World Need Gandhi," *New York Times*, October 2, 2019.

6. Live Reporting: Gandhi@150, Modi pays Tribute to Father of Nation at Sabarmati Ashram, *The Hindu*, October 2, 2019.

7. Michele L. Louro, *Comrades Against Imperialism: Nehru, India, and Interwar Internationalism* (Cambridge University Press, 2018), 92. Jawaharlal Nehru, "Press Statement Made in Brussels," *Selected Works of Jawaharlal Nehru*, vol. 2 (February 9, 1927) (Orient Longman, 1972), 270.

8. Judith Marshall, "The Worst Company in the World," *Jacobin*, December 11, 2015. See also Thiago Aguiar, *The Shifting Ground of Globalization: Labor and Mineral Extraction at Vale* (Brill, 2023).

9. The phrase "wolf warrior" comes from a Chinese action film starring Wu Jing released in 2015 that showed the power of the Chinese nation, its pride, and ability to stand up against

any enemies. Wolf warrior diplomacy is a shorthand for arrogant assertions of China in world politics. See Ye Min, "Wolf Warriors Blow Hot Before Cooling Down," *Global Asia* 15, no. 3 (2020): 102–6. The recent example of wolf warrior diplomacy is the first ministerial level meeting between China and the United States under the Biden administration when the Central Foreign Affairs Commission Director Yang Jeichi responded to Secretary of State Antony Blinken's claim that China is threatening "rules-based international order" with an angry rebuke that "Chinese people won't swallow this crap" (*Zhongguoren buchi zheyitao*). See GT Staff reporters, "China's 'Wolf-Warrior Diplomacy' in Alaska Meeting Impresses World; Behind It Is the West–East Battle: Observers," *Global Times*, March 21, 2021, https://www.globaltimes.cn/page/202103/1219387.shtml, accessed January 12, 2022. See also Nien-chung Chang-Liao, "Why Have Chinese Diplomats Become So Aggressive?," *Survival* 64, no. 1 (2022): 179–90, https://doi.org/10.1080/00396338.2022 .2032997. See also Peter Martin, *China's Civilian Army: The Making of War Warrior Diplomacy* (Oxford University Press, 2021). For claims of Russian imperialism from European Union and anti-imperial critics of EU's behavior in Africa, see, respectively, Wesley Dockery, "Germany Updates: Von der Leyen Received Charlemagne Prize," DW News, May 29, 2025, https://www.dw.com/en/germany-updates-von-der-leyen-receives -charlemagne-prize/live-72708796, accessed June 22, 2025. See Phil Hearse, "Critical Minerals and Genocide in the Congo," *Links: International Journal of Socialist Renewal* (June 13, 2025). For anti-imperial rhetoric in Azerbaijan, see Bahruz Samadov, "How Azerbaijan Uses 'Anti-Colonialism' to Authoritarian Ends," *OC Media*, December 22, 2023.

10. Matthew Duss, "Calling Trump an Anti-Imperialist Is Nonsense," *Foreign Policy*, April 18, 2023, https://foreignpolicy.com/2023/04/18/donald-trump-presidency-anti-imperialist -militarism-war/, accessed June 22, 2025.

11. William J. Robinson, "The Travesty of Anti-Imperialism," *Journal of World-Systems Research* 29, no. 2 (2023): 588.

12. See, for example, Nigel Biggar, *Colonialism: A Moral Reckoning* (William Collins, 2023). For a fantastic rebuttal, see Dan Hicks, "Beware of the Rise of Anti-Anti-Colonialism," *Hyperallergic*, April 24, 2023. For a superb critique of the glorifiers of British imperialism, see Sathnam Sanghera, *Empireland: How Imperialism Shaped Modern Britain* (Penguin, 2021).

13. Niall Ferguson, *Colossus: The Rise and Fall of the American Empire* (Penguin, 2005).

14. C. A. Bayly, *Recovering Liberties: Indian Thought in the Age of Liberalism and Empire* (Cambridge University Press, 2012), 105.

15. Tilly, "Contentious Repertoires in Great Britain"; Tilly, *Regimes and Repertoires*.

16. Stacie E. Goddard, *When Right Makes Might: Rising Powers and World Order* (Cornell University Press, 2018), 187.

17. Karl Marx, *The Eighteenth Brumaire of Louis Bonaparte*, 2nd ed. (1869; International, 1963), 15.

18. See, for example, Richard Seymour, *American Insurgents: A Brief History of American Anti-Imperialism* (Haymarket, 2012); Rohini Hensman, *Indefensible: Democracy, Counter-Revolution, and the Rhetoric of Anti-Imperialism* (Haymarket, 2018); Daniel Nexon, "Toward a Neo-Progressive Foreign Policy," *Foreign Affairs*, September 4, 2018; Van Jackson, *Grand Strategies of the Left: The Foreign Policy of Progressive Worldmaking*

(Cambridge University Press, 2023); Ayça Çubukçu, "On Left Internationalism," *South Atlantic Quarterly* 123, no. 3 (2024): 569–86.

19. Jan-Werner Muller, *What Is Populism?* (University of Pennsylvania Press, 2016).

20. John Ikenberry, *Liberal Leviathan: The Origins, Crisis, and Transformation of the American World Order* (Princeton University Press, 2011); Charles Kupchan, *No One's World: The West, the Rising Rest, and the Coming Global Turn* (Oxford University Press, 2012); Michael Zürn, *A Theory of Global Governance: Authority, Legitimation and Contestation* (Oxford University Press, 2018); John Ikenberry, *A World Safe for Democracy: Liberal Internationalism and the Crisis of Global Order* (Yale University Press, 2020); David Lake, Lisa L. Martin, and Thomas Risse, "Challenges to the Liberal Order: Reflections on International Organization," *International Organization* 75, no. 2 (2021): 225–57; Robert Kaplan, *The Tragic Mind: Fear, Fate, and the Burden of Power* (Yale University Press, 2023). For a useful corrective, see Amitav Acharya, *Constructing Global Order: Agency and Change in World Politics* (Cambridge University Press, 2018); Amitav Acharya and Barry Buzan, *The Making of Global International Relations: Origins and Evolution of IR at Its Centenary* (Cambridge University Press, 2019).

21. Jürgen Osterhammel, *The Transformation of the World: A Global History of the Nineteenth Century*, trans. Patrick Camiller (Princeton University Press, 2014), 432.

22. Daniel Levine, *Recovering International Relations: The Promise of Sustainable Critique* (Oxford University Press, 2013).

23. Jenny Edkins, Michael J. Shapiro, and Veronique Pin-Fat, eds., "Introduction: Life, Power, Resistance," in *Sovereign Lives: Power in Global Politics* (Routledge, 2004), 1–21; Jenny Edkins, *Trauma and the Memory of Politics* (Cambridge University Press, 2003); Vivienne Jabri, *The Postcolonial Subject: Claiming Politics/Governing Others in Late Modernity* (Routledge, 2013). For a good critique, see John M. Hobson and Alina Sajed, "Navigating Beyond the Eurofetishist Frontier of Critical IR Theory: Exploring the Complex Landscapes of Non-Western Agency," *International Studies Review* 19, no. 4 (2017): 547–72.

24. Stacie Goddard, Paul MacDonald, and Daniel Nexon, "Repertoires of Statecraft: Instruments and Logics of Power Politics," *International Relations* 33, no. 2 (2019): 304–21.

25. Patrick Thaddeus Jackson, *The Conduct of Inquiry: Philosophy of Science and Its Implications for the Study of World Politics* (Routledge, 2011) 142–55.

26. Friedrich Kratochwil, *Praxis: On Acting and Knowing* (Cambridge University Press, 2018).

27. For ontological security studies, see Jennifer Mitzen, "Ontological Security in World Politics: State Identity and the Security Dilemma," *European Journal of International Relations* 12, no. 3 (2006): 341–70; Brent Steele, *Ontological Security in International Relations: Self-Identity, and the IR State* (Routledge, 2008); Bahar Rumelili, ed., *Conflict Resolution and Ontological Security* (Routledge, 2015).

28. See Bahar Rumelili, "Integrating Anxiety into International Relations Theory: Hobbes, Existentialism, and Ontological Security," *International Theory* 12, no. 2 (2020): 257–72.

29. Rumelili, "Integrating Anxiety into International Relations Theory," 270.

30. Gilles Deleuze and Félix Guattari, *A Thousand Plateaus: Capitalism and Schizophrenia*, trans. Brian Massumi (University of Minnesota Press, 1987).

31. See Christian Bueger, "Territory, Authority, Expertise: Global Governance and the Counter-Piracy Assemblage," *European Journal of International Relations* 24, no. 3 (2018): 618. Important works in assemblage framework in international relations are Rita Abrahamsen and Micheal Williams, "Security Beyond the State: Global Security Assemblages in International Politics," *International Political Sociology* 3, no. 1 (2009): 1–17; Michele Acuto and Simon Curtis, *Assemblage Thinking and International Relations* (Palgrave, 2014).

32. Arjun Appadurai, "Mediants, Materiality, Normativity," *Public Culture* 27, no. 2 (2015): 234.

33. Alec Russell, "This Is the Hour of the Global South," *Financial Times*, May 19, 2023.

34. Sabina Lee and Susan Bartels. " 'They Put a Few Coins in Your Hand to Drop a Baby in You': A Study of Peacekeeper-Fathered Children in Haiti," *International Peacekeeping* 27, no. 2 (2020): 177–209.

35. Elian Peltier, "U.N. Peacekeepers in Haiti Said to Have Fathered Hundreds of Children," *New York Times*, December 18, 2019. See also Monica Hirst and Reginaldo Mattar Nasser, "Brazil's Involvement in Peacekeeping Operations: The New Defence-Security-Foreign Policy Nexus," *Report of the Norwegian Peacebuilding Resource Center*, September 2014, https://www.files.ethz.ch/isn/184486/1f05a3ed4e305be65263b1dd53f1bd64.pdf, accessed June 22, 2025.

36. Patricia Roberts-Miller, *Demagoguery and Democracy* (The Experiment, 2017), 33.

37. There are fertile debates within the study of transnational capitalism. See Leslie Sklair, *The Transnational Capitalist Class* (Blackwell, 2001); William Robinson, *A Theory of Global Capitalism: Production, Class, and State in a Transnational World* (Johns Hopkins University Press, 2004); William Carroll, *The Making of a Transnational Capitalist Class: Corporate Power in the Twenty-First Century* (Zed, 2010).

38. Robinson, "The Travesty of Anti-Imperialism," 598–97.

39. On the Gandhian way of power politics, see Karuna Mantena, "Another Realism: The Politics of Gandhian Nonviolence," *American Political Science Review* 106, no. 2 (2012): 455–70.

40. See Anand Chandrasekhar, "When Gandhi Visited Switzerland," *swissinfo.ch*, September 14, 2019, https://www.swissinfo.ch/eng/december-1931_when-gandhi-visited-switzerland/45225904.

41. Lucian Blaga, "An Encounter with Gandhi," in *Mahatma Gandhi: 125 Years*, ed. B. R. Nanda, 62–65 (New Age International, 1995).

42. For a recent analysis, see Nazmul S. Sultan, "Self-Rule and the Problem of Peoplehood in Colonial India," *American Political Science Review* 114, no. 1 (February 2020): 81–94; Nazmul S. Sultan, "Moral Empire and the Global Meaning of Gandhi's Anti-Imperialism," *Review of Politics* 84, no. 4 (2022): 545–69.

43. See Ronald R. Krebs, *Narrative and the Making of US National Security* (Cambridge University Press, 2015), 16.

44. It is hard to track down the precise source of this quote. See Jürgen Osterhammel, *The Transformation of the World: A Global History of the Nineteenth Century*, trans. Patrick Camiller (Princeton University Press, 2014), 837.

INDEX

affect, 148. *See also* emotions
Alawites, 166
Ambedkar, B. R., 75, 82
anticapitalist critique, 191
Aristide, 129, 133–35, 137–39, 144–46, 153, 154;
    overthrow, 135
Asian way, 183
Assad, Bashar al-, 162, 165–67, 169–70, 175,
    179–80, 182–85, 187, 201
audiences: evaluations of, 120; network, 197;
    reaction, 57; role of, 8, 16–17, 30, 32, 43,
    46, 51–52, 57–8, 62, 99, 104, 106, 108,
    110, 114, 116–27, 138–40, 143, 145–46,
    148, 149, 154, 156–57, 159, 163, 172, 174,
    178–81, 184, 186, 188, 194, 197–98, 200;
    types of, 117
authority: defined, 49; in high politics, 49;
    role of, 10, 12–13, 18, 26, 28–29, 34, 44,
    49, 50–51, 64, 98, 108, 138, 141, 163, 173,
    179, 193
autonomy, 18, 68, 80, 91–92, 96, 100–101, 112,
    116, 136, 165, 182

back foot, 15, 53
Backheuser, Everardo, 83

Bangladesh, 4, 60, 90, 96, 98, 100, 102, 107,
    108, 111, 123, 127
barbarians, 42, 68, 86; learning from, 69;
    rhetorical trope, 68
Barbosa, Ruy, 73, 75–76, 82–83, 95
binding: as strategy, 18
Bhutto, Zulfikar Ali, 101
Black: agency in Brazil, 21; epistemic violence
    and, 43
Bolsonaro, Jair, 3
BRICS, role of, 63
Buarque de Holanda, Sergio, 83

capabilities: assessment, 13, 26, 28–31; gap, 32,
    34, 36, 43–46; lack of, 134, 141, 143, 162,
    171, 184, 193; realism and, 20
capitalism, 12, 31, 81, 87, 171, 190–91, 202
Cardoso, Henrique, 136, 143
caste, 75, 82
Chatterjee, Bankim Chandra, 69
chemical weapons, 167–68, 173, 179–80
Chiang Kai-shek, 84, 86–88
Chinese nationalism, 85
colonial scripts, variations, 16
communists, 85–87, 165

community of practitioners, 23
Confucianism, 68–69, 77
conspiracy theories, 4
constructivist theories, 19–20, 27, 32, 36, 39,
    54, 123, 132
contestation, 11, 20–21, 154
contradictions, in liberal order, 1, 9, 11, 15–18,
    23, 27, 47, 52–59, 66, 71, 82, 89, 99,
    109–10, 114, 120–21, 123, 125, 132, 141,
    156, 163, 174–76, 180, 185–87, 189, 191,
    194–95
countershaming, 179–81, 187
covert military support, 107
creative, innovations to rhetoric, 118, 131, 150,
    182, 189, 194, 200; statecraft, 16, 27, 39,
    41, 59, 95

da Silva, Luiz Inácio Lula. See Lula
dialogue, 2, 17, 43, 57–58, 99, 110, 120, 122–23,
    126, 128, 141, 147, 171, 173, 182–83
disorder, 1, 7, 15, 19, 24, 29, 53, 164, 192, 203
double-standard. See hypocrisy
Du Bois, W. E. B., 6, 14, 53, 79

elites, and anti-slavery in Brazil, 75; global,
    202; intra-elite competition, 66;
    skillful role, 65; using selective
    tropes, 68
emotions, 141; affective performances,
    148, 183
epistemic violence, 20, 26, 95, 104, 156,
    193; definition, 43; not being heard,
    9, 109
Eurocentricism, 13, 20, 39, 196
exploitation of rules of international
    order, 16

frame, 28, 35, 84, 123, 132, 198; flip the scripts,
    16; rhetoric to flip the scripts, 27
Freyre, Gilberto, 83

Gandhi, Indira, 17, 57, 61, 96–99, 102–04,
    106–28, 194, 200

Gandhi, Mohandas, 203; appropriation
    of, 99; and Churchill, 12; exploited
    contradictions, 53; Mahatma, 189;
    matured rhetoric, 81; polemic, 74;
    rhetoric of, 31
genocide, 22, 51, 57, 96–97, 102–3, 106–7,
    114, 116–19, 122, 171, 173
geopolitics, 13, 70, 82, 88, 126, 196; Brazilian
    navy, 143; opponents of, 75; place
    in the sun, 71; Western militant
    nationalism, 71
Ghosh, Aurobindo, 74
global governance, 79, 177, 186
Global South, 200; ambitious, 7, 22, 25, 59, 157,
    163, 189; rising Global South, 19, 15;
    role of 2, 7, 24–25, 46, 49, 59–60, 163,
    178, 181, 190, 201, 202
Greater Indian Society, 80

Haiti, 4, 47, 58, 60–61, 66, 83, 92, 129–35,
    137–39, 145–55, 157–58, 194, 200
Haksar, P. N., 102, 108
hedging, strategy, 176
hegemony, 5, 29, 63, 67, 69, 94, 125, 131, 136–37,
    146, 154–55, 159, 169, 185
heterarchical arrangement, 108
hierarchy, 8–9, 13–16, 19–21, 26–28, 31,
    38–41, 43, 49, 51, 53, 55–57, 59, 61,
    64, 76, 95, 97–99, 108–09, 123–24,
    126–27, 130–32, 135, 140, 156–58, 161,
    163–64, 169, 174–75, 186, 188–89,
    192–93, 195–99; complex gradations
    of, 95; international system, 26;
    in legitimating principles, 42; of
    norms, 114
high politics, 8, 11–12, 23, 193
Hindu right, 82
Hu Shi, 77–78, 86, 95
human rights, 7, 35, 42, 46, 51, 56–57, 60–61,
    99, 107, 110, 112–14, 117–19, 121, 125–26,
    133–34, 138, 144, 155, 161, 171–72,
    174, 178; complicity in violations
    of, 178

humanitarian: definition of humanitarian crisis, 60; domain for research analysis, 61; politicization of humanitarian intervention, 168

hypocrisy, 4, 56, 108, 180

International Criminal Court (ICC), 167, 177–79, 183

identity, claims, 158. *See also* ontological security

ideological, 4, 14, 18, 33, 39, 55, 107, 119, 168, 190, 196–97, 199

imperial overreach, 160, 171

incompetence: example of Vietnam, 12; in high politics. 44, 46, 49, 50, 59; as prejudice, 61, 66, 97, 117, 125, 127, 130, 161, 164, 174, 185, 193, 199–200, 202; of non-Europeans, 11–12, 18, 23, 40; in using material capabilities, 45

indigenous communities, of Maoris, 22

institution, definition of, 131; relations in Latin America, 139; rules of the game, 149; shared conventions in, 140; solutions and evaluations, 143

interactions, 28, 30–31, 33–34, 55, 86, 98, 110, 114, 139

interconnections, between colonizers and colonized, 64; global space, 13–14; inter-imperial network for scrutiny, 67

international community, 71, 77, 113–14, 143, 146, 160, 178, 182, 186; skepticism of, 106

international order, 1, 4–7, 9–13, 15–18, 20, 23, 25, 27, 33, 44, 46–47, 49–50, 52, 61, 66, 70, 80, 83, 94–95, 108, 127–32, 137–38, 141, 156–57, 161–64, 169, 174–75, 182–83, 185–87, 192–93, 196–97; assumption of spontaneity, 33; change the, 25; flipping the scripts, 80; liberal ordering, 18; ordering, 27

international system, 5, 8–9, 13, 16, 19–21, 25–27, 29, 31, 35–36, 38–39, 41–43, 52–54, 57–58, 64–65, 68, 74, 76–78, 81–82, 86, 88–89, 97–99, 108–10, 113–14, 117–21, 123, 125, 130–32, 137, 140–42, 153, 156–57, 161, 163, 175, 185–87, 189, 194–97

interpretive: rejection as knowers, 46; research method, 23, 27, 50, 57, 59, 61–62; role of meaning in, 59; role of reflexivity in, 62

ISIS, 160, 167–68, 170–71, 173, 181

Kang Youwei, 77

Kautilya: in rhetoric, 74

Khan, Ayub, 100

Khan, Yahya, 100, 105, 119–21, 123

Kissinger, Henry, 46, 61, 97, 106, 116, 119

Kosygin, Alexei, 97, 121

leader: acknowledgment of Brazil's, 153; regional, 130

learning, 54, 182; learned in struggles, 55; under hierarchy, 55

legacies: continuous, 40, 50, 59, 94, 133, 164; imperial, 6–8, 19–20, 26, 34, 39

legitimating principle, 11, 42, 56, 70; geopolitics, 70, 186; Social Darwinist, 70

Li Hongzhang, 77

Liang Qichao, 73, 77–78, 95

liberal: complicity with Western imperialism, 21; hegemony of, 131; legitimating principles, 67

liberal interventionism, 138, 149

Lima, Oliveira, 76

Lin Zexu, 14

Lula, 3–4, 18, 55, 58, 61, 92, 129–32, 135, 137–38, 140–58, 190, 194, 200–202

Mao Zedong, 14, 55, 78, 84, 86–87, 93–95, 175–77; against humiliation, 87; rhetoric of, 55, 78, 84, 86–87, 93, 95, 175, 176

mediate, 105, 115, 167

mediation, 201
MINUSTAH, 129, 138–39, 150, 152, 154, 157
Modi, Narendra, 2–3, 17, 22, 55, 128, 189–190, 201–02
moral, conscience, 106, 173, 179, 181; dilemma, 173; framing, 173; panic, 173; pressure, 173
Movimento Sem Terra, 145

Nabuco, 73, 75–76, 95
narrative, 8, 10, 32, 37, 43, 65, 66, 71, 136, 145, 148
Nehru, Jawaharlal, 9–10, 48, 81–82, 89–90, 95, 104, 115, 126, 189–90; rhetoric of culture, 82
network structures: hierarchical, 16; ties, 54, 85, 108, 111, 124, 126, 139, 151, 165, 168, 196, 197
new materialism, 198–99
nonalignment, 48, 89, 104, 112; nonaligned idea 96
non-European: bias against, 48; discrimination, 42; ignorance of, 8; incompetence, 44; rejection of their authority, 49. *See also* non-Western; Global South
nonindifference, 149, 151–55
nonintervention, 52, 61, 113–14, 117–19, 138, 148–50, 171, 195
non-Western, 5, 7, 16, 22, 26, 33, 39, 40, 45, 47–48, 50–51, 59–60, 64, 126–27, 157, 189, 192, 194, 199, 202; agents not spectators, 40
norms: hierarchizing of, 118, 121; imperial, 10; manipulation of, 137; role in international order, 11; use of, 156

objective judgment, 13, 26, 44, 193
obligatory passage points, 55, 58
ontological insecurity: limits of, 39, 125; theory of 36–37, 198
Opium Wars, 14
ordering practices, 16, 26, 59–60, 157, 176, 193

Pan-American solidarity, 82
penholder system, 161
pivot to Asia, 169
pluralism, 18, 58, 182–84, 187
postcolonial: scholarship, 19; sensibilities, 26; studies, 13
power: bargaining, 30; Brazil's performance of, 143; constructions, 35; contested concept, 27; definition, 27–28; and hegemony, 29; of language, 32, 36; and legitimation, 34; neoclassical realism, 29; performative, 28; realist view of, 29; relational; understanding of, 28; Weberian definition, 28
power politics, 4–9, 11, 16–24, 26–41, 53–60, 63–64, 66, 87, 90, 93–95, 97–99, 107, 110, 115, 123–28, 130–33, 140–41, 147–50, 155–59, 162–64, 174–75, 178, 182, 184–92, 194–98, 200–203; anti-imperial and anti-colonial, 9
progressive politics, 195–96
protests, 11, 14, 72–76, 84, 94, 100, 160; in Syria, 160

Qing, 68–70, 73, 76–77, 84

race, weaponization of, 151, 153
radical uncertainties, 112
Rahman, Mujibur, 101–02, 110, 118, 121
Rai, Lala Lajpat, 74, 79
realism: complicit with imperialism, 33; and Global South, 20; in IR, 20; impoverished agenda, 34; limits of, 124, 184; theory of 19, 20, 23, 28–30, 32–33, 36, 53, 124, 132–33, 164, 198
realists, 20, 25, 30, 123
Realpolitik, 19–21, 26, 30–31, 33–34, 36–37, 39–40, 53, 64, 74, 76, 80, 89–93, 95, 98, 124, 154, 196, 197
recrimination, 178
refugees, 96, 97, 102, 105, 107, 111, 113–17, 119–20, 122–23, 145, 160–68, 173, 184, 194

regime change, 48, 160–62, 168, 170–74, 176, 184, 186; China against, 173; China's challenge to, 169

regional cooperation, 147

regional leadership: challenges to, 144

regional order, 57, 99, 103–4, 112–13, 117, 124, 127, 129, 135, 144, 183–84

repertoire: defined, 15; evolution of, 115; how it works, 15, 54; innovation to, 58, 118, 174; international politics, 54; learned from colonial and imperial past, 18–19; of statecraft, 9; of statecraft in Global South, 27; rhetoric and power politics, 54; updates to, 159

repertoire, 9, 54

reputation, 112, 116, 185

responsibility, 5, 21, 56, 106, 112, 138, 144, 149, 151, 152, 153, 154, 155, 157, 161, 172, 184

rhetoric: and affect, 51; anti-American, 58; anticolonial and anti-imperial, 4, 60, 66, 128, 162; antihegemonic, 142; against defanging, 55; against superiority of Western civilization, 70; and agency, 51, 56; art of persuasion, 188; of autonomy, 72; of Brazilian tradition and culture, 69; of British drain of wealth, 71; creative innovations to, 182; to challenge disempowerment, 52; of Confucian order, 69; defined, 8, 32, 51; and discourse, 32; to display multivocality, 38, 121; exceptionalism of Chile, 145; to exploit contradictions, 52–53; innovations to anti-Yankee, 155; innovations of the Lula administration, 141; of Indian culture, 69; is not empty, 188; and its necessity for subordinates, 51; necessity of, 27; of oppressed people, 94, 96, 98, 113, 116; as performance, 32; performance of non-performance, 121; role of emotions in, 51; for selective dialogue, 57; solidarity, 58; of strong state in China, 73; of swadeshi, 72

rhetorical ammunition, 113, 149, 180; cheap talk, 56

rhetorical coercion, 37–38; entrapment, 19–21, 23, 28, 38, 53, 56, 125, 133, 164; and its limits, 38

rhetorical innovation, 79, 83, 123, 125; anti-American, 4, 110, 132, 195; Xi Jinping's innovations to, 162

rhetorical repertoire, 40; ingenious use of, 98

Rio Branco, 55, 72–73, 75, 91, 95, 142

Roy, Rammohan, 67, 90, 95

Russia, 1–6, 12, 25, 33, 35–36, 41, 63, 160–64, 167–68, 170–72, 175, 176, 178–180, 184–85, 190, 201–2

Sarkar, Benoy Kumar, 80

scripts, flip the, 17

Self-Strengthening Movement, 77

shame, 18, 39, 43, 58, 81, 179–80, 198

Sheikh Mujibur Rahman. See Rahman

shrewdness, 3

silence: bias and prejudices, 46; challenging it, 51; long history of, 47; silencing, 9, 11–14, 16–21, 23, 26, 27, 40–41, 43–45, 47, 49, 51–52, 55, 64, 66, 70–71, 78, 88, 98–99, 108–10, 124, 132–33, 137, 140, 156–57, 163–64, 174, 185, 187–88, 192–96, 199, 201. See also epistemic violence

silent victims, 26; non-Europeans were not, 13

sincerity, questioning the, 176

solidarity: rhetoric, 18

South-South solidarity, 190

sovereignty, 1, 4, 35, 42, 56, 59, 80, 105, 107, 111, 113–14, 119, 142, 160–62, 165, 168–69, 171, 173, 176, 178, 180, 183, 186, 195, 202

statecraft: of China, 164; China's innovation to, 84; global, 81; Indian view of, 80; of Lula administration, 131 strategy, 6–9, 12, 16–17, 20, 22, 30–36, 49, 51–53, 56–58, 60, 64, 67, 69, 70, 80, 86, 89–90, 95, 98, 107, 109–11, 120–21, 124, 126, 136, 144, 153, 158, 170–71, 176, 181, 187, 201–2

structure, 19, 38, 104, 124–25, 137, 174, 193, 195, 202; pressures, 26

structural inequalities, 19

Sun Yat-Sen, 14, 70, 73, 77–78, 84–85, 87

superpower competition, 12, 98–99

Swaran Singh, Sardar, 102, 107, 115

Thass, Iyothee, 75

tradition: role of, 68

transnational capitalist class, 202. *See also* elites

transnational network, 11

treaty, 73, 78, 93, 108, 112, 116, 128

Trump, Donald, 6, 7, 22, 190–91, 201

TWAIL, 50–51

US imperialism, 83, 191

upend strategy, 9, 21, 27; rules and norms of international order, 164

Vargas, Getulio, 10, 61, 82–84, 91

Wang Yi, 4, 162, 176, 177, 179, 181, 183, 184

wedge, 17, 99, 119, 120, 194, 200, 201

West, the, 1, 4–14, 16, 18, 20–22, 25, 34, 36, 39, 41–43, 45–49, 55, 60, 65, 68, 73, 76, 78, 85–86, 88, 91–94, 97, 100–102, 105, 107, 110, 124, 137, 141, 153, 157, 162–63, 169–70, 173–74, 176, 178, 180, 184–87, 190–91, 193, 195, 196, 200–202

Western empires, collaborating against non-Europeans, 67

Western empires and imperialism histories of, 64

world-ordering, 26, 51, 59, 193; exclusion, 51; strategies in, 59

Xi Jinping, 3, 4, 18–19, 55, 58, 61, 94, 162–63, 171, 175, 177, 181–82, 185, 187, 194–95, 200

Yan Fu, 77

Yankee: anti-American, 18

GPSR Authorized Representative: Easy Access System Europe, Mustamäe tee
50, 10621 Tallinn, Estonia, gpsr.requests@easproject.com

www.ingramcontent.com/pod-product-compliance
Lightning Source LLC
Chambersburg PA
CBHW032119020426
42334CB00016B/1005